CRIME WAVE

The Filmgoers' Guide to the Great Crime Movies

HOWARD HUGHES

I.B. TAURIS

LONDON · NEW YORK

Published in 2006 by I.B.Tauris & Co Ltd
6 Salem Road, London W2 4BU
175 Fifth Avenue, New York NY 10010
www.ibtauris.com

In the United States and Canada distributed by Palgrave Macmillan,
a division of St. Martin's Press, 175 Fifth Avenue, New York NY 10010

ISBN 10:   1 84511 219 9
EAN 13:   978 1 84511 219 6

A full CIP record for this book is available from the British Library
A full CIP record for this book is available from the Library of Congress
Library of Congress catalog card: available

Typeset in Ehrhardt by Dexter Haven Associates Ltd, London
Printed and bound in Great Britain by TJ International, Padstow

CONTENTS

PREFACE

WELCOME TO THE UNDERWORLD

The underworld of crime, the 'city under the city', is a shadowy world, full of unpleasant, untrustworthy people. But for some reason, crime movies hold a special place in cinema audiences' affections. Many of the highest-grossing, most popular US films of all time fall into this category: *The Godfather* films, *Pulp Fiction*, and various stellar, all-action cops and robbers movies, often depicting the perfect crime. Something about breaking the law and getting away with it seems to appeal to everyone. The loveable outlaws *Butch Cassidy and the Sundance Kid* (1969), incarnated by Paul Newman and Robert Redford, were equally loveable when updated to thirties Chicago conmen in *The Sting* (1973), with equal box-office success. The aim of this book is to discover and enjoy this enduring appeal.

Inspired by Turner Classic Movies' annual *Crime Wave* season, the movies I've chosen for inclusion in this book are seminal Hollywood films, both in their genre and their respective eras. Crime is a feature of so many films, from westerns to horror movies, murder mysteries to historical epics: in fact any film in which the law is broken. As a guide, I've kept within certain genre boundaries, while discussing as many movies as possible. All the films examined in this book take place in the 'real world', and, in one form or another, look at crime fighting, corruption, thievery or vice.

Crime Wave includes the classic gangster flicks of the thirties and forties, often detailing bootlegging, robbery and smuggling: *The Public Enemy*, *High Sierra* and *White Heat*. I also trace the development of the post-war *film noir* style, from *The Maltese Falcon* and *Kiss Me Deadly* to the knowing post-modernism of *Chinatown* and *L.A. Confidential*. There are tough B-movies from the thrifty fifties, such as *The Big Combo*; tales of gangster revenge (*Point Blank* and *Get Carter*) and Quentin Tarantino's genre-referential *Pulp Fiction*. There are heist and caper movies, epitomised by *The Asphalt Jungle* and *Ocean's Eleven*. Also discussed are lone, rule-breaking cops (*Dirty Harry*), buddy cops (*Lethal Weapon*), global crime (*On Her Majesty's Secret Service*), blaxpoitation action (*Shaft*) and even a gangster love story: *Bonnie and Clyde*. And of course there are the four great gangster epics, directed by Martin Scorsese, Sergio Leone and Francis Ford Coppola: *GoodFellas*, *Once Upon a Time in America*, *The Godfather* and *The Godfather Part II*.

Each film is analysed in detail, with biographies and filmographies of key participants, accounts of the films' making (including details of sets and location filming), their critical reception, performance at the US and UK box office and influence on the crime genre. Where appropriate, there are notes on the films' literary inspirations or references to their historical period. Historical accuracy, particularly in B-movies, is often not one of the genre's strong points, while other directors, notably Coppola and Leone, are scrupulous within their eras.

Two notes concerning the text: firstly, when I refer to film and book titles, the film title is italicised, the book isn't. Thus: 'The Maltese Falcon' for Dashiell Hammett's book, *The Maltese Falcon* for John Huston's film. Secondly, a note on the ratings certification system in the UK and US. The system in the UK is governed by the BBFC: the British Board of Film Classification. Until 1951 the main ratings were simply U (Universal) and A (Adults); in 1951 the X-rating was introduced, for over 16s. After 1970, the ratings in the UK were U (Universal), A (suitable for under-14s), AA (suitable for accompanied over-14s) and X (suitable for 18-year-olds and over). In 1982, this changed to U, PG (parental guidance) and the age bands 15 and 18. In 1989, certificate 12 was added.

In the US, from the early thirties until 1968, films were subject to the strict Hayes Code. After 1968, the Motion Picture Association of America (MPAA) introduced a ratings system: G (general), M (suggested for mature audiences), R (restricted – under-17s must be accompanied), X (no one under 17 admitted). M was soon changed to GP (general audiences, parental guidance suggested) and then to PG (parental guidance). In July 1984, this became: G (general)/PG (parental guidance suggested)/PG-13 (no one under 13 admitted, unless accompanied)/R (restricted, under 17 years need accompanying)/NC-17 (no one under 17 admitted). I hope this helps to clarify any certificates mentioned in the text.

Finally, in these chapters you will find some of the great crime stars, in some of their greatest films: James Cagney on top of the world, Humphrey Bogart pursuing the black bird, Sterling Hayden prowling the asphalt jungle, Lee Marvin escaping Alcatraz, Clint Eastwood feeling lucky, Michael Caine spilling blood on the Tyne, Joe Pesci getting whacked, Robert De Niro being a wiseguy, George Clooney taking the pot and Marlon Brando making you an offer you can't refuse. Accept it, it's well worth the time.

ACKNOWLEDGEMENTS

I would like to thank Philippa Brewster, my editor at I.B. Tauris, for initiating the *Crime Wave* project, and for her ideas and support throughout its writing. Thanks also to Deborah Susman, Paul Davighi, Hannah Ross and Stuart Weir at I.B. Tauris, and to Robert Hastings at Dexter Haven Associates.

Thanks to Andrew Hanratty for additional research, for loaning me various essential source movies and for his restoration work on the posters and stills reproduced here. All illustrative material is from my own collection. Thanks also to Mike Coppack for extra research, tracking down rare source material and for offering insights on everything from the *Lethal Weapon* movies to the criminal psychology of the Zodiac Killer.

Thank you also to Andrew Collins, Alex Cox, Paul Duncan and Stuart Maconie, for taking the time to name their top ten crime movies. All their lists are totally different and I'm sure that each of them could easily have named their top twenty crime films – and still had difficulty pruning the list. Their favourites also remind us how many great films have been made in the genre.

Thanks too, to the following people who have contributed to the writing and research of *Crime Wave*: Belinda and Chris Skinner, Alex and Isabel Coe, Nicki and John Cosgrove, Rhian Thomas, Pen Kennedy, Sir Christopher Frayling, Paul Duncan, Gareth Jones, Tom Betts, Ann Jackson, Rene Hogguer, Chris and Roger Brown, David Weaver, William Connolly, Mike Oak and Tracey Mansell, Sonya-Jayne Stewart and Bob Bell, Nick Rennisson, Simon Hawkins and Lionel Woodman.

Thanks again to my parents, Carol and John, for their continued enthusiasm, help and support. And finally thank you to Clara, who not only sat through the entire *Lethal Weapon* series on consecutive nights, she has helped me with research, sourcing illustrations, books, videos and DVDs. Without her encouragement and support, this book would never have been finished.

CRIMINAL RECORD: AN INTRODUCTION TO CRIME MOVIES

Gangsterism and criminality in the nineteenth-century United States were associated with outlaws in the wild west; bandits such as Jesse James and Butch Cassidy, folk heroes fronting gangs named the 'Hole-in-the-Wall' and the 'Wild Bunch'. But in the east, in the big cities, with their rising immigrant populations, gangs such as the Dead Rabbits, the Shirt Tails, the Plug Uglies and the Roach Guards were fighting turf wars on the streets of New York, as depicted in Martin Scorsese's *Gangs of New York* (2002). Predominant among the street gangs were the immigrant communities of Irish, Italian and Chinese; the Chinese immigrants brought with them their Triad Societies, later renamed the Tongs, secret sects rooted in ritual, which gained a foothold in these nascent cities.

When crime became more organised, in the early twentieth century, it became more prominent. With the puritanical Volstead Act, declaring Prohibition in 1920, the sale and consumption of alcohol went underground and the criminals and bootleggers thrived. Irish and Italian gangsters battled it out for control of New York and Chicago. It was in the latter city that the most famous gangster atrocity

The Untouchables: gangster iconography adorns a fairground shooting gallery; Robert Stack as Tommy-gun-toting Eliot Ness (photograph Clara Hughes).

took place, after four long years of Beer War. On 14 February 1929, five gunmen, some disguised as cops, employed by mobster Al Capone ('Public Enemy Number One'), machine-gunned seven rival Irish gangsters. The victims were members of the North Siders, Bugs Moran's gang. They had met in Moran's bootlegging depot, the North Clark Street garage, to plan Capone's demise, when the killers struck. As a result of the St Valentine's Day Massacre, Sicilian gangster 'Lucky' Luciano organised 'Murder Incorporated', a self-regulatory gangland outfit, which killed mobsters who broke the criminal code. These enforcers thought they were doing the cities a favour. As James Woods's up-and-coming New York gangster says in *Once Upon a Time in America* (1984), when told that his form of urban crime is a disease: 'This country is still growing up…certain diseases it's better to have when you're still young.'

CRIME WAVE 30s

The thirties were the heyday of gangster movies, with Warner Bros Studios leading the way. There had been one notable silent crime movie, Joseph Von Sternberg's Chicago-set *Underworld* (1927). In Germany, Fritz Lang had directed *M* (1931), with the criminal underworld and the Berlin Homicide Squad joining forces to track down a child murderer, chillingly portrayed by Peter Lorre. Originally called *Murderers Among Us*, the film was retitled when the Nazi party sensed it referenced their infiltration of society. The killer is described as 'a danger often cloaked in a friendly disguise' and the sense of paranoia, as fear and suspicion spread through the city like a plague, vividly brings Lang's depiction of urban criminality to life. But with the advent of sound, the crime genre really took off in the US, concentrating on the topical subjects of bootlegging, racketeering, gang war, kidnap and murder.

The most fashionable type of early gangster movies was the Broadway crime movie, which looked at the links between the underworld and the theatre world. The relatively recent addition of sound ensured audiences heard their fair share of musical numbers, in films such as *The Lights of New York* (1928), *Tenderloin* (1928 – which concerned bootleggers, not butchers), *Broadway* (1929) and *Broadway Thru a Keyhole* (1933), with chorus girls on the ladder to stardom, mixing with mobsters. The influence of such early musical gangster movies can be seen throughout crime cinema; *The Girl Can't Help It* (1956), for example, featured Jayne Mansfield as a tone-deaf gangster's moll, who mobster Edmond O'Brien is convinced can be transformed into a singing sensation.

But in the thirties, a triumvirate of crime films quickly established a tougher side to the genre and ensured its global popularity. Each depicted a criminal's spectacular rise and equally dramatic fall, and all made stars of their leading actors. Edward G. Robinson starred as Cesare Enrico Bandello, alias Rico in *Little Caesar*

(1930). The film ended with the death of Rico on the steps of a church and his classic final line: 'Mother of God…is this the end of Rico?' (which was altered by the censors to 'Mother of mercy' in some prints). Rico was based on Al Capone, who was incarcerated that same year for the less-than-glamorous crime of three years' tax evasion; his defence was that he didn't think he'd have to pay tax on money garnered illegally. The second, and best, of the three crime films was William A. Wellman's *The Public Enemy* (1931), with James Cagney's dynamic turn as Irish hood Tom Powers, based in part on Bugsy Moran's associate, Dion O'Banion. This also climaxed with the mobster's memorable demise: here Power's trussed-up corpse is delivered to his mother's doorstep.

The third and most controversial of the three was *Scarface, Shame of a Nation* (1932), directed by Howard Hawks and starring Paul Muni as Tony Camonte and George Raft as his coin-tossing sidekick, Guido Rinaldo. Based on the novel by Armitage Traill, it was written for the screen by Ben Hecht and W.R. Burnett, as another thinly disguised biography of Al Capone. Hawks had trouble from the censors concerning the film's violence (one version ends with Camonte being hanged) and the movie was held back for over a year. Hecht was visited by Capone's heavy mob, who had heard it was about their boss. Hecht managed to convince them it was based on other mobsters and the 'Scarface' reference was simply to attract cinemagoers. Capone reputedly liked the film and even bought his own copy.

With the success of these three films, many imitations followed, though few equalled their power. Unlike the conflicting wild-west heroes and villains, these gangster badmen were completely amoral: violence is underhand and treachery rife. A code of honour, which existed in the film versions of the old west, is completely absent from the crime movie. Death comes with a knife in the back, or machine-gun ambush, and there are no rules in the urban jungle. It was ironic that for the first years of the thirties, these men were heroes.

As the decade wore on, James Cagney made two more films now regarded as classics. First he starred in *Angels With Dirty Faces* (1938), one of his most popular films. It is a highly moral version of the 'rise and fall' scenario, with a justly famous electric chair finale. Then Cagney released *The Roaring Twenties* (1939), which looked at how economic factors and unemployment following the First World War pushed men into a life of crime. In this period, future crime-movie icon Humphrey Bogart made his name as a supporting heavy, in Warners' films *The Petrified Forest* (1936) and *The Roaring Twenties* (1939), forever in the shadow of a star, which rankled with Bogart. There were also many spoofs of the genre, including Cagney and Robinson sending up their own gangster images in *Lady Killer* (1933) and *A Slight Case of Murder* (1938) respectively, while Buster Keaton parodied bootleggers with *What? No Beer?* (1933).

After their success in *Dead End* (1937) and *Angels With Dirty Faces* (1938), rough and tumble street urchins the Dead End Kids started a fad for juvenile crime gang films. These ranged from social dramas to knockabout comedies and horror spoofs. The Dead End Kids' imitators, competitors or spin-off projects included the 'Little Tough Guys' series (see *Little Tough Guy* – 1938, *Code of the Streets* – 1939, *You're Not so Tough* – 1940, and six further adventures), the East Side Kids (stars of 22 features, including *Spooks Run Wild* – 1941) and the Bowery Boys (who made 48 features between 1946 and 1958).

Stringent censorship and the reining in and dismantling of the real gangsters' power saw the on-screen G-men (government agents) fighting back from the mid-thirties onwards, spearheaded by Cagney's turn as James 'Brick' Davies in *G-Men*, based on the book 'Public Enemy No. 1' by Gregory Rogers. Released in April 1935, *G-Men* was a box-office smash and spawned many rushed-out sequels and derivatives: *Public Hero Number One* (1935), *Counterfeit* (1936 – featuring T-men, treasury agents), *Trapped by G-Men* (1937), *When G-Men Step In* (1937) and the western-set *Border G-Man* (1938).

CRIME WAVE 40s

Like everyone from Charlie Chan to Gene Autry, during the war years cinema cops tended to be combating Nazis, rather than their usual gangster opponents. Notable cop movies include *T-Men* (1948) and *Border Incident* (1949), both directed by Anthony Mann. Nevertheless, gangster biopics enjoyed a comeback. Some of the better-known examples include *Lady Scarface* (1941), *Johnny O'Clock* (1947) and *Dillinger* (1945), starring Lawrence Tierney, who was later to become the boss of the *Reservoir Dogs* (1992). Looming over all forties crime biographies and looking down from the top of the world was Cody Jarrett in *White Heat* (1949), given the definitive portrayal by James Cagney, in his most-remembered gangster role.

With the economic cutbacks and pessimism of the Second World War came the popularity of *film noir*, with mysteries, haunted antiheroes and *femmes fatales* to the fore. The male lead in *film noir* was often a private eye or cop, drawn into a spider's web of power, corruption and lies. This suffocating web of intrigue is often reflected in the films' photographic style, with dark shadows and sinister atmospherics, more in the manner of Universal's horror movies or German expressionism. But often, such style was a direct result of wartime thriftiness. The heroes have a fatalistic awareness of their own doom, which suited the films' dark morality tales, often with downbeat finales. The creeping tendrils of mystery often emit from a *femme fatale* (literally 'deadly woman'), who through her own obsessional kismet leads the hero to face his fate. The stories often take place in flashback, and the past tends to be something to be escaped and forgotten, rather than recalled nostalgically. Some of these *noirs* were little more than thin melodramas with a surfeit of style; others have stood the test of time and are perceptive and stylish works of art. Outstanding examples include *Double Indemnity* (1944), *The Blue Dahlia* (1946), *The Spiral Staircase* (1946), *The Big Combo* (1955) and *Touch of Evil* (1958).

Humphrey Bogart kicked off the forties by shedding his second-from-the-left, blink-and-you'll-miss-him, bad-guy image by playing what for many is the definitive screen detective: Dashiell Hammett's Sam Spade in *The Maltese Falcon* (1941). Following *Casablanca* (1942), Bogart returned to the genre with *The Big Sleep* (1946), where he enacted the most famous incarnation of private eye Philip Marlowe in Raymond Chandler's mystery. Chandler himself became involved with the film industry and co-scripted *Double Indemnity* and *The Blue Dahlia*. Other mysteries of the period included *The Mask of Dimitrios* (1944) and *The Glass Key* (1942).

The best screen adaptation of Chandler's work was *Farewell My Lovely* (1944 – *Murder, My Sweet* in the US), with Claire Trevor as the murderous Mrs Grayle and former musical star Dick Powell as Marlowe. Much was made of Powell's new incarnation on posters: 'Two-fisted, Hardboiled, Terrific – Meet the New Dick Powell!' *Noir* posters, like their subjects, were very stylish, featuring wispy smoke, the fog of dreams and the past, guns, dames and tangled cobwebs. The *femme fatale* was invariably the most important ingredient in forties crime movies. As the poster to *Farewell My Lovely* stated, 'Forget that Feeling... She's got Murder in her Heart!'

Other forties films had a mobster as the central character, some of which incorporated a *noir* flavour. These included Bogart's transitional *High Sierra* (1941), the Robert Mitchum vehicle *Out of the Past* (1947 – also called *Build My Gallows High*) and *Kiss of Death* (1947 – worth seeing for Richard Widmark's wired debut as murderous Tommy Udo). *Key Largo* (1948) boasted an unhinged performance by Edward G. Robinson, while the 1946 film version of Ernest Hemingway's short story 'The Killers' featured the steamy pairing of Ava Gardner and Burt Lancaster (in his film debut). There was also *Force of Evil* (1949), *Panic in the Streets* (1949 – in which bubonic plague represents the spread of crime) and the cult classic *Gun Crazy* (1949), concerning a pair of Bonnie-and-Clyde-style hoods.

CRIME WAVE 50s

In fifties Hollywood, the success of *The Asphalt Jungle* (1950) gave rise to a new breed of urban *noir*, the heist movie. Other examples include *Armoured Car Robbery* (1950), *Crime Wave* (1953), *5 Against the House* (1955 – a casino robbery), *Violent Saturday* (1955) and Stanley Kubrick's justly famous racetrack robbery, *The Killing* (1956). In France, *Rififi* (1955) set a new standard for heist movies, with its silent 30-minute jewel robbery.

There was also renewed popularity in the gangster biography, now using real names yoked to predominately invented narratives. In *The Bonnie Parker Story* (1958), Dorothy Provine starred as the title gangster, according to the posters, a 'Cigar smoking Hellcat of the Roaring Twenties' – Parker's life of crime started in 1932. Other criminals given the big-screen treatment were *Baby Face Nelson* (1958), *Machine-Gun Kelly* (1958) and *Al Capone* (1959). The decade saw Humphrey

Bogart's last work, with *The Enforcer* (1951), *The Harder They Fall* (1956 – his last film), and a return to his villainous thirties roots with *The Desperate Hours* (1955). There were also memorable B-movies from RKO (*Roadblock* [1951] and *The Narrow Margin* [1952]), United Artists (*Kansas City Confidential* – 1952) and Republic (*Hoodlum Empire* – 1952).

The cops were still in evidence, but for a while it was difficult to see whose side they were on. This was a feature of Hollywood cinema in the fifties, which had an uneasy political atmosphere. Big John Wayne moseyed into town as *Big Jim McClain* (1952), an investigator for the House of Un-American Activities, rooting out Communists in Hawaii; *I Was a Communist for the FBI* (1951) covered similar ground. *The Big Heat* (1953) and *The Big Combo* (1955) were both condemned for their violence. Orson Welles's much-tampered-with *Touch of Evil* (1958) depicted police corruption in a sleepy, sleazy Mexican border town that would have probably benefited from employing a sheriff like John Wayne.

There were some crime oddities in the fifties, with Robert Aldrich's *Kiss Me Deadly* (1955) proving to be one of the strangest. Ostensibly an adaptation of a Mickey Spillane novel about the search for a case full of drugs, it was transformed by Aldrich into something very stylish, different and topical. Here a case containing an atomic bomb is used as a metaphor for nuclear war and the end of mankind, creating a new genre along the way: apocalyptic sci-fi *noir*. Following on from the Dead End Kids, juvenile delinquency kept the cops busy across town, with *Crime in the Streets* (1956) and a *Rumble on the Docks* (1956), and reached its height in the choreographed gang wars of *West Side Story* (1961).

The fifties saw several gangster spoofs, though the humour was often rather laboured; only two films really hit the mark. The first was the UK Ealing comedy *The Ladykillers* (1955), with five shifty robbers posing as a classical quintet and planning their heist while staying in a boarding house with dear old Mrs Wilberforce. Among the crooks are Peter Sellers and Herbert Lom, later reunited in the 'Pink Panther' crime series, and the gang's leader, Professor Marcus, played by Alec Guinness. In Billy Wilder's *Some Like It Hot* (1959), two out-of-work musicians, Tony Curtis and Jack Lemmon, go on the run after witnessing the St Valentine's Day Massacre and hide out in drag, on tour with Sweet Sue's all-girl jazz band, including their 'Jell-O on springs' lead singer, Sugar Kane (Marilyn Monroe). The film included a humorous cameo by thirties star George Raft as 'Spats Colombo', the gangster on their trail.

CRIME WAVE 60s

With huge TV audiences, cinema audiences dwindled, and most of the best crime entertainment in the sixties was in TV shows such as *The Untouchables*, with Robert Stack as tough-as-nails Eliot Ness, and *Danger Man* (shown in the US as *Secret Agent*), with Patrick McGoohan as John Drake. Such was their popularity that *The*

Untouchables released a spin-off feature, *The Scarface Mob* (1959), while two colour *Danger Man* episodes ('Koroshi' and 'Shinda Shima') were glued together into a feature (released in the US as *Koroshi* in 1966).

In 1962, United Artists adapted Ian Fleming's 'Dr No' for the big screen, with Sean Connery in the lead as British superagent James Bond. The film and its sequels were a huge global success. Bond was a new type of hero – suave and sophisticated: brutal, clever and smartly turned out. He replaced the scruffy private sleuth and the explosive G-man as a new type of wisecracking antihero. In the US, such escapism was an antidote to the early sixties gloom following the assassination of President John F. Kennedy.

The Bond films started their own spy-movie industry. The most successful were a pair of Derek Flint films starring James Coburn (*Our Man Flint* [1966] and *In Like Flint* [1967]), four Dean Martin 'Matt Helm' films (*The Silencers* [1966], *Murderers Row* [1966], *The Ambushers* [1968] and *The Wrecking Crew* [1969]), based on the books by Donald Hamilton, and a very hip resurrection of Bulldog Drummond in the superior, exotic *Deadlier Than the Male* (1967 – and its lesser sequel *Some Girls Do* in 1969). On US TV there was *The Man from UNCLE* (Ian Fleming contributed the name Napoleon Solo to the series), *I Spy* (with Bill Cosby and Robert Culp as the undercover agents posing as tennis stars), *Mission Impossible* (detailing the exploits of the Impossible Mission Force) and *Get Smart!* (a US Bond spoof written by Mel Brooks).

If they weren't trying to emulate the success of the Bond franchise, crime movies in the sixties were dominated by a new kind of European cinema that took the American crime movie as a template. They were spearheaded by the directors of the French New Wave (the 'Nouvelle Vague'). François Truffaut's *Les Quatres Cents Coups* (1959 – *The 400 Blows*) detailed juvenile delinquency in a poetic, moving way. Jean-Luc Godard's *À Bout de Souffle* (1959 – *Breathless*) told of the relationship between a young American woman in Paris and a small-time hoodlum. Godard's science fiction *Alphaville* (1965) satirised French spy movies, such as those starring Eddie Constantine as secret agent Lemmy Caution; Constantine sent up Caution, his trench-coated, chain-smoking antihero, to great effect in Godard's film. But it was Jean-Pierre Melville who created the finest French gangster movies of the decade, with *Le Deuxième Souffle* (1966 – *Second Breath*) and his slow-burning story of a hitman, *Le Samouraï* (1967), starring Alain Delon. Italy also made some distinctive gangster movies, often based on real-life gangsters and bandits: *Salvatore Giuliano* (1962), *Wake Up and Kill* (1966), *The Violent Four* and *Day of the Owl* (both 1968). Internationally, even Japan made their own brand of crime thrillers, dubbed 'Yakuzas', the best of which were two films produced by the Nikkatsu Studio and directed by Seijun Suzuki: *Tokyo Nagaremono* (1966 – *Tokyo Drifter*) and *Koroshi no Rakuin* (1967 – *Branded to Kill*).

US crime movies began to show a stylistic and narrative influence from Europe, especially *Bonnie and Clyde* and *Point Blank* (1967), an existential revenge drama with Lee Marvin. Both these films also highlighted a sudden rise in the US of on-screen violence, in films such as *Johnny Cool* (1963), *The Killers* (1964), *Madigan, Bullit, Coogan's Bluff* and *The Detective* (all 1968).

In the US, gangster biopics were still popular, from *Ma Barker's Killer Brood* (1960) and *The Rise and Fall of Legs Diamond* (1960) to *The St Valentine's Day Massacre* and the phenomenally successful *Bonnie and Clyde* (both 1967). There was even *The George Raft Story* (1961 – also called *Spin of a Coin*). But these biographies became few and far between and rare seventies additions included Warren Oates as *Dillinger* (1973), *Melvin Purvis – G-Man* (1974 – also called *The Legend of Machine Gun Kelly*) and its sequel, *The Kansas City Massacre* (1975 – both originally made for TV), *Capone* (1975 – with Ben Gazzara in the title role) and *The Private Files of J. Edgar Hoover* (1977).

The sixties was the one era when to be an 'international jewel thief' was a valid occupation. Caper films were immensely popular; they were a lighter, more ingenious and less believable version of heist movies such as *The Asphalt Jungle* and *The Killing*. Caper movie escapism began with *Ocean's Eleven* (1960), a ridiculous movie about 11 army buddies who rob five Las Vegas casinos in one night. The trend continued throughout the decade and into the seventies. The best examples include the UK-made *The League of Gentlemen* (1960), Istanbul-set *Topkapi* (1964) and the classic *The Italian Job* (1969). Euro-heist movies include *Operation San Genarro* (1966), *Operation Saint Peter's* (1967), *After the Fox* (1966), *Grand Slam* (1967), *They Came to Rob Las Vegas* (1968) and *The Sicilian Clan* (1969). A rash of flashy US productions included *Assault on a Queen* (1966), *The Biggest Bundle of Them All* (1967) and *The Thomas Crown Affair* (1968).

CRIME WAVE 70s

The most successful robbery caper at the box office was the multimillion-dollar star vehicle *The Sting* (1973), George Roy Hill's follow-up to *Butch Cassidy and the Sundance Kid* (1969). Paul Newman and Robert Redford played a pair of Chicago conmen (Henry Gondorff and Kid Hooker) out to fleece mobster Doyle Lonnegan, 'The Big Mick' (Robert Shaw), in a cleverly conceived betting scam. Hill's film is now best remembered for the rearrangements of Scott Joplin's rag 'The Entertainer'; a further sequel, *The Sting II* (1983), with Jackie Gleason and Mac Davis in the Newman and Redford roles, hinged on a rigged boxing match.

Undoubtedly the biggest crime box-office hits of the seventies were the *Godfather* Mafia films, *Parts I* and *II* (1972 and 1974), whose influence and success were immense. Significantly, the first film was based on a best-selling novel by Mario Puzo, the producers hoping for a ready-made audience, but the film's success was by no means guaranteed. Moreover, the four Best Picture Oscar winners, 1971–74 were all crime movies: *The French Connection*, *The Godfather*, *The Sting* and *The Godfather Part II*, proving the genre's renewed popularity.

Private eyes were also back in style in the seventies. There was James Garner as *Marlowe* (1969), an update of Raymond Chandler's 'The Little Sister', and Warren Oates as private eye *Chandler* (1971), named after the novelist himself. Robert Mitchum played a period Marlowe in *Farewell, My Lovely* (1975) and *The Big Sleep* (1978). Robert Altman's offbeat *The Long Goodbye* (1973) cast Elliott Gould as a down–at–heel, scruffy seventies Marlowe. Altman's film was a precursor to the everyday threat and menace depicted in Roman Polanski's *Chinatown* (1974), the foremost private eye movie of the decade, with Jack Nicholson as J.J. Gittes, investigating the Water and Power company. All these films included the usual *noir* touches – a *femme fatale* who hires the hero, the dark side of the human psyche, a mystery element – and added a post-modern knowingness to the proceedings; this is particularly true of *The Long Goodbye*, a film that upset many Chandler purists.

The seventies also saw a vogue for thirties and forties vintage stories, with authentic period settings. These ranged from the children's musical *Bugsy Malone* (1976), with Tommy-guns that fire gunk, to comedies such as *Lucky Lady* (1975). There were serious, brutal treatments such as *The Grissom Gang* (1971) and *Thieves Like Us* (1974 – a remake of *They Live by Night* – 1948), and violent crime biographies: *A Bullet for Pretty Boy*, *Bloody Mama* (both 1970), *Dillinger* (1973) and *Big Bad Mama* (1974).

In France, Alain Delon became a big international star, via his retro gangster movie *Borsalino* (1970). The finest Italian crime film of the decade was Francesco

Marlon Brando as Don Vito Corleone, with Robert Duvall as Tom Hagan, his *consigliere* (negotiator and adviser), in Francis Ford Coppola's 1972 hit *The Godfather*.

Rosi's *Cadaveri Eccellenti* (1976 – *Illustrious Corpses*); based on Leonardo Sciascia's 1971 novel 'Il Conteso' (retitled 'Equal Danger'), with Lino Ventura playing Inspector Rogas, investigating a labyrinthine series of murders of the judiciary. Rosi also directed *The Mattei Affair* (1972) and *Lucky Luciano* (1973), topical, fact-based scenarios that chimed with Italian audiences.

The most reliable crime star of the seventies was Charles Bronson, whose films made a fortune worldwide. He was one of the top ten box-office stars from 1973–76; his highest ranking was 4th in 1975, beaten only by Robert Redford, Barbra Streisand and Al Pacino. He made films in many action genres, including several crime movies, often starring opposite his wife, Jill Ireland. *The Valachi Papers* (1972) was based on the real-life 1963 case of Joseph Valachi, Mafioso whistle-blower on the workings of the Mafia. *Violent City* (1970) was a tale of hitman revenge set in New Orleans, and *Death Wish* (1974) was the ultimate vigilante movie. Bronson also made *Cold Sweat* (1971), *The Stone Killer* (1973), *Mr Majestyk* (1974) and *Breakout* (1975). It is a safe assumption that, with Bronson in the title role, *The Mechanic* (1972 – UK title *Killer of Killers*) didn't repair many cars; 'mechanic' is a slang term for hitman.

With the arrival of Clint Eastwood's cop movie *Dirty Harry* and Michael Caine's Newcastle-set revenge thriller *Get Carter*, 1971 was a watershed year for crime movies. The same year Richard Roundtree starred as *Shaft*, opening the floodgates for the blaxpoitation explosion of black action heroes and heroines. *Dirty Harry* was also the epitome of a new breed of crime-busting rogue cops, heralded by the arrival of 'Popeye' Doyle, not on the trail of spinach, but heroin, in William Friedkin's *The French Connection* (1971) and its sequel *The French Connection II* (1975). *Badge 373* (1973) used the same source material as *The French Connection*. A variation of the formula saw Al Pacino as the eponymous unconventional cop in *Serpico* (1973), in the true story of an officer who tried to expose police corruption in the NYPD.

There were several oddball seventies crime fads, such as the minor craze for 'gang' movies, after John Carpenter's *Assault on Precinct 13* (1976) and Walter Hill's *The Warriors* (1979). Another craze was the backwood's 'moonshine' cycle, which produced at least one cult movie, Burt Reynolds's *White Lightning* (1973). Reynolds also kick-started the good-old-boy car chase series, with his immensely popular *Smoky and the Bandit* (1977), featuring much burning rubber, impressive stunts and colourful language, y'all.

CRIME WAVE 80s

In the eighties, with cinema audiences on the wane, period gangster films were much less successful than their seventies' counterparts had been. *City Heat* (1984 – uniting Clint Eastwood and Burt Reynolds), the troubled production of *The Cotton Club* (1984 – from the *Godfather* team of Robert Evans and Francis Ford

Coppola) and *The Sicilian* (1987 – with Christopher Lambert as Salvatore Giuliano) struggled at the box office. The ultimate retro gangster movie of the decade was Sergio Leone's labyrinthine *Once Upon a Time in America* (1984), with its authentic art design and settings; unfortunately that too died at the US box office. By far the most satisfying period piece of the eighties was Brian De Palma's no-nonsense *The Untouchables* (1987), which resurrected TV's Eliot Ness, portrayed by Kevin Costner, and pitted him against Al Capone, played by Robert De Niro. This was a return to classic form for the genre, aided by Ennio Morricone's powerful score and Sean Connery's Oscar-winning supporting turn as Irish cop James Malone. Experts in their field, the Untouchables were a real organisation – nine agents who in the murky Prohibition-era Chicago police were incorruptible, or 'untouchable'.

Bad guys were well served in the eighties. *Manhunter* (1986 – also called *Red Dragon*) was the first in a series of serial killer investigations culminating in *The Silence of the Lambs* (1991), with Anthony Hopkins as Dr Hannibal 'the Cannibal' Lecter, who means what he says when he remarks, 'I'm having a friend for dinner.'

Eighties law enforcers were popular too, be they futuristic mechanical policemen in multimillion-dollar productions, such as *Robocop* (1987), or blood-laced B-movies, such as William Lustig's *Maniac Cop* (1988). There were tough cops – Burt Reynolds in *Sharky's Machine* (1981) – and hip loners, such as Eddie Murphy in *Beverly Hills Cop* (1984). Dirty Harry Callahan reappeared in *Sudden Impact* (1983) and *The Dead Pool* (1988). Vigilantism was as popular as ever with grim, flame-thrower-wielding Robert Ginty as *The Exterminator* (1980).

Buddy cop movies were raised to an art form in the eighties. Crime-fighting teams were commonplace on TV, with literally dozens vying for popularity, including *Starsky and Hutch*, *Charlie's Angels*, *Cagney and Lacey*, *Miami Vice*, *The A-Team* and *Dempsey and Makepeace*. On the big screen, we had cops teaming up with crooks – for example, Eddie Murphy and Nick Nolte in *48 Hours* (1982). Alternatively, there were cop pairings that were poles apart from one another. By far the most successful example is *Lethal Weapon* (1987), starring Mel Gibson and Danny Glover, initiating the most popular buddy cop screen partnership of recent years.

The big crime biography of the decade was Brian De Palma's remake of Howard Hawks's *Scarface, Shame of a Nation* (1932). Adapted by Oliver Stone, De Palma's film, retitled simply *Scarface*, cast Al Pacino as Tony Montana, a Cuban ex-pat trying to make it in the USA, who rises to be a Miami drugs baron. The film looks great (it was photographed by John A. Alonzo from *Chinatown*) and Pacino crackles with tension, but the gloomy synthesiser score and downbeat, unsympathetic characters make the story heavy going, as does its infamously explicit violence. *Scarface*, in its uncut version, is probably the most violent crime film ever made. An early sequence sees Montana and three accomplices arriving at the apartment of a Colombian gang for a cocaine pick-up, but they are double-crossed. Their rival's boss turns out to be anything but a mellow Colombian and revs up his chainsaw; much bloody action ensues. It is the finale that secures the film's notoriety. Ensconced in his luxury estate, with his own personal bodyguards, Montana waits. A rival drug gang infiltrates the compound and a blood-splattered pitched battle ensues, resembling Sam Peckinpah's *The Wild Bunch* (1969). Montana takes on all comers with an automatic rifle until he is blasted with a shotgun. The finale of the original *Scarface* saw Tony Camonte (Paul Muni) dying near a travel sign reading 'The World is Yours'; here, what's left of riddled Montana swandives into his indoor ornamental pool, decorated with a garishly tasteless cod-Art Deco statue, with a globe motif reading 'The World is Yours'.

In France, there was a distinctively French resurgence of cop movies, called *Policiers*, with for example the phenomenally successful *La Balance* (1982), directed by ex-pat American Bob Swaim. But the protagonists are far from the stylishly dressed heroes of their influential sixties and seventies cousins; now they are scruffy cops in blue jeans, wearing Walkmans on their heads instead of Borsalinos. As well as *Policiers*, there was a new New Wave, including such films as Jean-Jacques Beneix's opera-mystery *Diva* (1980) and Luc Besson's cult *Subway* (1985), which were particularly popular in UK arthouses; the *Subway* poster joined Beatrice Dalle's *Betty Blue* as a must-have on every student's wall.

There were many eighties parodies and crime-film comedies, but despite huge box-office grosses, they haven't worn well. *Police Academy* arrived in 1984; its

'The World is Yours': Al Pacino, as Tony Montana, in
Brian De Palma's controversial *Scarface* (1983).

massive success inspired countless terrible sequels. *Prizzi's Honor* and *Wise Guys* (both 1986) lampooned Mafia movies, *Tough Guys* (1986) saw two ageing gangsters (Burt Lancaster and Kirk Douglas) being released from prison after 30 years, into a world that is unrecognisable to them. *Johnny Dangerously* (1984) failed to parody Cagney's *The Public Enemy*, *Dragnet* tried to ridicule old TV cop shows, while *The Naked Gun* began where the much funnier TV series *Police Files* left off, with Leslie Nielsen cast as Lt Frank Drebin, attempting to foil an assassination attempt on Queen Elizabeth during a royal visit to the US. Two sequels followed: *The Naked Gun 2½: The Smell of Fear* (1991) and *Naked Gun 33⅓: The Final Insult* (1994).

CRIME WAVE 90s

Crime movies in the nineties were dominated by two filmmakers: Martin Scorsese and Quentin Tarantino. Scorsese, a native New Yorker, had made the highly influential *Mean Streets* in 1973 and returned to the streets with his masterpiece, *GoodFellas* (1990), followed by *Casino* (1995) and *Gangs of New York* (2002). Tarantino directed *Reservoir Dogs* in 1991, which caused a furore on its release in 1992. His non-stop mix of John Woo action, hip culture references, sharp dialogue and the nostalgic pop soundtrack immediately found an audience. The follow-up, *Pulp Fiction* (1994), won the Palme D'Or at the Cannes Film Festival. Tarantino also scripted Tony Scott's lovers-on-the-run *True Romance* (1993) and Oliver Stone's bloodfest *Natural Born Killers* (1994), which saw Mickey and Mallory Knox (Woody Harrelson and Juliette Lewis) promoted by the media as superstars. Both films marked an MTV-era re-evaluation of Bonnie and Clyde mythology.

In the eighties frenetic Hong Kong crime films, directed by John Woo and Ringo Lam, gained massive cult popularity worldwide and made a star of Chow Yun Fat. In the nineties Woo made *Hard Boiled* (1992) in Hong Kong, then went to the US for *Broken Arrow* (1996), detailing the theft of a stealth bomber, and *Face/Off* (1997), one of the most bizarre Hollywood crime films of recent years. Here, FBI agent Sean Archer (John Travolta) tracks down Castor Troy (Nicholas Cage), who shot his son five years previously. During the manhunt they literally change faces, but in a psychological twist, they actually swap lives, with the cop trapped in prison at one point, unable to prove his identity.

Crime biography took an interesting twist with the comic book *Dick Tracy* (1990), featuring heavily made-up actors as cartoon characters. It starred Warren Beatty as Tracy, Madonna as singer Breathless Mahoney and Al Pacino as gangster Big Boy Caprice. Beatty also appeared in *Bugsy* (1991), as the title gangster, Bugsy Siegel. In the UK, Ronnie and Reggie Kray got the big-screen gangster treatment with *The Krays* (1990), a tale of the terrifying London mobster brothers, played by Gary and Martin Kemp, from eighties 'new romantics' Spandau Ballet.

The nineties saw the release of *Con Air* (1997), an airborne reworking of *Riot in Cell Block 11*, and Walter Hill's attempt at 'Red Harvest', *Last Man Standing* (1996). More interesting was the dark, claustrophobic atmosphere of *Copland* (1997), with Sylvester Stallone as a small-fry cop trying to swim with the big fish in the city, as corruption permeates; a strong cast included Harvey Keitel, Robert De Niro and Ray Liotta. *Boyz 'N the Hood* (1991) was *The Public Enemy* for the rap generation; in fact the most famous eighties rap act was named Public Enemy.

Pacino followed the final instalment of the *Godfather* story, *The Godfather Part III* (1990), with *Carlito's Way* (1993) and *Donnie Brasco* (1997). *Carlito's Way*, another gangster biography directed by *Scarface*'s Brian De Palma, saw Pacino cast as seventies Puerto Rican mobster Carlito Brigante and Sean Penn as his lawyer, David Kleinfeld (wearing what appears to be an Art Garfunkle wig). *Donnie Brasco* (1997) was based on a true story; Johnny Depp is the title character, actually Joe Pistone, an undercover FBI man, who is taught the ways of the mob by Pacino's Lefty Ruggiero.

Undoubtedly the most anticipated crime pairing since Bonnie met Clyde saw Robert De Niro and Al Pacino sharing the bill in Michael Mann's modern crime thriller *Heat* (1995 – a remake of his own TV movie, *L.A. Takedown* [1989]), filmed in an ultra-stylish, steely blue Los Angeles. *Heat* features the least subtle heist in crime movie history, with De Niro and company ramming an articulated lorry cab into the side of the targeted armoured car, which impacts with such force that the armoured car rolls onto its side. De Niro played Neil McCauley, a robber out for one last job; Pacino is his cop nemesis, Vincent Hanna, with a wife who is permanently stoned on grass and Prozac. *Heat* features many such personal problems: marriages break down, stepdaughters attempt suicide and families fracture. De Niro and Pacino share two scenes together: the central dialogue between McCauley and Hanna in a coffee shop, in which the pair grudgingly acknowledge mutual respect, and the final shootout near Los Angeles airport. Mann also stages an incredible firefight following a bungled bank robbery: Pacino and his heavily armed squad ambush McCauley and his three-man gang on the streets of Los Angeles; only McCauley and gang member Chris Shiherlis (Val Kilmer) escape. Pity the bystanders in this fiery exchange, as all the participants are wearing bulletproof vests. The heavy artillery on display in this machine-gun shootout and Mann's fluid camerawork, taking the audience to the heart of the firestorm, seems part bullet-ridden *First Blood*, part jumpy Kennedy assassination footage – 'criminal vérité' for the nineties. *Heat* is enhanced by an eerie score, composed by Elliot Goldenthal and performed by the Kronos Quartet.

The finest crime movie of the nineties was Curtis Hanson's fifties period *noir*, *L.A.Confidential* (1997), an adaptation of James Ellroy's terse, hard-boiled novel, which threw politics, tabloid journalism, celebrity, murder and corruption into the Los Angeles melting pot. There were also several blockbusting thrillers and their rolling sequels, which used hijacking and robbery in a broader action milieu, including *Die Hard* (1988), *Die Hard 2* (1990), *Speed* (1994), *Die Hard With a Vengeance* (1995), *Mission: Impossible* (1996), *Speed 2: Cruise Control* (1997) and *Mission: Impossible 2* (2000). These films rely heavily on spectacular stunts and CGI special effects to engage the audience's attention. For example, in *Speed*, a superior example of the genre, Keanu Reeves is pitted against extortionist Dennis Hopper, who demands a $3.7 million ransom from the city of Los Angeles. He has planted a bomb on a bus, which will detonate if the bus's speed isn't maintained at a steady 50 mph. Reeves and Sandra Bullock take the wheel for a nail-biting ride.

European crime movies produced *La Femme Nikita* (1990), Luc Besson's story of a female assassin. Besson's US film, *Leon* (1994), saw hitman Jean Reno teaming up with 12-year-old Natalie Portman to gain revenge on the murderer of Portman's father, a corrupt cop, played by Gary Oldman. In the UK there was renewed popularity in domestic crime movies, with the success of Guy Richie's *Lock, Stock and Two Smoking Barrels* (1998) and *Snatch* (2000). *Lock, Stock* mixed the brutality of *Get Carter* and the Cockney charm of *The Italian Job*, and even spawned a short-lived TV show, with episodes entitled 'Lock, Stock and Four Stolen Hooves' and 'Lock, Stock and A Fistful of Jack and Jills'. *Snatch* was better, featuring protagonists with descriptive names such as Turkish, Frankie Four Fingers and Brick Top, in a tale of jewel heists and fixed boxing matches: 'Stealing Stones and Breaking Bones' ran the tagline. Richie has since followed this with the crime drama *Revolver* (2005).

CRIME WAVE: 21st-CENTURY COPS

Entering the new century, crime films continue to diversify. They keep surprising audiences with further twists and turns, proving how flexible, adaptable and recyclable the genre is. To take some disparate examples: *Gone in 60 Seconds* (2000) featured Nicholas Cage stealing cars, but like the high-octane remake of *The Italian Job* (2003), the film was running on empty. There was the easygoing charm of Steven Spielberg's *Catch Me if You Can* (2002), with a con artist (played by Leonardo DiCaprio) chased by Tom Hanks's resolute FBI man. Shane Black, the writer of *Lethal Weapon*, directed the neo-*noir Kiss Kiss Bang Bang* (2005), starring Val Kilmer and Robert Downey Jnr, while the same year saw the release of *Sin City* (2005), a monochrome, violent comic strip *noir* starring Bruce Willis, Clive Owen and Mickey Rourke, and based on Frank Miller's urban gothic work. *Sexy Beast* (2000) features a Ronnie Biggs-style British crook hiding out in Southern Spain. Here, Ray Winston's sunbathing is interrupted by the arrival of Ben Kingsley, as Don Logan, possibly the most offensive and frightening British crook ever to appear in a crime movie; it is little wonder Winston suffers nightmares about being machine-gunned by an evil-looking giant rabbit.

The Colombian/US co-production *Maria Full of Grace* (2004) saw the teenage Colombian heroine smuggling condoms full of heroin in her stomach. Steven Soderbergh's *Traffic* (2000), based on a UK miniseries, looked at cocaine smuggling across the Mexican border; it won Soderbergh the Best Director Oscar. Soderbergh went on to direct *Ocean's Eleven* (2001), one of the slickest heist movies of the genre. Other super-smart heist thrillers include the superior *The Thomas Crown Affair* (1999), which pitted the audience against some of the most intricate plotting in the history of cinema, a trend initiated by the brain-teasing *The Usual Suspects* (1995).

Something of a step back for the genre, *Chicago* (2002) was a musical drama set in the twenties. Renee Zellweger appeared as Roxie Hart, with Catherine Zeta-Jones as Velma Kelly, a pair of cabaret singers mixed up in a murder case, based on a real incident. This film, with its authentic gangster milieu and production numbers, was inspired by mobster musicals set in the theatre, such as *Broadway* (1929), and sees the crime genre coming full circle.

One of the best and most distinctive recent crime movies is *City of God* (2003 – originally called *Cidade de Deus*), directed by Fernando Meirelles. Set in Rio de Janeiro's worst slum, cynically christened 'City of God', it tells the story of street gang violence and drug turf wars, which ravaged the city in the seventies. The main character is Winston Rodrigues, known as Rocket, a young man who dreams of being a photographer, a career that will allow him to escape the slums. His brother, a hood, is killed early in the film; his other contemporaries 'get religion' or work honestly, but most end up joining street gangs and being swept into crime. The most notorious and bloodthirsty of the gangstas is L'il Ze and his level-headed partner Bene, who sell drugs in town. Their only competition is 'Carrot', who teams up with Knockout Ned, a local hero, to stand up to L'il Ze. With stories entitled 'The Story of the Tender Trio', 'Flirting with Crime' and 'The Story of Knockout Ned', and Rocket's voiceover narration, *City of God* looks back to 'rise and fall' crime biographies, such as *The Public Enemy* and *GoodFellas*, but in an original way, with its intense action, brothel robberies and drug dealing (all beautifully photographed by Casar Charlone). To offset the brutality, Meirelles also depicts the community's flourishing nightlife, with sequences set in a vast nightclub pumping out James Brown tracks and 'Kung Fu Fighting', by Carl Douglas. The opening chicken chase scene is among the most arresting in modern cinema, as a mob of pistol-packing kids, the Runts, chase a hapless hen (making a bid for freedom) hell for leather through back street slums, only to round a corner and confront the police in a stand-off. *City of God* is breathtaking, but uncompromising; be warned: it is unlike any other crime film you will have seen.

Crime movies have used many settings, from the slums of Rio, the terraces of Newcastle and the towering neon palaces of Las Vegas, to the streets of San Francisco, the back streets of Paris and the mean streets of New York. To begin the movie gangster's story, we must look back to the thirsty thirties of Prohibition, when the public enemies first appeared, riding the crest of a crime wave…

CRIME WAVE TOP TENS

The films, selected from international sources, are arranged in order of preference; director and original release year in parenthesis.

Andrew Collins:
Andrew is a writer and broadcaster, and film editor at the *Radio Times*. He is the author of *Heaven Knows I'm Miserable Now*, *Where Did It All Go Right?* and *Billy Bragg: Still Suitable for Miners*.

The Godfather/The Godfather Part II (Francis Ford Coppola, 1972/74)
Chinatown (Roman Polanski, 1974)
Key Largo (John Huston, 1948)
Double Indemnity (Billy Wilder, 1944)
The French Connection (William Friedkin, 1971)
Reservoir Dogs (Quentin Tarantino, 1992)
GoodFellas (Martin Scorsese, 1990)
The Ladykillers (Alexander Mackendrick, 1955)
Get Carter (Mike Hodges, 1971)
The Silence of the Lambs (Jonathan Demme, 1991)

Alex Cox:
Alex Cox is a writer, broadcaster and filmmaker. His films include *Repo Man* (1984), *Sid and Nancy* (1986), *Walker* (1987) and *Highway Patrolman* (1993). His documentaries include *Kurosawa: the Last Emperor* (1999).

Rififi (Jules Dassin, 1954)
Deuxieme Souffle (Jean-Pierre Melville, 1966)
Branded to Kill (Seijun Suzuki, 1967)
Point Blank (John Boorman, 1967)
White Heat (Raoul Walsh, 1949)
Kiss Me Deadly (Robert Aldrich, 1955)
High and Low (Akira Kurosawa, 1963)
Bonnie and Clyde (Arthur Penn, 1967)
Get Carter (Mike Hodges, 1971)
Dead Presidents (The Hughes Brothers, 1995)

Paul Duncan:
Paul Duncan is editor of the Taschen Film Series and *The Third Degree: Crime Writers in Conversation*. He is also author of *Film Noir: Films of Trust and Betrayal*, *Martin Scorsese* and *Noir Fiction*.

Night and the City (Jules Dassin, 1950)
Le Samouraï (Jean-Pierre Melville, 1967)
Kiss Me Deadly (Robert Aldrich, 1955)
Touch of Evil (Orson Welles, 1958)
Branded to Kill (Seijun Suzuki, 1967)
GoodFellas (Martin Scorsese, 1990)
Point Blank (John Boorman, 1967)
Shadow of a Doubt (Alfred Hitchcock, 1943)
Ghost Dog – The Way of the Samurai (Jim Jarmusch, 1999)
The Insider (Michael Mann, 1999)

Howard Hughes:
Howard Hughes is a film writer, and the author of *Once Upon a Time in the Italian West*, and Pocket Essential guides to *The American Indian Wars* and *Spaghetti Westerns*.

Chinatown (Roman Polanski, 1974)
Point Blank (John Boorman, 1967)
Get Carter (Mike Hodges, 1971)
Dirty Harry (Don Siegel, 1971)
Le Samouraï (Jean-Pierre Melville, 1967)
The Public Enemy (William Wellman, 1931)
On Her Majesty's Secret Service (Peter Hunt, 1969)
Illustrious Corpses (Francesco Rosi, 1976)
The Godfather Part II (Francis Ford Coppola, 1974)
Bonnie and Clyde (Arthur Penn, 1967)

Stuart Maconie:
Stuart Maconie is a writer, broadcaster and journalist. He is also the presenter of *The DVD Collection* and *The Cinema Show*. His books include *3862 Days: the Official History of Blur*, *James – Folklore: the Official History* and *Cider with Roadies*.

Get Carter (Mike Hodges, 1971)
Strangers on a Train (Alfred Hitchcock, 1951)
House of Games (David Mamet, 1987)
White Heat (Raoul Walsh, 1949)
Dog Day Afternoon (Sydney Lumet, 1975)
The Private Life of Sherlock Holmes (Billy Wilder, 1970)
Homicide (David Mamet, 1991)
That Sinking Feeling (Bill Forsyth, 1979)
The Lavender Hill Mob (Charles Crichton, 1951)
The Big Sleep (Howard Hawks, 1946)

1

'I ain't so tough'

— *The Public Enemy* (1931)

Credits:

DIRECTOR – William A. Wellman

EXECUTIVE PRODUCER – Darryl F. Zanuck

STORY – John Bright and Kubec Glasmon

SCREENPLAY – Kubec Glasmon, John Bright and Harvey Thew

DIRECTOR OF PHOTOGRAPHY – Dev Jennings

EDITOR – Ed McCormick

ART DIRECTOR – Max Parker

COSTUME DESIGNERS – Earl Luick and Edward Stevenson

MUSIC CONDUCTOR – David Mendoza

Black and white

Interiors filmed at Warner Bros

A Warner Bros-Vitaphone production

Released by Warner Bros

84 minutes

Cast:

James Cagney (Tom Powers)/Jean Harlow (Gwen Allen)/Edward Woods (Matt Doyle)/Joan Blondell (Mamie)/Beryl Mercer (Ma Powers)/Donald Cook (Mike Powers, Tom's brother)/Mae Clarke (Kitty)/Mia Marvin (Jane)/Leslie Fenton (Samuel 'Nails' Nathan)/ Robert Emmett O'Connor (Patrick J. Ryan, alias Paddy Ryan)/Rita Flynn (Molly Doyle)/Frank Coglan Jnr (Tom as a boy)/Frankie Darrow (Matt as a boy)/Adele Watson (Mrs Doyle)/Murray Kinnell (Putty Nose)/Clark Burroughs (Dutch, member of Ryan's gang)/Robert Homans (Police Officer Pat Burke)/Mia Marvin (Jane, girl at hideout)/Purnell Pratt (Tom's father)/William H. Strauss (Pawnbroker robbed by Tom)/Lee Phelps (Bullied bartender)

*   *   *

Rico Bandello, alias *Little Caesar*, may have beaten Tom Powers, alias *The Public Enemy*, into theatres, but James Cagney's kinetic portrayal of a psychopathic gangster is pre-eminent among the 'rise and fall' tales of gangsterdom that dominated thirties Hollywood productions. Powers's final revenge for the death of his best friend, walking into the lions' den with a pair of pistols and subsequently staggering into the gutter, bullet-ridden, muttering, 'I ain't so tough', is far more effective than Edward G. Robinson's reedy 'Mother of God – is this the end of Rico?' demise. Cagney is *the* movie gangster and *The Public Enemy* is a pivotal film, though it was not Cagney's first contribution to the genre.

James Cagney was born James Francis Cagney Jnr in New York in 1899; he grew up on the Lower East Side in Yorkville and knew very well the kind of upbringing and background that could 'turn kids bad'. He worked in a variety of jobs, including boxing, but eventually joined a revue, finding his way into the chorus on Broadway in 1920 and from there graduated to lead roles. He appeared in the musical *Penny Arcade* and his first film appearance was recreating this role. Warners' film version, spicily retitled *Sinners' Holiday* (1930), was a carnival romance between a barker and a penny arcade girl. Bit-parts for Cagney followed – his next film was *Doorway to Hell* (1930 – released as the much lighter-sounding *A Handful of Clouds* in the UK), a topical tale of bootleggers, released a month before *Little Caesar* changed the gangster movie map. Lew Ayres starred as the kingpin, with Cagney as his henchman. Cagney also made *Other Men's Women* (1931 – a railroad drama) and *The Millionaire* (1931 – Cagney's first comedy), before screen-testing for the role of Matt Doyle in *The Public Enemy*. Young actor Edward Woods was to play the lead, Tom Powers, but almost immediately director William A. Wellman realised the actors were in the wrong roles and reversed them. The casting swap of Cagney and Woods is most apparent with the two young actors who were chosen to play Tom and Matt as children. Frankie Darro (as Matt) is a dead ringer for a young Cagney, while Frank Coglan Jnr (as Tom) closely resembles Woods.

The Public Enemy was based on the novelette 'Beer and Blood' by Baltimore-born John Bright, who had been a crime reporter in Chicago, the setting for his story. Bright's unauthorised biography of Chicago's mayor, 'Hizzoner Big Bill Thomson', led to him being sued by the mayor. *The Public Enemy* was his first film script. He wrote it with Kubec Glasmon, a Polish-born pharmacist, who became his writing partner at Warners, with the novel's dialogue adapted by Harvey Thew.

In the story, Tom Powers and Matt Doyle grow up together in Chicago. As slum urchins they fall into petty crime and when they grow up become involved with a small-timer named Putty Nose, who convinces them to take part in a robbery on the Northwestern Fur Trading Company. The job is a mess and in making their escape, Tom kills a policeman. Putty Nose vanishes and leaves Tom and Matt to face the music. The pair become involved with Irish racketeer Paddy Ryan, a bootlegger and liquor-runner, who is in business with Nails Nathan, a dapper mobster from 'the West Side'. Tom and Matt rise through the ranks of racketeers and become rich and notorious (when they catch up with Putty Nose, Tom executes him); all the while, Tom tells his mother that he is working in local politics, until his disapproving elder brother Mike discovers otherwise. Nails Nathan is killed in a freak riding accident and rival 'Schemer' Burns and his mobsters try to muscle in on his turf. In an ambush, Matt is machine-gunned down and Tom goes looking for revenge, attacking Burns's headquarters and killing the kingpin, but getting badly injured. While he recovers in hospital, Tom is kidnapped by the Burns faction; one night, as his mother prepares the bed for his homecoming, his brother answers the door and Tom's trussed-up corpse flops face down into the hallway.

The Great American Depression of the thirties, with falling output and massive unemployment (at some points 33 per cent of the population), coincided with the new vogue for gangster movies, spearheaded by Warner Brothers' Studio. The recent advent of sound meant that you could hear screeching wheels, approaching sirens and Thomson Submachine-gun fire and the wisecracking, quick-fire dialogue crackled with menace. When *The Public Enemy* was made, the US was still under the rules of the Volstead Prohibition (1920–1933) and the protagonists' activities were remarkably contemporary. Jack Warner liked to make films that had

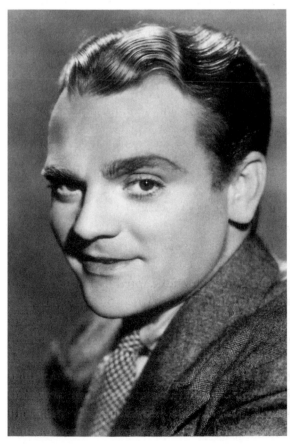

Early thirties Warners promotional portrait, published in the *Picturegoer* series, of fresh-faced James Cagney: Public Enemy Number One.

contemporary social thrust. The Prohibition act outlawed the manufacture, distribution or retail of alcohol. This led to bootlegging, or 'alky-cooking', as depicted in *The Public Enemy*, where organised crime, financed by illegal booze, resulted in inter-gang rivalry and turf wars (a bootlegger was originally a wild-west term referring to the way traders carried bottles of firewater in their boots to sell to the Indians). *The Public Enemy* is set between 1909 and 1920. The date captions include 1915 (the year of the fur heist), wartime 1917 (the US declaration and Mike enlisting in the Marines) and the Prohibition scenes in 1920, which begin with a sign in the Family Liquor Store – 'Owing to prohibition, our entire stock must be sold by midnight' – prompting a stampede by the locals to fill every available vessel with 'hooch'.

Director William Augustus Wellman had previously made the silent World War I film *Wings*, which won the very first Best Picture Academy Award in 1927 (it was re-released in 1929 with sound). In *The Public Enemy* Wellman cast Liverpudlian Leslie Fenton as spruce gangster Nails Nathan; Fenton himself later became a director in the fifties. Mae Clarke, who in the most famous scene in the film has a grapefruit thrust in her face, also appeared in James Whales's *Frankenstein* (1931), as Henry Frankenstein's fiancée, Elizabeth. Errol Flynn lookalike Edward Woods, the victim of Cagney's promotion to leading man, was only appearing in his second film (his debut had been in *Mother's Cry* – 1930) and his film career was short-lived. By contrast, Joan Blondell, as Matt's girl Mamie, had appeared with Cagney in *Sinners' Holiday* (her Warners' debut) and *Other Men's Women*, and was one of the most popular and prolific actresses of the era.

The most famous of Cagney's co-stars was Jean Harlow, the original platinum blonde screen goddess, who had caused a stir in *Hell's Angels* (1930) – her looks were so influential that the two movies she made after *The Public Enemy* were *Goldie* and *Platinum Blonde* (both 1931). She died tragically in 1937, aged 26, of a cerebral oedema (fluid on the brain), but her iconic impact was immense.

In 1928, Warners had bought the Stanley Corporation of America, owner of 250 cinemas across the US, and First National, another chain. *The Public Enemy* was filmed at Warner Bros' Studios between January and February 1931; Vitaphone's involvement was the relatively current sound-mixing elements and the Vitaphone Orchestra, conducted by David Mendoza, recorded the score. The Warners' Studios had formerly been First National Studios, which had been wired for sound in 1928. *The Public Enemy* features several authentic street-scene sets (with drays piled with kegs, a Salvation Army band and kids on the sidewalk swigging beer) and some stock location footage of railways, cattle pens and thriving streets choked with trams, automobiles, horse-drawn carriages and pedestrians. Interiors accurately evoked the era, with one sign in a spit-and-sawdust social club warning: 'Don't Spit On the Floor!'

During the making of the film, Cagney had a near miss during a machine-gun ambush; real bullets peppered the cornerstone of a building and one almost hit the actor (a hazard of filmmaking that recurred in *Angels With Dirty Faces*). The scene when Cagney pushes a grapefruit into Mae Clarke's face, after she accuses him of being unfaithful, was based on a real-life incident involving Chicago gangster Hymie Weiss, who used an omelette. On set it was decided that a grapefruit would be a good substitute. There are three versions of how the scene was filmed. Initially Cagney was going to throw it, but Wellman and Cagney changed their minds when Clarke would only allow them one take. Alternatively, Clarke had a cold and wanted to fake the shot with a stand-in, but the director insisted they do it for real, much to Clarke's displeasure. Finally, the most widely believed and plausible version was that Clarke and Cagney were larking around on set and the scene was never meant to appear in the finished film.

A brief foreword introduces the film's moral stance on 'the evils associated with prohibition'. Following the titles (accompanied by a staccato march arrangement of the standard 'I'm Forever Blowing Bubbles') we are introduced to each character, captioned with their character names: Tom mimes a punch (a gesture he repeats throughout the film) and Matt wipes his nose on his sleeve (his trademark, presumably in a joking effort to 'keep it clean'). Another caption then says the film is about to 'honestly depict an environment that exists today in a certain strata of American life', rather than 'glorify the hoodlum or the criminal'. In the US, the Hayes Code was introduced in 1930, which led to much more stringent censorship restrictions; until then films were covered by a simple do's and don'ts outline. Under the new guidelines, *The Public Enemy*, without such a disclaimer, would have clearly breached the code.

Playing safe, Warner Brothers Pictures claim that the story is true, but 'all names and characters appearing therein are purely fictional'. Many of the film's events were based on Charles Dion 'Deannie' O'Banion, an Irish Catholic mobster, and his gang, the Irish North Siders in Chicago (O'Banion was executed in classic gangland fashion in his florist's shop, when a rival mobster's men called in to collect a specially ordered wreath). In *The Public Enemy*, the brutal scene when Tom Powers shoots Rajah, the horse that kicked Nails Nathan in the head, is inspired by a true incident from the career of Louis 'Two Gun' Altieri, an O'Banion hoodlum. Nails Nathan was based on Samuel J. 'Nails' Morton; Morton was killed when his horse threw him and trampled him to death. Altieri, plus three other O'Banion men, kidnapped the horse, took it to the scene of the accident and shot it dead in revenge.

The central relationship between Tom and Matt, from teens to tombstone, is well delineated by Cagney and Woods. They begin as kids, having a crafty swig of beer on the street outside a saloon and with petty pilfering from department stores, but with maturity comes responsibility and far more serious crimes. The fur robbery is scotched by edgy Tom taking a shot at a stuffed bear caught in the torchlight. The shot alerts the police, who shoot the getaway driver, Lippy Larry. As they escape, Tom commits his first murder, with a Smith and Wesson given to him by Putty Nose – an exploitative and untrustworthy fence who even tried to swindle them when they were kids. As Tom notes later, 'You taught us how to cheat, steal and kill... If it hadn't been for you, we might've been on the level.' Following the fur robbery, Larry's wake is a poignant moment that sees sheepish Tom and Matt introduced as 'some of Larry's nicer friends', while elder relatives tut that Larry was 'a no-good boy'.

Prompted by alcohol being sold for $30 a gallon, they begin in the illicit liquor trade. Working for Irish bootlegger Paddy Ryan, they set up a brewing company (Lehman's) with Nails Nathan and his pack of hoods, making sure that local pubs and saloons 'buy our beer or they don't buy any beer'. Tom and Matt are the 'trouble squad', the muscle, threatening bartenders that if they don't comply, they will drop by and 'kick your teeth out, one at a time'. Their first foray into bootleg robbery is one of the film's highlights. Having cased the layout while working as deliverymen, the gang arrives at the booze warehouse in a tanker truck marked GASOLINE. Two cohorts pose as telegraph men and climb into the building, put taps on the storage kegs and syphon the beer into the tanker with a length of hosepipe.

Tom's relationship with women (his mother excepted) and the awkwardness of the romantic scenes are *The Public Enemy*'s biggest failing. Apart from his *grapefruit-à-tête* with Kitty, Tom's snappy dating technique sees him uttering the immortal lines, 'Hello baby, you're a swell dish – I think I'm going to go for you!' with his 'date' seemingly having little say in the matter. His relationship with Harlow, as out-of-town Texan 'merry-go-round' Gwen, is more complicated, but he certainly isn't in love, and she eventually decides to skip town. By contrast, Matt and Mamie get married; 'Matt's decided to take something lawful... a wife,' jokes Nails. But the night of their celebration is the night they run into Putty Nose again and the party is forestalled. It seems the bond between the two men is the singularly most important factor in their lives.

As the voice of the film's moral stance, so as not to make *The Public Enemy* too attractive to moviegoers deprived of drink and low on cash, Wellman has Tom's brother Mike. Their father is a police officer, but even when they were kids it was Tom to whom he had to 'give the strap'. As adults, with their father dead, Mike discovers Tom's nefarious activities from policeman Pat Burke and refuses any kindness from his brother; even a keg at Mike's homecoming from the war is described as being filled with 'beer and blood'. Later, Tom brings his family some money, but Mike has other ideas – 'Get an earful of this: that money's blood money and we want no part of it.' Tom says money is valueless to him (which suggests he does his job for enjoyment). His brother answers, 'With no heart and no brains it's all you've got... you'll need it.' Unfortunately this is not an entirely convincing argument: Mike works as a 'ding-ding' on tramcars, joins the war-bound Marines, comes back a shaking wreck and goes to night school (in Tom's words, 'learning how to be poor'). Tom meanwhile drinks beer and champagne throughout the decade-long drought, gets the girls, dances in tuxedos and drives the largest convertible ever seen on film. But his brother's pontificating is shown to be moral, when Tom's corpse is delivered to their doorstep, trussed up with rope, still in the hospital blanket and bloodied head bandage: mummified and ready for entombment. In the background, a gramophone plays 'I'm Forever Blowing Bubbles', then reaches the repetitive click of the endless run-out groove.

We don't actually see Tom's death, and for a film that is so black-hearted, there is surprisingly little on-screen violence perpetrated by the Public Enemy. Wellman keeps the most graphic instants of death to the narrative margins, supplying all we need to know from actors' reactions to events off-screen. When Tom finds out Putty has run out on them, he whines: 'Why that dirty, no good yellow-bellied stool...I'm gonna give it that Putty Nose right in the head, first time I see him.' When Tom and Matt do catch up with him, Putty tries to rekindle their friendship with a sense of nostalgia; he even plays a song from the good old days in the Red Oaks Social Club. As the camera follows Matt to the door, Tom shoots Putty off-screen; our only indication of the events are a gunshot and a discordant piano crescendo as Putty slumps on the keyboard.

The more conventional action scenes, like the moment Ryan's premises are obliterated by grenades tossed from Burns's speeding cars, offset the crueller elements of the film and reinforce its authenticity. Though some of the tough-guy

Rise and Fall: Tom (James Cagney) and Gwen (Jean Harlow) living the high life in William A. Wellman's *The Public Enemy* (1931).

language has dated badly ('Are you looking for a smack on the button?'/'Four pineapples tossed at us in three days'), the list of brutality is potent, especially for a film of 1931. Any film that can boast a protagonist who shoots people in the back, kills cops, lies to his mother, threatens bartenders, hits women and shoots a racehorse is violent fare for any era. Cagney was so effective in his portrayal of Tom Powers that by 1933 the Production Code Authority stated that gangsters should not be idolised or glamorised in the cinema; in 1935 Cagney himself made *G-Men*, starring as a gangbusting government agent, to redress the balance.

Tom is a cocky, grinning punk, who bullies the opposition and, until the final gun battle, always wins – unfair and square. The baby-faced gangster is turned by Cagney's gracefulness and élan into an angelic killer, for whom we almost feel sympathy in the dénouement; in one extraordinary moment the ex-dancer executes a light-footed pirouette, with a couple of half-skips thrown in, as he gets back in his car after chatting up Gwen. Later, at the ambush, the image of him standing in the lashing rain, waiting for Schemer Burns's mob to arrive at their 'front', the 'Western Chemical Company', is one of the film's most effective. Tom can hardly contain his loathing, Cagney's face sneering and twitchy, overcome with hatred and a feral instinct for revenge; just like when they were kids, when he was described as 'the meanest boy in town'. As the rival mob emerge from two cars and file in, Tom purposefully walks across the street, hands on pistols in his jacket pockets, collar up, hat low, and bursts in, unleashing his vitriol in a fusillade of shots. A moment later he emerges; in the background, screams and moans from Burns's crew follow in his wake. No more the angel, he staggers, bloody and drenched. Tom throws both his pistols through the shop windows and collapses in the gutter with the realisation 'I ain't so tough…' A final epilogue sternly gives the audience something to think about on the way home: 'The end of Tom Powers is the end of every hoodlum. The Public Enemy is not a man, nor is it a character – it is a problem that sooner or later, WE, the public, must solve!' No wonder it was called the Great Depression.

The Public Enemy was released in 1931. The trailer simply featured a pistol firing directly at the screen, with the slogan 'A few scenes cannot do justice to the most powerful picture of the year'. Posters depicted Harlow and Cagney embracing, or Cagney brandishing a pistol, with the effective tagline 'The Killer-Boss who Riddled, Roared and Terror-reigned his way across the DECADE OF DEATH'. For her prominent deployment in the publicity, Harlow is actually only on screen for three scenes. The film was condemned for its violence; even if most of it happens off-screen, the savage implication is clear. *Picture Play* called the film 'a grim and terrible document, with no attempt to soften or humanise the character. Of all racketeer films it is the most brutal and least like movie fiction. For this reason it is the most arresting.' *Time* magazine reckoned the film's intensity was 'relieved by scenes of the central characters slugging bartenders and slapping their women across the face. US audiences, long trained by the press to glorify thugs, last week laughed loudly at such comedy and sat spellbound through the serious parts.' Of the finale *Time* noted that it 'carries to its ultimate absurdity the fashion for romanticising gangsters, for even in defeat the public enemy is endowed with grandeur'. It was a huge hit in the US, even though Warner Bros were currently operating at a net loss of $7,918,604 – but it was the Depression and the studio did not begin to show a profit until 1935.

The original US print distributed ran 96 minutes, but all subsequent releases have been 84; TV prints from the seventies list the running time as 90 minutes. When it went for its general release in Britain, self-censorship was rife and the film was refused a certificate. In a famous case, Beckenham Council had its own film censorship board in the early thirties and banned nine films, including Paul Muni's *Scarface* and *The Public Enemy*. The latter was after the grapefruit scene had already been removed by the British censors; in another example, a moral-minded Cornish borough council took it upon itself to ban films throughout the decade, even though it didn't have a single cinema. *The Public Enemy* was retitled *Enemies of the Public* for the UK, broadening the focus to Tom and Matt, and their attendant mobsters' rogues gallery. Everywhere else the film was known by literal translations of its title: *Nemico Publico* in Italy; *Der Öffentliche Feind* in Germany.

Glasmon and Bright were nominated for an Oscar for Best Original Story for their work on *The Public Enemy* (John Monk Sanders won for *The Dawn Patrol*). They worked at Warners for the next few years and wrote several Cagney vehicles: *Smart Money* (1931); *Blonde Crazy* (1931 – with Cagney and Blondell as con artists masquerading as a bellhop and a maid); *The Crowd Roars* (1932 – Howard Hawks's motor racing drama) and *Taxi!* (1932). In 1933 Bright and Glasmon were two of the founders of the Screen Writers Guild and Bright was later blacklisted by the House of Un-American Activities. Bright also collaborated again with Harvey Thew; their greatest success was adapting 'Diamond Lil' to the screen for Mae West at Paramount as *She Done Him Wrong* (1933); made for $200,000 in 18 days, it grossed $3 million.

With the runaway success of *Little Caesar* and *The Public Enemy*, Robinson and Cagney were teamed in their next movie, the mediocre *Smart Money* (1931), with Robinson as a barber with a sideline in gambling and Cagney as his sidekick. The film also featured Boris Karloff, and was a massive success; it was the only time the two gangster greats co-starred together. In 1931, Cagney was on $450 a week, according to his Warners' contract. Shortly after the success of *The Public Enemy* he refused to work until it was revised: this resulted in a new five-year, $1000-a-week deal. In an indication of his power, Cagney pulled the same stunt in 1932. He lobbied for even more money, finally winning his case and earning $1,750 per week. Cagney's output throughout the thirties was generally average in quality, but he remained popular; typical was the boxing saga *The Irish in Us* (1935). He made *Lady Killer* (1933), which reunited him with Mae Clarke and Leslie Fenton from *The Public Enemy*, and parodied his tough-guy image. In *Taxi* (1932) Cagney uttered his most famous line, a favourite with Cagney impersonators, and anyone who narrowed their eyes, clenched their teeth and whined, 'Come out and take it…you dirty rat'.

One legacy of *The Public Enemy* was that Cagney never again had to buy a grapefruit – every time he walked into a restaurant, someone would send one over. Although Cagney worked hard, and even played a good guy in the highly successful *G–Men* (1935 – by which time he had hiked his salary up to $4,500 per week), it was seven years before Cagney made a film to equal *The Public Enemy*'s impact, and for that role he would once more have to play an angel with a dirty face.

2

'Just rushing towards death'

— *High Sierra* (1941)

Credits:

DIRECTOR – Raoul Walsh

EXECUTIVE PRODUCER – Hal B. Wallis

ASSOCIATE PRODUCER – Mark Hellinger (for First National)

STORY – W.R. Burnett

SCREENPLAY – John Huston and W.R. Burnett

DIRECTOR OF PHOTOGRAPHY – Tony Gaudio

EDITOR – Jack Killifer

ART DIRECTOR – Ted Smith

COSTUME DESIGNER – Milo Anderson

MUSIC COMPOSER – Adolph Deutsch

Black and white

Interiors filmed at Warner Bros Studios

A Warner Bros-First National production

Released by Warner Bros

100 minutes

Cast:

Ida Lupino (Marie Garson)/Humphrey Bogart ('Mad Dog' Roy Earl)/Alan Curtis ('Babe' Kozak)/Arthur Kennedy ('Red' Hattery)/Joan Leslie (Velma)/Henry Hull ('Doc' Banton)/Henry Travers (Pa Goodhue)/Elizabeth Risdon (Ma Goodhue)/Barton MacLane (Jake Kranmer, the ex-cop)/Jerome Cowan (Healy, reporter from the *Bulletin*)/Minna Gombell (Mrs Baughmann)/Cornel Wilde (Louis Mendoza)/Willie Best (Algernon)/Donald McBride (Big Mac)/Paul Harvey (Mr Baughmann)/Isabel Jewell ('Blonde', Jake's girl)/Spencer Charters (Ed, gas station owner)/John Elredge (Lon Preiser, Velma's beau)/George Meeker (Pfiffer, victim of car accident)/Robert Strange (Art)/Sam Haynes (Radio Announcer at siege)/Frank Cordell (Slim, the sniper)/Zero the Dog (Pard)

*   *   *

Based on Chicago author William Riley Burnett's book of the same name, *High Sierra* reveals how much the gangster hero had matured in the 10 years since the screen version of Burnett's *Little Caesar* and Cagney's Tom Powers in *The Public Enemy*. Roy Earle, a lifer, wins a pardon and is released from Mossmore Prison, Chicago, but finds that he is out of step with the times. He visits Jake Kranmer, an ex-cop, who informs him that he has been sprung from prison by his old boss, Big Mac, who has him earmarked for a job. Earle travels out to Shaw's Camp, a fishing resort in the High Sierras of California, and meets the gang: drinker 'Babe' Kozak, jumpy 'Red' Hattery and Marie, a refugee from LA who is tagging along with the duo. Earle discovers that they are to knock over the strong boxes in the luxury Tropico Hotel Resort, which at the height of the horseracing season will be brimming with diamonds. Their insider will be Louis Mendoza, who works at the hotel.

When the gang carry out the job, they clear the boxes, but Earle shoots a cop and they flee in two cars; the one carrying Red, Babe and Mendoza careers off the road and only Mendoza survives. On the run with the diamonds, Earle and Marie find that Big Mac has died and Kranmer is a turncoat, so Earle kills him – but is wounded in the process. While waiting for the fence to sell on the diamonds, Mendoza squeals, so Earle puts Marie on a bus to safety. With roadblocks springing up across the region, Earle is chased by the police back into the sierras, but a closed road forces him to abandon his car. He hides out in the mountains but is trapped; Marie hears the news on the radio and goes to the siege, in time to see Earle killed by a sniper. Woven into the story is a subplot revealing a completely different side to Earle. On his way to Shaw's Camp, he meets a couple and their granddaughter Velma travelling to LA. Earle becomes attached to Velma, who has a club foot. Once in LA, Earle pays for an operation to have her ankle corrected, and asks her to marry him, but she tells him she is in love with Lon, from back east, humiliating Earle and destroying what little faith he has in human nature.

Toupee-wearing, 41-year-old Humphrey De Forest Bogart had appeared in many movies throughout the thirties, usually in a supporting role, and mostly in gangster flicks. Warners cast him in *The Petrified Forest* (1936) as 'Duke' Mantee, a killer on the loose from prison, and it proved to be his breakthrough role. He also appeared in *Bullets or Ballots* (1936), with Edward G. Robinson as a cop who pretends to be disgraced and infiltrates the underworld. Between 1936 and 1940, Bogart made 28 films; because of his contract he was seldom given a choice as to which assignments he took, which explains his awful appearance as the black-clad bandit Whip McCord in the western *The Oklahoma Kid* (1939), with James Cagney. Bogart had to deliver lines such as 'Fork over dem moneybags' and recalled that his co-star's large white hat made him look like 'a mushroom'. He also appeared with Cagney in the documentary-styled *The Roaring Twenties* (1939) and as the truck driver brother of George Raft in *They Drive by Night* (1940 – *The Road to Frisco* in the UK), both for director Raoul Walsh. Bogart tended to get lead roles turned down by other actors and *High Sierra* was no exception. The role of Earle was offered to Warners' crime greats – Muni, Cagney and Robinson – but they all refused. Raft passed because he didn't want to die at the end, so the role was Bogart's.

One-eyed Raoul Walsh had started as an actor and assistant to D.W. Griffith, appearing as assassin John Wilkes Booth in *The Birth of a Nation* (1915). Working at Warners from 1939 to 1951, he made some of their most famous films of the time, including *The Thief of Bagdad* (1924) starring Douglas Fairbanks and *The Big Trail* (1930) with John Wayne. He would later work with Errol Flynn (*They Died with Their Boots On* and *Objective Burma!*) and made the gangster classic *White Heat* with Cagney in 1949.

Opposite Bogart, Walsh cast Ida Lupino, a striking actress and powerful screen presence, who had reproachful eyes and a sense of inner sadness that defined her screen persona. The pair had just appeared together in the successful *They Drive*

Mad Dog Earle: Humphrey Bogart in John Huston's *High Sierra* (1941).

by Night; Lupino played the wife of a trucking baron in love with Raft, whose brother (Bogart) loses his arm in an accident. Born in London and trained at RADA, Lupino had made her film debut aged 15 in *Her First Affaire* (1933), a Lolita-type role for which her actress mother, Connie Emerald, had also been in the running. In Hollywood from 1934 on contract at Paramount, she was signed by Warners in 1940, but found herself typecast as molls and villains. Of Marie in *High Sierra*, Lupino said, 'It was a damn good role…Bogart was a killer and no good and I was in love with him. Perfectly normal and natural for us.'

Imposing former male model Alan Curtis played thuggish 'Babe' Kozak. Arthur Kennedy, as 'Red' Hattery, was brought to Hollywood by James Cagney, to star in *City for Conquest* (1940) as Cagney's sensitive brother; *High Sierra* was only his second film, but he went on to make movies for the next five decades. Joan Leslie debuted on stage aged nine, and made several films in her teens under her real name of Joan Brodel. In 1941 she was signed by Warner Bros, and her role as selfish Velma in *High Sierra* was her contract debut. For *High Sierra*, Cornel Wilde was also on contract at Warners, but was constantly typecast as a heavy; he later left for 20th Century Fox and comparative fame, playing the lead in several successful pictures, including the cult crime classic *The Big Combo* (1955). Willie Best, as Algernon, had made a series of unfunny comedies under the derogatory stage name 'Sleep 'n Eat' and his sketchy portrayal in *High Sierra* did little to improve role models for black actors in Hollywood in the thirties and forties. Henry Hull, as 'Doc' Banton, was a reliable character actor, who appeared in *The Werewolf of London* (1935), *Jesse James* (1939), *The Return of Frank James* (1940) and later Hitchcock's *Lifeboat* (1944) and *Objective Burma!* (1945).

The crisp script was written by Burnett in collaboration with John Huston, who struck up a friendship with Bogart on set during the film's making. Warners allotted the film a modest $455,000 budget. *They Drive by Night*, Bogart and Lupino's previous film, was budgeted at $500,000. Filming began on 5 August 1940. The desert and car chase sequences were shot in the Alabama Hills, around Lone Pine, California; the area in the vicinity of Lone Pine and Independence was a popular location for shooting westerns. The 'Tropico Hotel Resort' was the Arrowhead Springs Hotel in San Bernardino (near Lake Arrowhead). Other scenes were shot at Warner Brothers Studios, Burbank; Stage 19 at Warners was transformed into the Tropico Hotel lobby for the robbery scene. Shaw's Camp was filmed on location, with cabin interiors at Warners. For the climax of the film the crew travelled to the High Sierra region of east-central California, to shoot the location scenes around Mount Whitney (then the highest peak in the US). The crew's equipment had to be brought in on horses and pack-mules. Stuntman Buster Wiles played both the dying Roy Earle (plummeting down the slope) and Slim, the sniper who kills him. Bogart was irascible on location and Walsh dubbed him 'Bogie the Beefer'. After a 44-day shoot, the film wrapped in September.

Some sources claim that 'Mad Dog' Roy Earle was based on a real-life member of the Dillinger gang. In Burnett's book, he's named Roy Earldon and Dillinger is name-checked in the film. Earle is probably the unluckiest gangster of all time. The robbery fails because of his cohorts' inexperience; as Earle says, 'Small-timers for small jobs…this one was just too big.' Earle falls in love with a girl who doesn't love him, finances her corrective surgery and then watches her selfishly run off with someone else. To Earle she's 'pretty…and decent', but he's only half right.

Earle's gang – which he's presented with, rather than chooses – are a bunch of 'jitterbugs', nervous and inexperienced. Babe is a drunken bruiser with a temper, Red is jumpy but keen and Mendoza is the one most likely to foul up. Earle doesn't like him at all: 'The cops'll punch him and he'll sing' – and of course he does. The gang are honoured to be in such 'fast company', but the reality is they're out of their depth. As 'Doc' Banton, himself a crook, now involved in 'the health racket', notes of Earle, 'You may catch lead any minute.' There aren't many of the 'old bunch' left (at least the good ones) and Earle himself concedes: 'All the A-one guys are gone…dead or in Alcatraz.' Even Big Mac, the brains behind the operation, is worn out and dying, 'like a kid's toy that's running down'. This sense of the end of the great gangsters is unusually melancholic for a genre piece, a melancholy that resonates in the film's finale.

The robbery itself is well handled by Walsh, with Huston and Burnett's hard-boiled dialogue adding to the planning and execution of the heist, and the subsequent manhunt. They hear there are 'plenty of rocks in the strongbox' and Earle calmly cases the joint with a tennis racket tucked under his arm, rather than a machine-gun (which he keeps hidden, according to genre convention, in a violin case). Later Big Mac is found 'cold as a mackerel' and Earle goes on the run. The frantic car chase into the sierras is an action highlight, with the dusty convoy of police motorbikes and squad cars zooming though the desert and up winding mountain hairpins, captured by Walsh's 360-degree pivoting camera. For these pursuit scenes, the camera was under-cranked, to increase the speed of the vehicles, with the rapidly swirling dust a give-away.

The final stand-off beneath Mount Whitney is presented as a media circus, with the cops and sharpshooters mingling with hyperbolic newsmen; 'One is awestruck by the gruesomeness of this rendezvous with death,' says one announcer. Nearly out of ammo, Earle hunkers down behind the rocks, while the law sends Slim, a sniper with a high-powered rifle and telescopic sight, to manoeuvre behind the fugitive. When Marie refuses to help the police negotiate a surrender, Pard, their dog, hears Earle's voice and scurries up the mountain. Seeing the dog, Earle rushes out looking for Marie and allows the sniper a shot at his back. Newspaper headlines have christened Earle 'Mad Dog'; over his corpse, a bystander sneers, 'Big-shot Earle…he ain't much now is he?' He's a tough man and a killer, and killers must be seen to pay. The ending, with sobbing Marie carrying Pard towards the camera, is pure melodrama, but is very effective nonetheless.

But it is this wistfully sentimental aspect of the film, and of Earle's personality in particular, where the film really scores, and where Huston's involvement is most prevalent. Bogart could sleepwalk through performances as a cold-blooded convict and bank robber, but to colour his portrayal of Earle to elicit sympathy for 'Mad Dog' was impressive. There are references to Earle's childhood as a farm boy in Indiana; on his way to the sierras, he nostalgically visits his old house, as though he senses that time is running out. Earle's first action when he gets out of prison is to go to the park and reassure himself that nothing has changed in the outside world. But Earle is kidding himself: the world is very different. While he sits in the park, a discarded newspaper tells us who this character really is: 'Desperado Released – Roy Earle, Famous Indiana Bank Robber, Wins Pardon'.

Earle's sympathetic relationship with club-footed Velma would have been unthinkable in earlier Bogart incarnations. She knows him as 'Roy Collins', staying 'up in the mountains for my health'. Perhaps because of his duplicity, their relationship is doomed. For his kindness in paying $400 for her operation, her grandfather says that Roy is 'The best man who ever lived', but 'Doc' Banton, quoting Dillinger, notes that men like Earle are 'just rushing toward death'. Earle and Velma are completely mismatched. She has a sweetheart back home named Lon and as soon as she is well, she is seen in gaudy dress and makeup. She wants to 'live a little' and is soon to marry Lon. 'That's swell,' says Roy with a face like thunder. These and other scenes in the film show Earle for the 'sap' he is – too trusting of human nature and equally resentful when he is treated untrustworthily.

Marie is his salvation and soulmate. During the making of the film, Bogart said to Lupino, 'You and I were born to be bad, but we're really saints, Ida'; Lupino replied: 'Who? You and me? Impossible! The halos wouldn't fit . . . our horns would be enormous!' Earle's relationship with Marie starts off on the wrong foot. Warily, he doesn't want her as part of the gang, but gradually she, and Pard, the stray mutt she adopts, become a surrogate family to Earle – Pard's 'got no home, got nobody' either. As they set off on the robbery Pard follows them and Marie pleads that he be allowed to come along. 'Of all the 14-carat saps,' says Earle, 'starting out on a caper with a woman and a dog.' But he grows to like her, especially after his treatment by Velma, and later, he places one of the rings stolen from the Tropico on the little finger of Marie's left hand; a gesture that reduces her to tears of joy: 'Of course, you would put it on the wrong finger,' she fusses.

There was a rumour around Shaw's Camp that Pard was bad luck. Earle and Marie initially laugh off such suggestions, but the way events unfold they begin to suspect they are indeed jinxed, Earle finally rattily conceding, 'OK, it's all Pard's fault.' Bogart's own dog Zero played Pard. In the final scene, Earle's riddled corpse is played by stuntman Buster Wiles, with cookies hidden in his palm, so the dog licks the dead man's hand. Finally, as Earle has 'crashed out' and is free, the dog remains by his master, a silent goodbye – and Marie, in tears, loves him too.

Prior to *High Sierra*'s release, the stars' billing was reversed. Bogart was originally to have received top billing, but Lupino was promoted by the studio – Bogart, who took the project partly because it was his first starring role, wasn't very impressed. *High Sierra* was premiered in the US on 21 January 1941 and put on general release the following week. The poster was an exciting depiction of the mountaintop shootout, with the line 'He killed…and there on the crest of Sierra's Highest Crag…He Must Be Killed!' Reviewers were gushing; the *Motion Picture Herald* noted that 'By painting a character with streaks of white which do not dilute the black, Huston and Burnett drive home their point with power and conviction'. The *New York Times* said the film had 'Speed, excitement, suspense and that ennobling suggestion of futility that makes for irony and pity'. Less seriously, the *New Republic* noted: 'This is what I should call a film worth exposing negative for…like it or not, I'll be damned if you leave before the end or go to sleep'. As part of the film's promotion, Bogart and his wife Mayo (known as 'the Battling Bogarts') undertook two weeks' worth of lucrative public appearances at Warners' prestigious first-run cinema, the Strand. A stage show review followed each evening's showing of *High Sierra*, with other performers including the stars of TV's *Ozzie and Harriet* and an Egyptian magician called Galli Galli. The film was a huge success in the US, but still didn't gross as well as Raft's and Cagney's films, which irked Bogart. In the UK, it was rated an A. The film was renamed throughout

Warners Bros' publicity still of two-gun Humphrey Bogart.

Europe: in Italy it was *Un Pallottola per Roy* ('A Bullet for Roy'); in Spain *El Ultimo Refugio* ('The Last Refuge'); and in Germany *Entscheidung in der Sierra* ('Decision in the Sierra'). In France it was known as *La Grande Évasion*: 'The Great Escape'.

Walsh remade *High Sierra* in 1949 in a western setting as *Colorado Territory* starring Joel McCrea and Virginia Mayo as the lovers (Mayo played a half-breed squaw), and Dorothy Malone as Velma. Another remake, *I Died a Thousand Times* (1955), also released by Warner Brothers, starred Jack Palance in the Roy Earle role, Shelley Winters as Marie, Lori Nelson as Velma, Lee Marvin as Babe, Earl Holliman as Red and Lon Chaney Jnr as Big Mac. It was written for the screen by Burnett and photographed in CinemaScope and WarnerColor. Palance overacts as usual; the film's success rests very much on your tolerance of Palance, and the strong supporting cast helps.

Sam Peckinpah's *The Getaway* (1972), based on a novel by crime writer Jim Thomson, was Steve McQueen's homage to *High Sierra*, with its robbery and chase structure. McQueen, as bank robber Doc McCoy, even dons a black Bogart-style suit and visits the park immediately following his release from the Texas penitentiary, with his wife Carol (Ali MacGraw). He plans the robbery of the First Bank of Beacon City, but the job goes awry. Doc and Carol flee towards Mexico with the proceeds, but vengeful hoods and the cops are in hot pursuit. Filmed with familiar Peckinpah élan, memorable scenes include shotgun-wielding Doc's slow-motion destruction of a squad car and the El Paso finale, when the hoods catch up with Doc for a hotel showdown. With McQueen and MacGraw on top form, *The Getaway* was a box-office smash, grossing $19 million in the US.

In 1941, Bogart and Lupino were to have starred again together in their next film, *The Gentle People*. For whatever reason Warners couldn't get them back together and the film was eventually made without Bogart (replaced by John Garfield) as *Out of the Fog*. Garfield played a crook who robs two elderly men of their savings for a fishing boat, but gets his just desserts when he falls overboard. The film is appropriately titled, as Warners had just invested in a new billowing smoke machine, which worked overtime throughout the shoot.

For many, *High Sierra* marked the end of an era for gangster cinema. With the coming of the Second World War, the nation was preoccupied with the occupation of Europe and the Far East. The *New York Times*, in their review of *High Sierra*, summed it up best. 'We wouldn't know for certain whether the twilight of the American gangster is here, but the Warner Brothers have apparently taken it for granted and, in solemn Wagnerian mood, are giving that titanic figure a send-off befitting a first-string god. It's a wonder the American flag wasn't wrapped around his broken corpse.' And of course, in keeping with Warners' history, he went out with a bang.

3

'The shortest farewells are best'

— *The Maltese Falcon* (1941)

Credits:

DIRECTOR   John Huston

EXECUTIVE PRODUCER – Hal B. Wallis

ASSOCIATE PRODUCER – Henry Blanke

STORY – Dashiell Hammett

SCREENPLAY – John Huston

DIRECTOR OF PHOTOGRAPHY – Arthur Edison

EDITOR – Thomas Richards

ART DIRECTOR – Robert Haas

COSTUME DESIGNER – Orry-Kelly

MUSIC COMPOSER – Adolph Deutsch

MUSIC DIRECTOR – Leo F. Forbstein

Black and white

Interiors filmed at Warner Bros Studios

A Warner Bros-First National production

Released by Warner Bros

100 minutes

Cast:

Humphrey Bogart (Sam Spade, the private eye)/Mary Astor (Brigid O'Shaughnessy, alias 'Miss Wonderly', alias 'Miss Leblanc')/Sydney Greenstreet (Caspar Gutman, 'The Fat Man')/Peter Lorre (Joel Cairo)/Elisha Cook Jnr (Wilmer Cook, the Fat Man's thin henchman)/Gladys George (Iva Archer)/Barton MacLane (Detective Lieutenant Dundy)/Ward Bond (Detective Sergeant Tom Polhaus)/Walter Huston (Captain Jacobi of the *La Paloma*)/Jerome Cowan (Miles Archer)/Lee Patrick (Effie Perine, Spade's secretary)/James Burke (Luke, hotel detective)/Murray Alper (Frank Richman)/John Hamilton (DA Bryan)

*   *   *

'The Maltese Falcon' was first published in 1930. Its author was born Samuel Dashiell Hammett on 27 May 1894, in St Mary's County, Maryland. He left school aged 14 and worked in many menial jobs. He eventually became a Pinkerton's Detective agent, where he worked on the scandalous Hollywood Fatty Arbuckle case, in which the comedian was accused of murdering a starlet. Following the First World War, Hammett returned to work as a detective, then began his writing career. Hammett became a highly successful author, and many of his books have been adapted for the screen. He created the detectives Nick and Nora Charles (the protagonists of 'The Thin Man' [1934]), Sam Spade ('The Maltese Falcon') and the nameless 'continental op'. His other novels include 'Red Harvest' (published 1929), 'The Dain Curse' (1929) and 'The Glass Key' (1931). He also published many short stories, with evocative titles like 'Corkscrew', 'The Gatewood Caper' and '$106,000 Blood Money'. Raymond Chandler wrote that Hammett 'gave murder back to the kind of people that commit it for reasons, not just to provide a corpse; and with the means at hand, not with handwrought duelling pistols, curare, and tropical fish'.

In the film adaptation of Hammett's 'The Maltese Falcon', San Francisco private investigating partnership Spade and Archer are approached by Miss Wonderly to locate her sister, Corrine. Trailing Corrine's lover, Floyd Thursby, Archer is shot dead and Thursby is also gunned down later that night. Spade visits Wonderly and finds her real name is Brigid O'Shaughnessy; she hires him to hide her from the police. Meanwhile, Spade is contacted by Joel Cairo, a dubious character, who wants help locating a black enamelled ornament, the Maltese Falcon, which has been stolen from a collector in Istanbul. Spade eventually realises that the falcon is the object of everyone's lust, including Brigid, Cairo, corpulent Caspar Gutman (known as the 'Fat Man') and his henchman Wilmer Cook. The *La Paloma* freighter docks in 'Frisco harbour from Hong Kong and is gutted by fire. Hours later, Jacobi, its captain, delivers a large package to Spade's office, before dropping dead, and Spade places the packet in the Union Bus Depot left luggage. At the climax, in Spade's apartment, they discover the falcon is a lead fake. Gutman, Cook and Cairo leave and Spade calls the cops to pick them up. Frightened, Brigid spills the beans: she stole the falcon and killed Spade's partner, to implicate Thursby, and get him out of the picture. The Fat Man's henchman had then killed Thursby, to warn Brigid they were on her trail. Even though he has fallen in love with Brigid, Spade turns her in too.

In 1931 Roy Del Ruth directed a rather chic version of Hammett's story for Warners, with Ricardo Cortez as Sam Spade, a suave man-about-town. The cast included Bebe Daniels playing 'Ruth Wonderly', Dudley Digges as a much slimmer Gutman, Una Merkel as secretary Effie, Dwight Fry (the hunchback from Universal horror films) as henchman Wilmer and Otto Matieson, billed as Doctor Joel Cairo; it was also released as *Dangerous Female*. In 1936 it was remade, again for Warners, as *Satan Met a Lady*, with Bette Davis (who views the film as the nadir of her career) in the Miss Wonderly role and Warren William as the rechristened detective Ted Shayne, hired to locate a gem-filled ram's horn. Directed by William Dieterle as a send-up, one of the many changes made to the film was Gutman's re-imagining as Madame Barabbas (Alison Skipworth).

In 1941, John Huston wanted to make his directorial debut with another adaptation of Hammett's classic story; he'd previously had much success at Warners, having worked on several scripts, including the highly successful *High Sierra* earlier that year. As for *High Sierra*, George Raft was again approached to be the lead, but refused (citing untried Huston's inexperience in direction), and Humphrey Bogart ended up incarnating Hammett's most famous detective. Mary Astor, as Brigid, had been a beauty queen at 15, appeared in many silent movies and was involved in a very public divorce case in 1936, with her diary brought into the proceedings. She had just appeared as a Tchaikovsky-playing concert pianist in the soapy *The Great Lie* earlier in the year (for which she would win the Best Supporting Actress Oscar) and thought *The Maltese Falcon* script 'a humdinger'. Other possibilities for the Brigid role were Olivia De Havilland, Rita Hayworth, Geraldine Fitzgerald and Ingrid Bergman. Gladys George, as Archer's widow Iva, had appeared with Bogart in *The Roaring Twenties* (1939). Director Huston cast his father Walter in the small role of Captain Jacobi, who delivers the falcon to Spade; Walter remembered that he ended up badly bruised after the scene took a whole day to film (some twenty takes); all the captain does is stagger in, drop the falcon and fall down dead.

Born in 1879, British stage actor Sydney Greenstreet was 61 when he made his screen debut in *The Maltese Falcon*; he was perfect for the role of Caspar Gutman, though he would never have been approached to play another of Hammett's creations, 'The Thin Man'; Greenstreet weighed 280 pounds. As soon as cane-toting Joel Cairo walks into Spade's office, we know he's crooked – we know this mainly because he is played by Peter Lorre. Lorre (real name László Löwenstein) appeared in films from 1928, but became associated with villainous roles through his lauded performance as Hans Beckert, the child murderer in Fritz Lang's *M* (1931). Lorre fled the Nazis in 1933 and went to Hollywood, becoming familiar as Mr Moto, a bargain basement Charlie Chan, in eight adventures (1937–39), before his performance for Huston. Elisha Cook Jnr played nervous, gun-happy Wilmer. These actors, especially shifty-eyed Lorre and Cook Jnr, visually summed up Hammett's 'trust no one' ethos.

Warner Brothers' success in the thirties was reined in during the early forties, partly due to the economy enforced by the Second World War. Firstly the European and British film markets were considerably reduced; then in December 1941 all Far Eastern film revenue vanished after the Japanese bombed Pearl Harbor. But it was exactly during this period that Bogart became the highest-paid star of his generation. *The Maltese Falcon* was budgeted at $381,000 and was shot from 9 June to 18 July (two days under its 36-day schedule) in chronological order.

Producer Henry Blanke said: 'Make every shot count. No detail can be overlooked.' Huston meticulously pre-planned the filming and the eventual cost was only $327,000. The entire film was shot at Warner Brothers' Burbank Studios. Some outdoor shots were filmed as process shots (for instance, the conversation between Spade and Sergeant Polhaus at Archer's embankment murder scene on the junction of Bush and Stockton) or on sound stages (such as the firefighters battling the *La Paloma* blaze).

There are several minor differences between the film and the book, but in the main they are identical. Warners' producer Henry Blanke backed writer John Huston for the project; Huston prepared a scene-by-scene breakdown of the book, printing the dialogue verbatim (his secretary simply photocopied the book). This accounts for the fact that Jack Warner was very pleased Huston had 'retained' Hammett's style – at some points it is possible to follow the book like a film script. The actors deliver Hammett's distinctive phraseology and vocabulary very well: a cop notes that Archer has been shot 'right through the pump'; Spade says he 'won't squawk' if the cops search his room and tells threatening henchman Cook, 'People lose teeth talking like that.'

Film Noir: in *The Maltese Falcon* (1941), Sam Spade (Humphrey Bogart) finally gets his hands on the black bird.

The relationships between Spade and Iva (Archer's widow) and Effie Perine, his secretary, are de-emphasised in the script version, while the presentations of Gutman and Cairo are slightly different. Hammett writes that Gutman speaks with a 'throaty purr', completely different to Greenstreet's clipped tones, while the implication is that Joel Cairo is even more of a dandy. In the book, the 'Levantine' (an old term, meaning of eastern Mediterranean origin) drifts in with 'the fragrance of chypre' (a unisex scent from Cyprus). Gutman's 17-year-old daughter Rhea, who in the book is found drugged in Brigid's suite, is missing completely. Bogart's memorable final line, his description of the falcon ('The stuff that dreams are made of'), doesn't appear in the novel, and is a quote from Shakespeare's 'The Tempest'.

Samuel Spade broke Bogart's typecasting as a villainous gangster and like occasional moments in *High Sierra* introduced something deeper and more virtuous to his character. Hammett's description of Spade is very similar to Bogart's physiognomy, with the exception that in the book he's blond: 'His chin a jutting V under the more flexible V of his mouth. His nostrils curved back to make another smaller V ... the V motif was picked up again by thickish brows ... He looked rather pleasantly like a blond satan.' Hammett later notes, 'He smiled without separating his lips. All the V's in his face grew longer', which just as aptly described a Bogart smile.

With the dialogue being so closely based on Hammett's, Bogart's style and voice became the epitome of the cinema private eye. This is especially noticeable with his distinctive speech pattern, a slight lisp and a tight-lipped manner, as he intones, 'The namesh Sham Shpade'. This inflection was caused by his scarred, partially paralysed lip, an injury he sustained during the First World War aboard the ship *Leviathan*. Unfortunately there are quite a few difficult pronunciations for him during *The Maltese Falcon*, including Miss Wonderly, Floyd Thursby and the pistol that shot Archer, the Webley-Fosbery (which Bogart gives up on and mumbles under his breath). Like Cagney, Bogart became a favourite with mimics, for his delivery of lines such as 'Where'sh the black boid?'

The love story between Brigid and Spade is much less of a central theme than advertising material for the film would have audiences believe. Spade instantly sees through her story and her 'schoolgirl manner, stammering and blushing'. As Brigid, Astor lies through her teeth and Astor achieved this edginess in her demeanour by breathing fast to hyperventilate. 'It gave me a heady feeling of thinking at cross-purposes.' Spade helps her and they begin to fall in love, but when she realises that he's been hired by Cairo to find the falcon, she says there is no future for them ('If I have to bid for your loyalty'), though Spade points out that all she has given him is money – no trust or confidence. In the book, Brigid is strip-searched in a bathroom by Spade for a missing thousand-dollar bill, which the Fat Man has palmed. In the film version, a greater degree of trust builds up between them and he takes her word for it. When he finally turns her in to the police (and she descends the elevator, literally 'going down'), he reasons that he had to turn her in because she killed his partner. It's all about loyalty – it doesn't matter what Spade thought of Archer, 'He was your partner and you're supposed to do something about it.'

In Hammett's world, nothing – especially relationships and loyalty – can be taken at face value, and characters are never what they first appear to be. A frightened woman turns out to be a conscienceless thief and liar; Archer's widow is also Spade's lover; Wilmer the gunman, for all his big talk, is a coward and incompetent at his job. Even the 'Black Bird' is a fake, prompting Cairo to whine, 'No wonder we had such an easy time stealing it.'

The Maltese Falcon's narrative is fast-paced, with most of the dialogue spoken at breakneck speed. Abridgements and omissions made to Hammett's plot are often papered over with brief explanatory telephone calls. The audience picks the clues up, as Spade discovers them – a Hong Kong label in Brigid's hat, for instance – but the plot is still a maze of dead and loose ends. As Spade notes while he speeds from one suspect to the next: 'I've got to keep in some sort of touch with all the loose ends of this dizzy affair, if I'm going to make heads or tails of it.'

Spade's adversaries are the best aspects of *The Maltese Falcon*. Lorre's performance almost steals the film as sneaky Cairo, who decides to throw in his lot with Gutman. Cairo's verbal sparring with Spade makes for some memorable scenes. The detective tells him at one point, 'When you're slapped you'll take it and like it.' Later, Spade quickly lies his way out of a tight spot with Cairo, who notes, 'You always have a very smooth explanation ready'; 'What do you want me to do?' responds Spade, 'learn to stutter?' Gutman is also a worthy adversary, his corpulent frame dominating scenes, with Huston filming him seated, often from a low angle, smoking a cigar. With his catchphrase ('By Gad sir!'), he spins lines such as 'I'm a man who likes talking to a man who likes to talk' and then surreptitiously slips Spade a Mickey Finn. Gutman's henchman Wilmer, whom he looks on as a son, is a jumpy, trigger-happy hood – 'Young wild-west', according to Spade. When it becomes apparent that Wilmer is to be the fall-guy to the police, Gutman reasons, 'If you lose a son, you can always get another – there's only one Maltese Falcon.'

Much of the action in the film is clever, rather than violent, though the film has its share of brutality. The violence comes quickly and unexpectedly – as with Archer's swift murder, when Wilmer kicks drugged Spade in the head, or more humorously, the moment when demur Brigid goes for Cairo with a swinging kick and Cairo shrieks. Later, *La Paloma* is set alight by Wilmer, on Gutman's orders, to literally smoke the falcon out. The captain is carrying the statue for Brigid and has to make a run for it when the ship catches fire – hence his arrival at Spade's office. The final scene, set in Spade's apartment and which takes 25 minutes of screen time, wraps up the plot surprisingly well, leaving Spade alone, but morally justified, in the fadeout.

After test-screening the film (under the trial title *The Gent from Frisco*), Jack Warner insisted that a scrolling foreword be added after the shivering-lettered title sequence, filling in the background story of the falcon – details that in the book are recounted by Gutman to Spade midway through the story. 'In 1539 the Knight Templars of Malta paid tribute to Charles V of Spain, by sending him a golden falcon encrusted from beak to claw with rarest jewels – but pirates seized the galley carrying this priceless token and the fate of the Maltese Falcon remains a mystery to this day.' In Hammett's book the pirate admiral is named as Barbarossa ('Red Beard') and the origins of the falcon are much more detailed.

The Maltese Falcon was premiered in New York on 4 October and released generally on 18 October 1941. The trailer was particularly effective, with its swooping animated falcon 'wiping' the screen. Greenstreet introduces the history of the falcon and looks almost exactly like Hitchcock's TV appearances in *Alfred Hitchcock Presents* in the fifties. During the trailer, Bogart is described as 'Topping his smashing success in *High Sierra*' and 'He's as fast on the draw as he is in the drawing room'. He's also 'the most ruthless lover you've ever met' and Astor 'the most exciting woman he's ever met'. It features much action from the film (including fisticuffs and the *La Paloma* ablaze) and some extra scenes not present in the final cut, including a mysterious hand holding a knife letter-opener and a shadowy strangulation, to spice up the proceedings. In the UK it was a certificate A. The posters blared, 'A Story as Explosive as his Blazing Automatics', with an illustration of Bogart brandishing a pair of pistols. Astor also featured prominently in the ad work, and a tagline linked the two characters: 'A Guy without a Conscience…a Dame without a Heart!'

The Maltese Falcon was a huge hit for Warners and 1941 was a good year for the studio, with the jingoistic *Sergeant York* winning Best Actor for Gary Cooper and net profit of over $5 million, almost double the previous year. It was a great success in the US and UK: the *New York Times* said the film was 'a combination of American ruggedness with the suavity of the English crime school – a blend of mind and muscle'. *Variety* called it 'perfection', the *New York Herald and Tribune* 'a knockout job', while in the UK the *New Statesman* surmised that '*The Maltese Falcon* has nearly everything a mystery film should have' and 'belongs to the vintage period of American gangsterism'. In Italy it was released as *Il Mistero del Falco* ('The Mystery of the Hawk', falcon is *falcone*), in Germany *Die Spur Des Falken* ('The Trail of the Falcon'), and literally *El Halcón Maltés* in Spain. The best alternative title is the Portuguese-Brazil *Reliquia Macabra*: 'Macabre Relic'. The 'masterpiece of mystery' was hugely popular worldwide, its classy *noir* imagery became ingrained in all cultures and Bogart became a global star.

Lorre and Greenstreet also did particularly well out of *The Maltese Falcon*. They made eight more films together at Warners, becoming a sort of Laurel and Hardy of international mystery movies. *Casablanca* (1943) and *Passage to Marseilles* (1944) both co-starred Bogart. They also made *Background to Danger* (1943 – a *Casablanca* rip-off set in Turkey); *The Mask of Dimitrios* (1944 – which saw the pair retracing the career of master criminal Zachary Scott); *The Conspirators* (1944 – another *Casablanca* clone, this time set in Lisbon); the foggy London-set period murder mystery *The Verdict* (1946 – director Don Siegel's first film); *Three Strangers* (1946 – a tale of winning sweepstake tickets, co-written by John Huston); and cameos in the all-star propaganda showcase *Hollywood Canteen* (1944); the Canteen was founded by Bette Davis, John Garfield and other stars, as a place for meals and entertainment for the troops.

Hammett's work continued to provide filmmakers with inspiration. 'The Dain Curse' was adapted for TV under the same name in 1978, and 'The Glass Key' was filmed in 1935, and again, with Alan Ladd, in 1942. 'Red Harvest' has inspired many films, including *Buchanan Rides Alone* (1958), *Yojimbo* (1961), *A Fistful of Dollars* (1964) and *Last Man Standing* (1996). Most famously, 'The Thin Man' led to a series of 'screwball mystery' hybrids concerning the detective adventures of the husband and wife team of Nick and Nora Charles, played by William Powell and Myrna Loy. The series began in 1934 with *The Thin Man* (made in two weeks) and continued with *After the Thin Man* (1936), *Another Thin Man* (1939), *Shadow of the Thin Man* (1941), *The Thin Man Goes Home* (1944) and *Song of the Thin Man* (1947). They were massively successful and the advertising copy summed up their appeal: 'A laugh tops every thrilling moment! A new kind of mystery with more laughs than chills … more warm-blooded romance than cold-blooded murder! Hilariously Gay! Breathlessly Exciting!'

All that 'breathless excitement' wore audiences out, so *The Big Sleep*, directed by Howard Hawks, was a welcome arrival in 1946. Bogart portrayed Philip Marlowe, another great fictional detective, in the adaptation of Raymond Chandler's first novel. Notoriously difficult to follow, the film was most memorable for the scenes between Bogart and his co-star, Lauren Bacall, who were married in real life. The plot is so convoluted that there is one murder (the chauffeur's) that is never solved; Hawks asked Chandler, 'Who did it?' 'How should I know?' Chandler responded.

In 1953, Huston and Truman Capote adapted James Helvick's novel 'Beat the Devil' into a parody of genre films like *The Maltese Falcon*, set in Italy in Porto Vento (actually shot in Revello). It features a caricature of Greenstreet's Fat Man, with Robert Morley as Peterson, a criminal who arrives in town to rendezvous with his three accomplices – O'Hara (Peter Lorre), Ravello (Marco Tulli) and Major Ross, the 'Galloping Major' (Ivor Barnard – with a knife hidden in his swagger stick). They team up with an American ex-pat-in-hiding, Billy Dannreuther, a 'middle-aged roustabout', played by Bogart (who due to biting his tongue in a car accident was dubbed by Peter Sellers). The plot sees the group shadowing Mr and Mrs Chelm, an English couple (Edward Underdown and Jennifer Jones, 'refugees from Earl's Court'), and concocting a plan to steal their East African uranium mine. The humour is quite subtle, with the shady characters delivering lines such as 'Say what you like about Hitler, he had his points', and 'Remember: every breath is a guinea in the bank of health', as they sit plotting among the Peroni and Cinzano signs. They take the SS *Nyanga* to Africa, but it sinks on the way and they are marooned. As the party land, Paterson and his men bury their passports on the beach

– their last scheme had been selling the Arabs rusty guns and dud ammunition. They are captured by the North African locals, who during the inquisition claim: 'We of this country have had 4000 years' experience in asking questions and getting answers.' *Beat the Devil* was a commercial failure, with its tongue-in-cheek tagline falling flat: 'You have seen "Colour" – "Dimension" – "CinemaScope". But Now We Proudly Present On the Small Flat Screen *Beat the Devil* In Glorious Black And White!' *Beat the Devil* was underrated and is celebrated today as a cult classic; it's well worth seeking out as a companion piece to *The Maltese Falcon*.

In 1942, Warners attempted to repeat *The Maltese Falcon* formula, with Bogart, Astor and Greenstreet reunited under Huston in *Across the Pacific*, a wartime tale of Japanese sabotage. But audiences preferred 'Bogey' on solid ground. Bogart was the pre-eminent post-war Hollywood star; in 1946 his contract at Warners was $5,000 a week, on the proviso he made one film a year. Original *Falcon* choice George Raft was reputedly not very impressed with the film's success and left Warners shortly afterwards, his career in ruins.

Via Chandler and Hammett, Bogart epitomised crime film private eyes, the down-at-heel 'gumshoe' out of his depth in a convoluted case, and is still the reference point most often associated with the genre. The two best parodies of the Spade character appear in *Murder by Death* (1976) and *The Cheap Detective* (1978), with Peter Falk as Sam Diamond. There was also a lazy parody of *Falcon* called *The Black Bird* (1975), with the usually reliable George Segal as Sam Spade Junior and Elisha Cook Jnr and Lee Patrick from the original movie. *Dead Men Don't Wear Plaid* (1982) features Steve Martin in a detective story, which cleverly intercuts Martin with clips from many forties classics, including *The Big Sleep* and *The Glass Key*. Bogart made *Casablanca* in 1943, donning trenchcoat and trilby – the 'Bogey' trademarks. This classic love story was a massive success, despite its sometimes cliché-ridden script, with Ilsa (Ingrid Bergman) uttering dialogue like 'Was that cannon-fire, or is it my heart pounding?' It won the Oscar for Best Picture, forever enshrining Bogart in movie history. But it is *The Maltese Falcon* that remains Bogart's best film and the beginning of a great career for Huston, one of America's finest post-war directors.

4

'Made it Ma! Top of the world!'

— *White Heat* (1949)

Credits:
DIRECTOR – Raoul Walsh
PRODUCER – Louis F. Eldelman
STORY – Virginia Kellogg
SCREENPLAY – Ivan Goff and Ben Roberts
DIRECTOR OF PHOTOGRAPHY – Sid Hickcox
EDITOR – Owen Marks
ART DIRECTOR – Edward Carrere
COSTUMES – Leah Rhodes
MUSIC – Max Steiner
Black and white
Interiors filmed at Warner Bros Studios
A Warner Brothers-First National production
Released by Warner Bros
110 minutes

Cast:
James Cagney (Arthur Cody Jarrett)/Virginia Mayo (Verna Jarrett)/Edmond O'Brien (Hank Fallon alias 'Victor Pardo')/Margaret Wycherly (Ma Jarrett)/Steve Cochran (Big Ed Somers)/John Archer (T-Man Phillip Evans)/Wally Cassell (Giovanni 'Cotton' Valetti)/Fred Clark (Daniel Winston, the fence)/Ford Rainey (Zuckie Hommell)/Fred Coby (Happy Taylor)/Marshall Bradford (Chief of Police)/G. Pat Collins (Michael 'Reader' Curtin)/Perry Ivins (Dr Simpson)/Mickey Knox (Het Kohler)/Harry Lauter (Mobile radio operator)/Ian MacDonald (Bo Creel)/Robert Osterloh (Thomas Reilly)/Paul Guilfoyle (Lloyd Parker)/Gradon Rhodes (Dr Harris)

*   *   *

Following the success of *The Public Enemy*, Cagney became the most famous gangster star on the Warners' lot. In *G-Men* (1935) he was on the side of the law – but it was two classics, *Angels With Dirty Faces* (1938) and *The Roaring Twenties* (1939), that cemented his popularity as the leading gangster bad guy. By this point in his career, Cagney received $150,000 for each film, plus 10 per cent of the profits. *Angels With Dirty Faces*, directed by Michael Curtiz, told the story of William 'Rocky' Sullivan, from Skid Row to Death Row. As childhood friends, slum kids Rocky and Jerome 'Jerry' Connolly fall into petty pilfering, but Rocky can't run as fast as Jerry and is caught. He winds up in reform school, beginning a cycle of crime, which will shape his whole life, while Jerry becomes a priest. Years later Rocky returns to his neighbourhood, but continues to dabble in the underworld; he tries to reclaim a hundred grand owed to him by a crooked lawyer, Frazier (Humphrey Bogart) and becomes a hero to a sextet of street urchins, the Dead End Kids (named Soapy, Swing, Bim, Patsy, Crab and Hunky), each on their way to becoming the next Rocky. Finally, Jerry launches a moral crusade to sweep the streets clean of corruption and vice; in the process he brings down Rocky, who kills Frazier and is captured in a gunfight at the El Toro casino. Rocky is sentenced to the electric chair and Jerry pleads with him to scream for mercy before his execution, so the kids won't see him as a martyr: 'They've got to despise your memory... be

Hollywood Gangsters: Rocky Sullivan (James Cagney) has a quiet word with crooked lawyer James Frazier (Humphrey Bogart) in *Angels With Dirty Faces* (1938).

ashamed of you.' Rocky concedes and breaks down before his electrocution; in a moving epilogue Jerry visits the kids and counts his lucky stars: 'Let's go and say a prayer for a boy who couldn't run as fast as I could.'

In interviews Cagney said there were three ways of getting out of the slums: prizefighting, crime or show business. Cagney was a boxer, then a dancer and finally a 'hood', albeit only an on-screen one. For Cagney's criminal roles, he recreated hoodlums from his Lower East Side childhood in New York. In *Angels* Cagney based Rocky on two men from the Yorkville ('Yonkers') district where he grew up; one was a pimp with the catchphrase 'What d'ya hear? What d'ya say?'; the other was Peter Hessling, a childhood friend, who ended up in the electric chair. Cagney used such personal knowledge to create his characters, which paid dividends when he won an Oscar nomination for Best Actor. *Angels* was such a success that the Dead End Kids made a series of cash-ins, including *Angels Wash their Faces* (1939) and *Dead End Kids on Dress Parade* (1939).

The Roaring Twenties was an homage to the gangster movie style of the thirties and was directed by Raoul Walsh, who later made *High Sierra* and *They Drive by Night*. The story follows three First World War soldiers, who become friends in France in 1918, and their lives back in New York following the armistice. Eddie Bartlett (Cagney) can't get his old mechanic's job back, so becomes a taxi driver. During the Prohibition years, he falls in with bootleggers and uses his 'Red & Blue Cab Company' as a front for distributing alcohol. Trainee lawyer Lloyd Hart (Jeffrey Lynn) gets him out of scrapes with the law and joins the bootlegging racket as an accountant, while George Hally (Humphrey Bogart) betrays his own boss and throws in with Bartlett. But eventually wealth, mistrust, lies and deceit destroy the gang and the good times come to a catastrophic end with the Wall Street Crash, on Tuesday 29 October 1929. Bartlett is ruined, Hally buys him out and Hart runs off with Bartlett's girl. The ending sees Bartlett, now a drunken bum, shooting Hally, when he threatens to kill Hart, now a respectable assistant DA about to expose Hally's rackets. On New Year's Eve 1929, Bartlett is gunned down on the snow-covered steps of a nearby church by Hally's gang. 'He used to be a big shot,' notes a bystander.

From the jingoistic Nazi-bashing of its opening, to its unwelcome romantic subplots, *The Roaring Twenties* isn't a patch on *The Public Enemy* or *Angels With Dirty Faces*. The 'March of Time' montages are the most memorable aspect of the film; they were assembled by a young Don Siegel, who used all kinds of stock footage (plus clips from *The Public Enemy*), optical effects and symbolism, including an extraordinary shot of the concrete canyons of Wall Street melting. These montages deployed John Deering's resonant narration imparting such facts as: 1924 saw the arrival of the Thomson Submachine-gun, the Tommy-gun – 'a deadly, wasp-like machine-gun and murder henceforth is parcelled out in wholesale lot'. According to Byron Haskin, Warners' special effects expert, without these montages *The Roaring Twenties* was 'a real sad sack'. Apart from Cagney, Lynn and Bogart, the cast was nondescript, the evocative 'speakeasy' locales were underused and the few good shootouts and robberies (including an ambush in an Italian restaurant and a huge liquor warehouse heist) were few and far between by Cagney's shoot-'em-up standards. But *Twenties* did boast the typically flamboyant Cagney persona, from rags to riches and back again, who declares at the height of his powers, 'While the gravy's flowing, I'm gonna be right there with my kisser under the faucet.'

Gangster films were changing throughout the forties. Many of its major stars abandoned the genre. Bogart, for example, moved into romantic melodrama, scoring massive hits with *Casablanca* (1942), opposite Ingrid Bergman, and *To Have and Have Not* (1947), opposite his new wife, Lauren Bacall. George Raft drifted out of the public's focus, due to a fatal combination of the poor choices of roles he did take and the great roles he turned down, including the Bogart role in *Casablanca*. Meanwhile, James Cagney, the tough killer of *The Public Enemy* and the bane of G-men everywhere, revisited his vaudevillian roots, winning an Oscar for his portrayal of the famous showman George M. Cohan in *Yankee Doodle Dandy* (1942). Cagney's success at the box office didn't depend on him snapping like a terrier and machine-gunning hoods to death – the film grossed $4.8 million in the US. In 1942 Cagney left Warner Bros and formed Cagney Productions with his brother, William (an associate producer on *Yankee Doodle Dandy*), distributing the films through United Artists. After seven years working independently, Cagney returned to the studio in 1949 for *White Heat*, a blistering crime drama and Cagney's greatest film.

White Heat was 'suggested' by a story authored by Virginia Kellogg, who also wrote 'T-Men', the inspiration for Anthony Mann's 1948 film of the same name. *White Heat* shares *T-Men*'s subplot, which saw two Treasury agents infiltrating counterfeiters. In *White Heat*, Cody Jarrett and his gang, including his mother, 'Ma', rob the Southern Pacific mail train. But one of their number is badly scalded in the hold-up; later the police find the scalded body, and fingerprints on a cigarette packet connect him to Cody's bunch. Treasury agents ('T-men'), led by Phillip Evans, plan to trap Cody, but the crook turns himself in for a robbery on the Palace Hotel that he didn't commit, which provides him with an alibi for the railroad robbery. In jail, Jarrett is befriended by Vic Pardo; while he's incarcerated Jarrett finds out that his mother has died, and his wife, Verna, has run off with his lieutenant, Big Ed Somers. Livid, he vows to escape and hatches a plan with Pardo and two other cons. About to be committed to a psychiatric institution, Jarrett breaks out and goes on the run, hiding out in New Mexico. He tracks down Verna, shoots Big Ed, and hooks up with his gang. Organised by a fence called Daniel Winston, they plan to rob a $426,000 payroll from a Long Beach chemical plant. But Pardo is actually a T-man, who manages to tip off his comrades. Tracked by Pardo's radio transmitter, the gang are trapped inside the works as they attempt to pierce the safe with an oxyacetylene torch. His confederates are tear-gassed and soon only Jarrett is left alive. He is cornered atop a chemical silo and, badly wounded, he shoots into the silo, igniting the volatile contents and blasting himself to kingdom come.

Cody Jarrett is based on Arthur 'Dock' Barker; Jarrett's first name, never used in the film except by a judge, is Arthur. Ma Jarrett is based on Arthur's mother, Kate Barker, known to crime history as 'Ma' Barker, the leader of a gang consisting of her four sons: Fred, Lloyd, Herman and Arthur. She was shot by the FBI at her hideout in Oklawaha, Florida, on 15 January 1935. In the film version of the story, she is shot in the back by Jarrett's wife Verna when Ma is about to liquidate Big Ed; when Jarrett catches up with them, Verna blames Big Ed, who dies by Jarrett's hand without revealing the truth.

With Cagney back on screen as a violent criminal, the rest of the cast had to work overtime to wrestle the audiences' attention from the lead. St-Louis-born blonde actress Virginia Mayo was cast as Verna, Jarrett's greedy, disingenuous wife, draped in mink coats and fur stoles; her beauty prompted the Sultan of Morocco to say that she was 'tangible proof for the existence of God'. Steve Cochran played Big Ed; Cochran and many of the supporting cast were genre actors, making a living in crime thrillers and B-movie westerns. For instance, Ian MacDonald, playing convict Bo Creel, was later Frank Miller, the villain who arrived by train in *High Noon* (1952).

Edmond O'Brien played Hank Fallon, alias 'Vic Pardo', the undercover T-man who spends more time in jail than he does out: 'Eight sentences in five years,' he moans. When he made *White Heat* he had recently married his second wife, Olga San Juan, an entertainer known as the 'Puerto Rican Pepper Pot'. O'Brien later went on to appear in *Seven Days in May* (1964) and *The Wild Bunch* (1969). There was grim humour in casting Margaret Wycherly, who had previously played the mother of war hero Alvin C. York in the Oscar-winning *Sergeant York* (1941), as the domineering, cadaverous Ma Jarrett. Wycherly had just recently appeared in the Rita Hayworth vehicle *The Loves of Carmen* (1948), billed as 'the old crone': excellent preparation for her turn as crotchety old Ma.

The film was shot on location around Los Angeles, with interiors at Warner Bros. During the famous prison mess hall scene, when Jarrett hears of his mother's death and goes berserk, slugging guards and running amuck, the extras' shocked reaction is real, as Cagney and Walsh hadn't told them what was going to happen. The opening railroad hold-up was filmed at the Southern Pacific railroad tunnel near Chatsworth. Urban street scenes and the Milbanke Motel were lensed around Van Nuys, while the chemical plant finale was shot at an actual oil refinery on 198th Street and Figueroa, in Torrence, Los Angeles.

Walsh employed a score by the prolific Austrian composer Max Steiner. It is most effective in the eerie scenes out at Big Ed's dust-blown New Mexico hideaway, with Verna and Big Ed nervously awaiting Jarrett's revenge. Steiner had also worked on *Angels With Dirty Faces*, *Gone with the Wind* (1939), *Casablanca*, *The Big Sleep* (1946) and *Key Largo* (1948), while his stock music was used unaccredited in many other productions. Cinematographer Sidney Hickox, whose *noir* flourishes add both atmosphere and realism to *White Heat*, had photographed *The Big Sleep* and *To Have and Have Not* (1947). He'd just worked with Walsh on the director's *High Sierra* remake, *Colorado Territory*, with Virginia Mayo in the Ida Lupino role.

With *White Heat*, Cagney returned from musicals to his gangster roots, but as a new type of rural gangster. The opening scenes recall the mountainous desert locale of *High Sierra*, with Jarrett and his men screaming along the mountain hairpins in a car, in pursuit of a steam locomotive on the High Sierra railroad line. The Jarrett gang consists of Cody, Ma, Verna, Big Ed Somers, Happy Taylor, Zuckie Hommell, Het Kohler and 'Cotton' Valetti; Hommell is the one who is badly scalded by steam during the train robbery and spends the early scenes bandaged up like the Invisible Man. The Southern Pacific railroad hold-up harks back to westerns, rather than the urban felonies and bootlegging of Cagney's previous crime films; Jarrett jumps off a tunnel onto the roof of the train and the gang park a car across the track. Jarrett's bunch are certainly larger-than-life figures, who closely resemble outlaws of the lawless old west. But Jarrett is much more complex than conventional rural western villains. He is untrusting to the point of paranoia, and a raging, violent homicidal maniac when riled. For example, there's a flurry of gunshots during the train hold-up. 'Sounds bad, Cody,' says Hommell, within earshot of the two train engineers. 'Why don't you give 'em my address too?' whines Jarrett, before gunning down the witnesses.

The character of Ma Jarrett and her umbilical relationship with her son takes the film into really interesting psychological territory. Ma is cranky, blunt and in her battered black hats, embroidered dresses and fur coats looks as though she should be living in the Klondike. Jarrett's oedipal fixation and his intense migraines would reappear in later crime films, as a popular excuse for deviant behaviour, but such derivatives never had the driving force and impact of *White Heat*. The weird scenes of Ma, soothing her adult son in her lap, are unique to forties cinema; Cagney was 50 years old and the effect is deeply unsettling. The source of the headaches is strange: as a child, Jarrett faked the headaches to wrest his mother's attention from his siblings, until they became real, and Ma's attention is now literally undivided. With his Ma beside him he's always 'Top of the world'; 'When you're around Ma, nothing can stop me,' Jarrett assures her. But the balance of their relationship indicates that Ma is in the driving seat; as a cop says: 'Where Ma goes, Cody goes', and Ma's death triggers a catastrophic imbalance of Jarrett's mind. He soon finds himself in a straightjacket in the psychiatric wing and is about to be committed when he manages to break out.

Cagney is plumper and older now, but still an exceptional screen presence. He was a great physical actor; his wonderful choreography is seen at its best in *Angels With Dirty Faces*, for example, when he referees the Dead End Kids' irreverent basketball game. But perhaps most significantly, in his crime films of the forties, Cagney is no longer a self-sufficient, confident hoodlum, but an older, mother-dependant psychopath to whom no one has ever shown any love. The snapping delivery and wired wisecracks are still there, but Cagney's 'Jarrett' persona, with grinning, sickly manner and hooded eyes, is darker and the film is among the most violent of its era.

One critic noted, 'the screenwriters have seen to it that death and savagery dominate the tale'. When a gang member is overusing the radio, vital for gauging how the police manhunt is progressing, Jarrett threatens, 'If that battery's dead, it'll have company.' Elsewhere, Jarrett pushes Verna off a chair, the same kind of petulance Cagney demonstrated when he shoved a grapefruit into Kitty's face in *The Public Enemy*. Later, Big Ed plans to have Cody killed. He hires Parker, a convict on the inside, to drop some heavy machinery on Jarrett in the workshop, but Pardo saves his life; later Jarrett exacts revenge by taking Parker hostage, then locks him in the trunk of a car and shoots him when Parker requests some 'ventilation'.

Pardo, working for T-man Evans, befriends Jarrett in prison with a view to breaking up the gang and locating the $300,000 taken from the mail train. Jarrett still suffers his headaches in prison and it is Pardo who becomes his surrogate 'mother', soothing away the pain. Later Jarrett begins to confide in Pardo and accepts him as an ally; they break out together and plan to split the payroll haul fifty-fifty, only for Jarrett to be betrayed by the only man he's ever put his complete trust in. In prison, a fine tension builder is that ex-convict Bo Creel was arrested by Fallon/'Pardo' four years ago and would recognise him instantly; later Winston hires now-paroled Creel as the tanker driver, cranking up the tension in the final robbery.

Mother's Little Helper: Cody Jarrett (James Cagney) and his wife Verna (Virginia Mayo) in Raoul Walsh's *White Heat* (1949).

The idea of a 'Trojan Horse' tanker filled with crooks recalls the tanker robbery of the brewery in *The Public Enemy*; Winston, the money-launderer, notes, 'We might all profit by a closer study of classical literature.' But the plan is scuppered by the T-men. Pardo manages to attach a makeshift radio transmitter to the bottom of the tanker, for the cops to track the vehicle, then he writes a message in a garage restroom: 'Attention Police, Call Evans – Treasury, Radio Signal Fallon'. This tips off Evans to alert the police radar trackers, who pick up the signal and are able to surround the chemical works with cops and flush the hoods out with tear gas. Earlier, Jarrett had had imaginary conversations with Ma since her death; in the finale he shouts out to her, calling on her in heaven to look down and watch him in action one last time, as he goes out in a blaze of glory. As Pardo notes: 'He finally got to the top of the world and it blew up right in his face.'

White Heat was released in the US in September 1949 and proved popular with critics and audiences. *Life* called it 'a wild and exciting mixture of mayhem and madness'; *Time and Tide* said the film was 'tense and grimly unpleasant' and 'a streamlined essay in hoodlum depravity ... the sort of film which Hollywood does so well'. The trailer stated: 'It's your kind of Cagney ... it's his kind of story ... Blazing his way to the top of the world'. In the UK, the *Sunday Times* noted that '[Walsh] has seen to it that the audience never has time to lose interest in the record of murder'. At the 1950 Academy Awards, Virginia Kellogg was nominated for an Oscar for her original story. Posters depicted Cagney brandishing a pistol, with the headlines 'Cagney is Red Hot in *White Heat*' and 'Pick up the pieces folks ... Jimmy's in action again!' Much was made of the reteaming of Cagney and his old studio for 'His New Hit Film from Warner Bros'. In the UK it was passed an A certificate, after some minor cuts. But the film's graphic style and unsettling subject matter was deemed too strong for some audiences. For instance, in 1950, both Finland and Sweden banned it. In Germany it was released as *Maschinenpistolen* ('Submachine-guns'), in Italy *La Furia Umana* ('The Human Fury') and in France as *L'Enfer est à Lui* ('Hell is with Him').

White Heat, with its iconic ending, is a pivotal American movie. For its DVD release in 2005 there was a special documentary made called *Top of the World*, containing interviews with Virginia Mayo and others, including Martin Scorsese, a huge fan of the film. There is also a documentary on Cagney's life, the aptly titled *A Tough Act to Follow*, which traces his extraordinary career. Cagney's fame and screen image is predominantly associated with gangster films, although he preferred musicals, saying, 'Once a song and dance man, always a song and dance man'. The ending of *White Heat* ensured Cagney took his place 'on top of the world' as a showman in cinema history. For Jarrett's curtain line, Cagney's stance – feet apart, arms outstretched – represents Cagney's twin careers merging as one: the gangster and the entertainer. He shouts the line 'Made it Ma! Top of the world!' heavenward, like the climax of a musical, and the subsequent explosion is the ultimate showstopper.

5

'If you want fresh air, don't look for it in this town'

— *The Asphalt Jungle* (1950)

Credits:

DIRECTOR – John Huston
PRODUCER – Arthur Hornblow Jnr
STORY – W.R. Burnett
SCREENPLAY – John Huston and Ben Maddow
DIRECTOR OF PHOTOGRAPHY – Harold Rosson
EDITOR – George Boemler
ART DIRECTORS – Cedric Gibbons and Randall Duell
SET DECORATION – Edwin B. Ellis and Jack D. Moore
MUSIC COMPOSER – Miklos Rozsa
Black and White
Interiors filmed at MGM Studios
An MGM production
Released by Metro-Goldwyn-Mayer
112 minutes
Cast:

Sterling Hayden (William 'Dix' Handley)/Louis Calhern (Alonzo 'Lon' D. Emmerich)/Jean Hagen ('Doll' Conovan)/ James Whitmore (Gus Minissi)/Sam Jaffe ('Doc' Erwin Riedenschneider)/John McIntire (Police Commissioner Hardy)/Marc Lawrence ('Cobby' Cobb)/Barry Kelley (Lieutenant Ditrich)/Anthony Caruso (Louis Ciavelli)/Teresa Celli (Maria Ciavelli)/Marilyn Monroe (Angela Phinlay, Lon's mistress)/Strother Martin (Karl Anton Smith)/Brad Dexter (Bob Brannom, the detective)/William Davis (Timmons)/ Dorothy Tree (May Emmerich)/John Maxwell (Doctor Swanson)

*   *   *

The Asphalt Jungle is the prototype *film noir* heist movie. Though robberies were an integral part of most crime films, *The Asphalt Jungle* was the first to concentrate completely on the recruiting for and planning of a robbery, treating this as important as the job itself. *The Asphalt Jungle* is set in a subterranean world, with the characters drifting aimlessly through the gothic 'city of night'. The heist is carefully calculated with mathematical precision, but the robbers' scheme unravels, with farcical misfortune overtaking the venture. Anything that can go wrong, does.

The Asphalt Jungle's 'worst-case scenario' was written by John Huston and Ben Maddow, based on the novel by William Riley Burnett. Burnett was the author of *Little Caesar* and *High Sierra* and was a writer of the 'hard-boiled' school, who lived in the asphalt jungle of Los Angeles. The film shares several themes and plot nuances with *High Sierra*: an aged ex-con released from prison finds himself caught out of time and place; a gallery of untrustworthy conspirators; a farm boy who dreams of going back home; and the meticulous jewellery robbery ending in tatters.

In an unnamed city, 'Doc' Riedenschneider is released from prison and approaches bookmaker 'Cobby' Cobb with an idea for a half-million-dollar diamond heist of Belletier's, the jewellers. Cobb is an acquaintance of Lon Emmerich, a crooked lawyer, and the Doc needs finance. Emmerich is about to go bankrupt and his detective ally, Bob Brannom, suggests they get the unwitting Cobby to bankroll the job, with an eye to double-crossing everyone involved. Doc hires a team of criminals: Louis Ciavelli is an expert safe-cracker, Gus Minissi a getaway driver and Dix Handley a street-smart Kentucky country boy. The trio learn Doc's complicated plan and then carry out the heist. They access the vault and steal the haul, but as they leave, a guard wounds Ciavelli in the stomach. Handley and the Doc visit Emmerich and Brannom, who try to dupe them. Handley kills Brannom, but catches a bullet in his side. Handley and Doc strike a deal with Emmerich – he'll arrange a 'buy-back' from the insurance company, ensuring them a quarter of a million dollars. A corrupt cop, Lieutenant Ditrich, convinces Cobby to rat on his friends; under questioning, Emmerich's alibi disintegrates and he shoots himself. Cobby and Minissi are rounded up by the cops, and Ciavelli dies; Handley and Doc hide out with Handley's girlfriend, Doll. Handley and Doll drive towards his childhood ranch home in Kentucky, while Doc heads for Cleveland in a taxi. At a way-station diner, Doc tarries too long, watching a teenage jitterbugger, and the police arrest him. To Doll's dismay, having reached Hickory Wood Farm, Handley slumps dead in a field.

Since his success with *The Maltese Falcon*, Huston had directed several more films, including two with Humphrey Bogart now regarded as crime classics. In *Key Largo* (1948), war veteran Frank McCloud (Bogart) arrives at the Largo Hotel on Key Largo, one of the remote Florida Keys, a chain of coral islands on the southern tip of the Florida peninsula. He's there to visit Nora and James Temple (Lauren Bacall and Lionel Barrymore), the widow and father of a war comrade, who has been killed at Casino in Italy. Soon afterwards, the weather turns: a hurricane is brewing and they batten down the shutters. There's tension in the air and not just because of the approaching storm – the hotel has been taken over and terrorised by Johnny Rocco (Edward G. Robinson – an exiled crook just in from Cuba), his alcoholic moll Gaye Dawn (Claire Trevor) and a gang of mobsters. They plan to use the hotel as a rendezvous to pass on counterfeit dollars. But the storm strikes first and, in its fury, almost destroys the hotel. Eventually it subsides, and Rocco meets Ziggy, his contact, passes on the money and leaves aboard a boat, piloted by McCloud. Out at sea, McCloud manages to kill the gang, and returns to Key Largo and Nora.

Claire Trevor won a Best Supporting Actress Oscar, in a cast that is uniformly excellent. Huston piles on the tension, while Robinson delivers one of his best performances, as a washed-up gangster trying to return to the big time. His gang includes two pugnacious thugs – Curly (Thomas Gomez) and Angel (Dan Seymour) – and a dapper, black-and-white-clad punk – Toots (a menacing turn by Harry Lewis).

The art design was by Leo K. Kuter, with the Largo Hotel wreathed in shadows, then suddenly strobed with lighting. The décor is tropically evocative: perpetually rotating fans, potted palm leaves casting ominous shadows and wall-mounted trophy

Mr and Mrs Bogart in *Key Largo* (1948); Frank McCloud (Humphrey Bogart) protects Nora Temple (Lauren Bacall).

fish – you can almost taste the stale air in the stifling bar. Outside, there's a quay, a moored boat (named *Santana*, after Bogart's real-life yawl) and the battered palm trees, twisted and bent into arcs in the powerful wind. *Key Largo* left Bogart overshadowed somewhat by his fellow actors and he was similarly upstaged in his next film with Huston.

The Treasure of the Sierra Madre (1948) was another huge hit. Based on the novel by the mysterious Bruno Traven (who was reputedly present during location filming, under the name Hal Croves), the film recounted a disastrous Mexican treasure hunt in which Fred C. Dobbs (Bogart) teams up with Curtin (Tim Holt) and Howard (scene-stealing, Oscar-winning Walter Huston, John's father). *Sierra Madre* was voted New York Film Critics' film of the year in 1948. Huston then made *We Were Strangers* (1949), with John Garfield and Jennifer Jones mixed up with Cuban revolutionaries.

In *The Asphalt Jungle*, Huston returned to the murky urban environment with which he had made his name in *The Maltese Falcon*. For *The Asphalt Jungle*, billed as 'A John Huston Production', he again assembled an exemplary company. As the director once said, 'The trick is in the casting', and the players deployed aptly sum up Burnett's grimy, subterranean world as fittingly as *The Maltese Falcon*'s cast reflected Dashiell Hammett's. For the central character of William 'Dix' Handley, Huston cast six-feet-five-inch New Jersey-born actor Sterling Hayden, even though MGM didn't like the choice. Hayden had been a seaman, model and contract player at Paramount, before joining the US Marines; he was also a special operations agent under the name John Hamilton (some biographies list this as his real name, which is actually Sterling Relyea Walter). He joined the Communist Party in 1946, after fighting with Yugoslavian partisans (his Party membership eventually got him into trouble with the House of Un-American Activities). The 1949 edition of *Film Parade* annual included a shot of bare-chested Hayden at the helm of his yacht, in a section designated 'He-men of Hollywood'. According to Huston's biography, in 1949 Hayden was battling alcoholism and was 'under psychiatric care', but his towering presence and imitation thick Kentucky drawl made this one of his best performances.

Patrician Louis Calhern had been appearing in movies since the silent twenties and had played Buffalo Bill in the screen version of *Annie Get Your Gun* the year before being cast as lawyer Lon Emmerich in *The Asphalt Jungle*. Broadway actress Jean Hagen, as Doll Conovan, had only recently signed a contract with MGM. Huston cast maths-teacher-turned-theatre-actor Sam Jaffe as Doc Riedenschneider, the brains behind the operation. Jaffe had also appeared as the Lama in *Lost Horizon* (1937) and played the title role in *Gunga Din* (1939). James Whitmore, as hunch-backed getaway driver Gus, was an ex-Marine, like Hayden. Police Commissioner John McIntire had been a radio actor and the voice of the *March of Time* newsreels. Strother Martin had a bit part in *The Asphalt Jungle* in a police line-out. Marc Lawrence, previously counterfeiter Ziggy in *Key Largo*, played nervous, duped bookie 'Cobby' Cobb. Reliably tough Brad Dexter (later the one no one can remember in *The Magnificent Seven*) made his debut as duplicitous private eye Brannom. Lola Albright was originally cast as Emmerich's mistress, Angela Phinlay, but she was too expensive. Instead, Angela was portrayed in familiar breathy style by a young Marilyn Monroe, who gets to deliver lines such as 'Imagine me on this Cuban beach in my green bathing suit – yipes!' An early quintessential Monroe moment sees her calling a cop 'You big bananahead!'

Originally slated to direct *Quo Vadis?* in Rome, with Gregory Peck and Elizabeth Taylor in the leads, Huston planned and filmed *The Asphalt Jungle* while they were waiting for Peck to recover from an eye infection. *The Asphalt Jungle* was shot just before Christmas 1949. The final scene at Hickory Wood Farm, of Handley's corpse surrounded by horses, was actually shot in Kentucky. The 'Asphalt Jungle' itself was photographed on location around Los Angeles and at MGM Studios. During the making of *The Asphalt Jungle*, Monroe's drama coach, Natasha Lytess, stood just off camera to encourage her pupil. Monroe's last scene, as she breaks down when Emmerich is cornered, was rated by the actress as the best scene she ever played. *The Asphalt Jungle*'s trendsetting brassy score was provided by Hungarian Miklos Rozsa, who later specialised in bombastic compositions for biblical spectacles, including *Quo Vadis?*, which was eventually made, without the participation of Huston, Gregory Peck or Elizabeth Taylor, in 1950.

The visual style of *film noir* photography, which could be termed 'urban gothic', was initiated due to budgetary constraints and economies enforced by the Second World War. In fact many of these *films noirs* were B-movies, with low budgets and sparse sets; the dark shadowy corners swallowed the periphery of the screen, hiding the fact that often the sets had little or no furniture. These dimly lit interiors, with their layered curtains of light, graded in shades of grey, fade into black. Elsewhere, a deserted railway marshalling yard is wreathed in fog, continuing the claustrophobic environment.

The setting for *The Asphalt Jungle* depicts the lowlife characters' nocturnal world – a metropolitan subculture of bookies, thugs and crooked lawyers. As Paul Duncan notes in *Noir Fiction: Dark Highways*, the essence of *noir* is 'not about the people standing on the edge of the abyss looking in, but about the people in it, forever writhing'. Huston's cinematographer was Harold Rosson. Rosson films down dark corridors with slivers of light chinking in the darkness, through doorways and curtains, or deploys light bulbs and other sources of illumination to inventive effect. Huston also uses the pyramidal light canopy thrown by suspended lamp-shades to accentuate facial features, as in the planning sequence, with drifting smoke and the tabletop littered with a map of Belletier's, an ashtray and drinks, edged with Handley, Ciavelli and Minissi, listening intently to Doc. But even on the edges of these pools of light, the characters can never escape the 'dark abyss'.

Although Rosson was most famous for lensing *The Wizard of Oz* (1939) and *Duel in the Sun* (1947) in Technicolor, his black and white work, particularly on *The*

Asphalt Jungle and Huston's next film, the severely abridged *The Red Badge of Courage* (1951), was equally stylish. Rosson was especially adept at close-ups, with the camera trained on the gang's strained faces for much of the robbery. Rosson's perspectival photography accentuates spatial trios within the frame, accentuating the depth of focus on the screen. These compositions reflect trio alliances in the story: Cobby, Emmerich and Brannom; Doc's three-man gang; and Emmerich, his wife and mistress. Another distinctive photographic effect was *The Asphalt Jungle*'s rain-slicked streets, an image borrowed from Carol Reed's *The Third Man* (1946), while a shining getaway car, reflecting the night lights, gleams as though it is infused with neon.

If, as the Doc mentions, 'Crime is only a left-handed form of human endeavour', then the crooks assembled for the Belletier's job are over-achievers. One of the most distinctive and influential aspects of Burnett's plotting was the disparate group assembled for a special crime. In later films this 'job' often became a mission (as in *The Dirty Dozen* – 1967). The identification between a character and his particular skill also began with *The Asphalt Jungle*; in a later variant such as *The Magnificent Seven* (1960), the character's skill would be his only defining feature. Interestingly, Burnett also collaborated on the screenplay of *The Great Escape* (1963), the template of which is clearly influenced by Burnett's earlier crime work: a Second World War prison breakout is engineered by a strategic mastermind ('Big X'), a forger, a tunneller and a scrounger, and characters with nicknames such as 'the Mole', 'the Ferret' and 'the Cooler King', each of whom bring their expertise to the plan – except that this time the protagonists are trying to get out of somewhere.

The centrepiece of *The Asphalt Jungle* is the well-executed, high-wire heist on Belletier's. Doc hires a three-man gang: a 'box man', a driver and a hooligan ('a hoolie') to take a consignment of diamonds that is like 'a ripe plum ready to fall'. Safe-cracker Ciavelli breaks into the sewers through a manhole then smashes through a brick wall into the jeweller's, letting Handley and Doc in. The trio manoeuvre under the electric eye, pick the lock on the vault door and blow up the safe. Their dialogue is full of authentic underworld vernacular: a pistol's a 'heater', a police van is a 'meat wagon', while the 'box man' blows the safe with a special explosive mixture – referred to as 'soup' – noting, 'It's gonna take a lot to blow this baby'. But almost as soon as the diamonds are theirs, their luck changes for the worse.

The Asphalt Jungle's catalogue of errors, leading to the gang's downfall, sets the tone for future heist movies. Doc terms such providence 'blind accidents'; individually these hiccups are no obstacle, but combined they cause the meticulous planning to go seriously awry. The first hint of danger is when the drill bit snaps as Ciavelli riddles the safe. The explosion blows the vault door and the gang clears the diamonds, but the blast sets off jangling alarms, which sound all over town. This cacophony brings both a sense of foreboding and dozens of cops into the locality. A snooping nightwatchman disturbs the gang's escape; Handley slugs the guard, who then drops his pistol, which shoots Ciavelli in the stomach.

When Emmerich and Bob Brannom try to cross the gang, the plan descends
into chaos. Brannom is shot by Handley, and Emmerich has to dispose of Brannom
in the river, which eventually leads the police to his door. Emmerich's opulence,
finery and class is a front – he's got no money and his debtors won't pay up. He has
a bedridden wife in whom he has no interest and Angela, a mistress who is many
years his junior, who unsettlingly refers to him as 'Uncle Lon'. Emmerich is known
as 'the Big Fixer', but he's out of his league and adrift, egged on by his 'muscle',
private eye Brannom. Hoping to make more out of the deal, Emmerich says he can
fence the jewels. When the cops atomise his alibi and Angela breaks down under
questioning, rather than suffer a public humiliation, he shoots himself.

'Doc' Erwin Riedenschneider, 'Herr Doktor', or 'the Professor', has a precise
approach and a calculated coldness, resembling the look and deliberate manner of
a war criminal, with his thick spectacles and briefcase full of plans. His unhealthy
fondness for pretty young women is initially evident in the way he leafs through
Cobby's pin-up calendar. During his escape to Cleveland he spends too long
watching a teenager dance to a jukebox record. Cops watch him through the window

Planning and Execution: Doc Riedenschneider (Sam Jaffe, left) briefs his gang on
the Belletier's job. Left to right: Sterling Hayden, Anthony Caruso and James
Whitmore (standing) in *The Asphalt Jungle* (1950).

(revealed in a clever tracking shot through the blinds by Huston), and as he leaves, they pounce. Doc asks how long they have been outside and is told two or three minutes – just the duration of the phonograph record. Doc's weakness, like that of all the other protagonists, leads to his undoing.

Horse-loving country boy Dix Handley is a nostalgic idealist; all he wants is enough money to buy back his father's 160-acre Hickory Wood farm. The city is choking him; he dreams of escape and his first action would be to jump in the farm creek and 'get this city dirt off me'. Even safe-cracker Ciavelli notes: 'If you want fresh air, don't look for it in this town.' Handley wistfully recalls to Doll his younger days spent riding, then his mood changes. He remembers his family's fall from grace: his father died, they lost the corn crops and their prize colt broke its leg and had to be shot. 'That was a rotten year,' drawls Handley. He's waiting for his luck to turn, but of course it doesn't: he's a loser and he's killed, like Emmerich and Brannom, by the Asphalt Jungle. A cop says Handley's 'a hoolie…a man without human feeling or human mercy'. The final shot of the film shows that Handley has both of these, as well as dignity; as he collapses and dies in the field at Hickory Wood farm, three colts gather around the fallen country boy. In *The Asphalt Jungle*, by humanising the gang, and especially the thuggery of Handley, Huston elicited sympathy for a seemingly dislikeable bunch.

Huston also deploys some keenly drawn background characters, trying to survive in the *noir* city. Getaway driver Minissi stakes his friend Handley with money; there are people you can rely on, but in Huston's world, the richer and more 'respectable' they are, the more corrupt they seem to be. Safe-cracker Ciavelli is a family man, who initially refuses to become involved in the plan, then looks at his sleeping wife and child, and changes his mind. His accidental death is the true tragedy of the film: a man forced to steal to provide for his family. When the cops get a lead and try to arrest Ciavelli, they arrive just in time to see him laid out in his coffin.

In Huston's cynical worldview, there is no honour among thieves and even the cops are on the make. Bookie Cobby's a coward, who is frightened by corrupt Lieutenant Ditrich into betraying his associates. 'They'll call me a fink!' pleads Cobby, but he still squeals. Huston presents the cops very unsympathetically, with Commissioner Hardy single-minded and soulless, and Ditrich an overweight, intimidating bully. At a press conference, Hardy switches on four police radio channel speakers, abuzz with activity; the overlapping racket demonstrates the police's over-stretched resources. 'Listen,' says the Commissioner, 'they're cries for help.' Then he turns the radio speakers off – that is what it would be like if there was no law and order: 'The battle's finished, the jungle wins… the predatory beasts take over.'

The Asphalt Jungle was first released in the US, in May 1950, with the slogan 'The City Under The City'. The trailer called Handley 'A hooligan with a twisted dream', and Doll 'The dime-a-dance dame who wanted to share that shabby dream'. Monroe's Angela was trailed as 'The easy-living, green-eyed blonde'.

Advertising was also endorsed by famous crime authors, including Stephen Longstreet, Gerald Fairlie and Richard Brooks. Original posters depicted the title written on the tarmac in white lettering, resembling road markings. Re-release posters from the late fifties have moved Monroe up the billing somewhat, in keeping with her star status – one Italian poster (entitled *Giungla di Asfalto*) is simply a portrait of Monroe, with her name top-billed; Hayden and Calhern barely get a look-in. In France, where Huston was immensely popular, the film was released in 1951 as *Quand La Ville Dort* ('When the City Sleeps'). *The Asphalt Jungle* was released in June 1950 in the UK, rated A (after the film had been slightly trimmed), and was a huge hit. MGM studio head Louis B. Mayer said, 'That *Asphalt Pavement* thing is full of nasty, ugly people doing nasty ugly things. I wouldn't walk across the room to see a thing like that.' *Time* was kinder: 'Even with its shortcomings, the picture succeeds to a remarkable extent in understanding its criminals, and creating a kind of perverse sympathy for them, without condoning their crimes. To have accomplished that…lifts *The Asphalt Jungle* high above the run of melodramas that do not score half as well on targets much easier to hit.' *Cue* called it a 'beautifully constructed film', while the *Hollywood Reporter* said it was 'almost a classic of its type', a view that has endured.

In 1949, comedies and westerns were the most popular Hollywood genres, with Bob Hope and Bing Crosby, Abbott and Costello, John Wayne and Gary Cooper the biggest stars. But *The Asphalt Jungle*, despite its bleakness, was one of MGM's hits of the year, along with the lighter *Annie Get Your Gun* and *Father of the Bride*. Jaffe won the Best Actor Award at Venice and an Oscar nomination for Best Supporting Actor. Other Oscar nominations included Huston as Best Director, Huston and Maddow for their screenplay and Harold Rosson for his black and white cinematography; none of them won.

Released in the UK on the same day (8 June 1950) as *The Asphalt Jungle*, *Armoured Car Robbery* was another post-war *noir* heist movie. Directed by Richard Fleischer, it featured an even more downmarket bunch of lowlifes: Calhern and Monroe's characters from *The Asphalt Jungle* became mastermind William Talman and his stripper girlfriend Aldele Jergens, who, as the title implies, rob an armoured car. Charles McGraw (from the classic 1952 sleeper hit *The Narrow Margin*) played the detective on their trail who foils the caper, with Talman being run over on a landing strip.

In 1961, following the huge success on TV of the series *The Untouchables*, a weekly TV series appeared in the US called *The Asphalt Jungle*, which bore no resemblance to Huston's film other than the title. To add to its influence on other heist movies and its many imitators, *The Asphalt Jungle* was directly remade three times by MGM. In 1958, Delmer Daves reworked it as a western, *The Badlanders*, with the Belletier's job replaced by an Arizona gold-mine robbery perpetrated by fresh-out-of-jail Alan Ladd and Ernest Borgnine. Ladd is the Doc equivalent 'the Dutchman', a mining engineer and geologist. In 1962, *Cairo* saw a team of thieves attempt to lift King Tut's relics from an Egyptian museum. MGM's first blax-ploitation cash-in on *Shaft* was a remake of *The Asphalt Jungle* entitled *Cool Breeze*, with Jim Watkins in the Dix Handley role.

One of the best known of *The Asphalt Jungle*'s derivatives was Stanley Kubrick's *The Killing* (1956), the young director's third film. Sterling Hayden was cast as Johnny Clay, who with his inexperienced gang tries to rip off a racetrack. They are going to steal the betting money, while one of the gang causes a diversion by shooting a racehorse, mid-race. Stitched together by a timescale voiceover and flashing back and forth through time, *The Killing* is much more complicated than *The Asphalt Jungle*. It was based on the novel 'Clean Break' by Lionel White, with the film's dialogue written by *noir* novelist Jim Thomson. The wife of one of the gang members decides to betray them, so she and her lover can run off with the money, but her plan, like everyone else's in the film, is doomed. Promotion for the film stated: 'In all its Fury and Violence…Like no other picture since *Scarface* and *Little Caesar*.' Kubrick's title is deliberately ambiguous, as the thieves plan to make 'a killing' on the horses, but due to extraordinary bad luck, some of them are killed. The final twist is particularly memorable, as the case containing the cash hits the tarmac at the airport and crashes open, bills whirling far and wide.

Heist movies later evolved into caper movies, where the jokey unbelievability of the action excused moral outrage at the thieves' plan succeeding. Ideally heist movies should prove that crime isn't the answer – even if the job is successful, there's always something just waiting to go wrong. Remember: no one wins in the asphalt jungle.

6

'The liar's kiss that says I love you'

— *Kiss Me Deadly* (1955)

Credits:
DIRECTOR AND PRODUCER — Robert Aldrich
EXECUTIVE PRODUCER — Victor Saville
STORY — Mickey Spillane
SCREENPLAY — A.I. Bezzerides
DIRECTOR OF PHOTOGRAPHY — Ernest Laszlo
EDITOR — Michael Luciano
ART DIRECTOR — William Glasgow
MUSIC — Frank DeVol
Black and White
Interiors filmed at Sutherland Studios
A Parklane Pictures production
Released by United Artists
105 minutes
Cast:
> Ralph Meeker (Mike Hammer)/Albert Dekker (Doctor G.E. Soberin)/Paul Stewart (Carl Evello)/Maxine Cooper (Velda Wickman)/Gaby Rogers (Gabrielle/Lily Carver)/Wesley Addy (Homicide Lt Pat Murphy)/Juano Hernandez (Eddie Yeager)/Nick Dennis (Nick, the mechanic)/Cloris Leachman (Christina Bailey)/Marian Carr (Friday, girl at mansion)/Jack Lambert (Sugar Smallhouse)/Jack Elam (Charlie Max)/Jerry Zinneman (Sammy)/Percy Helton (Morgue doctor)/Fortunio Bananova (Carmen Trivago)/Silvio Minciotti (Furniture mover)/Leigh Snowdon (Girl at pool party)/Madi Comfort (Singer in club)/James Seay and Robert Cornthaite (FBI men)/Mara McAfee (Nurse)/James McCallian (Horace, apartment superintendent)/Jesslyn Fax (Horace's wife)/Mort Marshall (Ray Diker)/Strother Martin (Harvey Wallace, the truck driver)/Marjorie Bennett

(Manager)/Art Loggis (Bartender in club)/Robert Sherman (Gas station attendant)/Keith McConnel (Hollywood Athletics Club clerk)/Paul Richards (Hood in street)/Yvonne Doherty (Doctor Soberin's secretary)

*   *   *

At night, on a lonely road, private eye Mike Hammer picks up a woman dressed only in a trenchcoat. Her name is Christina and she has escaped from an insane asylum, where she was being kept prisoner. At a gas station she posts a letter, but shortly afterwards Hammer's car is stopped and they are kidnapped; Hammer is drugged, Christina tortured to death and the two are put in a car and run over a cliff, in a faked accident. Hammer survives and with his secretary, Velda, attempts to find out who the girl was. Their search leads them to Carl Evello, a hood, who tries to car-bomb Hammer's speedster. Hammer finds Christina's room-mate, Lily Carver, and hides her in his apartment. The letter, posted by Christina to Hammer, tells him she has swallowed a key. The key leads Hammer to a locker with a mysterious case inside. The trail of suspects ends at Doctor Soberin, who is also after the box and who takes Velda hostage. It turns out that Lily Carver is actually Soberin's lover, Gabrielle (the real Lily was fished out of the harbour weeks earlier), and they manage to get the suitcase. Hammer arrives at Soberin's beach house, but is too late: Gabrielle has shot Soberin and although she has been warned not to, she opens the box. It contains volatile radioactive material, which explodes, killing Gabrielle and blowing up the house before Hammer can save Velda.

This intricate story, considerably simplified above, was based on a novel by Mickey Spillane, a writer of pulp crime novels from the late forties onwards. His work was noted for its sensationalism, its sexual content and its extreme violence; as Spillane's protagonist, Mike Hammer punched, kicked and shot his way through bad guys, often in revenge for the death or kidnapping of a close friend or associate. The first Mike Hammer books were 'I, the Jury' (published in 1947), 'My Gun is Quick' (1950), 'Vengeance is Mine' (1950), 'One Lonely Night' (1951), 'The Big Kill' (1951) and 'Kiss Me, Deadly' (1952). The film's plot sticks fairly closely to Spillane's 'Kiss Me, Deadly', but in the book the suitcase package contains drugs. Also missing from the film version was the comma in the title.

Kiss Me Deadly was financed by production company Parklane Pictures. They had already produced adaptations of two of Spillane's books – *I, the Jury* (1953) and *The Long Wait* (1954) – and would follow *Deadly* with another, *My Gun is Quick* (1957), which was originally to have been made in 1954, with Robert Aldrich at the helm. In *I, the Jury* onomatopoeic Biff Elliot played Mike Hammer. The film was shot in 3D, but released 'flat', which better summed up the material. Peggy Castle appeared as a psychiatrist, helping Hammer to solve a friend's murder. *The Long Wait* is the only one of the Parklane series not to feature Mike Hammer;

Anthony Quinn starred as McBride, who is accused of a murder he didn't commit, but following a subsequent car crash he conveniently loses his memory and his fingerprints. In *My Gun is Quick*, Hammer (Robert Bray) solves a murder case and busts a jewel heist. All three of these films are straightforward formula crime movies, something that certainly can't be said of *Kiss Me Deadly*.

Ralph Meeker was cast as the tough, bullying hero, Michael Hammer, PI. Meeker (real name Ralph Rathgeber) had previously stepped into Brando's shoes on Broadway in *A Streetcar Named Desire* and had been in the 1953 stage version of *Picnic* (later a movie with William Holden in the role). He began in films in 1951 and his best early roles were in westerns, often as a bullying character: the conniving adventurer out for a slice of reward money in *The Naked Spur* (1953) and the cocky Union officer whose double shooting bookends *Run of the Arrow* (1957). Albert Dekker, as the briefly-seen-but-threatening Doctor Soberin, also worked in theatre, but memorably appeared in a variety of movies, notably *Doctor Cyclops* (1940 – as a doctor in the Peruvian jungle conducting miniaturisation experiments on humans) and *The Killers* (as gang leader Jim Colefax in the 1946 version of Hemingway's story). Paul Stewart, playing Carl Evello, appeared on

Kiss Me Deadly: sultry 1955 promotional shot of Ralph Meeker as Mike Hammer and Maxine Cooper as his secretary, Velda.

radio in the famous, panic-inducing *War of the Worlds* transmission and made his screen debut in *Citizen Kane* (1941), as Kane's valet. Maxine Cooper, as Hammer's secretary Velda, had appeared extensively on TV and later played in *Zero Hour* (1957), a plane drama, with pilots struck with ptomaine poisoning, which was the straight-faced model for the *Airplane* series. A former Miss Chicago, Cloris Leachman made her film debut as Christina, the petrified woman on the loose from an insane asylum. Evello's henchmen Sugar and Charlie were played by two Jacks: thin-faced Lambert and wall-eyed Elam. Both actors specialised to great effect as heavies, almost exclusively in westerns and gangster movies.

Kiss Me Deadly's 21-day shoot began on 27 November 1954; it wrapped on 23 December. It was shot on location in and around Los Angeles, California, for $410,000. The final beach shack scene was lensed on Malibu Beach; two specially built sets (Hammer's and Velda's apartment interiors) were filmed at Sutherland Studios. The explosive special effects in the finale were executed by Complete Film Service, with a miniature model of the beach house.

Much was expected from Aldrich's new film. He had just made two exciting, highly successful movies with Burt Lancaster: *Apache* and *Vera Cruz* (both 1954). In contrast to these films, colourful, big-budget adventures shot in Technicolor (*Vera Cruz* was also in SuperScope), *Kiss Me Deadly* was low-budget black and white, photographed by Aldrich's regular cameraman of the period, 50-year-old Hungarian Ernest Laszlo. Laszlo captures admirably Spillane's universe; his location filming adds immensely to *Kiss Me Deadly*'s atmosphere, with much of the action taking place around seedy hotels, apartment blocks and seamy clubs or out of town, on deserted highways and secluded beaches.

Hammer's character is as hard and thuggish as the hoods he faces. In his novel 'I, the Jury', Spillane introduces Hammer on the trail of his friend's killer: 'When this kind of thing happens, it makes me want to hit out; watch the killer crawl, hear him beg for mercy as my finger tightens on the trigger. When I catch up with him, I'll be the jury, and the judge, and the executioner.' In the finale of 'I, the Jury', Charlotte, the murderer, strips in an attempt to convince Hammer not to shoot her. As they embrace, Hammer fires. Her eyes are 'a symphony of incredulity' – 'How c-could you?' she gasps. 'It was easy' is the answer. But in *Kiss Me Deadly*, Hammer is presented less as a caped avenger and more as a small-time operator, concerned with divorce cases and minor investigations, who uses his secretary Velda Wickman as 'woo-bait' to honey-trap unfaithful husbands. This seems to pay well. Not only does Hammer have a spacious apartment and a flashy sports car, he also has a very early answering machine rigged up to his phone, a huge reel-to-reel contraption built into the wall, which seems at odds with the low-key nature of the movie.

Hammer is drawn into the web of radioactive intrigue by chance. He's driving home and is stopped by a hitchhiker. She says her name is Christina, named after Christina Rossetti; following her death, Hammer finds an anthology of Rossetti's poems on Christina's bedside table, bookmarked on a poem. The letter Christina posted to Hammer says simply 'Remember Me', the first line of the poem, which reveals in code that Christina had swallowed a key, which opens the locker containing the radioactive package. Only when Hammer discovers the box is lethal do we realise why Christina's bird died in its cage in the contaminated flat. This and other subtleties of the plot were largely ignored at the time of its release.

The trail of suspects is labyrinthine: the mysterious Dyker (facially scarred and hiding alone in his apartment); 'Lily Carver' (presented as Christina's ex-room-mate, but really an enemy agent); Carl Evello and his sport-obsessed hoodlums (perpetually listening to boxing or horse racing on the wireless); Carmen Trivago, an opera buff; a crooked morgue doctor who wants a share of the 'treasure'; an easily bribed clerk at the Hollywood Athletics Club; William Mist, an 'art dealer'; and finally shadowy Doctor Soberin, the prescriber of sleeping pills and injector of Sodium Pentathol. The investigation is initially slow-paced, but picks up as the pile of bodies grows.

Spillane's books were thought to be unfilmable, because of the explicit sex and violence, but Aldrich made a good attempt at depicting Spillane's bad apple examples of humanity, rotten to the core. They are less graphic by today's standards, but packed a punch in the forties and fifties; Spillane's prolific sex scenes in particular would have caused problems. Moreover, Hammer's attitude is sexist rather than sexy, and his amorous effect on women in the film is difficult to fathom. His only meaningful relationship is with his secretary Velda – they share a beaten world-weariness. Throughout the film a fateful song seems to follow Hammer around: in the opening, over the titles, Hammer's radio plays 'Rather Have the Blues', composed by Frank DeVol and sung by Nat King Cole. Later in a bar, singer Madi Comfort performs the song again and Hammer ponders his predicament and listens intently: 'The web has got me caught, I'd rather have the blues than what I've got.'

The violence is hammered home by Aldrich and is the most objectionable aspect of *Kiss Me Deadly*. Hammer has a sadistic streak: he slaps around suspects, including women, and threatens informants – at one point he puts the frighteners on a Caruso fan by snapping his collectable records and traps a morgue attendant's fingers in a drawer. Evello's heavies fight back by rigging Hammer's car with two bombs, which he discovers in time ('We keep underestimating you,' says the chief hood), tie him to a bed and inject a dose of truth serum Sodium Pentathol ('Pleasant dreams, Mister Hammer'); this battle of wits seems to anticipate the Bond films. The villains even squash Hammer's excitable Hispanic mechanic Nick (whose catchphrase is 'Va Va Voom!') under a car, by letting down the hydraulic jack. In the most horrible sequence, they torture naked Christina; all we see are her legs (sitting on a table), her trenchcoat lying on the floor, and hear her terrible screams, while one of the hoods walks past drugged, immobile Hammer, holding a pair of pliers.

The major change to Spillane's original story, replacing the drugs with radioactive material, introduces a topical element to the film. In 1955, the Cold War and nuclear paranoia were at their height, as were the Communist witch-hunts. *Kiss Me Deadly* even name-checks the Manhattan Project, Los Alamos and Trinity. The implication is that the foreign-sounding Doctor Soberin represents 'the other side', who want to get their hands on this valuable material (never identified, but perhaps plutonium or some other fissile element in a lead box). When Hammer first locates the prize, referred to by Velda as 'the great whatsit', the case is hot to touch, and when he tries to open it, a blinding white light flashes forth and burns Hammer's wrist. When Soberin warns his lover Gabrielle not to open the box, he calls the much-prized contents 'the head of Medusa' and makes reference to Lot's wife and Pandora. He also mentions Gabrielle's 'feline perception', and it is this perception, and proverbial curiosity, that kills her. She shoots Soberin, then as she is about to open the case, Hammer bursts in. 'Kiss me Mike,' says Gabrielle. 'The liar's kiss that says I love you. You're good at giving such kisses.' She wounds him, before opening the box and being engulfed in a pillar of flame. The apocalyptic ending, with Hammer and Velda trapped in the exploding house, is often seen as their moral comeuppance: Hammer pays for his selfishness and brutality, Velda for her immorality.

The Parklane Pictures production was issued, like all their Spillane adaptations, through United Artists. It was released in Los Angeles on 18 May 1955, but two versions of the film exist. The full version runs at 105 minutes (101 on video) and includes several scenes of extreme brutality, including the torture and murder of Christina. Cut versions of the film (running at 96 minutes) remove or abridge the violence: in the short version, Hammer is knocked out when Christina is kidnapped and then wakes up in hospital, removing the entire sequence where she is killed, while he lies drugged on a bed. It also makes nonsense of Hammer later recognising Doctor Soberin's shoes, as in the short version he has never seen them. This cut does also work in the film's favour, creating an air of mystery around events during the three missing days and what exactly happened to Christina. This cut version was also issued in the UK, gaining a certificate A. The ending of the film is also different to the one Aldrich originally shot. In all release versions, Hammer and Velda die in the atomic explosion in the house and 'The End' appears over a shot of the house being destroyed. Subsequent reissues add over a minute of footage, which shows Hammer rescuing Velda from the room, running down the beach and into the sea; here 'The End' appears on the couple embracing, looking back at the explosion and lit by flashes from the blast.

When *Kiss Me Deadly* was released, the alluring poster depicted a big pair of lips with 'Kiss Me Deadly' written across them. The blurb declared, '*I, the Jury*, *The Long Wait* And Now Mickey Spillane Strips Down To Naked Fury!' (but only as naked as the censors would allow). In the accompanying artwork Hammer and Velda get cosy on the couch, with the caption 'I Don't Care What You Do To Me Mike – Just Do It Fast!' In keeping with the nuclear themes in the film, other copy unsubtly announced the film as 'Blood Red Kisses! White Hot Thrills! Mickey

Spillane's Latest H-Bomb!' The film was generally regarded as another thick-eared detective yarn by most critics and reviled for Aldrich's brutal, misogynistic approach, which was already present in the books. *Variety* said it was 'A series of amorous dames, murder-minded plug-uglies and dangerous adventures that offer excitement, but have little clarity to let the viewer know what's going on'. But *Kiss Me Deadly* was popular with the US public: advertising pointed out that the film was 'Tops in Thrills! Tops in Suspense! And Tops in Boxoffice!' The *New York Times* reckoned the film depicted a 'vision of a Southern California so spiritually parched that a single match struck at the wrong moment could unleash the fires of hell'.

But in France the critics responded very differently. *Kiss Me Deadly*, with its style and allusions to classical literature, was a massive influence on the gangster movies of the *Nouvelle Vague* (the 'New Wave'), in particular Jean-Luc Godard's *Breathless* (1959) and the science-fiction/*noir* hybrid *Alphaville* (1965), which saw Paris, glittering city of blinding lights, become a convoluted otherworldly *noir* maze, as Lemmy Caution (Eddie Constantine, in trenchcoat and trilby) travels from the 'Lands Without' to search the metropolis of Alphaville for evil Doctor Von Braun. *Kiss Me Deadly* was also a commercial success in France, where it was released as *En Quatrième Vitesse* – 'In Fourth Gear' – with one critic noting 'the release, in quick succession, of *Apache*, *Vera Cruz* and *Kiss Me Deadly* was perhaps the single most exiting cinematic event of the mid-fifties'. But as Aldrich noted, 'It isn't that deep a piece of piercing philosophy as the French thought it was'; for years Aldrich didn't even like the finished film and found its European appeal difficult to fathom. In Italy it was released as *Un Bacio e una Pistola* ('A Kiss and a Gun'); in Spain *El Beso Mortal* ('The Mortal Kiss'); and in Germany the pulpy *Rattennest* ('Rats' Nest').

Several films have paid direct homage to *Kiss Me Deadly* in the decades following its release. In Quentin Tarantino's *Pulp Fiction* (1994), which often seems straight from the pages of Spillane, a mysterious case, the contents of which emit a golden glow, are again the target for seedy gangster types. Another film that uses the nuclear (plot) device is Alex Cox's punky *Repo Man* (1984). 'We stole the structure of *Kiss Me Deadly*,' notes writer-director Cox; *Repo Man* features the inventor of the neutron bomb carrying it around in the boot of his '64 Chevy Malibu and stating at one point: 'Radiation, you hear the most outrageous lies. Everyone can stand 100 chest X-rays a year,' as he runs his fingers through his hair, which comes out in clumps. In *Pulp* (1972), Michael Caine played Mickey King, a Spillane parody, who has written books called 'The Organ Grinder' and 'My Gun is Long'.

Following *Kiss Me Deadly*, Aldrich continued in a cynical vein and directed *The Big Knife* (1955 – about Hollywood corruption), *Attack!* (1956 – a powerful anti-war movie) and *Ulzana's Raid* (1972 – a realistic portrayal of Apache warfare). He also made one of the most successful action films of the sixties, *The Dirty Dozen* (1967), and one of the seventies, *The Longest Yard* (1974), called *The Mean Machine* in the UK, which added a new slant to the usual prison drama, with Burt Reynolds leading a lunatic team of convicts in a crunching, no-holds-barred game of American football against the guards. On a quieter note, in 1971 Cloris Leachman won a Best Supporting Actress Oscar for Peter Bogdanovich's *The Last Picture Show*, while *Kiss Me Deadly*'s star Ralph Meeker never fulfilled the great promise he showed in the mid-fifties, with a selection of mediocre roles.

Spillane went on to write several more Hammer books: 'The Girl Hunters' (1962), 'The Snake' (1964), 'The Twisted Thing' (1966), 'The Body Lovers' (1967), 'Survival…Zero' (1970), 'The Killing Men' (1989) and 'Black Alley' (1996), and many other books besides. In the British film version of *The Girl Hunters* (1963), directed by Roy Rowland, Spillane himself played Mike Hammer. The film recounted Hammer's search for his missing secretary, Velda (played by Shirley Eaton, pre-*Goldfinger*). There were also two TV series devoted to Hammer's exploits, both called *Mickey Spillane's Mike Hammer*. One ran from 1958–59, with Darren McGavin as Hammer, and the other from 1984–85, with Stacey Keach as the hero and Lindsey Bloom as Velda.

It is easy to see Hammer's cynicism as the prototype for many modern crime antiheroes. His hatred of the meandering law process, his complete disregard for human rights and his womanising seem way ahead of their time, pre-empting various traits in Bond, Flint, Bullit, Shaft, Dirty Harry and Popeye Doyle, among many others, all of whom owe something to Spillane's hard-nut creation. In *Kiss Me Deadly*, Hammer drove a nail in the coffin of outmoded, meandering crime thrillers and brought them bang up to date.

7

'First is first and second is nobody'

— *The Big Combo* (1955)

Credits:
DIRECTOR – Joseph H. Lewis
PRODUCER – Sidney Harmon
SCREENPLAY – Philip Yordan
DIRECTOR OF PHOTOGRAPHY – John Alton
EDITOR – Robert Eisen
PRODUCTION DESIGNER – Rudi Feld
COSTUMES – Don Loper
MUSIC – David Raskin
Black and white
Interiors filmed at Allied Artists Studio
A Security-Theodora production
Released by Allied Artists Productions
89 minutes
Cast:
Cornel Wilde (Lieutenant Leonard Diamond)/Richard Conte
(Mr Brown)/Brian Donlevy (Joe McClure)/Jean Wallace (Susan
Lowell)/Robert Middleton (Captain Peterson)/Lee Van Cleef
(Fante)/Earl Holliman (Mingo)/Helen Walker (Alicia Brown, alias
'Anna Lee Jackson')/Jay Alder (Sam Hill, detective)/John Hoyt
(Nils Dreyer, antique shop owner)/Ted De Corsia (Bettini)/Helen
Stanton (Rita, Diamond's girlfriend)/Roy Gordon (Mr Audubon)/
Whit Bissel (Doctor)/Steven Mitchell (Bernie Smith, boxer)/
Baynes Barron (Young detective)/James McCallion (Lab
technician)/Tony Michaels (Photographic technician)/Brian
O'Hara (Mr Malloy, Brown's lawyer)/Rita Gould (Nurse)/Bruce
Sharpe (Detective)/Michael Mark (Fred, hotel clerk)/Philip Van
Zandt (Mr Jones)/Donna Drew (Miss Hartleby)/Jacob Gimpel
(Concert piano soloist)

*   *   *

Made in 1954 and largely ignored on its original release, Joseph H. Lewis's *The Big Combo* is now regarded as one of the most influential and trailblazing crime movies of the fifties. It is also the epitome of B-gangster movies, the so-called 'Grade-Z' junk that propped up the bottom half of double bills. In retrospect many of these were superior to the A-movies they accompanied. As renowned B-movie director Andre De Toth noted: 'I despise any discrimination…the B designation came from the studios' code for the low-B-udget pictures and not as any prejudgement of quality.' Today *The Big Combo* looks years ahead of its time, in style and tone, while simultaneously harking back to the classic *film noir* themes and stylistic milieu of the forties, including the *femme fatale*, the tormented hero and the larger-than-life, shadowy villain, circling each other in the urban jungle.

The Big Combo was written by Philip Yordan, who also scripted or co-scripted the fifties westerns *Johnny Guitar* (1954), *The Man from Laramie* (1955) and *Day of the Outlaw* (1959). He later worked on Samuel Bronston's epics, including *King of Kings* and *El Cid* (both 1961), *55 Days in Peking* (1963) and *The Fall of the Roman Empire* (1964). But he also allowed his name to be used as a 'front', or pseudonym, for blacklisted, supposedly Communist, screenwriters, so it is difficult to ascertain which scripts are entirely his, what his real style is and how much input he had on those scenarios he put his name to.

The Big Combo details the investigations of Lieutenant Leonard Diamond, of the 93rd Precinct, the Los Angeles Police Force. He is trying to break a crime syndicate, or 'combination', called the Bolemac Corporation headed by Mr Brown, a murky figure who owns the city. During his investigations, Diamond has fallen in love with Brown's girl, Susan Lowell, whom he has had under surveillance. The mainstays of the Bolemac Corporation are Brown, Joe McClure and two bodyguards, Fante and Mingo, who do Brown's bidding. Trapped in her relationship with Brown, Susan tries to commit suicide and the police take her into custody, but the only information they glean from her is the name 'Alecia'. Diamond discovers that Alecia is Brown's wife. Ten years ago, Brown became head of the organisation when its previous boss, Mr Grazzi, retired to Sicily. Alecia went missing around the same time and a body was dumped overboard on their way to Sicily. As Diamond collates evidence, Brown panics and Diamond's girlfriend Rita, a burlesque dancer, is mistakenly killed in Diamond's apartment. Diamond finds Alecia alive in a 'rest home' and figures out that Brown murdered Grazzi, enabling him to gain control of the syndicate. McClure tries to double-cross Brown and kill him, but is shot down. Brown covers his tracks, even blowing up Fante and Mingo with a booby-trapped cigar box. Brown kidnaps Susan and plans to flee; he waits at the airport for his private plane, but Diamond arrives and arrests him, putting an end to the Big Combo.

Lewis had directed a prototype Bonnie and Clyde scenario, the cult classic *Gun Crazy* in 1949. He followed it up with *The Big Combo*, casting Cornel Wilde as

Lieutenant Diamond. Wilde had been a contract player at Warner Bros (he had appeared in *High Sierra* with Humphrey Bogart); he left for 20th Century Fox, then Columbia, becoming a star playing Frederic Chopin in *A Song to Remember* (1945). By the fifties, however, he was down in the B-movie jungle, appearing in titles like *Beyond Mombasa* (1957) and *Hot Blood* (1956). The latter, with Jane Russell cast as a gypsy girl, was advertised with the memorable tagline: 'See Jane Shake her Tambourines…and Drive Cornel Wilde!' He formed his own production company, Theodora Pictures, in 1955, which co-produced *The Big Combo*. Jean Wallace, who resembled Grace Kelly, was cast in *The Big Combo* as Susan Lowell; since 1951 she had been married to Wilde.

The supporting cast was typically 'B'. Richard Conte was typecast as villainous Mr Brown. Conte was a regular in racketeer narratives such as *New York Confidential* (1954) and mystery dramas such as *Call Northside 777* (1948), *Hollywood Story* (1951) and *The Blue Gardenia* (1953). New Jersey-born, but of Italian descent, Conte had been a performing waiter, before being spotted by Elia Kazan. He later appeared alongside Frank Sinatra in a couple of caper movies (*Ocean's Eleven* and *Assault on a Queen*, robbing respectively a casino and the *Queen Mary*) before heading to Italy to make violent gangster films such as *Big Guns* and *The Violent Professionals* (both 1973). He also appeared in *The Godfather* (1972), as mobster

Lieutenant Diamond (Cornel Wilde) and Susan Lowell (Jean Wallace) in the foggy airport finale of Joseph H. Lewis's *The Big Combo* (1955).

Barzini, who doesn't like having his picture taken at the Rizzi–Corleone wedding. Mr Brown's jealous sidekick McClure was played by Brian Donlevy, another perennial heavy, often in genre movies. Brown's bodyguards, Fante and Mingo, were portrayed by two omnipresent fifties rogues, Lee Van Cleef and Earl Holliman, both of whom appeared in numerous westerns and crime dramas. Former stage actor Robert Middleton was well cast as Diamond's sympathetic boss, Captain Peterson. Helen Walker, who played Alicia Brown, had a promising career until a serious car accident in 1946; *The Big Combo* was her last film appearance – she retired shortly afterwards.

The Big Combo was made by Allied Artists Productions. Allied was formed in 1946 and was the 'A'-movie wing of Monogram Pictures, even if its A-movies were actually B-movies like *The Big Combo*. Jean-Luc Godard dedicated *Breathless* (1959) to Monogram Pictures, in homage to their B-movie roots. Monogram became known as Allied Artists from 1953 and released many horror movies and westerns, in addition to gangster flicks such as *The Phenix City Story* (1955), *Al Capone*, *The Purple Gang* and *Crime and Punishment USA* (all 1959), an *Al Capone* sequel, *Pay or Die!* (1960), *The George Raft Story* and *King of the Roaring Twenties – The Story of Arnold Rothstein* (both 1961). In its late fifties/early sixties heyday, Allied made well-observed, well-acted crime melodramas, often in a biographical, documentary style.

Although some of Allied's later movies had bigger budgets and better casts than *The Big Combo*, Lewis's film has worn far better than any of them. Location photography was briefly done around Los Angeles, but most of *The Big Combo* was filmed at Allied Artists' studio facilities. Even the fog-bound airport at the climax is obviously a studio set, with the dialogue recorded live; the voices have a hollow, stagey quality. Sparse set décor was by Jack McConaghy. A brassy score was provided by David Raskin, described in Eddie Muller's 'Dark Cities' as 'like a burlesque band summoning a stripper'. This score and Lewis's seedy snapshots of the city's underbelly give the film a distinctive edgy quality.

The Big Combo is a typically eye-catching B-movie title. The slang 'combo' refers to the 'combination', an all-powerful crime syndicate of mobster gangs, known as the 'Bolemac Corporation'. This resembles the syndicate created by Lucky Luciano when he became 'boss of bosses' of the underworld. 'Big' is a classic B-movie prefix, usually used to title low-budget, small-scale films suggesting magnitude and expense. It was particularly popular with crime films – titles included *The Big Fight* (1930), …*Heat* (1953), …*Money* (1956), …*Snatch* (1962) and …*Switch* (1968).

Film noir's photographic elegance was born out of economy, but perpetuated for effect. *The Big Combo* is classily shot, with the accent on style and the dark sets minimally lit. The settings are back alleys, burlesque clubs and deserted airports choked with fog. Characters are glimpsed through shadows as they dart through pools of light. Many scenes are totally reliant on artificial lighting for their impact and there are virtually no daylight scenes; the drive up to the 'rest home' is one of the few sun-drenched moments. When Brown blows up Fante and Mingo with dynamite and a grenade concealed in a cigar box, the aftermath is economical yet effective. The gloomy room is wreathed in smoke, a hole in the ceiling reveals twisted reinforcing irons and shattered concrete. Rooms and corridors are riven with bright shafts of lamplight or subtly illuminated by EXIT signs, while machine-gun barrels protrude from the darkness and mow down victims. Flashing neon burlesque adverts filter through curtains or blinds. The airport is strafed with a watchtower's revolving lighthouse beam, while Brown is finally trapped, like a petrified animal, when Susan catches him in the swivelling car headlamp. Director of photography John Alton is the author of several books on his craft, including 'Painting With Light', and his work on *The Big Combo* is a masterclass in *noir* technique.

The Big Combo also bears several trademarks of B-movie ingenuity, demonstrating both the advantages and disadvantages of the sub-genre. The all-powerful syndicate is depicted entirely through suggestion; even the plane at the airport is mentioned but never appears on-screen. In the same way that B-westerns deploy small advanced parties of Indians, hardly any horses and lots of bushes, and B-war films send small 'crack units' on a special mission behind sparsely populated enemy lines, *The Big Combo*'s Bolemac Corporation is represented by Brown, McClure and two bodyguards. A sole plaque in an elevator bears the legend 'Bolemac Hotel', hinting at the combination's vast assets, which we never see.

Diamond's chief motivation is his love for Susan: a *film noir* rather than a gangster movie motivating force. The *femme fatale* here is in danger and suicidal; Diamond sees fragile Susan as a way of getting to Brown, by coaxing him out of the shadows. The rivalry between Brown and Diamond – and the latter's love scenes with Susan – are intensified somewhat by the obvious chemistry between married actors Wilde and Wallace. In a perverse scene, Diamond tells Susan that the mink she's wearing is made of 'the skins of human beings… people beaten, sold, robbed, doped, murdered by Mr Brown'. More conventionally, Diamond's lusty relationship with burlesque dancer Rita resembles Mike Hammer's with Velda in *Kiss Me Deadly*: they need, rather than want, each other.

The main action is often pushed into the background by Lewis's zeal for his subplot. Diamond first hears the name Alecia from a delirious, suicidal Susan. Brown is hauled in on a phony charge and given a polygraph test; his heart rate goes through the roof when Alecia is mentioned, though Brown claims it is the name of a racehorse. Diamond discovers that Alecia is Brown's wife; he finds the terrified woman in a mental home, under the name 'Anna Lee Jackson', but there is nothing wrong with her. She tells Diamond, 'I'd rather be insane and alive, than sane and dead.' Diamond later realises that it was Grazzi, Brown's boss, who was thrown overboard on the way to Sicily, not, as he suspected, Alecia. The boat's skipper had to stop in the Azores to buy a new anchor; Grazzi is on the bottom of the Mediterranean attached to the old one.

The film's script is sometimes patchy and there is some risibly clichéd genre dialogue: Rita is machine-gunned to death and Diamond articulates his remorse: 'I treated her like a pair of gloves. When I was cold I called her up.' 'Don't blame yourself,' says cop Sam, 'you'll go crazy.' Conte as Mr Brown is an effective villain and gets all the best lines; his credo is 'First is first and second is nobody'. Later Diamond threatens Brown: 'I'm gonna open you up and I'm gonna operate.' Brown tries to stop Diamond arresting Susan for attempted suicide. 'It happens to be against two laws,' says Diamond, 'God's and man's... I'm booking her under the second.' Brown is impervious to threats; he informs sidekick McClure, 'You're a little man with a soft job and good pay... you may live to die in bed.' Brown says of himself: 'All I had was guts; I traded them for money and influence.' In his best put-down, he informs square-cut cop Diamond: 'You'd like to be me. You'd like to have my organisation, my influence, my fix. You can't, it's impossible. You think it's the money? It's not, it's personality. You haven't got it.'

B-movie violence is often more intense than mainstream offerings, but *The Big Combo* is one of the most sadistic films of the fifties. Hard-of-hearing henchman Jim McClure's hearing aid is used in two scenes to vicious effect by Brown. In a darkened room, Brown and his men tie Diamond to a chair and torture him. Brown demonstrates his 'technique': 'We're going to give the lieutenant a little concert,' sneers Brown, inserting the hearing aid earpiece into Diamond's ear. Brown turns the volume up on the device and barks questions into the receiver. Then Mingo screams into the device, almost blowing Diamond's head off. Brown places the receiver next to a wireless on full volume: 'Do you like crazy drums, lieutenant?' asks Brown. A drum solo booms out and Diamond soon falls unconscious. The gang pour 40-per-cent-alcohol-content hair tonic down his throat and deliver him shattered to Captain Peterson's door. The mob are clever – there isn't a mark on Diamond's person to say he has been tortured. When McClure tries to usurp his boss, Brown exacts his revenge: 'I'm gonna do you a favour,' Brown tells cornered McClure, pulling out his earpiece. 'You won't hear the bullets.' This scene is overtly stylised. Lewis cuts the soundtrack to silence; we only see the flashes of the hoodlums' guns, with no sound effects, as though we are inside McClure's mute world.

The Big Combo's poster tagline was 'The Most Startling Story the Screen has Ever Dared Reveal!'; it is certainly one of the cruellest. The poster's image depicted Conte passionately kissing scantly clad Jean Wallace, with a large image of Wilde looking over Conte's shoulder, visualising the central tug-of-love triangle. *The Big Combo* was released in the US in February 1955 – exhibited on the bottom half of double bills and then quickly forgotten. In the UK, cuts were required to gain an A certificate in April 1955. A financial disappointment at the time, it was re-released in the eighties on the repertory circuit in the UK and enjoyed much more success. Its European release was in 1956. Only in France was it popular on initial release, titled *Association Criminelle* ('Criminal Association'). It was a key influence on Jean-Luc Godard and the French New Wave, and cemented Lewis's reputation, following *Gun Crazy*, as an *auteur*. In West Germany *The Big Combo* was called *Gegeimring 99* ('Ring 99'); in Spain *Agente Especial* ('Special Agent'); in Portugal *Rajada De Morte*

('Gust of Death'); and in Italy it was *La Polizia Bussa alla Porta*: 'The Police Knock on the Door'.

The Big Combo is a fine combo of *film noir* and fifties B-movie gangster film. Fifties crime B-movies were usually budgeted between $200,000 and $400,000. Robert Aldrich made his 'B' *Kiss Me Deadly* for $410,000; the year before he made the 'A' production *Vera Cruz*, starring Burt Lancaster and Gary Cooper, for $1.7 million. The reason some of these B-films have enjoyed such longevity is that many of them boasted appearances by pre-stardom superstars or on-their-way-down has-beens. B-movies also had an irritating habit of reappearing once their actors became famous, with theatre exhibitors prominently displaying the actors' names, as though they were showing a prestigious new release.

The better B-movie crime films include Joseph H. Lewis's own *Gun Crazy* (1949) and the tension-filled train journey in *Narrow Margin* (1952), in which cop Charles McGraw escorted key witness Marie Windsor, a B-genre regular, to a grand jury hearing. 'A Fortune if they Seal her Lips,' said the posters, 'A Bullet if they Fail!' Don Siegel's *Riot in Cell Block 11* (1954) raised the B-movie bar, by being both a critical and commercial success. Titles were often 'Confidential' (*New York Confidential* [1955], *Chicago Confidential* [1957]), or they incorporated the names of notorious gangsters in deliberately sensationalised biopics – Mickey Rooney appeared in *Baby Face Nelson* (1958), Dorothy Provine starred in *The Bonnie Parker Story* (1958) and Rod Steiger was Al Capone in the 1959 film of the same name. *Gangster Story* (1960) was Walter Matthau's bargain-basement directorial debut, while Robert Mitchum's moonshine movie *Thunder Road* (1958) was a roaring success. *Cry Baby Killer* (1958), Jack Nicholson's film debut, was described by a UK critic as 'the type of picture the average British audience – certainly family audience – could well do without'. *The Great St Louis Bank Robbery* (1958 – tagline: 'Planned like clockwork, it went off like a timebomb') boasted a young actor named Steve McQueen in the cast. *Inside the Mafia* (1959) depicted the exploits of the euphemistic 'Black Hand' society; *Vice Squad* (1959) told the cops' side of the story. The students in the Mamie Van Doren vehicle *High School Confidential* (1958) were indeed at 'high' school, with a marijuana racket exposed.

Roger Corman was truly the 'King of the Bs' and the peak of the crime B-movies was Corman's *The St Valentine's Day Massacre* (1967), made with a $1 million budget from 20th Century Fox. Economical Corman reused prestigious Fox sets for his twenties gangster movie: a bar from *The Sand Pebbles* became a brothel, the *Sound of Music*'s Austrian manor became Capone's house and the Chicago street scenes were filmed on sets ready to shoot *Hello, Dolly!* Even better, Corman had a cast that included Jason Robards as Al Capone, Ralph Meeker as Bugs Moran and Clint Richie as Machine-Gun Jack McGurn, with George Segal, Bruce Dern and Jack Nicholson in supporting roles (the original casting was to have been Orson Welles as Capone and Robards as Moran). *The St Valentine's Day Massacre* looked back to the Warners gangster classics of the thirties with a sixties knowingness:

even the clichéd narration, voiced by Paul Frees, adds to the referential atmosphere, while simultaneously mocking it. This was a common Corman device, as was the sarcastic *Dragnet* pastiche voiceover that accompanies the gangsters hiding out on a boat in *Creature from the Haunted Sea* (1960).

Corman's best comic strip crime B-movie was *Machine-Gun Kelly* (1958), produced by the legendary Samuel Z. Arkoff and starring Charles Bronson in the title role. It was shot in Superama for $200,000 in eight days; Bronson received $5,000, his highest pay packet so far for his first starring role. Written by R. Wright Campbell, it told the story of George F. Barnes, called 'Machine-Gun Kelly' (Bronson), and his ambitious partner, Flo Becker (Susan Cabot), loosely based on Kathryn Thorne Kelly, Barnes's wife. With their gang, Howard, Maize and Fandango, they rob the Lebanon Bank of $41,000. Later they try to rip off a construction payroll in Elizabethtown, but Kelly panics and ruins the plan, decimating the gang. Kelly and Flo hide out at Flo's parents' brothel. Flo wants Kelly to hit the big time, so they kidnap the nine-year-old daughter of Andrew Vito, a steel executive (in reality, Kelly kidnapped 43-year-old oilman Charles F. Urschel). They demand $100,000, but are double-crossed by Fandango, who tips off the cops. As the police close in, mythmaker Flo says, 'I made you.' 'I didn't want to be Public Enemy Number One,' whines Kelly, discarding his machine-gun. The cops burst in and take him into custody: 'Come along, Pop-Gun Kelly.'

'Pop-Gun Kelly': Charles Bronson and Susan Cabot as the cowardly gangster and his ambitious moll, in Roger Corman's B-movie *Machine-Gun Kelly* (1958).

Sharply photographed in black and white by Floyd Crosby, *Machine-Gun Kelly* is a minor masterpiece, made with panache by director-producer Corman. The costumes, sets and vehicles are exact for the period, though the lively jazz score by Gerald Fried disguises quite a macabre film. Kelly tortures Fandango with a wildcat, who eats his arm. Later Kelly mows down Howard and his gang while they play cards – as a cop puts it, 'The mob was sieved.' Kelly aims his machine-gun at a henchman named Apple and threatens: 'Go ahead Apple...and I'll peel and core you.' Earlier, Howard pulls a flick-knife on Kelly: 'I'm gonna carve a map of Hell across your kisser.'

Kelly is scared of death and dying – an undertaker's coffin spooks him during the Elizabethtown Merchant's Bank raid and later he wakes up in a panic on the lower level of a bunk bed, convinced he's trapped in a coffin. Bronson is memorable in the title role; the same year he also starred in *Gang War*, as a schoolteacher whose wife is killed by a gangster. His stand against gang violence anticipates Bronson's highly successful *Death Wish* movies of the seventies.

The *Monthly Film Bulletin* review of *Machine-Gun Kelly* could be applied to any crime B-picture: 'The pace of the action is so fast as to be almost frantic and the acting is more than adequate to the occasion... but this apart, the film is in all other respects highly unpleasant'. A review like that was pure gravy to exploitation producers, churning out movies high on action and gunplay, low on motivation and dialogue. They played in grind-, not art-, houses. In the US, *Machine-Gun Kelly* played on double bills with *The Bonnie Parker Story*, but in Europe it was a success in its own right; in France it was even shown at film festivals. The stylish French poster depicted Bronson in snap-brimmed hat and brandishing a Tommy-gun, with the title '*Mitraillette Kelly* – Un Charles Bronson Explosif!' The Bronson cult was massive in France, where he was known as 'le Sacre Monstre' ('the Holy Monster'). These 'ugly-beautiful' screen heroes – often fifties B-villains such as Bronson, Lee Van Cleef, Jack Palance and Henry Silva – went on to be highly successful in continental action movies.

With the modern cinema distribution network, the B-movie is dead. *The Big Combo*'s equivalent these days would be an 'Indie' film, or even straight-to-video. But B-movies are a hugely important part of cinema history, providing historians with a more representative depiction of contemporary society than is often the case in bigger-budget, higher-profile pictures. That is the great thing about B-movies: film books often ignore them, distributors release them cheaply on video and DVD, and every once in a while you stumble across a movie as startling as *The Big Combo* – a real cult classic.

8

'Somebody's got to pay'

— *Point Blank* (1967)

Credits:

DIRECTOR – John Boorman
PRODUCERS – Judd Bernard and Robert Chartoff
STORY – Richard Stark
SCREENPLAY – Alexander Jacobs and David and Rafe Newhouse
DIRECTOR OF PHOTOGRAPHY – Philip H. Lathrop
EDITOR – Henry Berman
ART DIRECTOR – Albert Brenner and George W. Davis
COSTUME DESIGNER – Margo Weintz
MUSIC COMPOSER – Johnny Mandel
Panavision/Metrocolor
Interiors filmed at MGM Studios
A Judd Bernard/Irwin Winkler production
Released by Metro-Goldwyn-Mayer
92 minutes

Cast:

Lee Marvin (Walker)/Angie Dickinson (Chris)/Keenan Wynn ('Yost', alias Fairfax)/Carroll O'Connor (Brewster)/Lloyd Bochner (Frederick Carter)/Michael Strong ('Big John' Stegman)/John Vernon (Mal Reese)/Sharon Acker (Lynne Walker)/James B. Sikking (Hired sniper)/Sandra Warner (Sandy, 'Moviehouse' waitress)/Roberta Hayes (Carter's wife)/Kathleen Freeman (Woman at function)/Victor Creatore (Carter's henchman)/Guy Way (Brewster's chauffeur)/Lawrence Hauben (Used car salesman)/Susan Holloway (Miss Stewart, woman buying car)/Sid Haig and Michael Bell (Huntley lobby guards)/Pricilla Boyd (Receptionist)/John McMurtry (Messenger with Lynne's pay-off)/Roger Walter and George Stratten (Men tied up in apartment)/Nicole Rogell (Carter's secretary)/Roland LaStarza and Rico

Cattini (Reese's guards)/Bill Hickman and Chuck Hicks (Guards)/
Ted White (Football player)/Felix Silla (Bellhop at Huntley)

*   *   *

Point Blank marked a major innovation in crime movies in Hollywood. During the early sixties, the French New Wave had adopted and adapted the plots and trappings of American gangster movies and reinvigorated them. Narratives were slim; it was the way the characters looked, talked, acted and reacted that was paramount. Jean-Luc Godard and Jean-Pierre Melville were the foremost purveyors of this style, with loving homages to Hollywood juxtaposed with stylised cinematography and jump-cut, non-linear editing, leaving the audience to fill in the blank points of their puzzling, elliptical stories.

Shepperton-born director John Boorman had been an assistant film editor on TV and by 1962 was the head of the BBC's documentary unit in Bristol. In 1965 his directorial debut was the Dave Clark Five pop movie *Catch Us if you Can* (released in the US as *Having a Wild Weekend*), one of many life-on-the-run beat movies released in the wake of *A Hard Day's Night* (1964) and *Help!* (1965). Boorman, aged 33, met actor Lee Marvin the following year, while the latter was in London at MGM's UK studios making *The Dirty Dozen*, and they immediately struck up a relationship; to Boorman, tough Marvin was the 'essence of America'. When Marvin finished filming, Boorman travelled to MGM US in late 1966 to direct Marvin's next film.

Point Blank was written by Alexander Jacobs, David Newhouse and Rafe Newhouse, based on the 1962 novel 'The Hunter', by 'Richard Stark' (whose real name was Donald E. Westlake). It was the first in a series of books detailing the adventures of antihero Parker, in the film scenario renamed Walker.

Walker, a gangster, is shot and left for dead by his wife Lynne and his partner in crime Mal Reese during a hold-up of mob money at a drop-off in the disused prison on Alcatraz Island, San Francisco Bay. But Walker survives, manages to swim the straits and a year later embarks on a trail of revenge in LA to recover the $93,000 owed him by Reese, who is now in 'the big time' as a respectable member of a crime syndicate known as the 'Organisation'. Walker is aided in his search by the mysterious 'Yost', who also seems to want to exact vengeance on the Organisation. Walker contacts his wife Lynne, who has since split up from Reese, but she commits suicide soon after their reacquaintance. Walker discovers that other members of the Organisation include John Stegman, a used car salesman, and Frederick Carter, a respectable public figure. With Lynne's sister, nightclub owner Chris, Walker manages to get to Reese, hiding out at the Huntley Hotel, but Reese accidentally falls from the penthouse before he can pay Walker. Stegman and Carter are killed in an ambush meant for Walker, who later finds out from Brewster, the most powerful man in the Organisation, that Fairfax, the gang's accountant, will arrange for Walker to be recompensed. In a night-time drop-off on San Francisco Bay, Walker and Brewster wait for the helicopter to arrive with the cash, but Yost is also there. It transpires that Yost is Fairfax and has been stage-managing his own rise through the Organisation. The Organisation's hitman shoots Brewster, but Walker remains in the shadows; Fairfax, now head of the Organisation, leaves Walker the package of blood money for services rendered.

Boorman assembled a strong ensemble cast for the film. Ex-Marine sniper Lee Marvin was cast as Walker, the indomitable antihero. Marvin had served in the Pacific War but was badly wounded and shipped home; asked in 1984 on UK TV's *Wogan* how he won his Purple Heart, he answered: 'You don't win them, you get them when you get hit – so in other words I'd rather not have it.' Marvin appeared throughout the fifties and early sixties as an unhinged supporting heavy in some of the best westerns, war films and gangster movies of the era, including *Bad Day at Black Rock* (1955), *Violent Saturday* (1955) and *Attack!* (1956). Known for his violent portrayals, he had famously disfigured Debby (played by Gloria Grahame) with bubbling hot coffee in Fritz Lang's crime movie *The Big Heat* (1953). These striking portrayals reached their zenith in John Ford's *The Man Who Shot Liberty Valance* (1962), with Marvin as the demonic, whip-wielding title villain.

In the early sixties Marvin's rough comedy roles in *The Comancheros* (1961), *Donovan's Reef* (1963) and his Oscar-winning portrayals in *Cat Ballou* (1965 – as drunken hero Kid Sheleen and artificial-nosed killer Tim Strawn) were offset by his stony performance in Don Siegel's thriller *The Killers* (1964). Based on the Hemingway story, and originally made for NBC TV (but released in cinemas due to its violence), *The Killers* featured Marvin and Clu Gulager as two hitmen, hired to shoot Johnny North (John Cassavetes). The film begins with the assassins arriving at a school for the blind and coldly shooting teacher North dead, who accepts his fate without struggle or escape. The two decide to uncover the reason for North's odd behaviour. The film, in colour, is very stylised, as the action unfolds in flashback reminiscences. Marvin gave a stoic performance, but it was Siegel's accent on framing and potent emphasis on guns that proved most influential. Marvin's pistol, fitted with a huge silencer, seems to dominate the frame at the expense of all else. By the mid-sixties, Marvin's star was rising, and he was cast in *Point Blank* immediately after two memorable roles as specialists in killing: Henry 'Rico' Farden in *The Professionals* (1966) and US Major Reisman, the leader of *The Dirty Dozen* (1967).

Opposite such a dominant lead, Boorman deployed an array of powerful supporting players. Angie Dickinson, who achieved fame as gambler Feathers in *Rio Bravo* (1959), had established her strong screen persona opposite male leads in films like the Rat Pack-dominated *Ocean's Eleven* (1960). She had also appeared in *The Killers*, as Sheila Farr, the mistress of powerful gang boss Ronald Reagan. At one point Marvin dangles her out of a window by her heels. The business-suited Organisation in *Point Blank* is peppered with fine actors. Carroll O'Connor, later

US TV's 'Archie Bunker', played Brewster, the blustering head of the group. Lloyd Bochner played smoothy Carter, a thug in sheep's clothing, and newcomer John Vernon (in his second film appearance) was cast as snivelling misogynist Mal Reese, the worst turncoat of all, who tries to take everything from his partner – his cut of the money, his wife and his life. Michael Strong was the cowardly yes-man Stegman, used car dealer and general factotum, while James B. Sikking was suitably viperous as the Organisation's hitman. Stuntmen Chuck Hicks and Bill Hickman played hotel guards. New Yorker Keenan Wynn was Yost. He had appeared on Broadway, then moved to film versions of Broadway productions – the Betty Hutton barn-stormer *Annie Get Your Gun* (1950) and *Kiss Me Kate* (1953). He also made two gangster films: *The Scarface Mob* (1959 – the pilot for Robert Stack's TV series *The Untouchables*) and *King of the Roaring Twenties – The Story of Arnold Rothstein* (1961), released as *The Big Bankroll* in the UK. As the vague Yost, who sidles into the story at key moments, he had one of his best roles.

Budgeted at $3 million, *Point Blank* was filmed from December 1966 to April 1967, on location and at MGM Studios. The film is bracketed by two night-time scenes set on San Francisco Bay, at Alcatraz Island and Fort Point (with its distinctive parallel arches, below Golden Gate Bridge). Alcatraz Island Prison, also

Magnum Force: Walker the avenger takes on the Organisation
in John Boorman's *Point Blank* (1967).

known as 'The Rock', was a federal maximum-security prison from 1934–63. It is routinely shrouded in fog (the so-called 'Alcatraz Symphony' of foghorns drove inmates insane) and the bay is chilly even in the summer – the water temperature making escape near-impossible. The once brightly lit main corridor of the cell block was jokingly christened 'Broadway' by the prisoners, but by 1967 America's 'Devil's Island' had fallen into disrepair and looked even more ghostly and foreboding than it had when in use, with its silent watchtowers and ominous wire fences. At the end of the schedule, while shooting the heist on Alcatraz early one April morning, Boorman couldn't figure out how to stage the action. Marvin could see the young director was in trouble and feigned drunkenness on set, stalling the production until Boorman had focused his resolution. Boorman then gave Marvin a nod and the actor made a 'miraculous recovery'.

Other location shooting was completed in Los Angeles, at the international airport and the vast open LA storm drain that has been seen in so many films (most famously in the drag race in *Grease*). Huntley House (now the Radisson Huntley), the coastal hotel and apartments resort at 1111 Second Avenue, Santa Monica, was used for Reese's penthouse hideout. Philip H. Lathrop's cinema tography lensed the skyscrapers and island prison evocatively, his Panavision nocturnes of LA capture the monolithic, moonlit Huntley or pan slowly across desolate 'Frisco Bay. He also photographed sunlit structures beautifully: the concrete and glass architecture, with bright white perpendicular lines, chequer-board reflective windows and shadowed arches.

White-haired Marvin delivers his best performance in a career filled with memorable portrayals. In his moving documentary *Lee Marvin – A Personal Portrait*, John Boorman recalls theirs was an 'intense and inspiring collaboration...and scary'. Marvin was 'always pressing for the truth...the essence of a scene...always searching for a gesture that would replace a line of dialogue, the perfect move to express an emotion'. Marvin was a tough actor to work with; during rehearsals at Marvin's house he hit John Vernon so hard Vernon burst into tears. Walker's physical violence is best depicted in a punch-up in Chris's psychedelic 'Moviehouse' go-go club, while the Stu Gardner Trio belt out 'Mighty Good Times', a frantic, screaming soul number. Walker takes on two of Stegman's toughs behind the stage's projection screen, hitting one with a bottle and savagely punching the other in the groin, among the trippy light projections and spools of overturned celluloid.

Walker gives us hardly any details about himself, not even his Christian name: his vengeful motivation is enough, though, as Chris points out, his quest for the money is morally wrong: 'It wasn't yours in the first place.' Walker finds himself alone at the beginning of the film, lying wounded in a prison cell; his voiceover murmurs, 'Cell...prison cell...how did I get here?', then later: 'Did it happen? A dream?', further suggesting that the whole film may be a figment of Walker's imagination. He begins his vendetta trying to take revenge on Reese and Lynne, but ends up taking down the multimillion-dollar Organisation, with a little help from Yost. Brewster can't believe that Walker is going to all this trouble for $93,000. 'What do you really want?' asks bemused Brewster. 'I really want my money.' But once Walker starts, building up momentum and fuelled by Yost, he's unstoppable.

Boorman saw the film as a biography of Marvin, with the Alcatraz double-cross an allegory for his wounding on Saipan during the Second World War. In the film, the implication is that Walker is an ex-seaman – he wears a USN jacket in a flashback at a marina with Lynne and in two sequences it is stressed he is a strong swimmer (an idyllic surf reverie and his escape, wounded, across the Alcatraz straits). A year later, he's back there, a changed man. Once trusting, now all he wants is his money. Walker is a machine, the Organisation term him 'a pro', unbalanced and lethal. Marvin, an ex-army sniper, knew instinctively how to handle weapons – his Smith & Wesson .44 Magnum seems to be a part of him, an extension of his persona. Oddly for a vengeful action hero, he doesn't actually kill anyone in the whole film, though he certainly hurts a few.

Walker's revenge told as linear narrative would have been very similar to any standard mob flick, no more ambiguous than an episode of *The Man from U.N.C.L.E.* But it is Boorman's assured style and his disorientating editing strategy that makes the film so groundbreaking, balanced precariously between flashback, reality and dream. In the most notorious and stylised scenes in the film, Walker strides down a seemingly endless corridor. This is intercut with Lynne lying in bed, then getting dressed, applying mascara and going to a beauty salon; meanwhile Walker is seen driving towards her flat – all the while his footsteps echo incessantly on the soundtrack like a metronome. As Lynne arrives back at her apartment, Walker rushes her in the hallway, throwing her to the floor and pulling his pistol, before storming into the bedroom and riddling the empty bed with bullets; Reese isn't home. He slumps on her sofa and tips the spent shell casings onto the marble tabletop. This ritualised behaviour is further emphasised later, when moments from this confrontation are recalled in Walker's sleep. In this slo-mo replay, Boorman noted that Marvin 'invests [the pistol] with a recoil it doesn't possess', as though the gun is uncontrollable, a metaphor for Walker's own psyche.

Boorman's sound design is equally innovative, with overlapping dialogue, disembodied monologues and sudden amplified sound effects. Elsewhere there is the eerie use of an unaccompanied female vocal (almost a spiritual), echoing down Alcatraz's dimly lit 'Broadway', or the disorientating delay on the Alcatraz boat tour tannoy, which brings the film's introduction into the present day.

Some of the editing and imagery hint at Walker's psychological state and imply that he may be suffering from mental illness. He's a bad sleeper and the recurring images, disorienting angles, chopped-up fragments of thought mixed with reminiscences, bewilder the viewer, while everything he encounters seems to remind Walker of something else, suggesting depression. For example, an empty bed at Brewster's pad prompts thoughts of Lynne's suicide, while spilt perfume and scent bottles smashed in a bath, colourfully running into one another, like an artist's pallette, reminds Walker of shed blood. Sometimes we hear Lynne's echoing singing on the soundtrack, taking us inside Walker's head. He can't erase recent events from his mind, even when he's awake; these symptoms are consistent with trauma associated with combat.

Opposite psychotic bursts of violence, Marvin uses silence and stillness to great effect; Walker is one of the great underplayed roles of modern cinema. There are many scenes with long dialogue pauses, sometimes accentuated by Johnny Mandel's subdued score, incorporating ghostly flute, trumpet and brass. Characters stare off-screen into the middle distance, lost in their own thoughts (as if Antonioni had remade *The Killers* as an existential mystery), while delivering dialogue like 'How good it must be, being dead'. In one scene, Walker and Lynne sit on a sofa. Walker doesn't say a word, while his wife tells him everything he needs to know about events since his betrayal, telepathically answering his unasked questions. She kills herself shortly afterwards and Walker sheds no tears for his betrayer, though after checking her body for signs of life, he poignantly takes off his wedding ring and slips it on her finger.

Walker only trusts two people in the film. The first is Yost. He is a marginal figure who talks like a cop; on the Alcatraz tour boat he tells Walker, 'You want Reese and I want the Organisation.' Yost begins by giving Walker Lynne's current address in LA, which she's supposedly sharing with Reese. Whenever the trail goes cold, Yost appears to reinvigorate Walker's quest with another 'clue'. Yost is finally revealed to be Fairfax, the Organisation man who 'signs cheques'. By skilfully manipulating Walker, he has manoeuvred himself to the top of the mob ladder. His motives are muddied and it's never fully explained what his grudge against the Organisation is (he may even be a police officer or government agent). But it seems that Brewster is preparing to oust him from power and Yost wants the Organisation rubbed out, and Walker's revenge spree gives him the excuse.

His other ally is Lynne's sister, Chris. When he first sees her, he thinks she's taken a sleeping pill overdose too, but she awakens and comments: 'You're supposed to be dead.' Even though Reese makes her 'flesh crawl', she agrees to sacrifice herself to him, to distract him long enough for Walker to capture him. She dislikes Reese and disliked her sister, but after seeing Walker's ruthlessness, she comments, 'You died at Alcatraz.' Walker hides out at Chris's, then takes her to Brewster's luxury spread, overlooking LA. In their most famous scene they discuss what Walker will do with Brewster. Chris says, 'You'll ask him for the money, he'll say no and you'll kill him.' Walker flippantly answers that this isn't 'a pitch'; Chris completely loses control and takes out her frustrations on him, furiously lurching at him with fists, slaps and handbag. But Walker simply stands there, immovable, absorbing her punishment, until she slumps, exhausted on the floor. Shortly afterwards, emotional mood swings are juxtaposed: Chris furiously hits Walker with a pool cue, then moments later they kiss. When they spend the night together, Boorman cuts between Walker and Chris, Walker and Lynne, Reese and Lynne, and Reese and Chris, linking the protagonists together in a *ménage à quatre*. It may even be yet another figment of Walker's aimless imagination, as he is awoken by a dreamt gunshot. After their intimacy, Chris asks, 'What's my last name?', and Walker answers, 'What's my first name?'; neither can answer.

Walker's violent revenge on the Organisation is the backbone of the movie. They are dispatched in turn, in brutal set pieces, with each hood's death passing the buck to his superior. With the help of Chris, Walker traps Reese in the Huntley penthouse, Reese panics and accidentally plummets naked off the rooftop patio. Carter, the respectable head of 'the Multiplex Company', arranges for Walker to be paid off by Stegman at a rendezvous in the open concrete storm drain, but it's a set-up. Walker avoids catching a hired sniper's high-velocity bullet, turning the tables on Stegman and Carter, both of whom are killed. Walker checks Carter's wallet for cash and only finds a cascade of laminated credit cards. On his quest, Walker is mindlessly destructive too, shooting phones, stamping on communication cables or smashing perfume bottles; in the best example, Walker deliberately demolishes John Stegman's car during a test-drive, lurching forward and reversing between two concrete freeway stilts until the vehicle is a wreck. For the finale, the action shifts back to San Francisco, and again depicts a cash drop and a betrayal, while wiser Walker fades into the shadows. The plot's circularity is echoed in the film's final ironic shot; the camera pans away from Brewster's body, rises over the ramparts of Fort Point and zooms slowly into the distance, focusing on the bleak mound of Alcatraz Island, where the story began.

Point of View: outside the Huntley Hotel, Walker (Lee Marvin) and Chris (Angie Dickinson) set their sights on Reese's penthouse, in *Point Blank* (1967).

When the rushes were screened for MGM, they were very disappointed with the results, and director David Lean had to convince the executives to retain Boorman as director. Their faith in him was rewarded. *Point Blank* was released in the US on 30 August 1967. Oddly there is no hyphen in the title ['point-blank'], as would be grammatically correct. All UK and US poster art depicted Marvin and his Magnum; the US version, with key art by Serrano, also incorporated a spiralling target motif, the sprawled figure of Angie Dickinson and the banner 'That *Dirty Dozen* Man Is Back!' The questionable tagline ran: 'There are Two Kinds of People in His Up-tight World: His Victims and his Women. And sometimes you can't tell them apart.' The violence ensured the film was rated R in the US; it was granted an X certificate in the UK in September 1967. The critical response was predominantly positive, with *Life* saying that 'One leaves a blank, pointless movie like *Point Blank* feeling cheapened by it', but 'it will win this year's sweaty palm award – hands down'. In the UK, the *Guardian* called it 'Riveting; the screenplay is intelligent...an absolute must'. On 8 December 1967, *Time* magazine put a still from *Bonnie and Clyde* on the cover, with the strap-line 'The New Cinema: Violence...Sex...Art', which looked at several contemporary examples of 'Europeanised' American cinema, including *Bonnie and Clyde*, *Point Blank* and *The Fox* (1968), a sexually provocative adaptation of D.H. Lawrence's novella. *Point Blank* garnered $3.5 million in the US and was released throughout Europe in 1968. In West Germany it was *Point Blank – Keiner darf Überleben* ('Point Blank – No One Will Survive'); in Italy it was *Senza Un Attimo di Tregua* (literally 'Without a Moment's Respite'); in France it was retitled *Le Point de Non-retour* ('The Point of No Return'). Its Spanish title, *A Quemarropa*, translated as 'At Point-Blank'. In Poland the film was titled *Zbieg Z Alcatraz* ('Escape from Alcatraz').

Though immensely influential, its only direct film connection was *Payback* (1999), a remake of Stark's source novel, with Mel Gibson in the Walker role (here named Porter) out to recover $70,000 and armed with exactly the same Magnum. In this version the Organisation are 'The Outfit', Mal Reese is named Val Reisnic, Stegman's first name is Arthur, but the plot is roughly the same. Kris Kristofferson appears as syndicate head Bronson, while uncredited James Coburn is Fairfax, who, when he hears the amount Porter is owed, quips, 'Hell, my suits are worth more than that.' Directed in dark, glacial style by Brian Helgeland (the screenwriter of *L.A. Confidential*), *Payback* is exceptionally violent, with one excruciating scene seeing Porter having his toes smashed with a lump hammer.

Marvin worked for Boorman again in 1968 with *Hell in the Pacific*, in which Marvin further referenced his war experiences. By 1969, Marvin had gone from rising star to 'Wanderin' Star', but he never recaptured the excitement of his mid-sixties work. An indication of his popularity by 1969 was the top-ten list of US exhibitors' biggest stars, which read Newman, Wayne, McQueen, Hoffman, Eastwood, Poitier, Marvin, Lemmon, Streisand and Katherine Hepburn. In a 1973 poll of the US box office's favourite stars of the last decade, topped by John Wayne,

Marvin came 10th. He died in 1987 of a heart attack and was buried in Arlington War Cemetery, with full military honours. Boorman himself went on to great success with his Oscar-nominated, ecological 'Heart of Darkness', *Deliverance* (1972), his best film. *Point Blank* and *Deliverance* even share a macabre image: a digger's back-actor shovel excavating graves – the modernisation and mechanisation of death.

Point Blank is one of the most strikingly shot and remarkable films of the sixties. Its visuals were highly influential and its style can be seen emulated in even the worst TV cop show. The most successful aspects were intelligent plotting melded with violent action, presented in an innovative manner. It was a new, existentialist approach to narrative, as the plot unravelled in slow motion half-memory. American cinema came of age with *Point Blank*, though not to massive commercial success. It would take another visionary director to take European style into the US main-stream, with a couple of little-known hoods named Parker and Barrow.

9

'We ain't heading nowhere, we're just running from'

— *Bonnie and Clyde* (1967)

Credits:

DIRECTOR   Arthur Penn
PRODUCER – Warren Beatty
SCREENPLAY – David Newman and Robert Benton
DIRECTOR OF PHOTOGRAPHY – Burnett Guffey
EDITOR – Dede Allen
ART DIRECTOR – Dean Tavoularis
COSTUMES – Theodora Van Runkle
MUSIC COMPOSER AND CONDUCTOR – Charles Strouse
Technicolor
Interiors filmed at Warner Bros Studios
A Warner Bros-Seven Arts Inc/Titira-Hiller co-production
Released by Warner Bros
111 minutes

Cast:

Warren Beatty (Clyde Barrow)/Faye Dunaway (Bonnie Parker)/
Michael J. Pollard (Clarence 'CW' Moss)/Gene Hackman ('Buck'
Barrow)/Estelle Parsons (Blanche Barrow)/Denver Pyle (Sheriff
Frank Hamer)/Dub Taylor (Ivan Moss, CW's father)/Evans
Evans (Velma Davis)/Gene Wilder (Eugene Grizzard, the
undertaker)/James Stiver (Grocery store owner)/Clyde Howdy
(Deputy)/Gary Goodgion (Billy)/Ken Mayer (Sheriff Smoot)

*   *   *

Bonnie and Clyde is one of the great American films of the sixties, and made Faye
Dunaway and Warren Beatty rebel icons for a generation. Their romantic pairing,
knocking off banks to the accompaniment of the bouncy, twanging banjo of
'Foggy Mountain Breakdown', represented a Depression-era America that was a

romanticised, stylised nostalgic fantasy. Nevertheless, the film struck a chord with US audiences already tired of the Vietnam War and beguiled by the simple tagline: 'They're young, they're in love…and they kill people'.

The screenplay for *Bonnie and Clyde* was written by Robert Benton and David Newman. Influenced by the carefree life of crime depicted in Jean-Luc Godard's *Breathless* (1959), they concocted a story based on two real-life rural criminals in Texas: Clyde Barrow and his partner in crime, Bonnie Parker. The pair terrorise the countryside, stealing money from banks that foreclose on farmers. They recruit CW Moss, a mechanic, as their getaway driver, and in a raid on the Mineola Bank, Clyde shoots a clerk. They are soon joined by Clyde's brother Buck and Buck's wife Blanche, and continue to carry out robberies. Eventually they are surprised in their hideout in Platte City; Buck is killed, Blanche blinded, and the other three escape. Both Bonnie and Clyde are badly wounded and CW takes them to his father's farm to recuperate. But CW's father tips off their nemesis, Sheriff Hamer, who arranges an ambush on a quiet Arcadia country road; the lovers die horribly, peppered in a staccato burst of machine-gun fire.

Benton and Newman used John Toland's 1963 book 'The Dillinger Days' for research; in fact some of Bonnie and Clyde's exploits in the film were carried out in reality by Dillinger. They tried to get François Truffaut to direct, but US studios weren't interested in the New Wave director making a Hollywood movie. Jean-Luc Godard was also approached to direct, but he made *Alphaville* (1965) instead. Then Warren Beatty saw the script and immediately bought the rights. Beatty decided to produce the film and to star in it himself, and brought in Arthur Penn.

Penn had worked extensively in TV and had moved into cinema in the late fifties. His previous film, *Mickey One* (1965), starring Warren Beatty, had been a flop, but it dealt with a man on the run from the mob in Chicago in a distinctly stylised way. In his film debut, *The Left Handed Gun* (1958 – with Paul Newman as Billy the Kid), Penn had briefly used slow motion in an action sequence to heighten the moment of death, as Kurosawa had done in *Seven Samurai*. Robert Towne was brought in to work with Penn on the *Bonnie and Clyde* script. Towne had worked for Roger Corman at AIP, initially on *The Last Woman on Earth* and *The Creature from the Haunted Sea*, as writer of the first film, and as an actor in both; Corman reportedly couldn't afford to take a writer and an actor to the location shoot in Puerto Rico so Towne doubled up. Among Towne's alterations to Newman and Benton's screenplay was the removal of the *ménage à trois* element to the story, suggested by Truffaut's *Jules et Jim* (1961); here Bonnie attempted to seduce CW Moss to provoke Clyde romantically. Towne is billed in the titles as 'Special Consultant'.

Earlier film versions of the Bonnie and Clyde story included American International's *The Bonnie Parker Story* (1958), which saw Bonnie (dancer Dorothy Provine) hooking up with the 'Darrow Boys', with no mention of Clyde Barrow. Two films deployed the doomed-lovers-on-the-run motif reused in *Bonnie and Clyde*. The first was Nicholas Ray's directorial debut *They Live by Night* (1948 – also called *The Twisted Road*), adapted from Edward Anderson's novel 'Thieves Like Us'; Anderson apparently wrote the novel with the characters of Bonnie and Clyde in mind. An escaped convict, Bowie (Farley Granger), marries Keechie (Cathy O'Donnell) and attempts to go straight, but after a robbery he ends up on the run and is later killed, leaving behind Keechie expecting their child. The film was remade by Robert Altman as *Thieves Like Us* in 1974.

Even more influential, and one of the finest gangster movies ever made, is Joseph H. Lewis's *Gun Crazy* (1949), which depicts a true *Bonnie and Clyde*-style partnership, in love and crime. Bart Tare (John Dall) grows up obsessed with guns, but when he steals a pistol aged 14 he is sent to reform school. Returning to his home town years later, he joins a sharpshooting circus act with Annie Laurie Starr (Peggy Cummins). They marry and Annie convinces Bart that they should embark on a life of crime – knocking off stores, banks and payroll offices. But one job goes disastrously wrong and Annie shoots two bystanders. A manhunt ensues when they start circulating hot bank notes. Hiding out in a misty swamp, the police, rangers and bloodhounds close in on the duo. As Annie is about to shoot it out with them, Bart kills her and is then mown down by the law. Ironically, Annie is the first person Bart shoots in the entire film – he may be 'gun crazy', but he's not a killer.

Their doomed love affair and violent crime spree is well handled by Lewis. Annie is the driving force in their relationship (the film was also released as *Deadly is the Female*). With her blonde hair, beret and trenchcoat, her character had an influence on Dunaway's look in *Bonnie and Clyde*, and Cummins is one of the finest *femmes fatales* in *noir*, bewitching Bart and pushing him to greater immorality, through his love for her. Also noteworthy is the celebrated four-minute robbery sequence on the Hampton bank. Their approach into town, the heist itself and their speedy escape are filmed in one continuous take, from a camera positioned on the car's back seat. Bart and Annie are dressed as cowboys (their old circus outfits) but pack real guns. It is an extraordinary piece of *verité* filmmaking (*Gun Crazy* was a major influence on François Truffaut and Jean-Luc Godard). No one, except the two 'robbers', the people in the bank and a street cop on duty outside, knew they were making a film, and as the car drives away a woman shouts faintly in the background, 'A robbery!' *Gun Crazy* is Lewis's paean to the classic gangster motifs of love and guns; as Bart says of their bond: 'We go together...like guns and ammunition.'

Beatty, who was Shirley MacLaine's younger brother, was an up-and-coming actor with several critical successes to his credit. He appeared in *Splendour in the Grass* (1961 – opposite Natalie Wood) and *Lillith* (1964). He approached Warner Bros with the *Bonnie and Clyde* project; Warners seemed a good choice as it was the spiritual home of the classic gangster movies of the thirties, with Robinson, Cagney and Bogart. Beatty produced the film, for his own company Titira, for $200,000 and 40 per cent of the film's box-office gross; the budget for the whole project was only $1.6 million.

With handsome Beatty in the lead, the search was on for a suitably striking partner for the role of Bonnie. Blonde, Florida-born 25-year-old Faye Dunaway fitted the bill. She had debuted on screen in *The Happening* (1966), a hippy kidnap caper, and had appeared in the slated, Georgia-set *Hurry Sundown* (1966), of which *Esquire* said, 'to criticise it would be like tripping a dwarf'; Dunaway did at least get the chance to practise her southern accent. Her modish, Bardot pout was perfect for the French-influenced look of Bonnie, in her designer clothes, neckerchief and cocked beret. Some sources claim that Dunaway based her look on Brigitte Bardot's 'Bonnie' in the promotional film for the hit single 'Bonnie and Clyde', which Bardot recorded with Serge Gainsbourg (who played Clyde); but the song wasn't recorded until December 1967, after Penn's film was released. The rest of the gang was composed of largely unknown actors. Ex-Marine Gene Hackman had appeared in one scene with Beatty in *Lillith*; Beatty cast him as Clyde's brother Buck. Estelle Parsons, playing Buck's wife Blanche, was involved in local politics and TV's *Today* show before becoming an actress. Michael J. Pollard, as mechanic and Myrna Loy fan CW Moss, had appeared as Hell's Angel 'Pigmy' in Corman's *The Wild Angels* (1966), with Peter Fonda and Nancy Sinatra. Gene Wilder made his film debut in *Bonnie* as undertaker Eugene Grizzard, with Evans Evans as his betrothed, Velma.

Sharpshooter Clyde Barrow cases the joint; Warren Beatty in Arthur Penn's *Bonnie and Clyde* (1967).

Denver Pyle, cast as the gang's nemesis Sheriff Hamer, later enjoyed many more car chases accompanied by twangy banjo music, in his role as Uncle Jesse in the seventies TV series *The Dukes of Hazzard*.

Filming took place in spring 1967. The film was shot largely in Texas; locations included Dallas, Denton, Pilot Point, Ponder, Red Oak and Waxahachie. To add historical detail, a selection of authentic-looking automobiles were deployed, although their souped-up engines and impressive off-road performances occasionally look rather too contemporary for the period. Other filming was done at Warner Bros Studios in Burbank; interiors were also done at Warners, and process shots were used for the dialogue sequences in moving cars. The beautiful costumes were designed by Theodora Van Runkle. The locals are dressed in authentic Dustbowl dungaree rags, while Bonnie and Clyde look like they are about to appear in *Vogue* (Dunaway did shoot thirties-styled magazine promotional spreads in costume). The musical accompaniment to their adventures was Lester Flatt and Earl Scrugg's 'Foggy Mountain Breakdown', a bluegrass disk that provided the gang's exploits with a sense of adventure.

The titles commence with an old, faded Warner Bros shield logo, like a gangster film from the thirties, and the white lettering of *Bonnie and Clyde* fades ominously to red. There is no music, just the click-click-click of a photographer's shutter, as Penn's scene-setting images flash on the screen: family shots of Bonnie and Clyde as babies, children and teenagers. There follows several Walker Evans-style portraits of Dustbowl dwellers (Evans chronicled life in the Depression with documentary realism), intercut with some stranger images: kids with a snowman, a gas station porch full of gunmen, a group of women holding dead rabbits and eventually the real Bonnie and Clyde posing with firearms in front of a jalopy.

The narrative begins with two captions, accompanied by mock-up Evans-esque shots of Dunaway (in a simple white silk dress) and Beatty (in natty suit and hat). 'Bonnie Parker was born in Rowena Texas 1910 and then moved to West Dallas. In 1931 she worked in a café before beginning her career in crime'; 'Clyde Barrow was born into a family of sharecroppers. As a young man he became a small-time thief and robbed a gas station. He served two years for armed robbery and was released on good behaviour in 1931.'

In reality, Bonnie and Clyde first met in January 1930, before Clyde went to prison. On his release they became reacquainted in February 1932 and joined up as robbers in August of that year. Buck and Blanche were members of the Barrow gang, but CW Moss is fictitious; their accomplice on their early raids was named W.D. Jones, a Dallas teenager. Other members of the Barrow gang, not mentioned in the film, were Henry Methvin and Raymond Hamilton; it was Methvin's parents who actually betrayed Bonnie and Clyde to the law. The shootouts in Joplin (April 1933) and Platte City (July 1933), both in Missouri, are pretty accurate in the film, as is the kidnapping of the undertaker and his girlfriend, near Ruston, Louisiana. But missing from the film's narrative is the car accident Bonnie and

Clyde were involved in, near Quail, Texas, in June 1933; Bonnie was badly burned and recuperated in Fort Smith, Arkansas.

In his study 'Armed Robbery', Roger Matthews outlines the 'moralities and motivation' of armed robbers. Criminals involved in armed robbery take several moral decisions and often convince themselves with a 'technique of neutralisation' against the banks and their staff – 'it's not their money, no one will miss the money, they are insured, banks exploit people anyway'. They also justify violence against employees with the same rhetoric: 'They (the bank staff) asked for it … and they know the risks of working in such an environment.' The robberies in *Bonnie and Clyde* are given moral justification early in the film, with just such an argument. Bonnie and Clyde are hiding out at a ruined farmhouse. Outside they meet the former owner and his family, packed up and on the road: the bank has foreclosed. 'Well that's a pitiful shame,' says Bonnie. 'You're damn right ma'am,' answers the farmer. Clyde lets the farmers borrow his pistol and shoot up the sign ('PROPERTY OF MIDLOTHIAN CITIZENS BANK – Trespassers will be prosecuted') and smash the front windows. As they bid the farmers goodbye Clyde does the introductions: 'This here's Miss Bonnie Parker, I'm Clyde Barrow … we rob banks.'

Faye Dunaway is a revelation as Bonnie, either bemoaning one of their ramshackle hideouts in her drawling Texan accent, 'These accommodations ain't particularly dee-lurx', or posing for a photograph with a cigar and revolver on the fender of their car. Her delivery is ideal for the serio-comic style of the movie: she asks CW what type of car they are driving. 'This is a four-cylinder Ford Coupe'. 'No,' she says shaking her head, 'this is a stolen four-cylinder Ford Coupe.' We first see Bonnie getting ready for her shift at the local café; outside Clyde tries to steal her mother's car. They start to chat and he tries to guess what she does for a living: a movie star, a lady mechanic or a maid. 'What do you think I am?' she asks. 'A waitress,' he guesses correctly. She wants to escape this boring existence and is working out how she can get away from town: 'And now you know,' says Clyde, suggesting she travels with him. Clyde is her escape, her meal ticket out of nowhere, no matter what the price. 'What's it feel like?' she asks him. 'State prison?' 'Armed robbery,' she answers suggestively. 'It ain't like anything,' says Clyde, chewing on a matchstick. She doesn't believe he has committed the crime and he eventually loses patience, stalking into a store across the street and robbing it in front of her as proof.

Dunaway's portrayal aches with a sense of foreboding, especially in the second half of the film, epitomised by the terse goodbye from her mother: 'You try to live three miles from me and you won't live long honey.' When the gang take a couple of lovers hostage they laugh and joke, until they find out that Eugene (Gene Wilder) is an undertaker. Bonnie's smile fades and she says, 'Get them out of here.' Later, she manages to get some of her poetry published, but there is a sadness to the scenes, as one of her readers is shown to be Sheriff Hamer, plotting their demise.

Beatty's performance as Clyde is the best of his career. In reality the 30-year-old actor was nine years older than the robber, but Beatty's strutting egotist, who tells

Bonnie, 'I ain't good, I'm the best,' is a *tour de force*. He has grand ideas for them – and a fine sense of self-publicity and celebrity. Ostensibly they are Robin Hood figures, striking back at the banks in the name of the farmers (they even let a farmer keep a wad of cash during one of their raids), but as their notoriety grows, their motives become blurred – a sense of 'what have they got themselves into?' Also, for all his bravado, it is hinted early on that Clyde is impotent ('I ain't much of a lover boy'), though later, when they are in hiding at the Moss's farm, they consummate their relationship – a moment of real tenderness between the lovers on the run. When the spotlight moves from the central duo, with mechanic CW Moss recruited as getaway driver and Clyde's elder brother Buck and his wife joining them, the film is less successful; especially when compared with *Butch Cassidy and the Sundance Kid* (1969), which keeps the two heroes in focus throughout.

Bonnie and Clyde's plot is more linear and conventional than the other innovative crime movie of the period, John Boorman's *Point Blank* (1967), but Penn occasionally switches to odd moments of surrealism. This is especially noticeable in the soft-focus, blurred meeting between Bonnie and her family – both a reverie and an unsettling nightmare (with jump-cutting, cocked angles and disorientating silence).

The bank robberies are often treated as comedy sequences; this jars with the violence, which escalates throughout the film. On their first job, the Farmer's State Bank is empty of cash; on another Clyde is rugby tackled by a meat-cleaver-wielding butcher. During the Mineola hold-up, CW parks the getaway car and almost costs the gang their lives. In the next scene they hide out in a cinema and watch the 'We're in the Money' Busby Berkely sequence from *Gold Diggers of 1933*. In Mineola, Clyde shoots a bespectacled bank clerk clinging to the running board of their getaway car, point-blank in the face (the shattered glass image an homage to Eisenstein's *Battleship Potemkin*). But the law ambush the gang, firstly at Joplin and later, more effectively, in Platte City; in the latter, Buck is fatally wounded, while his wife is blinded in a bloody anticipation of the finale. In reality Blanche caught a bullet fragment in her forehead and a fragment of shattered glass lodged in her eye.

The most famous scene in the film is the celebrated, dreadful last scene – not so much a final shootout, in the way Sam Peckinpah would use such imagery, but a final massacre. Penn said: 'We're in the Vietnamese War. This film cannot be immaculate and sanitised bang-bang…it's fucking bloody,' and indeed it is. Originally the ambush scene was going to be an assemblage of stills with police machine-gun fire on the soundtrack, like the influential French 1963 sci-fi film *La Jette*, a photo-novel approach (as a bookend to *Bonnie and Clyde*'s similarly styled title sequence). The last image would have been of two farmers hurrying towards the wreckage of the car, with a reprise of 'Foggy Mountain Breakdown'.

Penn and Beatty decided instead for its graphic, gratuitous opposite. The ambush actually took place on 23 May 1934, eight miles out of Gibsland, Louisiana. In reality Bonnie and Clyde didn't stop the car and get out – it was perforated with

150 bullets as it rolled along the road, coming to rest against an embankment. Bonnie was so badly riddled she lost her right hand. In the film, both Beatty and Dunaway were rigged with dozens of 'squibs', condoms filled with red dye. These would be wired together under the actors' clothes and set off with an electrical impulse, exploding a tiny charge of black powder. The effect, recorded with four cameras by Penn in slow motion and edited for impact by Dede Allen, left audiences shocked, as Bonnie and Clyde were shot to pieces before their eyes. Critic Pauline Kael said the film 'put the sting back into death'. It was a harrowing end to the movie, hardly the light entertainment advertised, and the most violent piece of footage in mainstream cinema up to that point, instantly gaining the film notoriety. The film actually produced a change in the US ratings system; in 1968 the Hayes Code was abolished and films were rated G(eneral), M(ature, later PG), R(estricted) and X (no one admitted under the age of 17). In the UK the film, billed as *Bonnie and Clyde ... Were Killers*, gained an X rating.

Rough-cuts of the film ran 130 minutes; it was finally released at 111. Several scenes were cut from the final version and, although they all appear in the shooting script, there is conjecture as to whether all were shot. These include Clyde shooting the cleaver-wielding butcher; in the finished version he merely knocks him out, and the butcher is later shown identifying Clyde from a prison mugshot (no. 990830).

Bandit Chic: Faye Dunaway as Bonnie, outside the Mineola Bank, in *Bonnie and Clyde* (1967).

Also cut was a long scene where Bonnie and Clyde get drunk and muse on death – even to the extent of getting dressed in their Sunday best, applying death mask makeup and turning their bed into a coffin (Towne in particular says this scene was never shot).

Originally scheduled to premier in Denton, Texas, *Bonnie and Clyde* was first screened at the Montreal Film Festival on 4 August 1967. Its US premiere was in New York on 13 August. The trailers stated 'This is Bonnie…this is Clyde…their paths crossed like two hot wires', but Warners had little faith in the film. It went on general release on 13 September and a few weeks later vanished, having taken about $2.5 million. The reviews were terrible: *Newsweek* recommended it 'for the moron trade' and the *New York Times* called it 'a cheap piece of bald-faced slapstick'. But Pauline Kael in the *New Yorker* championed the film and when it was released in London in September 1967 it made a fortune. The *News of the World* called it 'exciting, disturbing and damnably clever'; *The Times* said, 'Don't miss it.' This led to *Bonnie and Clyde* being re-released in the US in February 1968. The film's exuberant overall tone overrode the downbeat ending and this time it made $16.5 million and ended up grossing almost $23 million; it rapidly became Warner Brothers' second highest moneymaker of all time (behind *My Fair Lady*).

In the wake of the film's success, a novelisation of the film by Burt Hirschfeld was published in the UK and US, based faithfully on the screenplay by Newman and Benton. Even Georgie Fame's 'Ballad of Bonnie and Clyde' cashed in and reached number one in the UK hit parade in late 1967. In the western *Shane* (1953), when Jack Palance shoots a farmer in a muddy street, the gunshot was mixed exceptionally loudly to make maximum impact on the audience. With the release of *Bonnie and Clyde* projectionists complained that they hadn't exhibited a film mixed this loudly since *Shane*; some projectionists made a note of when the gunshots were about to come in and adjusted the volume accordingly. Nearly 40 years later, in 2004, *Bonnie and Clyde* came 13th on the American Film Institute's list of the all-time best thrillers and it is the oldest film on the 50 highest-grossing gangster films of all time.

At the 1968 Oscars, *Bonnie and Clyde* had ten nominations: Estelle Parsons (supporting actress) and Burnett Guffey (cinematography) won; Pollard and Hackman (supporting actors), Dunaway (actress), Van Runkle (costumes), Penn (direction), Newman and Benton (screenplay) and Beatty twice (as actor, and producer of best picture) didn't. In 1991 Beatty again played a real-life gangster, this time Benjamin 'Bugsy' Siegel, to great effect in the hit movie *Bugsy* (1991), which was similarly nominated for several top Oscars, winning only for costume design, and art and set decoration.

In the mid-seventies *Bonnie and Clyde* had a Network Showcase premiere on US TV; for TV showings in the US and UK there have been some minor edits for violence and a sex scene between Bonnie and Clyde is often abridged. The film was known by its literal translation abroad – *Bonnie et Clyde*, *Bonnie und Clyde* – except in Italy, where it was released as *Gangster Story*. Its huge success led to a minor resurgence of Depression-era gangster flicks, such as John Milius's directorial debut *Dillinger* (1973), a film that shares *Bonnie and Clyde*'s fine sense of period. There were also many imitators: all-action, bloody shoot-'em-ups like Shelley Winters in *Bloody Mama* (1970), and Angie Dickinson in *Big Bad Mama* (1974) and *Bloody Mama II* (1987); these copyists tended to end with the obligatory slo-mo massacre/shootout. Other derivatives include two 1973 movies: *Little Laura & Big John*, intended as fifties singer Fabian's comeback film, and Terence Malick's spree-killing *Badlands*, based on the Starkweather–Fugate case, with Martin Sheen doing a fine James Dean impersonation in the lead.

More recently *Bonnie & Clyde: The True Story* (1992) attempted to re-examine the story, with Tracey Needham as Bonnie and Dana Ashbrook as Clyde, and rather a surprising amount of blood for an afternoon TV movie. There was a drama documentary called *The Other Side of Bonnie and Clyde*, made in 1968, which purported to tell the true story of their capture, and included much eyewitness testimony, including from Sheriff Frank Hamer. Other, more eclectic derivatives include a memorable Warner Brothers rabbit cartoon parody called *Bunny and Claude – We Rob Carrot Patches* (1968); an Italian version of the film (*Bonnie and Clyde Italian-Style* – 1982) and a high-school remake (*Teenage Bonnie and Klepto Clyde* – 1993).

Arthur Penn, George Roy Hill, Sam Peckinpah, George Romero all cite bloody TV news items reporting Vietnam as their inspiration for the deaths of the heroes in their late-sixties movies: respectively *Bonnie and Clyde*, *Butch Cassidy and the Sundance Kid*, *The Wild Bunch* and *Night of the Living Dead*. *Bonnie and Clyde* started this, with a dénouement where the heroes literally go out with a bang. It was a natural successor to Cagney's 'Made it Ma!' demise in *White Heat* – a morality tale warning that crime doesn't pay. But did Penn have to make his heroes so attractive? Cowboys, zombies or gangsters: the medium is the message.

10

'We have all the time in the world'

— On Her Majesty's Secret Service (1969)

Credits:

DIRECTOR – Peter Hunt
PRODUCER – Albert R. Broccoli and Harry Saltzman
ORIGINAL STORY – Ian Fleming
SCREENPLAY – Richard Maibaum and Simon Raven
DIRECTOR OF PHOTOGRAPHY – Michael Reed
EDITOR – John Glen
PRODUCTION DESIGNER – Syd Cain
ART DIRECTOR – Robert Laing
COSTUME DESIGNER – Marjory Cornelius
MUSIC – John Barry
Technicolor/Panavision
Interiors filmed at Pinewood Studio, Buckinghamshire
A Danjaq/Eon Production
Released by United Artists
140 minutes

Cast:

George Lazenby (Commander James Bond)/Diana Rigg (Contessa Teresa Di Vicenzo, known as Tracy)/Telly Savalas (Ernst Stavro Blofeld)/Ilse Steppat (Irma Bunt)/Gabriele Ferzetti (Marc Ange Draco)/Yuri Borienko (Grunther)/Bernard Horsfall (Campbell, MI6 agent)/George Baker (Sir Hilary Bray)/Bernard Lee ('M')/Lois Maxwell (Miss Moneypenny)/Desmond Llewelyn (Major Boothroyd, 'Q')/Angela Scoular (Ruby Bartlett)/Julie Edge (Helen, Scandinavian angel of death)/Jenny Hanley (Irish angel)/Mona Chong (Chinese angel)/Joanna Lumley (Sue-Ann, English angel)/Zara (Indian angel)/Anouska Hempel (Australian angel)/Catherina Von Schell (Nancy)/Sylvanno Henriques (Sylvano, Jamaican angel)/Ingrit Black (German angel)/Helena Ronee

(Denise, Israeli angel)/Dani Sheridan (American angel)/
Virginia North (Olympe, Draco's secretary)/Geoffrey Cheshire
(Toussaint, Draco's man)/Irving Allen (Ché Ché)/Terry Mountain
(Raphael)/James Bree (Gumbolt)/John Gray (Hammond)/Captain
John Crewdson (Draco's helicopter pilot)/Richard Graydon
(Draco's driver)

*   *   *

Of the six actors to play the famous British screen secret agent James Bond, George
Lazenby is probably the least remembered, and *On Her Majesty's Secret Service*, the
sixth in the series, is one of the most overlooked. And yet in its depiction of Bond's
battle with corruption, extortion and organised crime on a global scale, *OHMSS*
has aged much better than its contemporaries and remains one of the most elaborate
and exciting crime thrillers of the sixties.

The adventures of fictional MI6 secret agent James Bond (code-named 007, his
'licence to kill') are the second most successful film franchise in the world after the
'Star Wars' movies. In the early fifties ex-naval officer Ian Fleming began writing
books about Bond, naming him after the author of 'Birds of the West Indies'.
'Casino Royale' was written in four weeks in 1953 at his Jamaican house, 'Goldeneye'.
A moderate success in the UK, it was retitled 'You Asked for It' in the US.
Eventually it took off and Fleming wrote several sequels: 'Live and Let Die' (1954),
'Moonraker' (1955), 'Diamonds Are Forever' (1956), 'From Russia with Love'
(1957), 'Dr No' (1958), 'Goldfinger' (1959), 'Thunderball' (1961), 'The Spy Who
Loved Me' (1962), 'On Her Majesty's Secret Service' (1963), 'You Only Live Twice'
(1964) and 'The Man With the Golden Gun' (1965). They became immensely
popular; John F. Kennedy named 'From Russia with Love' among his favourite
books and their fast action and style led them to be adapted to the big screen.

The first of these adaptations was *Dr No* (1963), a fast-moving, Jamaican-set
thriller. Scot Sean Connery played Bond, Ursula Andress was Honey Ryder and
metal-handed Eurasian villain No was played by Joseph Wiseman. The film
established various series modal traits: the guitar-driven 'James Bond Theme' by
Monty Norman, the exotic locations, sexy *femmes fatales*, larger-than-life adventures
and irredeemable villains.

Though it earned nearly $60 million worldwide, *Dr No* was easily surpassed by
From Russia with Love (1963) and *Goldfinger* (1964). The series swiftly established
its emphasis on outlandish gadgetry and crimes: in *Russia*, Bond attempts to gain
possession of a Lektor decoding machine; in *Goldfinger* the eponymous master
criminal plans to detonate an atom bomb in Fort Knox. By this point James Bond
and the 007 logo was a licence to print money; *Thunderball* (1965), depicting the
theft of nuclear weapons from NATO by villain Largo, was the highest-grossing of
the sixties Bonds, earning $141 million worldwide. It was to have been followed by

On Her Majesty's Secret Service, with Connery in the lead, but the producers eventually decided on *You Only Live Twice* (1967). This was largely set in Japan and memorably featured cat-stroking master villain Blofeld's headquarters hidden in a dormant volcano. By the fifth outing a formula had been established of guns, girls and gadgets, which by now included an Aston Martin DB5 with machine-guns and a passenger ejector seat, a Bell-Textron one-man jet pack and a collapsible gyrocopter.

But Connery thought it rather too rigid a formula and went off to the Almerian desert to star in Louis L'Amour's *Shalako* (1968). In 1967 an anti-Vietnam demonstrator in Washington, DC held a placard with a cartoon of President Johnson brandishing a long, silenced pistol, with the caption 'Blood-Finger Johnson – 00$'. As well as comparing the US president to a government assassin with a 'licence to kill', it demonstrated how iconic Bond had become. Who could fill Connery's shoes?

Fleming had written 'On Her Majesty's Secret Service' in April 1963, while on location in Jamaica filming *Dr No*. Richard Maibaum closely followed the book's plotting for the film adaptation. On assignment in Portugal, Bond saves the life of suicidal Tracy, a widow with a taste for danger. Her father is Marc Ange Draco, a construction magnet and head of the Union Corse, a European crime syndicate. He promises Bond a £1million dowry, if he'll marry Tracy; Bond says he needs information on his arch-enemy, Blofeld, the head of SPECTRE. Back in London, Bond is taken off Operation Bedlam, the search for Blofeld; in protest he tries to resign, but is granted two weeks' leave. Bond travels to Draco's estate, where he and Tracy fall in love. He also learns that there is a connection between Blofeld and Gebrüder Gumbolt, lawyers in Bern. Bond discovers that Blofeld is claiming to be Balthazar, Count de Bleuchamp. Posing as Sir Hilary Bray, Sable Basilisk of the Royal College of Arms, Bond travels to the Bleuchamp Institute for Allergy Research atop Piz Gloria in the Swiss Alps. There he uncovers Blofeld's plot to release 12 'Angels of Death', young women carrying a Virus Omega, a bacterium causing infertility in all living animals and plants. Bond is unmasked, but escapes, with Blofeld and Irma Bunt, Blofeld's lieutenant, in pursuit. Tracy rescues him, but SPECTRE capture her; Blofeld contacts the United Nations and asks for recognition of his title and amnesty for his crimes. MI6 won't interfere, so Bond contacts Draco with a 'demolition deal'; they attack Piz Gloria by helicopter, save Tracy and destroy the institute, though Blofeld and Bunt escape. Months later, Bond and Tracy marry, but as they depart on their honeymoon, the SPECTRE agents drive past and shoot Tracy dead.

In 1968 the Bond producers set about the unenviable task of finding a new Bond for the new film. According to director Peter Hunt, 100 actors were auditioned, including future Bonds Roger Moore and Timothy Dalton. Eventually 28-year-old George Lazenby was chosen; an Australian ex-car salesman and model, he had achieved some degree of fame on TV in the 'Big Fry' chocolate adverts. He had also appeared in an Italian/Spanish spy movie called *Espionage in Tangiers* (1965). To secure the role, Lazenby bought one of Connery's suits from tailor Anthony Sinclair and had a Connery haircut at the Dorchester. Lazenby had scant acting experience, but looked the part and tested well for the action scenes.

Even though *OHMSS* was a UK production, the cast and locations were international. Both Brigitte Bardot and Catherine Deneuve were considered for Tracy, but the role was offered to 30-year-old Diana Rigg, who was famous on TV as karate-kicking, catsuited Emma Peel in *The Avengers*. Rigg took the role, claiming, 'I rather wanted to know what it was like to be in an epic'. Her Corsican father was played by respected Italian actor Gabriele Ferzetti, who had appeared in *L'Avventura* (1960) and had just played railroad baron Morton in *Once Upon a Time in the West* (1968). Telly Savalas made a first-rate Blofeld, though there was no attempt at continuity – in *You Only Live Twice*, he had been played by Donald Pleasance. Of Greek descent, bald Savalas had headed the news team for ABC TV in the US; he didn't turn to acting until he was 36, but was prolific, appearing in *Birdman of Alcatraz* (1963), *The Dirty Dozen* (1967) and several westerns and crime thrillers, often as the villain. He was later TV's lollipop-licking detective Kojak.

German actress Ilse Steppat was Irma Bunt; Russian wrestler Yuri Borienko played her SPECTRE sidekick Grunther. Series regulars Bernard Lee, Lois Maxwell and Desmond Llewelyn played respectively Bond's MI6 boss M, Miss

George Lazenby, as Ian Fleming's superagent hero, aims at Blofeld on location at Piz Gloria, in Peter Hunt's *On Her Majesty's Secret Service* (1969).

Moneypenny and armourer Q. George Baker, who played the real Sir Hilary Bray, dubbed Lazenby in the scenes at Piz Gloria, when Bond impersonated kilt-wearing Bray. A competition to determine who would play the 12 Angels of Death was announced as early as October 1965; in the book there are only 10 angels and they are all from the UK. In the film, the angels are an international mix. The eventual line-up included Angela Scoular, future *Magpie* presenter Jenny Hanley, Anouska Hempel, Hungarian Catherine Schell (later Maya in *Space 1999*) and former Miss Norway Julie Edge, who became a star via prehistoric Hammer movies. Joanna Lumley, who later starred on TV in *The New Avengers*, *Sapphire and Steel* and *Absolutely Fabulous*, has since described her small role as angel Sue-Ann as 'set dressing, like a vase'.

Filming a $7 million production on location was a vast logistical operation. Shooting began on 21 October 1968, first in Switzerland, then Pinewood Studios (late December 1968) and finally in Portugal (April 1969); it wrapped on 20 June 1969. The main unit (under Hunt) filmed Blofeld's mountaintop stronghold, Piz Gloria, at a half-completed revolving restaurant atop the 10,000-feet-high Schilthorn in the Swiss Alps, near Interlaken; the Bond producers installed a helipad, generators and the revolving 'Alpine Room'. The building still exists today, called Piz Gloria in honour of the movie. Its cable car was also used. Most of the skiing was filmed in the locality, some on a 12,000-foot glacier; the night-time scenes illuminated with magnesium flares were shot around the village of Winteregg. Base camp for the crew was the village of Mürren in the Lauterbrunnen valley below Piz Gloria. When Bond arrives, he steps off the train at Lauterbrunnen station. The town was also used for some car chase scenes (for instance the telephone box where Bond is ambushed). The 'Gloria Express' bobsleigh run was constructed by bob champion Franz Capose nearby, for second-unit director John Glen to shoot a chase scene. The Christmas Eve Grand Ice Carnival, with its stalls and skating rink, was shot in a car park in nearby Grindelwald; the skiddy stockcar race was filmed in Lauterbrunnen. A spectacular avalanche scene took some planning: during the summer of 1968, charges were planted above the valley, with a view to exploding them during the winter. Unfortunately the snow came down by itself before it could be filmed. A two-mile-wide staged avalanche, detonated by three bombs, was used in the finished film, combining Disney stock footage with optical effects, including cascading salt.

At Pinewood Studios, Iver Heath, interior sets were built for the Portuguese casino, Piz Gloria and Blofeld's ice cave laboratories, the College, and hotel rooms and offices. The exterior of M's 'Quarterdeck' home is 'Thames Lawn' in Marlow, near London; the Royal College of Arms and Heralds is in Queen Victoria Street, Blackfriars. In Portugal, Tracy's attempted suicide was filmed on Muchaxo Guincho beach; Bond stays at the Hotel Palacio at Estoril. Draco's estate, the bullring scene and the final wedding scenes were all filmed on the vast Vinhus private estate, near Setúbal. Tracy's murder was filmed on the Arribida Road on the

Portuguese coast (near the beach where they first meet) and was the last major scene to be filmed.

The skilled stunt crew were led by second-unit director John Glen (also the film's editor) and stunt co-ordinator George Leech. Vic Armstrong was the ski double for Bond; Joe Powell was the double for Blofeld. In the opening beach fight, Lazenby grappled with stuntmen Terry Mountain (Raphael, the gunman) and Bill Morgan (the knifeman). Bill Dean wore a special suit when he was set on fire for the flame-thrower scene. Stuntman Irving Allen had a role in the film as Draco tough Ché Ché ('Le Persuadeur'). The Bond hanging from the cable car wire as the wheel approaches is Chris Webb; for other cable shots Bond is played by Richard Graydon. The stock car race was directed by Anthony Squire, with Tracy's red Ford Cougar driven by Willi Neuner. Stunt driver Erich Glavitsa supervised; Ford Motors supplied several Escorts to be smashed up for the scene, the making of which features in the documentary *Shot on Ice*. In the bobsleigh chase, Robert Zimmerman doubled for Savalas and Heinz Lau for Lazenby. Aerial cameraman Johnny Jordon was suspended from a parachute harness beneath a helicopter to lens the ski chase and sections of the bob run. Ski cameraman Willi Bognor Junior skied backwards ahead of the actors, with a camera on his shoulder to get some fantastic ski chase shots. An on-set documentary *Above it All* depicted their working methods. His pilot was Captain John Crewdson, who can be seen in the finished film as Draco's pilot. The results, when intercut with Michael Reed's main-unit photography, are breathtaking.

Lazenby is highly convincing as Bond; his portrayal is closer to the character as written. Lazenby had a strong Australian brogue, but practised an upper-class English accent, which he even passed off in press interviews. He was told by Hunt to stop lolloping about and 'walk like Prince Philip'. Cinematographer Reed said that Bond needed to have 'the ruthlessness of Jack Palance and the charm of Cary Grant'. Lazenby also has the smugness of Connery, but with a violent streak, and is believable in the frequent hand-to-hand action. He's also a human Bond, a man capable of love, rather than Connery's selfish serial misogynist.

In the Connery films, some of the sixties high-tech gadgets now look clunky, whereas Hunt's downplaying of such gimmickry enhances the action. The 1969 Aston Martin DBS Bond drives in *OHMSS* doesn't have a smokescreen, emit an oil slick or fire its passengers through the roof. Hunt's point seems to be that if it was so equipped then Tracy would have survived – the bulletproof glass would have ensured that. But this is the real world: Bond uses a safe-decoder and photocopier for the heist on Gumbolt's offices and a miniature camera at Piz Gloria. He's also equipped with his trusty Walther PPK automatic pistol, described in *Dr No* as having 'a delivery like a brick through a plate glass window'. The only incongruous 'gadget' moment is when Q is talking to M about 'radioactive lint', fluff hidden in pockets to keep track of agents.

OHMSS is the darkest Bond film. It begins with an attempted suicide and ends with a wedding-day murder, the car bedecked with flowers. 'It's alright,' says Bond to the passing police patrolman, as he cradles Tracy's head in his lap. 'There's no hurry you see … we have all the time in the world,' as he kisses her wedding ring and breaks down. Hunt's original idea was to have the murder at the beginning of the next film; thus *OHMSS* would have closed on the wedding and *Diamonds Are Forever* would have opened with Tracy's death. There is certainly an 'autumnal' feeling to the film, even to the scenes set in sunny Portugal, and it is the most introspective and thoughtful of the series. Additional dialogue was written by Simon Raven, including a poetic scene between Blofeld and Tracy directly before the dawn raid on Piz Gloria, which misquoted from 'Hassan: A Soldier's Story' by James Elroy Flecker: 'Thy dawn,' says Tracy, 'O Master of the World, thy dawn; For thee the sunlight creeps across the lawn … for thee the poet of beguilement sings.' The snowy, picture-postcard 'Christmas in Switzerland' locale helps to lift the mood. But there's still a gnawing sense that a tragedy is unfolding. Tracy is the doomed heroine: tragic, beautiful and self-destructive, like Bardot in *Le Mepris* (1963). Our first glimpse of her is through the cross-hairs of Bond's telescopic sight: already she is a target – a target who later is fatally hit.

Bond is a crime-busting secret agent on a grand scale – a very distant relative of the G-man heroes of old. His opposition in this film is SPECTRE, an acronym of Special Executive for Terrorism, Revenge, Extortion; his opponents in other adventures were SMERSH ('Smiert Spionom'; Death to Spies), or freelance lunatics like Auric Goldfinger or Francisco Scaramanga. In the finale, SPECTRE is pitted against Draco's Union Corse, another crime syndicate; to access Piz Gloria's airspace Draco's helicopter Alpine troops pose as the Red Cross, on a mercy flight carrying blood plasma to victims of the Italian flood disaster.

Blofeld is dapper and elegant, as befits a budding count, while his employees wear distinctive orange and black uniforms: the armed guards are ostensibly to deter rival chemical companies. The villain's scheme in *OHMSS* sees Blofeld unleashing his brainwashed 'Angels of Death', who will release bacteriological warfare on the world from their gift set perfume atomisers. The angels think they are at the clinic to remedy their allergies to everyday things, such as chickens and potatoes. Blofeld's brainwashing techniques masquerading as aversion therapy include throbbing psychedelic lights and weird sound effects, while Blofeld purrs to one patient, 'I have taught you to love chicken.' In Fleming's book there is an outbreak of 'foul pest' affecting the turkey population in East Anglia, which leads Bond to Blofeld's scheme; there had actually been a massive foot and mouth outbreak in the UK from October 1967 to June 1968, which Blofeld topically claims responsibility for in the film. Blofeld's 'allergy research' is not for profit, but, according to his sidekick Irma Bunt, for 'the sake of mankind … he wants to leave his mark on the entire world'.

The film is intentionally littered with in-jokes and references, which make it fun for Bond buffs. The title sequence, designed by Maurice Binder, features stills from previous Bond adventures; later a janitor whistles the theme from *Goldfinger*.

Following a beach fight Lazenby even says directly to camera, 'This never happened to the other fellow.' When he walks into Miss Moneypenny's office, she comments, 'Same old James…only more so' as he pinches her bottom. When Bond clears out his desk, he finds Honey's sheath knife from *Dr No*, the watch with the wire garrotte from *From Russia with Love* and the underwater mouthpiece from *Thunderball*, with each item accompanied by a musical pastiche.

OHMSS boasts a superior John Barry score, recorded at CTS Studios, Bayswater in October 1969. Barry had made his name on the Bond films and with his scores to *The Ipcress File* (1965) and *Born Free* (1966). *OHMSS* is Barry's best Bond score and the one that most repays revisiting. The powerful 'OHMSS' main theme incorporates swirling strings, trumpets and cor anglais, propelled by a pulsating Moog synthesiser (a descending G minor/F/E-flat/D root), which is also used in chase scenes and the attack on Piz Gloria. Elsewhere Barry has the cool jazz piano of 'Try', as the neon casino sign reflects in a shimmering swimming pool. The composer uses blasts of brass and machine-gun percussion for fistfights, suggestive 'Carry On' saxophones for 'Bond meets the Girls' and lush horn and string arrangements for elegant snowscape ski chases. He deploys flutes, xylophone, tinkling bells and lush Mantovani-style strings, especially on the horn-

Mr Kiss Kiss, Bang Bang: Italian poster featuring Diana Rigg and George Lazenby, working *On Her Majesty's Secret Service* (1969).

and trumpet-led last post of 'Journey to Blofeld's Hideaway', or the eerie sonar of 'Over and Out'.

The song 'Do Your Know How Christmas Trees Are Grown?' was performed by Nina Van Pallandt; apparently 'They need sunshine and raindrops, but most of all, they need love'. 'We Have All the Time in the World', also written by Hal David and Barry, was the last song ever recorded by Louis Armstrong. It is an effortless composition and has since become one of the most popular wedding songs of all time; in the film it is cut to a quixotic montage of Bond and Tracy falling in love (Lazenby wanted Blood, Sweat and Tears to provide a suitable love song). The piece is a smooth blend of rolling bass, soaring violins and acoustic guitar with 'Satchmo's' molasses vocal: 'Time enough for life to unfold, all the precious things love has in store – nothing more, nothing less, only love'. There are also instrumental reorchestrations of this throughout, most movingly following the death of Tracy; the one unforgivable mistake is the reprise of the brazen 'James Bond Theme' at the close, shattering the poignancy.

When the film was edited together, two sequences were cut. The first is where Bond chases a herald from the College of Arms when he discovers he's been bugged. The second involves a subplot with MI6 agent Campbell (Bond's associate in the Swiss scenes), who is killed by Blofeld in a faked climbing accident; Campbell's scenes have since been restored. *OHMSS* was advertised as 'The Biggest 007 Adventure of them All'; TV spots announced: 'On a racing bobsleigh! On a ton of Dynamite! On one Ski! *On Her Majesty's Secret Service.*' The trailer promised '007 times more excitement…the name's Lazenby, George Lazenby' and unsubtly referenced the Angels of Death: 'If you think your girl's a good looker, take a good look at this guy's dolls'. It was rated M, for Mature Audiences. Poster copy marvelled 'Far Up! Far Out! Far More! James Bond 007 is Back!' with Lazenby and Rigg ridiculously portrayed skiing in eveningwear – at least Lazenby wasn't in his kilt. *Variety* said, 'Stunt arranger George Leech deserves an award'. It went on to praise the 'break-neck physical excitement and stunning visual attractions'. Lazenby was described as 'wooden', but when the *Daily Express* reported that *OHMSS* had broken records in the US and UK, Lazenby commented: 'That makes my knockers look like idiots'.

OHMSS was released simultaneously in the UK and US on 18 December 1969. It took nearly $23 million in the US and was the ninth biggest grosser of the year. It was rated an A certificate in the UK, after the film had been edited slightly. UK merchandise tie-ins included expensive replicas of Tracy's white guipure lace wedding dress (designed by Marjorie Cornelius) and wedding ring (inscribed 'We have all the time in the world'). Like all the Bond movies, *OHMSS* was massively popular throughout Europe and in Japan, making $82 million worldwide. It was first broadcast on US TV on 16 February 1976 and in the UK on 4 September 1978 (on ITV). Some seventies US TV prints begin with a prologue of the attack on Piz Gloria, then fade back to the beginning of the story, with a Bond 'voiceover' provided by George Baker. The film has since enjoyed a reappraisal on home video and DVD; in 1995 it was released in the UK as a limited edition boxed set – the only Bond film ever to be released in this format. In 1994, Louis Armstrong's song reached number 3 in the UK, while a punchy cover of 'Main Theme OHMSS' by David Arnold and The Propellerheads reached number 7 in 1997.

In 1970 Lazenby was nominated for a Golden Globe as 'Most Promising Newcomer'. He was quoted as saying, 'I'm not saying I'm a great actor, but it proves that the fans have accepted me as James Bond'. Unfortunately he hadn't accepted himself. *On Her Majesty's Secret Service* ends with the caption 'James Bond Will Return in *Diamonds Are Forever*'. He did, but Lazenby wasn't playing him. Lazenby's adviser, Ronan O'Reilly, thought the way forward was *Easy Rider* and the counterculture, but by the seventies the flower children were wilting. Lazenby arrived at the *OHMSS* premiere with long hair and a beard (the producers had managed to get him to remove an earring), which was certainly not the sort of image to be associated with the franchise. Lazenby had never signed his contract, so the producers fired him. Unsurprisingly, Lazenby now regrets the decision: 'I should have done two'.

Connery returned for *Diamonds Are Forever* and he received the then-record fee of $1.25 million. This was a good investment, as the film made $116 million worldwide. With *Diamonds* the series was back to the gadget-laden, Shirley Bassey-warbling super-production that *OHMSS* had subverted. Connery then left the franchise altogether, only returning as Bond in *Never Say Never Again* (1983), a remake of *Thunderball*. Connery was followed by Roger Moore, of TV's *The Saint* and *The Persuaders*, who introduced a lighter, self-mocking style into the series from 1973 to 1985 with *Live and Let Die*, *The Man With the Golden Gun*, *The Spy Who Loved Me*, *Moonraker*, *For Your Eyes Only*, *Octopussy* and *A View to a Kill*, each film bearing little resemblance to its literary inspiration. Timothy Dalton took over in 1987 for *The Living Daylights* and *Licence to Kill* (1989). But it wasn't until Pierce Brosnan stepped into the role that the series really equalled its sixties success. Brosnan was a very different Bond; the series couldn't pass off the sexism of the early films with humour any more. Brosnan's films to date are *GoldenEye* (1995), *Tomorrow Never Dies* (1997), *The World is Not Enough* (1999) and *Die Another Day* (2002). 'The World is Not Enough', as we find out at the Royal College in *OHMSS*, is the Bond family motto: 'Orbis non Suffict'. In 2005, Daniel Craig was announced as Brosnan's successor for the twenty-first film in the series, based on Fleming's 'Casino Royale'.

Thus the movies continue to thrive, with successive generations having their own personalised Bond, fashioned as much by his milieu as by Fleming's original creation. But by virtue of its 'one-off' nature, *OHMSS* stands alone in the series. Hunt recalled that he 'was intent on making the best James Bond film of all'. Lazenby may not be the greatest Bond, but *On Her Majesty's Secret Service* is the finest Bond film.

11

'I'm visiting relatives ...
a death in the family'

— Get Carter (1971)

Credits:
DIRECTOR – Mike Hodges
PRODUCER – Michael Klinger
STORY – Ted Lewis
SCREENPLAY – Mike Hodges
DIRECTOR OF PHOTOGRAPHY – Wolfgang Suschitzky
EDITOR – John Trumper
ART DIRECTOR – Roger King
PRODUCTION DESIGNER – Assheton Gorton
COSTUMES – Evangeline Harrison and Dougie Hayward
MUSIC COMPOSER AND CONDUCTOR – Roy Budd
Metrocolor
An MGM Production
Released by Metro-Goldwyn-Mayer
112 minutes
Cast:
Michael Caine (Jack Carter)/Ian Hendry (Eric Paice)/Britt
Ekland (Anna Fletcher)/John Osborne (Cyril Kinnear)/Tony
Beckley (Peter the Dutchman)/George Sewell (Con McCarty)/
Geraldine Moffatt (Glenda)/Dorothy White (Margaret, Frank's
lover)/Rosemarie Durham (Edna, 'Las Vegas' landlady)/Petra
Markham (Doreen Carter)/Alun Armstrong (Keith)/Bryan
Mosley (Cliff Brumby)/Glynn Edwards (Albert Swift)/Bernard
Hepton (Thorpe)/Terence Rigby (Gerald Fletcher)/John Bindon
(Sid Fletcher)/Godfrey Quigley (Eddie, mourner at funeral)/
Carl Howard ('J', hired assassin)/Maxwell Dees (Vicar)/Liz
McKenzie (Mrs Brumby)/Denea Wilde (Pub singer)/John
Hussey and Ben Aris (Architects)/Kitty Attwood (Old woman)/
Geraldine Sherman (Girl in café)/Joy Merlyn and Yvonne

Michaels (Women in post office)/Alan Hockey (Scrapyard dealer)/Reg Niven (Frank Carter)

*   *   *

The development of the British crime movie was very different to its American counterpart. British gangsterism, particularly following the Second World War, tended to be small-time racketeering, slot-machine and horse-racing scams, and protection; British filmmakers didn't have the rich underworld heritage or the iconic figures of the legendary American gangsters to identify with and depict. *Brighton Rock* (1947 – retitled *Young Scarface* for American audiences), the controversial James Hadley Chase adaptation *No Orchids for Miss Blandish* (1948), Jules Dassin's *Night and the City* (1950) and Val Guest's *Hell is the City* (1959) were notable exceptions. Into the sixties, British crime cinema tended to concern club owners, turf wars, narcotics and prostitution, in B-movies such as *The Challenge* (1959), *Beat Girl* (*Wild for Kicks* in the US) and *Too Hot to Handle* (both 1960); low-budget showgirl narratives mixed with drugs and guns.

Even when London had its own criminal royalty, with the Kray twins and their affiliates, films weren't made about them. As Peter Cook said of the capital in the sixties, 'London swings like a pendulum do' – crime films of the era were caper comedies, such as *The Jokers* (1966) or *The Italian Job* (1969), or else far-fetched international espionage, such as the Bond franchise and its derivatives. The most interesting British crime film of the period was *Performance* (1969), in which an East End skinhead gangster hides out with a reclusive hippy rock star at 81 Powis Square, with unusual consequences. But by the seventies, the atmosphere had changed. The gloss rubbed off, cynicism and realism showed through, like the truthful, angry young man dramas of the late fifties and early sixties. Mike Hodges's 1971 movie *Get Carter* was the epitome of this: *Point Blank*-meets-gritty 'kitchen sink' northern soul.

Bristol-born writer-director Hodges had worked at Granada TV on the *World in Action* programme, as well as arts programme *Tempo* (where he made profiles on several film directors, including Welles, Tati and Godard). He followed this with contributions to *New Tempo* (a series of nine short films, including 'Heroes', 'Noise', 'Nostalgia' and 'Violence') and a children's series called *The Tyrant King* (1967). He was writer-director-producer on two 80-minute *Playhouse* presentations for Thames Television: *Suspect* (1969), detailing a search for a missing girl and the breakdown of a marriage, and *Rumour* (1970), about a journalist drawn into the world of prostitution and scandal.

In January 1970, producer Michael Klinger approached Hodges to write and direct an adaptation of Ted Lewis's novel 'Jack's Return Home', for £7,000. He reworked the story, replacing the flashback structure with linear narrative, and retitled the piece *Get Carter*. Having decided to shoot the film around Newcastle (the town in the book is nameless), Hodges incorporated local locations and stories into the script, including a case where a hitman was brought up to Newcastle from London to rub out a crook involved in a slot-machine racket.

In Hodges's scenario, Jack Carter, a tough London gangster who works for the Fletcher brothers, travels to Newcastle to attend his brother Frank's funeral. Initially suspicious of the circumstances of Frank's death (Frank was blind drunk and involved in a car crash), Carter befriends Frank's daughter, Doreen, Frank's lover Margaret (a prostitute) and Keith, a family friend. At the funeral, the cortege is shadowed by a mysterious Land Rover. Carter checks into the 'Las Vegas' guesthouse and sets about looking for a local informant named Albert Swift. Carter goes to the races and runs into Eric Paice, another gangster, who claims to be going straight. The Londoner trails him and discovers that Paice is the chauffeur to crime boss Cyril Kinnear, who is locked in a gang war with rival Cliff Brumby. Thorpe, one of Brumby's associates, tries to get Carter to take the train back to London, but Carter stays. He gradually realises that Doreen has appeared in a Kinnear-financed porn movie and that Brumby saw the film; he told Frank, who was going to go to the police. Carter then wreaks revenge on both gangs, throwing Brumby off a multi-storey car park, stabbing Swift and informing the police of Kinnear's activities. At the climax, Carter discovers that Eric Paice was the one who propositioned Doreen and also killed Frank. On a slag heap, at a colliery on the coast, Carter bludgeons Paice to death and dumps his body in the sea, before Carter is also cut down, by an assassin in the pay of Kinnear.

After the first draft was written, Michael Caine was approached by Klinger to play Jack Carter. Born Maurice Joseph Micklewhite in Bermondsey, in the East End of London, Caine had risen to become one of the biggest worldwide stars – he had just been voted best actor of 1970, by *Films and Filming* magazine. After years in supporting parts, his first starring roles had been in *Zulu* (1964), as Harry Palmer in *The Ipcress File* (1965) and the eponymous antihero of *Alfie* (1966), three of the finest British films of the decade. He had also made two caper movies: *Gambit* (1966 – with Shirley MacClaine and Herbert Lom) and *The Italian Job* (1969 – with Noël Coward, Benny Hill and a fleet of Mini Coopers). But these successes were interspersed with some odd choices: he'd just played the Captain, a bearded, Germanic-accented leader of a group of mercenaries in *The Last Valley* (1970).

With Caine involved (he also became uncredited co-producer), MGM wanted big stars for the rest of the cast too. One reported early casting was Telly Savalas as Kinnear, a role eventually taken by playwright John Osborne. Osborne had adapted his own plays for the screen: *Look Back in Anger*, *The Entertainer* and *Inadmissible Evidence*; he also won an Oscar for rewriting Henry Fielding's *Tom Jones* for Tony Richardson in 1963. Osborne's performance as crime lord Cyril Kinnear is immoral and soulless, involved in pornography, gambling and slot machines. One can only imagine what Savalas would have done with the Geordie role ('Oo luvs ya beeby, like?'). But MGM did manage to get Britt Ekland, the blonde, Stockholm-born actress, who was cast as Anna, Carter's lover in London and the wife of Carter's boss, Gerald Fletcher.

Ian Hendry, as chauffeur–henchman Eric Paice, was a regular in British TV and films, including *The Hill* and *Repulsion* (both 1965). He had played Dr David Keel, opposite Patrick Macnee (as John Steed), in the first series of *The Avengers* (1961–62). Hendry, born in Ipswich, had a jaded, crafty voice, expert at delivering sarcasm and blunt wit. His persona was vilely ideal for the despicable Paice; he had been Hodges's original choice for Carter.

The supporting cast was made up of the cream of British acting talent, particularly from TV. Glynn Edwards (cast as Albert Swift) had appeared with Caine in *Zulu* and *The Ipcress File*, and was later Dave Harris, the Winchester Club barman, in ITV's *Minder*. Bryan Mosley, as industrialist Brumby, played Alf Roberts in *Coronation Street*; in fact several cast members reappeared in the long-running British soap opera at one time or another, including the three female leads, Geraldine Moffatt, Dorothy White and Rosemarie Durham. Cast as Con, a southern hood on Carter's trail, George Sewell later appeared on both sides of the law in many TV cop shows, including *Softly Softly*, *The Sweeney*, *Z Cars*, *Special Branch* and *The Bill*, and played the detective superintendent in Jasper Carrot's comedy series *The Detectives*. Snappily dressed henchman Tony Beckley had been

'With me it's a full-time job, now behave yourself': Michael Caine gets tough in *Get Carter* (1971).

elegant 'Camp Freddie' in *The Italian Job*, Alun Armstrong (as Keith) was making his film debut at the beginning of what has proved to be a long and distinguished career, while Reg Niven (producer Klinger's chauffeur) had a bit part as Frank Carter's corpse.

With a budget of £750,000, filming began in spring 1970. *Get Carter* was shot in 38 days, on locations in and around Newcastle, and Tyne and Wear. The boat-side shootout was filmed at Wallsend Ferry Terminal; the ferry scenes were added when Hodges saw the location. The ferry travels between Wallsend and Hebburn, the site of Ken Hailes 'Turf Accountant', where Carter knifes Albert Swift. Carter's rendezvous with Margaret is on the Tyne Bridge walkway and later he scores the drugs he'll kill her with on the Newcastle Swing Bridge. Frank Carter's house, where he's laid out to rest, is in Frank Street, Benwell; Edna's 'Las Vegas' guesthouse is located in Coburg Street, Gateshead, Tyne and Wear; the 'Demon King's castle' (as Brumby's prospective restaurant is referred to by Glenda) is Gateshead multi-storey car park, currently at the centre of a preservation order dispute. 'The Heights', Kinnear's mansion, was shot at Dryderdale Hall, which had once belonged to Vincent Lander, who had been involved in actual slot-machine scams in working men's clubs; below the house, the police fish Margaret's corpse out of the lake. The final beach scene was filmed at Blackhall Rocks, a colliery, complete with a coal bucket cable-car system, dumping slag (and Paice) into the North Sea.

Posters advertised the film with the tagline 'Caine is Carter', the same kind of star-vehicle symbiosis between actor and character attempted several times in eponymously titled crime movies of this period, including Steve McQueen's *Bullit*, Clint Eastwood as *Dirty Harry* or Richard Roundtree as *Shaft*. But Caine's virtuoso villain, adrift in a world of disorder and vice, was closer to Caine than one might think. Having lived in the East End, Caine had seen men like Carter, a type of gangster who had never been depicted in British movies. As the actor noted, gangsters in British movies 'were either stupid or funny...I wanted to show that they're neither'. The mobster Caine based Carter on told him years later that he disliked the finished film, complaining that Carter had 'no family life...I've got a wife, a mortgage, one of my kids is in hospital. All you showed was the fancy side.'

Fancy or not, Carter is a violent man, with moments of frightening rage. This isn't the criminal Caine of *The Italian Job*, berating his gang's ineptitude in cockney tones: 'You're only supposed to blow the bloody doors off!' Here Carter is a psychotic killer, with moments of overt politeness followed by extreme violence. When Brumby squares up to Carter, the Londoner warns, 'You're a big man, but you're in bad shape – with me it's a full-time job, now behave yourself,' before laying Brumby out when he fails to heed this advice.

Later, Carter watches the flickering Super-8 pornographic movie *Teacher's Pet* on Glenda's bedside projector. The on-screen participants are Glenda, Albert Swift and Doreen; Carter, crushed, begins to cry. Composing himself, he makes his way upstairs to where Glenda is taking a bath. 'I want to give you an Oscar,' he says. Carter questions her about the other girl appearing in the film: 'Did my brother Frank find out?' She claims she doesn't know anything, but Carter loses his temper, lurching at her in a frenzy, raging, 'You lying bitch!' as he pushes her under the bath water. Later, when he has the evidence to blackmail Kinnear he telephones the crime boss and spits down the phone, 'Now listen carefully, you hairy-faced git,' before posting the incriminating reel to 'The Vice Squad, New Scotland Yard'. This was not the Michael Caine audiences had come to love, and a long way from his previous incarnations. The only link is Carter's sartorial elegance. Caine's clothes were made by tailor Dougie Hayward, who made suits for many celebrities, including two famous Moores: Bobby and Roger. Arriving in Newcastle, Carter wears his black funeral suit and trenchcoat for the entire film.

The Tyneside setting is highly effective and Carter's arrival highlights the old rivalries between gritty northerners and southern softies. Carter is defiantly an outsider, ordering his beer in a thin glass and smoking distinctive white-filtered French Gitane cigarettes. Hodges, in deploying north-eastern clichés (working men's clubs, docks and slag heaps, flat caps, awful pub singers and bingo halls), throws in everything, including the kitchen sink. The settings are at once ordinarily real and extraordinarily vivid. The rows of back-to-back terraced housing, so many of which have now been levelled, are Coronation Street, with walled yards and an outside privy. The pubs filled with smoke and locals, or the girl majorettes' marching band (the Pelaw Hussars, with their motto 'For Youth and Valour') add colour to Hodges's environment, as does the multi-storey car park (the bland concrete house-of-cards design that's seen in every city), the dockyard cranes and red-leaded rivet and girder bridges. In one club, as Carter chases Thorpe, it's 'Big Beat Night', with the usual huddle of girls dancing around handbags. Hodges's exceptional eye for detail and *mise-en-scène* gives the film a huge advantage over its contemporaries.

The scenes between Caine and Ian Hendry, as Eric Paice, Kinnear's shades-wearing, uniformed chauffeur, crackle with tension and jet-black humour. Their reacquaintance at a racetrack has since passed into film mythology. 'On your holidays?' asks Paice politely. 'No, I'm visiting relatives,' answers Carter, equally politely. 'Oh, that's nice.' 'It would be, if they were still living…a bereavement, a death in the family,' adds Carter. 'Oh, I'm sorry to hear that.' 'That's alright Eric.' Carter, quietly menacing, reaches out and removes Paice's shades: 'Do you know, I'd almost forgotten what your eyes looked like? They're still the same…piss holes in the snow.' 'You've still got a sense of humour,' says Paice. 'Yes, I retained that Eric.' Ian Hendry arrived drunk to rehearse the racetrack scene the night before filming and became abusive, but the fact that he was the original choice for Carter probably rankled and brought out the best in his performance as Paice.

Hodges unsettlingly fuses gang violence with sex and vice. The film begins with the Fletcher brothers watching a dirty slide show and trying to dissuade Carter from attending Frank's funeral, perhaps already realising the trouble it's going to cause. But family honour is more important, even though it is insinuated later by Keith that Frank thought Jack was 'a shit' and may be Doreen's father. One scene sees Britt Ekland, as Anna, having phone sex with Carter. He also sleeps with Edna (the 'Las Vegas' landlady) and Glenda. Edna becomes suspicious when she finds a gun in his room: 'If you're a traveller, I'm bloody Twiggy.' Glenda is Kinnear's leading lady, who lives in a flat paid for by rival Brumby. The scene where she and Carter make love echoes the opening scene of *Performance* (1970), with the inter-cutting between a sexual encounter and a speeding car. In *Get Carter* shots of Glenda driving her white Sunbeam are fractured into a montage of details – her gloved hand changing gear, her foot pumping the accelerator, the rev-counter needle – cross-cut with her undressing and their lovemaking. Their post-coital conversation is stilted, accentuated by the eerie, out-of-context whistling wind on the soundtrack of an interior scene.

The violence in *Get Carter* is cruel, vicious and casual. There is a messy, sordid realism to the murders that reinforce their authenticity, making *Get Carter* one of the most intense films of its era. It is a violent hybrid of revenge thriller and detective story. Carter solves the case and Hodges references great detective fiction, with the gangster reading Raymond Chandler's 'Farewell My Lovely' on the train up from London (ironically, he also shares the carriage with his eventual killer, hired assassin 'J'). There are two rival gangs, as in Dashiell Hammett's 'Red Harvest', with Carter, like the Continental-Op, trapped between the two; Brumby tries to use Carter to get back at Kinnear, just as Brumby had used Frank. For this, Carter punches Brumby unconscious and drops him off the penultimate storey of a high-rise car park. Elsewhere, a hood has his head smashed through a car window; another is dragged along the street by his seatbelt. Carter is surprised in bed by Con and Peter, two London hoods, and turfs them out of the house at shotgun-point, still naked – 'Come on Jack, put it away,' quips Con, 'you know you won't use it.' 'The gun he means,' adds Peter. Later the pair, accompanied by Paice, shotgun-ambush Carter on the Wallsend ferry, before gleefully informing him that gang boss Gerald Fletcher has found out about Carter's affair with his wife. Carter shoots Peter, and in retribution the crooks shunt Glenda's Sunbeam into the river, unaware that she has been locked in her own boot by Carter – a casual moment where the story's grim ironies are at their most effective. In the most disturbing scene in the film, Carter drives Margaret into woodland, orders her to strip, gags her and then administers a lethal injection, before dragging her into the undergrowth.

Kinnear's underworld associates are reprobates. Albert Swift is a twisted, com-pulsive gambler and ex-schoolmate of Carter's, who is stabbed to death with a flick-knife by Carter in the back yard of a bookies. Eric Paice, the worst of the bunch, enticed Doreen to appear in blue movies and laughed 'Good' when he found out that Frank was Jack's brother, as he poured whisky down Frank's throat. This situation is reversed later, with Carter's horrific revenge on Paice atop a slag heap. Carter makes him down a bottle of scotch before caving his head in with the butt of a shotgun. But eventually the villains do 'Get Carter'. He's felled by a single assassin's bullet through the forehead (in a set-up reminiscent of the storm drain ambush in Boorman's *Point Blank*) and left lying on the beach, the oily sea and overcast sky fading to black.

Get Carter's music was composed by Roy Budd and performed by his trio for £450. Budd played piano and harpsichord, with Chris Karan (previously of the Dudley Moore Trio) on drums, percussion and tablas, and Jeff Cline on double bass and bass guitar. The title music, 'Carter Takes a Train', has become a classic. The double bass plays the same ascending ten-note riff throughout the entire piece, the tablas chattering off the beat, while a glacial harpsichord adds a haunting edge to the jazz groove. Later, a shaker and electric piano solo are overlaid on the looped, bass-driven rhythm, until finally the tablas stutter to a halt, as the train arrives in Newcastle. The incidental music is similarly effective. The cool boogie-woogie of 'The Girl in the Car' that accompanies Glenda speeding along in her Sunbeam Alpine sports car (Carter himself drives a less-than-glamorous H-Reg Ford Cortina) and the Bach-esque harpsichord toccata of 'Goodbye Eric', as Paice's body is spirited out to sea. Most effective is the shimmering, haunting harpsichord of 'Manhunt', as dawn breaks at Kinnear's debauched party, the police Rovers and Land Rovers spew officers around the property and Margaret's corpse is fished out of the lake.

There are also several songs featured on the soundtrack, again performed by Budd's trio. Additional musicians on these tracks include guitarists Brian Daly and

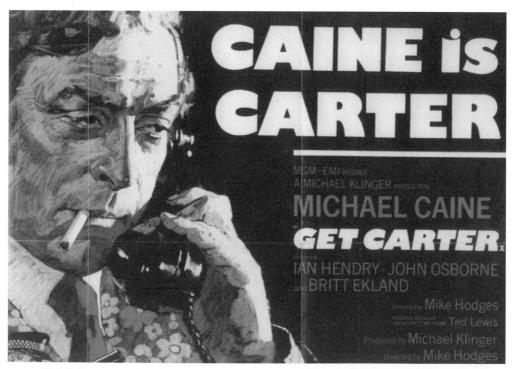

1971 UK poster advertising Mike Hodges's *Get Carter*.

Judd Proctor. 'Looking for Someone' and 'Getting Nowhere in a Hurry' are playing on the jukebox in the long bar-room Carter visits at the beginning of the film; elsewhere a pub singer belts out 'How About You?', 'Livin' should be that Way' plays in the Big Beat nightclub and 'Love is a Four-letter Word' accompanies Kinnear's house party. Mickey Gallagher and John Turnball sang vocals on some of the songs, all of which were co-written by Budd and Jack Fishman, the soundtrack's producer. The enduring popularity of the score is reinforced by the fact that a 2005 Budd career overview CD was titled 'Get Budd'.

Hodges notes that *Get Carter*'s entire creative process – from being contacted by producer Klinger to the film being screened for MGM production executives in October 1970 – was very quick, a mere 32 weeks. The advertising campaign asked 'What happens when a professional killer violates the code? Get Carter!' It depicted Caine with a cigarette dangling from his mouth, while on the phone to Ekland, or a low-angle shot of him brandishing a shotgun. *Get Carter* was released in the UK by MGM-EMI in March 1971. It was certified an X in November 1970, after the censor had trimmed Albert's stabbing. UK critics predominantly disliked it. George Melly equated the film with 'a bottle of neat gin swallowed before breakfast', while the *Evening News* called it 'a revolting, bestial, horribly violent piece of cinema'. The *Daily Express* was more forgiving, saying: 'I'd get Carter if I were you...he certainly got me.' Ian Hendry was nominated for a BAFTA as best supporting actor. Hodges recalls that following the film's release, 'Caine's cold eyes were everywhere, staring at me from buses, billboards, newspapers'. London double-deckers had matching posters on their rear windows – 'Caine is...Carter' – and business in the UK was fantastic.

Unfortunately, when it was released stateside in March 1971, it was rated 'Restricted' and stuck on a double bill with MGM's awful Frank Sinatra/Jack Elam time-waster *Dirty Dingus McGee*. But it was quite well received by critics. The *New York Times* said Caine 'tints and glints like a bomb encased in steel'. Pauline Kael in the *New Yorker* noted, 'There is nobody to root for but the smartly dressed sexual athlete and professional killer (Michael Caine) in this English gangland picture, which is so calculatedly cool and soulless and nastily erotic, that it seems to belong to a new genre of virtuoso viciousness. What makes the movie unusual is the metallic elegance and the single-minded proficiency with which it adheres to its sadism-for-the-connoisseur formula.' In Italy, the film was released simply as *Carter*; in Spain it was *Asesino Implacable* ('Relentless Assassin') and in France *La Loi de Milieu* ('The Law of the [social] Environment').

In Hodges's eyes at least, it really was grim up north, and *Get Carter*'s ultra-realism paved the way for *The Sweeney*, *The Professionals* and a host of other similarly gritty UK TV crime dramas throughout the seventies; *The Sweeney*'s two spin-off movies, *Sweeney!* (1976) and *Sweeney 2* (1978), prove what a popular and first-rate cop team Regan (John Thaw) and Carter (Dennis Waterman) were. Britain also produced some excessively violent and, after Cagney, mother-fixated psychopaths, epitomised by Richard Burton's turn in *Villain* (1971). Later British gangster derivatives, part of a crime film renaissance in the UK, include cockney Brit-flicks like *Lock, Stock and Two Smoking Barrels*, shot in the burnished nostalgic hues of a Guinness advert, with about as much soul. There was even an abominable remake of *Get Carter* (2000) starring Sylvester Stallone as Carter, avenging his brother Richie's murder; in typical Hollywood fashion, Carter survives. Mickey Rourke, looking like a waxwork of William Shatner, played villain Cyrus Paice; Caine himself played a brief role as Cliff Brumby and said of the film: 'I take responsibility for the ones where my name's over the title, otherwise...' 'The Truth Hurts' ran the tagline; so does watching this film.

In 1971 Hodges didn't really consolidate the success of *Get Carter*. He made *Pulp*, again with Caine, in 1972. Caine played a pulp fiction writer hired to ghost-write the autobiography of a real gangster, Preston Gilbert (Mickey Rooney), who plans to make certain revelations that could jeopardise the career of a high-powered politician, making Gilbert the target for assassins. Shot in Malta, *Pulp* was well received, *Variety* calling it 'a reasonably entertaining piece of rococo recall...at its best as visual camp', but it bombed at the box office. In 1977, Caine was supposed to make another film directed by Hodges, as Kim Philby, the notorious spy, but Philby himself vetoed the casting. 'It seemed he didn't like the idea of someone

'I'd almost forgotten what your eyes looked like': Carter gets reacquainted with Eric Paice during a day at the races; Michael Caine and Ian Hendry in *Get Carter* (1971).

of my class playing him, which I thought was spoken like a true Communist,' said Caine.

Hodges eventually returned to the crime genre, with the unusual *A Prayer for the Dying* (1987), with Mickey Rourke cast as an IRA hitman on the run. He then directed *Croupier* (1998), starring Clive Owen as Jack Manfred, a budding fiction writer embroiled in the seedy world of gangsters, gamblers and a casino knockover, when he becomes a croupier to make ends meet. This environment eventually provides him with plenty of material for his best-selling, autobiographical 'I, Croupier'. This was a return to form by Hodges, who worked again with Owen on the *Get Carter*-esque brotherly revenge flick *I'll Sleep When I'm Dead* (2003). But Hodges has never equalled the power of his film debut, a milestone in crime cinema. And *Get Carter* is Caine's finest film – it is unique in the history of British crime films and remains unsurpassed.

12

'We're all on the hustle'

— *Shaft* (1971)

Credits:
DIRECTOR – Gordon Parks
PRODUCER – Joel Freeman
ASSOCIATE PRODUCER – David Golden (for Shaft Productions)
STORY – Ernest Tidyman
SCREENPLAY – Ernest Tidyman and John D.F. Black
DIRECTOR OF PHOTOGRAPHY – Urs Furrer
EDITOR – Hugh A. Robertson
ART DIRECTOR – Emanuel Gerard
COSTUMES – Joseph Aulisi
MUSIC – Isaac Hayes
Metrocolor
A Sterling Silliphant-Roger Lewis Production
Released by Metro-Goldwyn-Mayer/Shaft Productions
98 minutes
Cast:
Richard Roundtree (John Shaft)/Moses Gunn (Bumpy Jonas)/
Charles Cioffi (Lieutenant Vic Androzzi, NYPD)/Christopher St
John (Ben Buford)/Gwenn Mitchell (Ellie Moore)/Lawrence
Pressmen (Sergeant Tom Hannon)/Sherri Brewer (Marcy Jonas)/
Joseph Leon (Captain Byron Leibowitz)/Arnold Johnson (Cul,
shoeshine man)/Dominic Barto and George Struss (Patsy and
Carmen, Mafia hoods)/Drew Bundini Brown (Willy, Bumpy's
lieutenant)/Tommy Lane and Al Kirk (Leroy and Sims, Bumpy's
men)/Lee Steele (Marty, blind newspaper vendor)/Robin Nolan
(Waitress in coffee shop)/Betty Bressler (Mrs Androzzi)/Gordon
Parks (Buford's ex-landlord)/Rex Robbins (Rollie, bartender)/
Camille Yarbrough (Dina Green)/Margaret Warncke (Linda)/
Shimen Rusjin (Sam, the doctor)/Antonio Fargas (Bunky,

informant)/Donny Burks and Tony King (Remmy and Davies,
Buford's men)/Clee Burtonia (Sonny)

*　　*　　*

In Hollywood in the late sixties and early seventies, there were several black leading
men, such as Harry Belafonte and Sydney Poitier. But it wasn't until the arrival of
ex-pro footballer Jim Brown that black American audiences had a genuine cinema
action hero. Raised in Manhasset, Long Island, Brown was a star player for the
Cleveland Browns, 1957–67. While still a player, he was cast in *Rio Conchos* (1964),
but retired from football in 1967, when he began appearing in films, including *The
Dirty Dozen* (1967), *Dark of the Sun* (1968 – *The Mercenaries* in the UK), *100 Rifles*
(1968) and *The Split* (1968), a prototype black crime drama, which fittingly featured
the robbery of a football stadium. In the early seventies a black American cinema, of
directors, crew members and technicians, still didn't exist, and on TV the Black
Entertainment Television channel (BET) was a very long way off.

An important film in the development of black cinema in Hollywood was *Cotton
Comes to Harlem* (1970), based on the 1964 novel by Chester Himes. Here, two
Harlem detectives, named Grave Digger Jones (played by Godfrey Cambridge) and
Coffin Ed Johnson (Raymond St Jacques), attempt to locate stolen charity money.
A sequel, *Come Back Charleston Blue*, followed in 1972. Through the popularity of
such films, and in particular the underground success of Melvin Van Peebles's *Sweet
Sweetback's Baad Asssss Song* (1971 – with director-producer-writer-composer
Peebles also starring as the title criminal, a pimp on the run having shot a cop),
black directors were able to attract finance for a new type of crime film, dubbed
'black-exploitation' film, or 'blaxploitation'.

Director Gordon Parks was at the forefront of this blaxploitation explosion. He
had worked as a pianist in a bordello in Minnesota and as a runner for drug gangs
in Chicago; he also had played professional basketball and spent 20 years as a
photographer for *Life*. He made his directorial debut in 1969 with *The Learning
Tree*, based on his own autobiographical book about his upbringing as the youngest
of 15 children in Kansas. His next project, an action movie called *Shaft*, couldn't
have been more different.

The screenplay for *Shaft* was written by Ernest Tidyman (the author of the
hugely successful *The French Connection*) and John D.F. Black, based on Tidyman's
1970 novel. In the script, New York private investigator John Shaft is attacked in
his office by two hoods, one of whom is thrown out of the window. Shaft discovers
they are in the pay of Harlem racketeer Bumpy Jonas. Questioned by police
Lieutenant Androzzi, Shaft is unco-operative, but is told that he will lose his
licence and gun permit if he doesn't co-operate – he has 48 hours on the streets to
find out what's going on. Soon afterwards Bumpy contacts Shaft and hires him to
locate his daughter, Marcy, who has been kidnapped by Ben Buford, a militant.

Shaft tracks down Buford and finds that he isn't the kidnapper. The two team up when some of Buford's men are killed in a Mafia ambush. It transpires the Mafia are trying to take over Harlem and have seized Marcy as bargaining power, forcing Bumpy to relinquish his monopoly. Shaft makes contact with the Mafia and arranges a meeting, but as he tries to save Marcy, he is wounded and her captors take her to a nearby hotel. Shaft, Buford and his gang, some posing as hotel staff, infiltrate the building and in a daring raid snatch Marcy from the Mafia. As cops swarm around the hotel, Shaft calls Androzzi and tells him: 'Your case just busted wide open,' leaving the cop to close it.

In Tidyman's original story Shaft was white, but Parks cast Richard Roundtree as the eponymous hero. An ex-*Ebony* magazine model, he had made his inauspicious screen debut in Allen Funt's X-rated spin-off from his *Candid Camera* TV show, called *What Do You Say to a Naked Lady?* (1970). Roundtree had the right blend of action man acting ability, charm and sex-appeal required for the role of Shaft; the fact that he was an ex-model meant he looked great in the Joseph Aulisi-designed clothes. Moses Gunn, a stage actor who moved into movies in the early sixties, was cast as crime kingpin Bumpy Jonas, who conveyed menace by perpetually puffing on a cigar; Jonas was partially inspired by Harlem's black godfather, Ellsworth 'Bumpy' Johnson. Christopher St John appeared as Buford, and Charles Cioffi was ideal for crotchety Lieutenant Androzzi, as was Drew Bundini Brown, as Bumpy's argumentative sidekick, Willy (who refers to Shaft as 'Snow White'). Two Mafia hitmen, Carmen and Patsy, who case Shaft's apartment from the 'No Name Bar' across the street, were threateningly played by George Straus and Dominic Barto. Antonio Fargas, as easily bribed informant 'Bunky', went on to great success replaying a similar persona as Huggy Bear in TV's *Starsky and Hutch*, while director Parks himself cameoed as a tenement landlord.

Modestly budgeted at just over $1 million, *Shaft* was made on location in early 1971 in Manhattan, New York City (the calendar in Shaft's office reads 'Jan and Feb 1971'). Shaft's bachelor pad apartment, the 'Café Reggio' and the 'No Name Bar' were in Greenwich Village. Shaft's office overlooked Times Square and Buford's Amsterdam Avenue hideout was in Harlem. In Bumpy's Harlem office, a model dustbin wagon with 'Bumpy's Sanitation Service' livery jokingly hints at Bumpy's efforts in keeping the streets 'clean'. As Shaft hails a taxi, cinema hoardings publicise *Love Story*, *Cotton Comes to Harlem* and Sidney Poitier's *They Call Me MISTER Tibbs*, while on his way to Harlem, Shaft passes an advertisement: 'Michael Caine – *Get Carter*'. Editor Hugh A. Robertson filmed *Soul in Cinema: Filming Shaft on Location*, a documentary of Parks's shooting of the 'No Name Bar' scene and the stairwell ambush of Buford's men, sequences that involved much shattered sugar glass and squibbed fake blood.

The title sequence was filmed on 42nd Street and into Times Square, under the film marquees emblazoned with *The Scalphunters* (starring Ossie Davis, the director of *Cotton Comes to Harlem*), *Rough Night in Jericho* and *Barbarella*, with Isaac Hayes's

'Theme from *Shaft*' scoring Roundtree's confident stride. The instrumental section, played by the Bar Keys and Movement, deploys pulsating bass, stuttering wah-wah guitar, Hayes's own distinctive piano playing, a descending four-note horn motif, ascending flute runs and the now famous *Pearl and Dean*-style blasts of brass and strings. 'Hot Buttered Soul Man' Hayes auditioned for Roundtree's role, but was contracted to compose the music instead. As the piece becomes more layered, a dialogue strikes up between Hayes's smooth, largely spoken, vocal and his backing singers: 'Who's the black private dick, that's a sex machine with all the chicks?' answered by a falsetto: 'Shaft!'; 'Damn right,' intones Hayes. 'Who is the man that would risk his neck for his brother man?' – 'Shaft!'; 'Can you dig it?'

Described by Bumpy as 'the spade detective', Shaft's actions aren't that different to the classic gumshoe detective heroes of Chandler and Hammett, though he is more upmarket and stylish. Shaft has a tastefully furnished Greenwich Village pad and keeps a spare gun 'on ice' in the fridge. Director Parks is familiar with genre convention and Shaft's informants are newspaper vendors, shoe-shiners and myriad fly-by-nights; the only real differences between Shaft and his predecessors are that he's black and that his search for Buford around the tenements of Harlem is scored by the moving Motown of 'Soulsville'. A later derivative of Shaft's Chandler-esque private eye was Fred Williamson in *Black Eye* (1974).

Although Hayes surmises in 'Theme from *Shaft*' that 'He's a complicated man, but no one understands him but his woman', Shaft has little psychological depth – he's as one-dimensional as James Bond. He is also as misogynistic as Fleming's hero, epitomised by a phone call from his girlfriend Ellie. 'I love you,' she confesses. 'Yea, I know,' answers Shaft, 'take it easy,' which is hardly a reassuring. 'I love you too.' But *Shaft* was publicised as a forceful mixture: 'Hotter than Bond, Cooler than Bullit', alluding to the hero's womanising charm and tough action facade.

The relatively small-scale action spots are spread thinly throughout the film and Parks sustains the tension well through dialogue, never allowing the pace to flag. Shaft throws an assailant through the window of his office and outwits two Mafiosi in a bar, but he has to play dirty – smashing one over the head with a bottle. For the finale, wounded Shaft recovers quickly; two scenes previously he has been hit at least twice with machine-gun fire. He abseils down the outside of the hotel, smashing through the window and saves Marcy from her captors, while Buford's men turn on a high-pressure fire hose in the corridor, then make their escape in a trio of yellow cabs.

In addition to its trendsetting score and fine action, *Shaft* has a superior script, with 'jive-talk' vernacular deployed to good effect; the dialogue is peppered with pithy jargon: a plethora of 'mans', 'asses', 'cats' and 'can you dig its?'. 'You're a cagey spook, Bumpy,' comments Shaft. 'You ride a tall horse, Mister Shaft,' is the boss's answer, when the detective wants more money. Androzzi wants Shaft to tell him what he thinks is brewing in Harlem, and the hero answers: 'You want me to pigeon? I just said, "Up yours baby".' 'One hand washes the other,' observes the cop.

The New York setting is highly effective. The general rule of thumb in blax-ploitation crime dramas is 'uptown' bad, 'downtown' good. Anyone from uptown (i.e. Harlem) is bad news and in *Shaft* those from uptown are obtrusive on the downtown streets, and vice versa. The subtext to the action is the turf war: Bumpy versus the Mafia. Bumpy has tried unsuccessfully to kidnap a Mafia operative as leverage and the Mob have taken his daughter as retribution – they want Harlem. The case is not really Shaft's scene, but he takes it when the money is too much to turn down. As Bumpy tells Shaft, 'A lot of cats hate my guts…I got money, you spend it and you find her.' Androzzi notes that the turf war is hood against hood, but unfortunately to the outside world it will look like black against white; it could mean war, with troops called out and 'tanks on Broadway', but this element of the plot is quite obscure – it's the resolution of the kidnapping that is important to Parks.

Similarly, Buford's gang are described as 'militants', though their agenda is politically cloudy. Androzzi mentions by name the Black Panthers and the Young Lords, and Buford's bunch are called the 'La Mumbas'. Shaft notes that Buford has lost his edge: 'When you lead that revolution, whitey better be standing still.' Buford's militants are Bumpy's army; he employs them at $10,000 a head against

Soul Man: Richard Roundtree as private eye John Shaft, on
the trail of kidnappers, in Gordon Parks's 1971 classic *Shaft*.

the Mafia for distinctly non-political ends. But politics aside, Bumpy comments to Shaft and Buford, 'We're all on the hustle.'

Probably the worst crimes perpetrated in the blaxploitation genre were against fashion, with huge, sidewalk-brushing flares, flapping, yacht-sail collars and voluminous Afros the norm. *Shaft* is relatively restrained in this department, with the Mafia sporting classic trench coats and fedoras, and Bumpy's mob slightly more stylish, with plaid and camel popular choices. Shaft himself dons a selection of turtlenecks, a long brown leather coat and an all-in-black leather combo that resembles Elvis's *1968 Comeback Special* outfit. Blaxploitation derivatives were guilty of far worse fashion *faux pas*, with King George (Robert DoQui), the pimp in *Coffy* (1973), possibly the worst example. He steps out of his limo sporting a canary yellow flared zip-up jump-suit and matching cape, a brown fedora (with a white feather in the hatband), giant Elton John saucer shades and a silver-topped cane, somewhat justifying his demise at the hands of a rival gang.

Shaft was released in the US in July 1971, rated R. The poster read SHAFT in huge lettering, with hardly a mention of Roundtree, or any other cast members. The public was encouraged to completely identify Roundtree with the hero – 'Shaft's his name, Shaft's his game' ran the advertising, adding, 'The Mob want Harlem back. They got Shaft...up to here.' The trailer closed on the strange line: 'If you wanna see *Shaft*, ask your mamma!' It was X rated in the UK, for violence and nudity. The *Monthly Film Bulletin* said of the film, 'In the main a highly workmanlike and enjoyable thriller,' while in *Newsweek*'s review of the copyist *Trouble Man* the following year, they called *Shaft* 'the Father Divine of the genre'. In the film, Shaft reclines on the sofa and reads a copy of *Essence* magazine (which was co-founded by Parks); the magazine's review of the film stated, '*Shaft* is the first picture to show a black man who leads a life free of racial torment. He is black and proud of it, but not obsessed with it.' Other publications noted that previous black actors – in particular Poitier and Brown – were still making films for white audiences. The attendance for *Cotton Comes to Harlem* the previous year was 70 per cent black, but *Shaft* was a huge crossover hit and grossed over $7 million in the US. Isaac Hayes received an Academy Award Nomination for Best Original Dramatic Score, but won the Oscar for Best Original Song with his 'Theme from *Shaft*', as writer of the music and lyrics. The 45-single release of the record topped the US charts, made number 4 in the UK and is still popular today, enjoying a new lease of life as a cellphone ring tone. In Italy the film was called *Shaft: Il Detective*, while in France it was *Shaft, les Nuits Rouge de Harlem* ('Shaft, the Red Nights of Harlem').

Ernest Tidyman wrote six 'Shaft' novel sequels, including 'Goodbye Mr Shaft' and 'Shaft's Carnival of Killers'. In addition, there were two more 'Shaft' films, neither capturing the soul of the original. *Shaft's Big Score* (1972), again directed by Parks, came closer, with a replay of the gang rivalry between Bumpy and the Mafia and including more explicit references to Shaft's two inspirations, Bond and Bullit. *Big Score* featured car, speedboat and helicopter chases and a finale in New

York harbour, with Shaft this time being hired to track down missing charity funds. *Shaft in Africa* (1973) saw John Guillermin take over as director and the Four Tops provided the catchy theme song ('Are you man enough? Big and bad enough?'). The film was shot partly in Ethiopia; this time Shaft found himself 'out of my turf', mixed up with slave traders. Such was the *Shaft* character's popularity, Roundtree reprised the role in an eponymous CBS TV series spin-off, which lasted for eight episodes from 1973–74 (rivals NBC countered with their own series, *Tenafly*). Both the *Shaft* film sequels closely resemble *Live and Let Die* (1973), the most blaxploitation-influenced of the Bond series. Roger Moore's first outing as Bond was a comic book adventure set in Harlem, New Orleans, the Louisiana bayous and the Caribbean island of San Monique. It mixed villainous gangsta Mr Big (and his double Dr Katanga), metal-clawed giant Tee Hee, mystic Baron Samedi and a voodoo subplot, with the usual motorboat and car chases, most memorably involving a double-decker bus and a low bridge.

But following *Shaft*'s success, blaxploitation really caught fire, and its popularity lasted until the mid-seventies. Genre regulars include Jim Brown, Ron O'Neal, Antonio Fargas, Vonetta McGee, Fred Williamson, Jim Kelly and Richard Pryor. Brown appeared in *Black Gunn* (1972), *Slaughter* (1972 – a vengeful Vietnam vet: 'It's not only his name…it's his business'), *Slaughter's Big Rip-off* (1973) and *Three the Hard Way* (1974 – about neo-nazis infecting the US water supply). Ron O'Neal starred in the controversial pro-drug-dealing *Superfly* (1972 – slang for cocaine), which saw him as a pusher named Youngblood Priest (complete with crucifix), who drives a custom-made Eldorado car. It had the advantage of a popular Curtis Mayfield score, was directed by Parks's son (Gordon Jnr) and is the all-time second-highest-grossing blaxploitation film, after *Shaft*.

Elsewhere there was the big-budget, Harlem-set *Across 110th Street* (1972 – with Anthony Quinn and Yaphet Kotto), featuring Bobby Womack's hit song of the same name. Other entries included *Hammer* (1972 – a boxing drama with Fred Williamson and Vonetta McGee), *Melinda* (1972 – a vendetta, with McGee and Calvin Lockhart) and *Hit!* (1973 – starring Billy Dee Williams and Richard Pryor), directed by Sydney J. Furie of *Ipcress File* fame. *Trouble Man* (1972) was the first venture of the writer and producer of *Shaft*, Black and Freeman, and starred Robert Hooks as 'Mr T', with the tagline 'He'll give you peace of mind – piece by piece'. In one of the most enduring films of the era, Tamara Dobson played the title role in *Cleopatra Jones* (1973), a CIA narc (she reprised the role in *Cleopatra Jones and the Casino of Gold* – 1975), while one of the most financially successful films, now largely forgotten, was *The Mack* (1973), concerning pimps, starring Max Julien and Richard Pryor. Prostitution was also the focus for *The Candy Tangerine Man* (1975). Stand-up comedian Rudy Ray Moore had a smash with his wild spoof karate-gangster movies *Dolemite* (1974) and *The Human Tornado* (1976 – *Dolemite II*).

In the seventies there was also a trend for black cast remakes of classic crime movies. These included *Cool Breeze* (1972 – a retread of *The Asphalt Jungle*, with Jim

Watkins and Thalmus Rasulala) and *Hit Man* (1972 – *Get Carter*, blaxploitation-style, with Bernie Casey in the Carter role). *Black Caesar* (1973 – also released as *The Godfather of Harlem*, thereby managing to rip off two immensely popular films in its title) was advertised as 'Hail Caesar…The Cat with the .45 calibre claws'; despite ending like the downbeat Edward G. Robinson classic, a sequel, *Hell up in Harlem* (1973), featured the same character. Also treated to a makeover was Warren Beatty's *Shampoo*, with *Black Shampoo* (1976), featuring John Daniels as a hairdresser up against gangsters, while *Thomasine and Bushrod* (1974) derived from another Beatty movie, *Bonnie and Clyde*.

Crime blaxploitation was blended with kung fu to create some popular hybrids. Jim Kelly, who had appeared in *Enter the Dragon* (1973), made *Black Belt Jones* (1973 – where the Mafia try to take over a karate school), Fred Williamson starred in *That Man Bolt* (1973) and Rockne Tarkington was *Black Samson* (1973). Ex-*Playboy* model Jeannie Bell starred as 'a one-mama massacre squad' in *TNT Jackson* (1975), described in advertising as 'TNT Jackson, she'll put you in traction'. Along similar lines, there was *Ebony, Ivory and Jade* (1976), also released as *Foxforce* (and name-checked by Uma Thurman in *Pulp Fiction*). *Shaft* composer Isaac Hayes even appeared in a couple of cash-in movies: the Italian/US *Three Tough Guys* (1974 – directed by Duccio Tessari) and *Truck Turner* (1974), as a modern-day bounty hunter with the cheery tagline 'If he gets you, you're cold meat'.

Apart from Richard Roundtree, probably the most famous exponent of the genre was Pam Grier, a beautiful, athletic actress who became a star via a series of action-filled escapades; as trailers assured – 'Have no fear…Pam Grier is here!' After a series of exploitative prison dramas, her 1973 breakthrough was as the eponymous heroine of *Coffy*, a nurse by day, who exacts bloody revenge on drug pushers by night. At the beginning of the film we find Coffy mourning her sister's addiction to narcotics, so she goes undercover in the seedy world of clubs and pimps, often in the guise of her sexy alter ego, 'Mystique'. With its good production values, *Coffy* remains the definitive Grier vehicle and one of the top films in the cycle – *Charlie's Angels* with ultraviolence and language to match, though recent DVD releases are still slightly cut (in particular a shotgun blast to the head), giving a fair indication of how uncompromising these films were. Grier also made *Foxy Brown* (1974 – 'Don't mess aroun' with Foxy Brown'), followed by *Sheba Baby* (1975 – as private investigator Sheba Shayne) and *Friday Foster* (1975 – based on a comic strip fashion photographer), two lighter, less violent outings. Grier was engaged to Richard Pryor (they made *Greased Lighting* together in 1977), but her career fizzled and she spent the eighties and most of the nineties in low-budget productions, which is astonishing when in 1975 she was named as the third most bankable female star in the US, after Barbra Streisand and Liza Minnelli.

In subsequent decades, there have been hundreds of parody references to blaxploitation movies, with huge Afro gags the most popular by far. The production design and soundtracks of the genuine article are sufficiently way-out not to need further stylisation. Probably the most sustained example is Keenen Ivory Wayans's *I'm Gonna Git You Sucka* (1988), set in 'Any Ghetto, USA' and starring Bernie Casey, Jim Brown, Isaac Hayes and Antonio Fargas (as 'Flyguy'). The most wretched is *Undercover Brother* (2002), with the hero escaping from the bad guys' lair in the climax with parachuting flares. Although it features clips from *Shaft* and *Foxy Brown*, stars Chris Kattan and Denise Richards are no Roundtree and Grier, nor even Jim Brown and Vonetta McGee. More successfully, in his UK TV show, comedian Lenny Henry married Roundtree's screen persona to Barry White's 'Walrus of Love' voice and Tom Jones's stage moves in a creation known as 'Theopholis P. Wildebeast'.

Blaxploitation movies continue to be acknowledged as influential. Roundtree won the 1993 MTV Movie 'Lifetime Achievement Award' for his role as John Shaft. Director Quentin Tarantino is a huge fan of the genre; he gave Samuel L Jackson a Ron O'Neal-style moustache in *Pulp Fiction* (1994) and cast the genre's female icon Pam Grier as *Jackie Brown* (1997), while referencing numerous key works of the genre in films and interviews. Today's gangsta rappers, with their conspicuous 'bling' wealth, perpetuate the memory of *Superfly* and *The Mack*, while R 'n' B stars Jay-Z and Beyoncé Knowles recorded a duet entitled '03 Bonnie and Clyde', complete with lovers-on-the-run promotional video.

The cycle came around fully in 2000, when Samuel L. Jackson starred as the hero's nephew in a *Shaft* sequel for the MTV generation. Detective John Shaft (Jackson) is on the New York police force. He investigates the racially motivated murder of a black youth outside a bar by Walter Wade Jnr, a rich kid racist, who later jumps bail. Two years on, Shaft is now a narcotics agent; when Wade is eventually re-arrested he makes bail again and Shaft quits, embarking on a personal vendetta against him. Wade is now involved with Hispanic drug dealer Peoples Hernandez. With the help of his uncle, private eye John Shaft (still played by Richard Roundtree), and a cop, Carmen Vasquez (Vanessa Williams), Shaft aims to put Wade in jail, or at least in hospital.

Shaft (2000) briefly looks at the difficulties of being a black cop, with racism on the street and in the force; policeman Shaft is 'Too black for the uniform, too blue for the brothers'. But most of the dialogue is along the lines of 'You the man, Shaft!' and 'His ass is mine', and after a promising opening, the film deteriorates. When Shaft turns in his badge by hurling it across a courtroom at a bail-granting judge, Bruce Lee throwing-star fashion, believability jumps out of the window, and the rest of the film is little more than a standard urban crime thriller. It is a TV movie with a big-name cast, though it was a nice touch to cast original *Shaft* director Gordon Parks in a cameo as 'Mr P', a patron in the Lenox lounge. As an older and wiser Shaft, Roundtree's charisma shines, proving that after all these years, he's still the man.

13

'Do I feel lucky?'

— *Dirty Harry* (1971)

Credits:

DIRECTOR AND PRODUCER – Don Siegel
EXECUTIVE PRODUCER – Robert Daly
STORY – Harry Julian Fink and Rita M. Fink
SCREENPLAY – Harry Julian Fink, Rita M. Fink, Dean Reisner and
    John Milius
DIRECTOR OF PHOTOGRAPHY – Bruce Surtees
EDITOR – Carl Pingitore
ART DIRECTOR – Dale Hennessey
MUSIC COMPOSER AND CONDUCTOR – Lalo Schifrin
Technicolor/Panavision
Interiors filmed at Universal Studios
A Malpaso/Warner Bros co-production
Released by Warner Bros
102 minutes

Cast:

Clint Eastwood (Inspector Harry Francis Callahan)/Harry
Guardino (Lieutenant Al Bressler)/Reni Santoni (Inspector
Chico Gonzalez)/Andy Robinson ('Scorpio')/John Vernon (The
Mayor)/John Larch (Chief of Police)/John Mitchum (Inspector
Frank Di Georgio)/Mae Mercer (Mrs Russell)/Lyn Edgington
(Norma)/Ruth Kobart (Marcella Platt, bus driver)/Woodrow
Parfrey (Mr Jaffe)/Josef Sommer (DA William T. Rothko)/
William Paterson (Judge Bannerman)/James Nolan (Liquor store
proprietor)/Maurice S. Argent (Sid Kleinman, radio expert)/Jo
de Winter (Miss Willis, secretary)/Craig G. Kelly (Sgt Reineke)/
Charles Washburn (Steve, police doctor)/Diana Davidson
(Rooftop swimmer)/Lois Foraker (Hot Mary)/Marc Hertsens
(Park Emergency doctor)/Debralee Scott (Ann Mary Deacon)/

Stephen Zacks (Boy fishing)/Albert Popwell (First bank robber)/
Ernest Robinson (Getaway driver)/Diane Darnell (Mayor's
secretary)/Bill Couch (Suicidal man) with Pamela Tanimura,
Richard Samuelson, Sean Maley, Derek Jue, Jack Hanson, Diane
and Denise Dyer (Kids on school bus)

*   *   *

Directed by Don Siegel in 1971, *Dirty Harry* is the most influential cop movie of
the seventies. It cemented star Clint Eastwood's popularity at the box office and
unleashed a whole series of 'rogue cop' vigilante movies that continue to spawn
imitators today. These are men and women who take the law into their own hands
and bend the rules, ignoring Escobedo, Miranda and the fourth amendment in
favour of Magnum-force heavy artillery – the heavier the better.

Don Siegel began directing in 1946. He made several crime movies, usually
involving characters outside the law, including *Baby Face Nelson* (1957) and *The
Lineup* (1958), but it was *The Killers* (1964), his violent take on Hemingway's short
story, that ensured the next two decades would be prolific for the director. Siegel
made *Madigan* (1968), starring Richard Widmark and Harry Guardino and set in
New York. Siegel then began collaborating with Clint Eastwood, who wanted to

Inspector 71: Clint Eastwood as
Harry Francis Callahan – Dirty
Harry to his friends...and enemies.

bring his cowboy hero into a contemporary urban environment. This he did, literally, with *Coogan's Bluff* (1968), the story of an Arizona cop coming to New York to extradite a prisoner. The cowboy meets and beats up hippies, and it is clear that the filmmakers' loyalties lay with the straight-laced cowboy cop, not the assorted reprobates. Siegel and Eastwood collaborated on two more films: *Two Mules for Sister Sara* (1970) and *The Beguiled* (1971). Eastwood then made his directorial debut with the obsessional *Play Misty for Me* (1971) and cast acting débutante Siegel in a bit part as Murph the bartender.

Their next project came together rather by accident. A script called 'Dead Right' by Harry Julian Fink and his wife Rita had been bought by Universal. This was refashioned into *Dirty Harry*. 'Scorpio', a sniper, is holding San Francisco to ransom. He has already shot a woman in her rooftop swimming pool and has left a note in his sniper's nest demanding $100,000 or he will kill 'a Catholic priest or a nigger'. Helicopters circle the rooftops, but Scorpio manages to kill a black boy, foils a stakeout at a church and then kidnaps Ann Mary Deacon, a teenage girl, and buries her alive. Brought in on the case (and with Chico, a rookie college boy partner in tow), Homicide Detective Inspector 'Dirty' Harry Callahan is hired to deliver the ransom (now upped to $200,000), but after a tense game of phone booth cat-and-mouse, Scorpio escapes without the money. Callahan tracks the killer to the Kezar football stadium and tortures him until he finds out the girl's whereabouts, but she's already dead. Because of Callahan's ruthless methods, Scorpio walks free, and Callahan trails him in his own time. Changing tack, Scorpio pays a thug to beat him up, claiming police brutality and then delivers the *coup de grâce*: he hijacks a bus full of school kids and demands $200,000 and a waiting jet plane at Santa Rosa airport. Asked again to be intermediary, Callahan refuses and goes after Scorpio himself. He waylays the bus and in a gun battle through a rock-crushing works he kills Scorpio, tossing his police badge after the killer's corpse into the quarry pit reservoir.

Dean Reisner worked on the script, as did an uncredited John Milius. Early drafts had the setting as Manhattan, then Seattle; originally Harry Callahan was much older (John Wayne, Robert Mitchum and Frank Sinatra had been offered the role) and the finale of the story took place in the airport, with a plane hijack and a marine sniper picking off Scorpio. Siegel came up with the new ending, though initially Eastwood refused to throw away his badge.

The character of serial killer Scorpio was based on the Zodiac Killer, who struck between December 1968 and October 1969. The Zodiac Killer slayed randomly throughout California (including the Bay Area of San Francisco) and contacted the police through newspapers, signing his name with a distinctive crossed circle target symbol. In *Dirty Harry* Scorpio passes on his demands via the San Francisco *Chronicle*; in his book 'Zodiac', Robert Graysmith notes that the film's ransom letters reproduce Zodiac's handwriting. Zodiac was never caught and over 40 unsolved murders have been attributed to him. One of his final threats, which he never carried out, was delivered to the offices of the *Chronicle* on 14 October

1969: he claimed he was going to hijack a school bus full of children. The real investigating officer, Homicide Detective Dave Toschi, has been touted as a model for Eastwood's character.

In cinema, John Frankenheimer's *The Manchurian Candidate* (1962) had shown a brainwashed sniper used as a political pawn in a senatorial assassination. The randomness of a spree sniper who strikes indiscriminately (as opposed to a serial killer) was best depicted in Peter Bogdanovich's *Targets* (1967), based on the 1966 Charles Whitman case and starring horror icon Boris Karloff. In *Targets* all-American Bobby Thompson (Tim O'Kelly) shoots his wife, his mother, a delivery boy and then climbs up a cooling tower and picks off motorists on the carriageway. In the final scene, he hides behind the screen in a drive-in and takes pot-shots at the audience, blurring the line between movie horror (the film showing is Roger Corman's *The Terror*, starring Karloff) and reality; *Targets* was pulled from release following the assassination of Bobby Kennedy in 1968.

With Eastwood as star, Siegel cast New Yorker Harry Guardino as Callahan's boss, Bressler. Guardino had appeared in *King of Kings* (1961 – as Barabbas) and was Dan Madigan's partner Rocco Bonaro in *Madigan* (1968). Canadian-born John Vernon had played treacherous Mal Reese in *Point Blank* (1967), but his distinctive, authoritarian voice was ideal for the Mayor of San Francisco; he'd previously been

Based on the real-life Zodiac Killer, and hidden by his silencer, rooftop sniper Scorpio (Andy Robinson) terrorises San Francisco in Don Siegel's *Dirty Harry* (1971).

the voice of Big Brother in the 1956 version of *1984*. John Larch, as the Chief of Police, had played investigating officer Sergeant McCallum in *Play Misty for Me*. Reni Santoni was cast as the Hispanic Inspector Chico Gonzalez, though the actor had already had small roles in some prestigious productions, including *The Pawnbroker* (1965). Offering a different slant on his clean–cut image, Audie Murphy was to have played the killer, but he was killed in a plane crash in 1971. Andy Robinson was a theatre actor who was spotted by Siegel in the play *Subject of Fits*. His role as the rooftop sniper was his screen debut; in the end titles he's billed only as 'Killer'. Robinson is no relation to Edward G. Robinson, though the rumour possibly originated from the publicity for this film.

Dirty Harry began shooting in April 1971. The Golden Gate Bridge appears several times, most memorably when, in the dim light of dawn, Harry watches as Ann Mary Deacon's naked body is recovered from a manhole. The neon stakeout at Saint Peter and Paul's Church is lit by a revolving JESUS SAVES sign. The Kezar football stadium (previously the home of the San Francisco 49ers), the cross in Mount Davidson Park and San Francisco City Hall also appear; San Francisco Mayor Alioto allowed the crew to film Eastwood's scenes with Vernon in his office. Scorpio is on top of the Bank of America building in the opening shooting, with the girl swimming in the rooftop pool of the Holiday Inn (which has since been dwarfed by the vast Pyramid building adjacent). The setting for the final shootout, the quarry of 'Hutchinson Company Crushed Rock', was shot at San Anselmo, Marin County. The only outdoor scene not shot on location was the foiled robbery of the United Bank of San Francisco, filmed at Universal Studios on a mocked-up street.

When Siegel was ill for a few days, Eastwood filmed the scenes depicting an attempted suicide and a brief encounter in the park between Callahan and the homosexual 'Alice'. The stunts were the responsibility of Wayne 'Buddy' Van Horne. A double for Scorpio performed the final plunge into the reservoir. Eastwood did his own jump from the Southern Pacific railroad trestle bridge onto the roof of the bus driving down Sir Francis Drake Boulevard and also went up in the fireman's lift for a night-time scene. Stuntman Ernest Robinson played the bank robbers' getaway driver; his car is fired into the air by a stunt cannon, activated when his vehicle hits a fire hydrant.

Eastwood's performance as Callahan (call name 'Inspector 71') is one of his best, striking the balance between taciturn sarcasm, and genuine anger and frustration. Since the death of his wife, killed in a car crash by a drunk driver, Callahan is an empty soul. His job fills the emotional void and has become his obsession. As he dispatches each punk with his Magnum he's thinking about the drunk who 'crossed the white line'. When he rendezvouses with Scorpio in Mount Davidson Park, he vengefully jams a switchblade into the criminal's thigh. Callahan carries out his job with relish; he gets 'Every dirty job that comes along', but more than anything else, 'Dirty Harry' earned his name because he has to play dirty to stay alive.

Equally, Callahan has no respect for the red tape and bureaucracy of City Hall; he even parks his car on a red-kerbed 'no parking at any time' space outside Jaffe's Burger Den, reserved for emergency vehicles. He treats the Chief of Police and the Mayor with equal disdain and can't understand why they want to 'play this creep's game'. Callahan doesn't believe criminals have any rights: 'Ann Mary Deacon,' says the inspector, 'she's raped and left in a hole to die... who speaks for her?' 'The District Attorney's office, if you let us,' answers DA Rothko. Having broken into Scorpio's room at Kezar stadium and confiscated a sniper's rifle, and then trodden on Scorpio's knife wound to extract her whereabouts, Callahan is lucky not to be indicted for assault, with intent to commit murder. Scorpio's 'Miranda' rights have been violated: by law he is owed a warning of his fundamental rights before any questioning should take place. Callahan should also have had a search warrant. 'Does Escobedo ring a bell?' asks Rothko. 'Miranda? I mean you must have heard of the Fourth Amendment... what I'm saying is that man had rights.' 'Well I'm all broken up about that man's rights,' answers Callahan. As it stands, Scorpio will soon be back on the streets; all Callahan's evidence is inadmissible; 'Well then the law's crazy.'

The facelessness of the sniper, who could strike with impunity at any moment, is chillingly portrayed in the film. The opening shot, of Scorpio training the cross-hairs of his high-powered sniper rifle on a girl in a swimming pool, is similar to Siegel's style in *The Killers*, with the silencer dominating the San Francisco roofscape. During their investigations, the police check 'all known extortionists, rifle nuts' and the like, but Scorpio doesn't look particularly distinctive in the cosmopolitan melting pot of San Francisco; the police even resort to checking their files for 'Natives of Scorpio'. This may be San Francisco, the bastion of hippiedom in the Age of Aquarius, but like *Coogan's Bluff*, the longhairs are definitely the villains. Scorpio looks like a beatnik, with his straggly hair and CND-symbol belt buckle. It was dangerous imagery for Siegel and Eastwood to play with – the peace movement was a potent force and didn't take kindly to the filmmakers' misappropriation of their cultural symbols. So much so that demonstrators' placards outside the 1972 Oscars read 'Dirty Harry is a rotten pig'.

Dirty Harry is now best remembered for its action sequences rather than its politics. Callahan's cavalier attitude to the law is best summed up in the scene where he foils a robbery on the United Bank in downtown San Francisco, which plays like a wild-west shootout. Callahan pulls up to his favourite eatery, the 'Burger Den', run by genial Mister Jaffe. Outside the bank, a tan Ford sits with its engine running. 'Tell No Lies, Girl', a slow Motown groove drifts from the car radio ('Just take your mask away... the hallowing season is gone'); its chain-smoking black driver drops another cigarette butt on the eight already lying in the road. Becoming suspicious of the vehicle, Callahan orders a jumbo hotdog and asks Jaffe to call the police and tell them there's 'a two-eleven in progress at the bank'. He settles back to enjoy his snack ('Now just wait till the cavalry arrives'), but no sooner has he taken a mouthful than the bank's alarm bell starts ringing, followed by a muffled shotgun blast. As one shotgun-toting robber emerges from the bank, Callahan strides outside, draws his Magnum and calls 'Halt', but the hood turns and shoots, as the inspector fires simultaneously and hits the robber in the shoulder. Chaos ensues and the general public run for cover as a second robber runs out and dives into the getaway car, which speeds off down the street. Callahan kills the driver, the car hits a fire hydrant and flips on its side, then Callahan kills the escaping passenger, sending him crashing through a clothes shop window.

With the situation under control and the street looking like a war zone (a great jet of water shoots into the air from the hydrant), Callahan walks to where the first bank robber (Albert Popwell) is lying slumped on the sidewalk. As the felon's hand creeps towards his shotgun lying nearby, Callahan raises his pistol and warns: 'Uh-uh. I know what you're thinking. Did he fire six shots or only five? Well to tell you the truth, in all this excitement I've kind of lost track myself. But being as this is a .44 Magnum, the most powerful handgun in the world, and would blow your head clean off, you've got to ask yourself one question. Do I feel lucky? Well do you, punk?' After a hesitation, the robber moves his hand away from the gun, Callahan retrieves it and turns to walk away. 'Hey,' says the wounded man, 'I gots to know.' Callahan points the pistol at him and pulls the trigger, which clicks on an empty chamber. Callahan laughs; the crook, failing to see the funny side, spits, 'Son of a bitch' at the departing cop.

Like *Coogan's Bluff*, this is Eastwood's western hero transposed to the big city. There are even a couple of in-joke references to Eastwood's cinematic past. As he walks out of the 'Burger Den' one of the shop signs reads 'Saloon', while a billboard on a local cinema advertises *Play Misty for Me*. In fact the larger-than-life scene is nearly out of place in a film that often looks like a piece of *cinema verité*, with Bruce Surtees's grainy hand-held camerawork, seedy settings and location shots backed by Lalo Schifrin's jazzy, underplayed score.

Publicity-seeking Scorpio appears on the six o'clock news (the Zodiac Killer once rang the live TV phone-in on Channel Seven's *The Jim Dunbar Show*). Later his psychopathic behaviour and treatment of seven children from Park Street School on the bus is chilling. His happy refrains of 'Old MacDonald had a farm, ee-eye-ee-eye-o' and 'Row, row, row your boat' give way to lunatic promises that they're on their way to the ice cream factory and finally the threat to sing or 'I'm gonna kill all your mothers', a threat stifled by the arrival of Callahan, wearing a dark suit and shades, standing on the railway trestle like an avenging angel. In the finale it's Callahan's Smith & Wesson Model 29 .44-inch Magnum, against Scorpio's 9mm Luger pistol. In the quarry, Scorpio takes a boy idly fishing hostage and Callahan accurately puts a bullet in Scorpio's shoulder. The murderer's pistol falls nearby and Callahan repeats his 'Did I fire six shots or only five?' monologue, but this time Scorpio takes the chance – and loses.

Dirty Harry was rated R and released in the US in December 1971. The posters, with repeated images of Eastwood aiming his pistol or firing through shattered glass, were accompanied by the slogans 'Detective Harry Callahan. He doesn't break murder cases. He smashes them' and 'You don't assign him to murder cases … you just turn him loose'. The trailer was equally hard-hitting: 'This is about a movie about a couple of killers. Harry Callahan and a homicidal maniac. The one with the badge is Harry.'

The *Los Angeles Times* said the film was 'a bluntly violent, very well made suspense thriller' and on a technical level critics found it hard to fault. Its ideology was another matter. Most outspoken was Pauline Kael in the *New Yorker*, who called it 'a right-wing fantasy', where the 'fascist potential' of the genre 'has finally surfaced'. Eastwood and Siegel argued that it was simply a story of a man doing his job. The film, like *The Lineup*, was dedicated to the San Francisco Police Department; Eastwood has said that 'Harry is a fantasy police officer who gets to do a few things that most police officers never get to'. Liberals meanwhile referred to Callahan's Magnum as an 'angry erection'.

Audience reaction was positive and everyone found something to cheer in the film. Even though she hated the film's 'fascist medievalism', Pauline Kael noted that Puerto Rican audiences 'jeered … when the maniac whined and pleaded for his legal rights'. Clint Eastwood's biographer Iain Johnstone remembered that the predominately black audience he saw the film with supported Harry, as did most

'Do I feel lucky … well do you, punk?'; Clint Eastwood as Harry Callahan in a Warner Bros' promotional portrait.

policemen. According to Eastwood, even the dawdling VW Beetle shunted off the road by Scorpio's hijacked bus got a cheer from audiences.

It was the fifth biggest movie of the year in the US and eventually became Eastwood's biggest hit so far. It also made many 'Ten Best' lists for the year and soon appeared in *Variety*'s all-time moneymakers. In its first year of release it earned $16 million domestically, almost $50 million worldwide and was a huge hit in Europe and the Far East; rather worryingly the police force of the Philippines used their 16mm print as a training film. There was also a novelisation of *Dirty Harry* written by Phillip Rock and published by Star Books, who published tie-ins for many Eastwood movies. In Rock's book, Callahan doesn't throw his badge away at the end.

Dirty Harry was also highly successful and influential abroad. In the UK it was rated X, for violent content. For initial TV showings on the BBC, the film was trimmed for violence and profanity; though ITV have since broadcast it uncut. In Spain it was released as *Harry, El Sucio* ('Harry, the Dirty One'). In France it was *L'inspecteur Harry*. In Italy it was released as *Ispettore Callaghan: il Caso Scorpio è tuo* ('Inspector Callaghan: the Scorpio Case is yours'). Its success led to dozens of imitators in Europe, with tough loners pursuing assorted killers, bombers, drug pushers, gangsters and extortionists, in films like *Fear in the City* (1976), *Forced Impact* (1976) and *Blazing Magnums* (1976), the re-releases of which clogged video shelves throughout the eighties.

When Eastwood's old friend Burt Reynolds directed and starred in *Sharky's Machine* (1981), Reynolds dubbed it 'Dirty Harry Goes to Atlanta'. Reynolds made it in response to Eastwood moving in on his *Smokey and the Bandit*, good-old-boy comedies with *Every Which Way but Loose* (1978). There was also an awfully *Dirty Harry*-ish US TV series called *Sledgehammer* that traded on Callahan's character. John Wayne got in on the act, with *McQ* (1974) and *Brannigan* (1975); *McQ* even borrowed the plot of *Magnum Force*.

As just about everyone had a go at playing a rogue cop, the vigilante aspect of the Harry Callahan films reappeared in Michael Winner's massively successful *Death Wish* (1974). It starred Charles Bronson as architect Paul Kersey, who stalked the streets of New York for the men who had raped and beaten his wife and daughter. Originally called 'Sidewalk Vigilante' the film was a glorified B-movie, but with backing from Dino De Laurentiis it made $22 million at the US box office and remains one of the most popular movies of the seventies, its abysmal sequels notwithstanding. At one point Kersey asks what you call people who do nothing when attacked, and is answered with 'civilised'. *Death Wish* shows what happens when the civilised start retaliating.

With its sensational returns and controversy, *Dirty Harry* resulted in four dirtier sequels over the next 17 years. *Magnum Force* (1973) began with a variation on the airport scene from the original *Dirty Harry* finale, as Callahan poses as a pilot to thwart a hijack. With a screenplay by Milius and Michael Cimino, the film saw Callahan facing a police death squad – a quartet of neo-Nazi motorcycle cops led by Davis (a pre-Hutch David Soul), who execute criminals beyond the law. They are working with Lieutenant Briggs (Hal Holbrook), but in reality are an excuse for several exceptionally violent action scenes, as various unsavoury criminal types (drug pushers, mobsters, pimps and syndicate royalty) are shot, stabbed, blown up and mangled in the name of justice. It was a shrewd move to put these neo-Nazi killers next to Callahan, who now looks positively liberal; when the gang ask Callahan to join them, he says, 'I'm afraid you've misjudged me.'

After *Magnum Force*, Eastwood should have asked himself one question: should he make any more needless *Dirty Harry* sequels? *The Enforcer*, advertised as 'The dirtiest Harry of them all', appeared in 1976. Initially re-teamed with Frank DiGiorgio and back working for Bressler, Callahan opens the film causing $14,379 worth of damage by driving his car into a liquor store hold-up. Callahan's persona here really is medieval, epitomised by his chauvinistic attitude to his new partner Kate Moore (Tyne Daly, pre-*Cagney and Lacey*). Some of the acting in *The Enforcer* is so bad it often looks like a *Police Academy*-style parody of the first film. Callahan's mayor-kidnapping terrorist opponents are particularly risible: the Peoples' Revolutionary Strike Force are kitted out in headbands, fatigues and leisurewear, like a militant keep fit class.

Eastwood directed himself in *Sudden Impact* (1983), a film that was advertised solely on one line of dialogue: 'Go ahead, make my day'. Callahan is shunted out of San Francisco down the coast to the resort of San Paulo to investigate a spate of mysterious murders – actually a series of revenge killings by rape victim Jennifer Spencer (Sondra Locke). Apparently sponsored by Coors and Budweiser, there's little to recommend a film that sees Callahan beaten up by three fishmongers, and his new, presumably comic relief, 'partner' is a farting dog.

Callahan had one last hurrah in 1988, floating around in *The Dead Pool*, which is probably where the script was conceived. The title refers to a sort of Tontine, a list of various high-risk San Francisco celebs: either through their age or lifestyle. Callahan makes the list, which takes him into the B-movie world of rock stars and horror video directors. A journalist wants to write Callahan's life story and presents him with a book of press cuttings depicting past glories: 'Callahan wins police contest 3 years in row' (from *Magnum Force*) and 'Scorpio Killer Captured' (*Dirty Harry*). One funny moment sees Chinese cop Al Quan getting a mystical tattoo to ward off evil spirits when he becomes Callahan's latest partner. But the four *Dirty Harry* sequels epitomised the law of diminishing returns, with some good moments and sound bites, but a lot of filler, which only highlighted what an exceptional team Eastwood and Siegel were.

Like the report from Callahan's .44 Magnum, the resonance of Eastwood's initial incarnation of Dirty Harry was loud and long-lasting. He paved the way for idiosyncratic rule-benders like Mel Gibson in the 'Lethal Weapon' series and later became something of a national icon, with 'Go ahead, make my day' entering the language. A Californian police officer even once asked Eastwood to etch his autograph on the cop's Magnum. With the public's general dissatisfaction with law and order, and Callahan the personification of a 'fantasy cop' making the streets safer for ordinary people, it seems oddly fitting that following the real-life 1974 'Zebra Murders' in San Francisco, graffiti read: 'Dirty Harry, where are you when we need you?'

14

'I'm gonna make him an offer he can't refuse'

— *The Godfather* (1972)

Credits:

DIRECTOR – Francis Ford Coppola
PRODUCER – Albert S. Ruddy
ASSOCIATE PRODUCER – Gray Frederickson
STORY – Mario Puzo
SCREENPLAY – Mario Puzo and Francis Ford Coppola
DIRECTOR OF PHOTOGRAPHY – Gordon Willis
EDITORS – William Reynolds and Peter Zinner
ART DIRECTOR – Warren Clymer
SET DECORATOR – Philip Smith
COSTUMES – Anna Hill Johnstone
MUSIC COMPOSER – Nino Rota
MUSIC CONDUCTOR – Carlo Savina
Technicolor
An Alfran Production
Released by Paramount Pictures
175 minutes

Cast:

Marlon Brando (Don Vito Corleone)/Al Pacino (Michael Corleone)/James Caan (Santino 'Sonny' Corleone)/Richard Castellano (Clemenza)/Robert Duvall (Tom Hagan)/Sterling Hayden (Captain McCluskey)/John Marley (Jack Woltz)/Richard Conte (Don Barzini)/Diane Keaton (Kay Adams)/Al Lettieri (Virgil Sollozzo, alias 'The Turk')/Abe Vigoda (Sal Tessio)/Talia Shire (Constanzia 'Connie' Rizzi)/Gianni Russo (Carlo Rizzi)/John Cazale (Frederico 'Fredo' Corleone)/Rudy Bond (Cuneo)/Al Martino (Johnny Fontane)/Morgana King (Carmella 'Mama' Corleone)/Lenny Montana (Luca Brasi)/John Martino (Paulie Gatto)/Salvatore Corsitto (Amerigo Bonasera)/Richard Bright

(Al Neri)/Alex Rocco (Moe Green/Tony Giorgio (Bruno Tattaglia)/Vito Scotti (Nazorine)/Tere Livrano (Theresa Hagan)/Victor Rendina (Phillip Tattaglia)/Jeannie Linero (Lucy Mancini, Sonny's mistress)/Julie Gregg (Sandra Corleone, Sonny's wife)/Ardell Sheriden (Mrs Clemenza)/Simonetta Stefanelli (Apollonia Vitelli)/Angelo Infanti (Fabrizio)/Corrado Gaipa (Don Tommasino in Palermo)/Franco Citti (Calo)/Saro Urzi (Vitelli, Apollonia's father)/Joe Spinall (Willi Cicci, Corleone hitman)/Sophia Coppola (Michael Rizzi)

*   *   *

Released in 1972, Francis Ford Coppola's film, based on Mario Puzo's novel, is the godfather of all crime movies and with its grander sequel, *The Godfather Part II* (1974), a seminal work. Puzo was born in New York in 1920. His early novels include 'Dark Arena' (1953) and 'Fortunate Pilgrim' (1964), but they weren't particularly successful. In the sixties, Puzo wrote a script with the working title 'The Mafia'; Robert Evans at Paramount Pictures acquired the film rights for $12,000 and Puzo reworked it as a novel, 'The Godfather'. It told the story of the Corleones, an Italian Mafia family in New York in the forties and fifties. A flashback section recounted the title character's arrival in America from Sicily, following the murder of his father. The paperback rights to the book were sold for a record $410,000 and it was published worldwide in 1969. By the time the film version was being shot in 1971, it was the number one bestseller in the world, with ten million copies in print.

Burt Lancaster was very keen to star in the film version as the title character, a character who Lancaster felt resembled his Sicilian Prince of Salina, Don Fabrizio, in Luchino Visconti's *The Leopard* (1963). Lancaster wanted it so badly that he was even willing to audition. Paramount pushed for Lancaster, but Coppola, the director assigned to *The Godfather* project by Evans, had other ideas.

Coppola was not an obvious choice as director. He had his first break in Roger Corman's B-movies, directing a horror called *Dementia 13* (1963). Coppola's first big Hollywood production was the musical *Finian's Rainbow* (1968), followed by the drama *The Rain People* (1969), neither of which was a commercial success. When he was offered *The Godfather* in 1970 he was sceptical, but accepted the project, writing the script with Puzo himself. Puzo, at Paramount's request, had updated the story to the seventies; period costumes and sets would send the cost rocketing and Paramount wanted a modestly budgeted film. Producer Albert S. Ruddy visited Charles Bluhdorn, the head of Gulf and Western, the owner of Paramount, and described what he wanted to do with *The Godfather*: 'I want to make an ice-blue terrifying movie about people you love'; Bluhdorn assigned Ruddy as producer. Paramount were reticent about investing in *The Godfather*, as a film called *The Brotherhood* (1968) had failed badly at the box office. Coppola eventually convinced Paramount to set the film in the forties and fifties, and received $110,000, plus 6 per cent of the net profits, to write and direct.

The film version of *The Godfather* takes place over a ten-year period (1945–55) and follows the Corleones, a criminal family of Italian-Americans of Sicilian ancestry, on Long Island, New York. Don Vito is the paterfamilias. His four children are the eldest Santino (called 'Sonny'), Frederico ('Fredo'), Constanzia ('Connie') and the youngest Michael, a recently demobilised soldier, who is dating Kay Adams. Michael is ambivalent towards his family and distances himself from their activities. Also working for the Corleones is their lawyer, almost an adopted son, Tom Hagan. On the last Saturday in August 1945, Constanzia Corleone and Carlo Rizzi marry and Don Vito throws a huge celebration. Soon afterwards, the Corleone clan is approached by the Tattaglias, a rival faction, and Sollozzo, a Sicilian mobster. They want the Corleones to join them in drug trafficking. The Corleones, already involved in the unions and gambling, refuse, even though they can see that drugs are one of the trades of the future. In response to the rejection, the Tattaglias kill Corleone man Luca Brasi and shoot Don Vito. The Don recovers, but in retribution, Michael wreaks revenge, killing Sollozzo and crooked police captain McCluskey. This precipitates the Five Families War and in 1946 Michael is forced into exile in Sicily, where he meets, falls in love with and marries Apollonia, a local girl. In 1947, back

Portrait of Power: Marlon Brando, prematurely aged by Dick Smith's intricate prosthetic makeup, in Francis Ford Coppola's *The Godfather* (1972).

in New York, the Corleones' power is weakening and, in an ambush, Sonny is shot dead. In Sicily, Apollonia is killed in a car bomb meant for Michael, so he returns to New York, where he marries Kay, in 1951. By 1954, the family have moved some of their interests to Las Vegas's gambling joints, with Fredo posted out there as their representative. Don Vito dies of a heart attack the same year and Michael assumes his mantle. He decides to wipe out his enemies in one fell swoop. While Michael attends the baptism of Connie's child, the heads of the rival families are assassinated, leaving the Corleones as the most powerful clan once again. As the family prepare to move out to Las Vegas, Michael orders that Connie's husband Carlo be killed because he was involved in Sonny's murder. Connie is shattered and Kay asks her husband if he ordered Carlo's death; 'No,' Michael lies. The new Don Corleone is ruthless; only those in his inner circle will be treated with complete respect and know the true workings of the family, as Kay begins to realise.

Coppola wanted either Lawrence Olivier or Marlon Brando for the title role. Olivier was ill and Brando was only 46, too young for the ageing Don. For his informal screen test, Brando pushed tissue paper into his mouth (to 'look like a bulldog'), blackened his hair with shoe polish and adopted a mumbled, raspy whisper. Brando was one of the great screen actors, but in the late sixties several of his films had failed at the box office, most recently Gillo Pontecorvo's political _Queimada!_ (1969 – released internationally as _Burn!_). Paramount were horrified to discover Coppola's choice, until they saw Brando's makeover in the screen test. For the actual film, Brando was convincingly transformed by Dick Smith's prosthetic makeup. The Don's famous rasping line, 'I'm gonna make him an offer he can't refuse', was already present in Puzo's book.

After much lobbying by Coppola, Al Pacino eventually won the role of Michael. Pacino, full name Alfredo Pacino, was born in New York in 1940. He attended Lee Strasberg's celebrated Actors Studio in New York. His role as a junkie in _Panic in Needle Park_ (1971) impressed Coppola, and Pacino was chosen over Paramount preferences Robert Redford, Ryan O'Neal, Alain Delon, Warren Beatty and James Caan, who was actually cast in the film as Michael's brother, Sonny. Bronx-born Caan had appeared in the motor racing drama _Red Line 7000_ (1965) and the western _El Dorado_ (1967), then played the dying footballer of TV movie _Brian's Song_ (1970). Stage actor Robert Duvall had appeared in _The Detective_ and _Bullit_ (1968), as the villain of _True Grit_ (1969) and in _MASH_ (1970), before being cast by Coppola as Corleone lawyer Tom Hagan; both Duvall and Caan had worked with Coppola on _The Rain People_ (1969). Diane Keaton (real name Diane Hall) was cast as Michael's girlfriend Kay Adams. _The Godfather_ was only her second screen role and she later went on to great success in films directed by Woody Allen, notably _Sleeper_ (1973), _Love and Death_ (1975), _Annie Hall_ (1977) and the more serious _Interiors_ (1978) and _Manhattan_ (1979). The lead actors were paid $35,000 each, while Brando received $50,000 (though some biographies claim $100,000).

Various reliable crime actors had cameo roles: Sterling Hayden played the corrupt police captain, McCluskey. Richard Conte was cast as rival gangster Barzini; he was originally in the running for the role of Don Vito. John Marley played Woltz, the ill-fated movie producer out to curtail the career of Johnny Fontane. Crooner Al Martino played crooner Fontane; Martino had the first ever UK number 1 on 16 November 1952, with 'Here in My Heart'.

Grim-faced Abe Vigoda was cast as traitorous Corleone henchman Tessio, with Al Lettieri as gangster Sollozzo. Lenny Montana, cast as Luca Brasi, was a wrestler who unfortunately wasn't very good with dialogue. Sicilian jazz singer Morgana King was cast as the Don's wife, Carmella. Coppola also used family members in the cast and crew. Talia Shire, who played Constanzia 'Connie' Rizzi, was Coppola's sister. Coppola's father Carmine composed the music to the tarantellas (whirling Southern Italian dances) at the opening wedding and appears in the film, playing the piano. Coppola's mother and other relatives lurked as wedding guests. At the baptism, baby Michael was played by the director's daughter, Sophia. For the Sicilian sequences, Coppola cast several Italian actors, including Simonetta Stefanelli as the beautiful Apollonia, and Angelo Infanti and Pasolini's lead actor Franco Citti, as Michael's two bandit bodyguards, Fabrizio and Calo.

According to Coppola, *The Godfather* was initially scheduled for a 53-day, $2.5 million shoot; with the added time and costs for making the movie in period dress, *The Godfather* actually took 62 days and $6.5 million. Coppola rehearsed his actors for two weeks prior to beginning in March 1971. Many interiors were filmed in Filmways Studio in Upper Manhattan, near Harlem. The assassination attempt on the Don at the fruit stand outside the Genco Olive Oil Factory was filmed on Mott Street in New York's Little Italy (this murder was inspired by the Bronx fruit stand murder of mobster Frank 'Don Cheech' Scalise in 1957). Don Vito's office interior was a studio set, with sheets of white paper placed outside the window blinds, giving the effect of daylight. The wedding mall and other Corleone residence exteriors were filmed on Staten Island. Radio City Music Hall and 'Best and Co' in New York were used for the Christmas shopping scenes. Woltz's mansion exterior was the Guggenheim estate (with doubles used for the exterior shots of Duvall and Marley). Woltz International Pictures studio was filmed by the second unit on LA sets, with interiors on the New York sound stage. The Statue of Liberty can be seen across the cornfield, when traitorous Corleone associate Paulie is murdered. The school where Kay is working when Michael returns from Sicily was in Ross, New England. The meeting of the five families of hoods was filmed in the boardroom of the New York Central Railroad, beneath a huge painting of a locomotive. The hospital exteriors were outside Bellevue Hospital; Luca Brasi was killed in the Art Deco Edison hotel, while the Don's funeral was held at the vast Calvary Cemetery, Woodside, in Queens, New York, with the sombre, flower-bedecked cortege winding through the tombstones. Louis's Restaurant, where Michael shoots McCluskey and Sollozzo, was a real location with a noisy L-train (elevator train) running nearby. The Sicilian sequences were filmed in Sicily, in the hillside village of Savoca. Filming was completed in August 1971, though some scenes, for example the New England school, were lensed over a year later.

Coppola chose Nino Rota to compose the music, again against the studio's wishes. Rota was the Milan-born composer who had worked in Italy in collaboration with director Federico Fellini, on *La Strada* (1954), *La Dolce Vita* (1959) and *8½* (1963), and Luchino Visconti on *Rocco and his Brothers* (1960) and *The Leopard* (1963). The main theme for *The Godfather* was a lilting, haunting seven-note trumpet melody, which is later reorchestrated for full orchestra in robust dramatic style. It is also set to a two-step, played by the oompah band, for Don Vito's dance with his daughter. The fragile 'love theme' is beautifully understated, as in the Sicilian courtship scenes, with Apollonia and Michael accompanied by a flock of black-clad chaperones and Michael's bandit bodyguards.

Significantly, the Mafia and their organisation, the 'Cosa Nostra' (which literally translates as 'This Thing of Ours'), is not mentioned by name in *The Godfather*. Earlier films had similarly played safe – for instance, the euphemistic 'Black Hand' society in *The Black Hand* (1949). American, even Italian-American, filmmakers working in the seventies had to be very careful they didn't offend anyone connected with the Mafia or the Cosa Nostra. The latter, with its membership rituals, is peculiar to the New York Mafia: for instance, in Chicago they are 'The Outfit', in Buffalo 'The Arm'. The term Mafia has been attributed to several different origins. Some sources state that it relates to banditry in Sicily; 'mafia' is the scrub grass covering hillsides on the island, which provides cover for fugitives from the law. Others say it is an acronym of 'Morte alla Francia Italia anela!' ('Death to the French is Italy's cry!'), used by Italian soldiers fighting the French in the thirteenth century, or it is the call of a vengeful Sicilian mother in 1282, who filled the streets of Palermo with shouts of 'Ma fia! ma fia!' ('My daughter'), following her daughter's rape at the hands of the French.

Coppola and Puzo were also cautious not to depict any real Mafia characters; the closest to one is Johnny Fontane, the cabaret singer with mob connections, allegedly loosely based on Frank Sinatra. The 'war movie' Fontane wants a role in could be *From Here to Eternity* (1953); Sinatra had to beg Columbia Pictures' Harry Cohn for a role in the film. In *The Godfather* showbiz has turned Fontane soft and he cries, disgusting Don Vito, who calls him a 'Hollywood *finocchio* [a 'queer']'. Studio head Woltz is persuaded to offer Fontane the part he desires, when he wakes up in his blood-stained satin sheets and discovers the severed head of Khartoum, his jet black racehorse, lying at the foot of the bed. Later we see Fontane living the high life in Las Vegas, with 'Sands' billboards advertising 'Jack Entratter presents Jerry Lewis and Dean Martin', so the Sinatra parallels are certainly present. Fontane is the Don's godson and features more extensively in Puzo's book.

Don Vito's informal title, 'godfather', with its religious connotations, links together the crime and family elements of the film. From Brando's introductory scene, where we simply see his hand gesturing for one of his men to give a visitor a glass of water, he presents Don Vito as godlike – it is he who is pulling the strings in the family. His sense of power, accentuated by his hefty desk, opulent room decor and cigars, suffuses the entire film. He is the aristocrat of screen crime lords.

The Godfather accentuates the two sides of the Don, the public and the private. This is immediately apparent from the opening scenes: the contrast between the darkness of the Don's office, a murky den, and the bright light and sunshine of the wedding party at the mall. 'I believe in America,' says Amerigo Bonasera, unconvincingly. He has come to ask the Don for revenge against the two men who have beaten his daughter (Puzo's book actually opens with Bonasera in court listening to the men receive suspended sentences). Bonasera has raised his daughter in the American fashion, but the American judiciary has failed him; now he wants Sicilian justice. So he comes to the Don's dark chamber, his inner sanctum, where fates are decided over cigars.

The family side to Don Vito is depicted in a melancholy scene ten years later. In the garden, one July afternoon, the Don puts an orange peel in his mouth, like scary teeth, and chases his grandson, Anthony. The little boy is obviously quite frightened, as he runs through the tomato patch. The boy then playfully sprays a water pump gun at the monster. When the Don clutches his chest and tumbles through the tomato canes, suffering a cardiac arrest, the little boy laughs at the death of the big bad wolf, running over to squirt him with water, until he realises that something is wrong and runs into the house. From the cold Godfather, who

Michael (Al Pacino), flanked by Tom Hagan (Robert Duvall, left) and Clemenza (Richard Castellano), arrives at the Corleones' Long Island estate in *The Godfather* (1972).

orders the death of men as though ordering a sandwich, to the granddad playing with his grandson, Brando's is one of the great screen performances.

What is perhaps most surprising about *The Godfather* is the broad tableau it depicts, including in it the Don himself, his children and their children. Aside from the male members of the family's numerous business meetings, the clan is depicted domestically as a normal family, almost of soap opera dimensions. The ongoing plot threads, certainly in relation to *The Godfather*'s sequels, contain dynastic soap opera elements. There is also prominence given to the enjoyment of food; European crime movies had already highlighted this: in *The Sicilian Clan* (1969), the title family enjoys spaghetti, Parmesan and breadsticks as they discuss 'business'. But Coppola integrates such scenes into the narrative more effectively and gives the patriarchal crime family another dimension. When we see Carlo Rizzi beating Don Vito's daughter Connie, having already been warned by Sonny to wise up, we know the family saga will take another twist. Here Carlo betrays Sonny to Barzini's men; familial squabbles spill over into public life and gang feuds.

The three Corleone sons are very different from one another. Michael is the dutiful son, the college boy who has been to war and has a relationship with Kay, his nice WASP girlfriend. Michael tells Kay the story of how Johnny Fontane ducked out of his binding contract with a bandleader; Don Vito and Luca Brasi went to see the bandleader. 'My father made him an offer he couldn't refuse,' said Michael. Brasi held a gun to the bandleader's head and Vito informed him that 'Either his brains or his signature would be on the contract...that's a true story'. Kay looks shocked: 'That's my family Kay,' Michael assures her, 'It's not me' – but eventually it is.

Sonny is a hothead. He has an impetuous, somewhat shallow, nature, and is having an affair with one of the bridesmaids at Connie's wedding. Sonny's recklessness leads to his death, when he goes to Connie's aid, only to be bushwhacked en route. Fredo is the weakest and least significant of the brothers; he fails to protect his father when they are ambushed and later is farmed off to Las Vegas to look after their casino interests. When Michael visits, in his new guise as don-in-waiting, Fredo sides with casino owner Moe Green against the Corleones. Michael, disgusted, quietly utters the warning: 'Fredo, you're my older brother and I love you, but don't ever take sides with anyone against the family...ever.'

The film's key scene is the subsequent exchange between Michael and his ailing father in the garden, written by Robert Towne. The Don says that the rival gangs will contact Michael and, whoever is Barzini's envoy, he is the traitor in their midst – the meeting with Barzini will be a trap and they will try to assassinate Michael. During the conversation, it becomes clear that Michael has been drawn into the family business, even though it is against the Don's wishes. The Don notes that during his time as patriarch, 'I refused to be a fool, dancing on a string held by all those big shots'. Then he adds regretfully that he had hoped, 'When it was your time, you would be the one to hold the strings – Senator Corleone, Governor

Corleone...something...there just wasn't enough time Michael'. 'We'll get there pop, we'll get there,' answers Michael. It is a very moving scene, beautifully played by Pacino and Brando, and was a late addition by Coppola, who suddenly realised that father and son didn't have a shared moment together during the film.

Opposite such tender moments, Coppola deploys some of the most violent murders of the seventies. Luca Brasi's demise is typically brutal, as befits the man who makes offers no one can refuse. He meets Bruno Tattaglia and Sollozzo in a bar, but ends up with his hand pinned to the bar with a knife and a garrotte looped around his neck. Coppola doesn't spare us the sight of Brasi's choking. Later the Corleones receive word of Brasi's death when two large fish wrapped up in Brasi's bulletproof vest arrive, a coded Sicilian message: 'Luca Brasi sleeps with the fishes'. When Michael shoots Sollozzo and McCluskey in the restaurant, with a pistol that has been earlier concealed in a toilet cistern, the deaths are again more realistic than one expects from a genre film. Sollozzo's brain sprays across the restaurant when hit in the head at close range, while McCluskey's squirming death spasm is equally distressing when he is hit in the throat. These killings are very realistic, unglamorous and disturbing. By contrast, Sonny's murder on the causeway, when he stops at a tollbooth and his car is riddled by Tommy-guns, is Coppola's bloody homage to the finale of *Bonnie and Clyde*. Hundreds of blood squibs and bullet hits explode across the car, and James Caan performs a twitching dance of death.

Michael's final revenge, and the climax to the film, is chilling. With the appropriate correlation between religion, family and crime that has been present throughout the film, Michael has been asked to become godfather to Connie and Carlo's son. The family attends the baptism, while several Corleone men, including Clemenza and Neri, surprise the rival family bosses and casino owner Moe Green in a series of hits. We see the assassins preparing for their contracts, intercut with the baptism ceremony. The priest intones the creed and other scripture, Bach's organ 'Passacaglia and Fugue in C Minor' and the baby's cries intensify the soundtrack and Michael is asked 'Do you renounce Satan?' to which he replies, 'I do renounce him'. This is intercut with the bloody murders, as a new Godfather emerges, a transformation that occurs right before our eyes. 'Go in peace and may the Lord be with you,' says the priest. 'Amen.'

In postproduction, two supervising editors worked on *The Godfather*: William Reynolds cut the first half, Peter Zinner the second, then the results were spliced together, at Coppola's own American Zoetrope studio facility in San Francisco. Coppola had trouble with Paramount, who wanted a film no longer than 135 minutes. The director chopped his almost-three-hour version down, then received complaints from Paramount that all the good material was missing, so according to Coppola, he simply reinstated it.

The Godfather was eventually released at 175 minutes. The film's full title, as it appears on screen, is *Mario Puzo's The Godfather*. It was premiered in the US in

March 1972, rated R. The trailer was made up almost entirely of stills, like a family album, while the famous poster artwork featured a simple, sinister shadowy facial portrait of Brando, or the distinctive Godfather logo, with the film's title suspended from strings controlled by an unseen puppeteer, in machiavellian style. *The Godfather*'s initial reviews were a mixed bag. The *New York Times* called it 'The year's first really satisfying, big commercial American film...that describes a sorrowful American dream as a slam-bang, sentimental gangster drama'; for *Time* it had 'warmth, violence, nostalgia...and the dynastic sweep of an Italian-American *Gone With the Wind*'. *Variety* said it was 'overlong at about 175 minutes (played without intermission) and occasionally confusing. While never so placid as to be boring, it is never so gripping as to be superior screen drama.' *New Republic* seemed particularly riled: 'Al Pacino rattles around in a part too demanding for him. Brando's makeup is poor, the score by Nino Rota is surprisingly rotten and the print has very washed-out colours.' *Vogue* said the film was 'a tedious three-hour, quasi-epic', which 'Warner Brothers would have made...35 years ago as a hundred minute feature', concluding 'gangsters have their *Greatest Story Ever Told*, but minus George Stevens'. *Cinema TV Today* reckoned the actors 'do all that can be done with their interchangeable puppet roles. Brando almost persuaded me that I was watching a great film...but it is not.' Released nationwide on 400 screens, *The Godfather* took $25 million in three weeks in the US, $86 million throughout its run and $126 million worldwide, beating the record set by *Gone With the Wind* in 1939 to become the biggest hit of all time.

At the 1972 Oscars, the film was nominated in 12 categories, including Caan, Duvall and Pacino all competing for the Best Supporting Actor Oscar; Joel Grey won for *Cabaret*. Jack Lemmon presented Coppola and Mario Puzo's daughter with the award for Best Adapted Screenplay. Clint Eastwood presented the Best Picture Oscar to producer Albert Ruddy for *The Godfather*, while Brando famously sent Sasheen Little Feather to receive his Best Actor Oscar; she read out a speech highlighting the plight and treatment of Native Americans in the US, to a chorus of boos.

Brando's mumbled, gesticulating performance as Don Vito also launched a thousand skits, with Peter Sellers incorporating a Godfather parody into the Pink Panther series, in *Revenge of the Pink Panther* (1978). In Burt Reynolds's speedy auto comedy *Cannonball Run II* (1984) Dom DeLuise performs a passable Brando *Godfather* send-up, as Don Canneloni, the head of a gang of mobsters up against rival families, the Rigatonis, Tortellinis, Fettuccinis and Raviolis. His son is named Don, who one day will take over the family as Don Don. Canneloni's henchmen are Sonny (Michael Gazzo, from *The Godfather Part II*), Caesar (Abe Vigoda, Tessio in *The Godfather*), Tony (Alex Rocco, casino owner Moe Green in *The Godfather*) and Slim (played by perennial Mafia movie hitman Henry Silva). Also, look out for a *Saturday Night Live* sketch, with Peter Boyle and John Belushi, both dressed as fifties-era Brandos, quoting famous lines of the actor's dialogue back and forth, entitled 'Duelling Brandos'.

   Massively successful and enduringly popular, *The Godfather* regularly wins 'best ever movie' polls, outgunning the phenomenally popular 'Star Wars' and 'Lord of the Rings' series. But perhaps *The Godfather*'s best recommendation comes from Henry Hill, a real gangster, whose story is depicted in *GoodFellas*. In his autobiography, Hill notes that he doesn't watch *GoodFellas* on TV any more, 'but I'll watch *The Godfather* for the 87th time it's on'. With *The Godfather* still garnering admiration and praise, it seems amazing that the *New York Post* reported in their 1972 review: 'Far from surviving as the *Gone With the Wind* of gangster movies, my guess is that *The Godfather* will be as quickly forgotten as it deserves to be'.

15

'Forget it, Jake, it's...'

— *Chinatown* (1974)

Credits:

DIRECTOR – Roman Polanski
PRODUCER – Robert Evans
EXECUTIVE PRODUCER – C.O. Erickson
SCREENPLAY – Robert Towne
DIRECTOR OF PHOTOGRAPHY – John A. Alonzo
EDITOR – Sam O'Steen
PRODUCTION DESIGNER – Richard Sylbert
ART DIRECTOR – Stewart Campbell
COSTUMES – Anthea Sylbert
MUSIC – Jerry Goldsmith
Panavision/Technicolor
Interiors filmed at Paramount Studios
A Long Road Production – presented by Paramount-Penthouse
Released by Paramount Pictures
125 minutes

Cast:

Jack Nicholson (Jake J. Gittes)/Faye Dunaway (Evelyn Cross
Mulwray)/John Huston (Noah Cross)/Perry Lopez (Lieutenant
Lou Escobar)/John Hillerman (Russ Yelburton)/Darrell
Zwerling (Hollis I. Mulwray)/Diana Ladd (Ida Sessions)/Roy
Jenson (Claude Mulvihill)/Roman Polanski (Mulvihill's
sidekick)/Dick Bakalyan (Detective Loach)/Joe Mandell and
Bruce Glover (Lawrence Walsh and Duffy, Gittes's employees)/
Nandu Hinds (Sophie, Gittes's secretary)/James O'Rear
(Lawyer)/James Hong (Kahn, Mulwray's butler)/Beulah Quo
(Mulwray's maid)/Jerry Fujikawa (Mulwray's gardener)/Belinda
Palmer (Katherine Cross Mulwray)/Roy Roberts (Mayor Bagby)/
George Justin (Barney the barber)/Don Erickson (Banker in

barber's)/Fritzi Burr (Mulwray's secretary)/Charles Knapp
(Morty, morgue attendant)/Federico Roberto (Cross's butler)/
Allan Warnick (Hall of Records clerk)/Burt Young (Curly)/
Elizabeth Harding (Curly's wife)/John Rogers (Mr Palmer, at
Mar Vista)/Cecil Elliott (Emma Dill, Mar Vista resident)

*   *   *

'You can't eat the venetian blinds, I just had them installed on Wednesday,' a private
eye tells a distraught customer who has just discovered his wife is having an affair.
This snatch of dialogue begins *Chinatown*, a post-modern *noir* mystery set in 1930s
Los Angeles. At first glance *Chinatown* doesn't look like *noir*: large portions are set
in the desert and orange groves, and on the coast around Los Angeles – lushly
photographed in Technicolor and Panavision. There is also plenty of humour;
traditional *noir* tends to take itself far too seriously. But here, in the sunshine and
among the tide pools, the darkness lies within the characters.

Paramount producer Robert Evans, who had recently had great success with
The Godfather, hired Robert Towne to write a treatment of his scenario *Water and
Power*, soon retitled *Chinatown*, for $25,000. It would be Evans's first solo production
credit. Towne had worked on the *Bonnie and Clyde* script; for *Chinatown* he concocted
a period mystery thriller. The story had echoes of conspiracy theory, being based
on a real scandal in Los Angeles history, the Owens River Valley incident of 1908.
Here a group of powerful businessmen redeployed the Owens River to serve arid
land, making the land worth a lot more than they had paid for it.

In 1937 drought-stricken Los Angeles, divorce case private eye J.J. Gittes and
his two associates, Walsh and Duffy, are hired by 'Mrs Mulwray' to spy on her
husband Hollis, head of the city's water and power department. Gittes discovers
that the department is about to build a dam to quench Los Angeles' thirst, but
Hollis is convinced the dam is dangerous; Gittes also discovers the water department is running off hundreds of tonnes of water into the sea without explanation.
Gittes photographs Mulwray with a young woman and the scandal hits the papers;
but Gittes is served with a writ from the real Mrs Evelyn Mulwray – the original was
an impostor. Soon afterwards Mulwray drowns in a reservoir and Gittes becomes
involved with Evelyn, who hires him to solve her husband's murder. He finds out that
the bogus Mrs Mulwray is a prostitute, Ida Sessions, who is later murdered. The
police investigation is led by Lou Escobar, an ex-colleague of Gittes, when they used
to work in the Chinatown district. Meanwhile, Gittes is also hired by Noah Cross, a
rich water executive and Evelyn's father, to locate Mulwray's mistress, who has gone
missing. Gittes uncovers a scheme to buy up arid swathes of desert for a fraction of
their worth and then to irrigate them, raising their value by $30 million. The tenant
farmers in the valley are being forced out; the land buyers are all residents of the
Mar Vista Rest Home. It is a huge cover-up by Cross to own the richest land in the

state. Meanwhile, Gittes trails Evelyn, with whom he is now having an affair, and discovers that she is holding Mulwray's mistress prisoner. But when he confronts her he discovers that the woman is both Evelyn's daughter and her sister; her own father is the incestuous culprit. Gittes arranges for Evelyn and her daughter Katherine to be whisked away to Mexico, but at their escape rendezvous in Chinatown, the cops and Cross intercept them. In the confusion, Evelyn wounds her father and drives off with Katherine, but a cop shoots Evelyn dead, leaving screaming Katherine in the care of the man she knows as 'grandfather'.

Evans brought in Roman Polanski to direct the film. Polish-born, he was the director of claustrophobic psychological thrillers *Knife in the Water* (1962), *Repulsion* (1965) and *Cul-de-Sac* (1966). He had also made *Dance of the Vampires* (1967 – a Hammer horror parody) and the massively popular *Rosemary's Baby* (1968 – with Mia Farrow giving birth to the devil's son). His *Macbeth* (1971), a grotesque, blood-drenched treatment of the bard, was a cathartic film for Polanski. On 9 August 1969, Polanski's wife, Sharon Tate (who was eight months pregnant) and four friends had been butchered at Polanski's Benedict Canyon house at Cielo Drive by Charles Manson's religious cult, while Polanski was in London.

Polanski hated Towne's script and the two men worked together in the summer of 1973 to improve it; Polanski said it was overlong (some 180 pages), over-wordy and over-complicated. According to Robert McKee in his BBC TV programme *Filmworks*, a comparison between Towne's version and the shooting script demonstrates how Polanski transformed the work, lifting it 'from good to great'. Towne originally had the story end with Evelyn killing her father; Polanski wanted Evelyn killed. As Towne noted: 'That's life. Beautiful blondes die in Los Angeles ... Sharon had.' One of Towne's ideas was to have a protagonist who is injured early in the film and doesn't recover immediately. Gittes wears an unsightly bandage on his nose for much of the action, having had his nostril slit by a switchblade thug, played with relish, at Evans's suggestion, by Polanski; in the original script, Gittes had his earlobe severed. Writer and director constantly disagreed throughout the rewrites, so much so that by the time shooting commenced, they weren't even speaking to one another. In particular, Polanski didn't like Gittes's too-linear, *noir* narration throughout the action and dispensed with it entirely. The shocking ending was actually written by Polanski only two nights before it was shot, with Jack Nicholson rewriting his own dialogue in 'Gittes-speak'.

New Jersey-born Jack Nicholson was a graduate of Roger Corman's informal, no-budget, B-movie film school. He had appeared in sixties gothic horror movies (*The Raven* and *The Terror*), westerns (*The Shooting* and *Ride in the Whirlwind*) and biker movies (*Hell's Angels on Wheels* and *Easy Rider*), before earning great reviews and Oscar nominations for more considered projects, including the character study *Five Easy Pieces* (1970) and Hal Ashby's *The Last Detail* (1973). Nicholson was interested in *Chinatown* from the beginning and Gittes was the surname of Nicholson's best friend.

The original casting for Evelyn Mulwray was Jane Fonda or, at Evans's suggestion, his then wife Ali McGraw, but the role eventually went to Faye Dunaway, at Polanski's insistence. Since *Bonnie and Clyde*, Dunaway had made *The Thomas Crown Affair* (1968 – opposite Steve McQueen) and *Little Big Man* (1970), both huge successes, but others, including *A Place for Lovers* (1970), bombed. Crispin Glover's father, Bruce Glover, was cast as Duffy; he'd memorably been hitman Mr Wint in *Diamonds Are Forever* (1971); Perry Lopez was excellent as Gittes's ex-partner on the Chinatown beat. Roy Jenson was suitably threatening as hulking ex-sheriff Claude Mulvihill, who with pint-sized knifeman Polanski, is Cross's strong-arm help. John Hillerman, later manservant Higgins in the TV series *Magnum PI*, appeared as Yelburton, Mulwray's deputy at Water and Power. The real casting coup was John Huston as Noah Cross, like Dunaway an inspired choice. The director of *The Maltese Falcon* and *The Asphalt Jungle* has never given a better performance, although in this period he was appearing frequently in such choice items as *Candy* (1968), *Myra Breckinridge* (1970), *The Deserter* (1971) and *Breakout* (1975 – as Charles Bronson's granddad). Cross's public persona was reputedly based on William Mulholland, the head of Water and Power, who installed miles of pipeline in the Owens River scandal.

The film was budgeted at $6 million; Towne received $250,000 plus 5 per cent of the gross for writing the screenplay. Filming began in September 1973, with the

J.J. Gittes can't help sticking his nose in other people's business; Jack Nicholson in *Chinatown* (1974).

orange grove sequences the first to be lensed. Several scenes were shot in the picturesque locale of Avalon, on Santa Catalina Island, including the distinctive circular casino exterior. The Council Chambers of Los Angeles City Hall appear, as does the Peninsula Equestrian Centre, in Portuguese Bend, where Gittes meets Cross. The Windsor Restaurant, behind the Ambassador Hotel, was the 'Brown Derby' rendezvous between Evelyn and Gittes. Pt. Fermin, near the Stone Canyon Reservoir, San Pedro, saw Gittes having his nose sliced; a retirement home in Brentwood is the Mar Vista, where the 'landowners' reside. Gittes and Duffy shadow Mulwray in a rowing boat on the lake in Echo Park. Mulwray's mansion stands in a five-acre plot in Pasadena; Katherine's residence is on Canyon Drive in Hollywood. Other locations include the Biltmore Hotel, the Bradbury Building and the Big Tujunga Wash, at Foothills Boulevard. The climax of the film was actually shot in Chinatown. Polanski was known for his hard working methods and driving, dictatorial style, answering Dunaway's enquiries for pointers as to her motivation with 'Your salary is your motivation!' Filming wrapped in early 1974.

The thirties-styled clothes were designed by Anthea Sylbert, the period set decoration by her brother-in-law, Richard Sylbert, who had also worked on *The Graduate* (1967). Nicholson looks immaculate in pinstripe suits and Borsalino. Dunaway was made up to look like Polanski's mother, with plucked eyebrows and 'cupid's bow' lipstick, and drives an authentic cream Packard convertible. The original cinematographer was Stanley Cortez, but he didn't understand the 'look' Polanski required. The director then chose John Alonso, the cinematographer of the hip road movie *Vanishing Point* (1971); he went on to co-photograph *Close Encounters of the Third Kind* (1977) and Al Pacino's *Scarface* (1983). His lush style and exquisite compositions lent *Chinatown* an otherworldliness, a dreamlike feel, invoking the stalking scenes of Hitchcock's *Vertigo* (1958). Polanski even deploys Hitchcockian imagery – for instance the reflection of the subject in the lens of Gittes's Leica camera – like a similar shot in Hitchcock's *Rear Window*.

Jerry Goldsmith's score, with its smoky trumpet theme, is partly an homage to thirties movies and partly a reaction against them. Goldsmith says it is his personal favourite, even though he wrote it in only ten days. The eerie, high-pitched violins, repetitive echoing piano and harp arrangements, and jagged piano arpeggios reference Bernard Herrmann's scores for Hitchcock's *North by Northwest*, *Vertigo* and *Psycho*, while creating a threatening ambience in keeping with Polanski's unusual, twisted take on classic Hollywood.

Though *Chinatown* appears to detail Gittes's investigations (first into a possible affair, then a murder, followed by a missing person's enquiry), the main narratives are two parallel plot lines: the 'water mystery' and the 'daughter mystery'. These are linked together by Noah Cross, Evelyn and Katherine.

Los Angeles is 'dying of thirst'. 'The heat's murder,' a barber points out, as he looks at a car radiator steamily overheating outside. Later, Mortician Morty jokes: 'Middle of a drought and the water commissioner drowns...only in LA.' In most crime films, according to Towne, the mystery element revolved around robberies, jewels and exoticism: 'water and power, that's unusual', and also mundane. Water kills Mulwray and drowns a tramp sleeping under a bridge on a 'dry' riverbed, which has been taking run-off water. This water, eventually discharging into the sea, is making it appear there is a water shortage to increase the chance of the forthcoming Alto Vallejo (High Valley) Dam and Reservoir project, which Mulwray opposes on safety grounds. Cross considerably simplifies this grand design: 'Either you bring the water to LA, or you bring LA to the water' and incorporate the soon-to-be-lush valley into the city. Only such a scheme could be hatched by a man called Noah. The land has been purchased unwittingly by elderly patients in the Mar Vista Rest Home. As Gittes notes, when he sees one of the new owner's names in the obituary column of the *LA Post-Record*: 'He passed away two weeks ago and one week ago he bought the land . . . that's unusual.' The real landowners are members of the Albacore Fishing Club, which Cross owns.

Water is key to the mystery, with many references throughout the film. The Albacore Club's symbol is a fish and 'Mar Vista' translates as 'Sea View'. Mulwray drowned in a freshwater reservoir, but had salt water in his lungs. The tide pool in Mulwray's garden is salt water and the pair of glasses Gittes finds reflecting in the bottom of the pool are bifocal: Mulwray wore normal lenses, but Cross's match. Cross remembers that Mulwray used to say of tide pools 'That's where life begins'; for Mulwray it also ends there.

In *noir* fiction, the *femme fatale* who hires the private eye is, according to Towne, more commonly a 'black widow', but here she's the heroine, trying to protect her daughter from evil 'grandfather'. Evelyn excuses her vagueness regarding the case to Gittes: 'It's very personal, it couldn't be more personal.' Later Gittes wants to know the truth about the woman he thinks Evelyn has kidnapped and roughs her up to make her talk. Thereafter she reveals her darkest secret: 'She's my daughter, she's my sister,' says Evelyn, eventually breaking down. 'She's my sister and my daughter. My father and I . . . understand?' Cross is an evil man whose affable presence masks his threat. His own daughter warns, 'My father is a very dangerous man.' On their initial meeting, Cross tells Gittes he's heard that the detective has 'a nasty reputation . . . I like that'. And although the old man says, 'Politicians, ugly buildings and whores all get respectable if they last long enough,' he is morally doomed. He also chillingly observes, 'Most people never have to face the fact that at the right time and the right place, they're capable of anything.'

The thirties setting is totally convincing, even down to period newspaper headlines featuring star racehorse Seabiscuit. Particularly interesting is Gittes's thirties-style detective work. He places pocket watches under the wheels of parked cars, then returns later to retrieve the smashed timepieces, thus discovering the hour the car drove off. Later, he smashes the red rear light cover of Evelyn's car, ensuring that it is distinctive for his night-time pursuit; the mismatched white and red lights recall Evelyn's flawed iris, an optical birthmark making her eye colours appear different.

Gittes's photographic evidence of various adulterous affairs recalls the tabloid hackwork of *Confidential* magazine, while vintage music such as Bunny Berigan's 'I Can't Get Started', 'Easy Living', 'The Way You Look Tonight' and 'Some Day' and authentic period names (Mulwray, Yelburton and Mulvihill) evoke thirties LA.

Chinatown is Polanski's first return to Los Angeles following the death of his wife and, judging by his depiction of the place, he hated it. Alongside the black humour, the violence, as in Robert Altman's detective yarn *The Long Goodbye* (1973), is jarring. Towne said Gittes's split nostril was apt punishment for 'a nosy detective'. Polanski's 'midget' thug sticks the point of his flick-knife up Gittes's nostril and jerks it back, then threatens that next time he'll 'cut it off and feed it to my goldfish'. The bandage on Gittes's nose is subsequently the butt of humour; Gittes tells Evelyn: 'I goddamn nearly lost my nose and I like it…I like breathing through it.' When water deputy Yelburton looks at Gittes's nose injury he notes: 'That must really smart.' 'Only when I breathe.' Nicholson delivers such humour with his usual charm, calling in to see 'Morty' the morgue attendant with the words 'Thought I'd drop by to see who dropped dead.' Dunaway is also coolly self-deprecating: when Evelyn Mulwray threatens to sue the PI, she tells him, 'I don't get tough with anyone…my lawyer does.'

The title *Chinatown* was suggested to Towne by a Hungarian vice squad cop, who when asked what he did when he patrolled Chinatown, said, 'As little as possible'; this line is spoken twice by Gittes in the film. He tells Evelyn that because of the cultural differences when he worked in Chinatown, he tried to do 'as little as possible'. In his last dealings there he tried to protect someone and 'ended up making sure that she was hurt'.

Only the finale takes place in Chinatown, but the implication is that the lawlessness of the district metaphorically permeates the whole movie, from corruption to incest. 'You may think,' says Cross to Gittes, 'you know what you're dealing with, but believe me, you don't.' Gittes smiles. 'Why is that funny?' asks Cross. 'That's what the District Attorney used to tell me in Chinatown,' answers Gittes. As *Chinatown* leads the audience deeper into the labyrinth, it gets darker, in atmosphere and tone. At the climax, all the key protagonists find themselves in the nocturnal jungle of Chinatown. Escobar has arrested Gittes's associates, Walsh and Duffy, and Evelyn is preparing to leave with Katherine for Mexico. In a monstrous moment, lumbering Cross whines, 'Please, please be reasonable…she's mine too,' as Evelyn ushers Katherine into the car. Evelyn pulls a gun and wounds Cross, then speeds off with Katherine. Police detective Loach fires after the car and the vehicle pulls up far down the street, the horn blaring and a woman screaming. Gittes, Escobar and the others sprint down the street to be greeted by a horrifying spectacle. Evelyn is slumped over the steering wheel, her head resting on the car horn. Her face is a mask of blood and her eye is missing; beside her is Katherine, screeching hysterically. Cross wails 'Oh Lord' and covers Katherine's eyes, then enfolds her in his arms and leads her away, still screaming. 'As little as possible,' murmurs Gittes, as he realises Cross is going to get away with murder. While the cops clear the streets, dazed Gittes is led away by Duffy and Walsh, the latter commenting, 'Forget it, Jake...it's Chinatown'.

Chinatown was released in the US in June 1974, rated R. The poster art depicted swirling, wispy smoke from Nicholson's cigarette forming Faye Dunaway's hair, with a stylised wave lapping against Nicholson's arm. It incorporates Art Nouveau style and was designed by Jim Pearsall. It was so good that it was used unchanged worldwide. A variation, by Amsel, had the tagline: 'He's a private eye. She's a case. It's inscrutable.' It was an X certificate in the UK. The trailer predictably played up the action, with much shooting and speeding cars, while a narrator ominously intoned: 'You get tender, you get close to each other...maybe you even get close to the truth'. *Village Voice* called Gittes 'Bogart for the age of rock 'n' roll'. *Films in Review* perceptively noted, 'Someone once said of Richard Strauss' *Salome* that it was composed of bits and pieces of fecal matter: the same is true of *Chinatown*; quickly, however, we must add that both are extraordinarily successful *tours de force*.' *Christian Century* said, 'Polanski merges Manson with Watergate as elements in the substance that now pervades and stains all our society', while *The New Republic* opined, 'If *Chinatown* were shorter and less consciously paradigmatic, it would be a good sinister thriller. But Towne and Polanski are insufficiently innocent.'

Art nouveau poster designed by Jim Pearsall advertising Roman Polanski's *Chinatown* (1974).

Best of all, *Newsweek* said conspiracy-riddled *Chinatown* was 'Watergate with real water'. It grossed $12.4 million in the US and £30 million worldwide.

Robert Towne hated the finished film and reputedly wanted to take his name off the credits. *Chinatown* received 11 Academy Award nominations, including Nicholson, Dunaway, Polanski's direction, Alonzo's cinematography, Goldsmith's score and the Best Picture award; it was up against *The Godfather Part II* (which won Best Picture, Director and Score) and ironically it was only Towne's Original Screenplay that triumphed. Some TV screenings slightly edit the unpleasant scene when Gittes gets his nose job; other prints have omitted expletives and in some cases the entire 'making love like a Chinaman' joke, which is both crude and racist.

In the seventies, thirties-style crime thrillers were in vogue, with directors if not audiences. Robert Altman's *They Live by Night* remake *Thieves Like Us* (1974) was a commercial disaster, while Dick Richards's UK remake of Raymond Chandler's *Farewell My Lovely*, with Robert Mitchum in the lead and Charlotte Rampling as the *femme fatale*, was more successful. Simultaneously, nostalgia-obsessed director Peter Bogdanovich unsuccessfully attempted to resurrect thirties-style musical comedy, with *At Long Last Love* (1975), starring Madeline Kahn, Cybill Shepherd and Burt Reynolds. According to reviewers, Reynolds 'sings like Dean Martin with adenoids and dances like a drunk killing cockroaches', while Shepherd 'apparently thinks badinage is something you put on a small cut', ensuring the thirties musical revival was brief. A more hip updating of Chandler's work appeared in Robert Altman's detective movie *The Long Goodbye* (1973), a marvellously skewed version of the private eye genre. At its most successful, a little of *Chinatown*'s underworld atmosphere also permeates *L.A. Confidential* (1997), another successful *noir*-ish mystery, set in the early fifties.

Chinatown was intended as the first part of a trilogy, to be followed by 'The Two Jakes' (with oil as the motivation rather than water) and 'Cloverleaf' (detailing a freeway construction). Only *The Two Jakes* was made, with the team of Nicholson as Gittes, Towne scripting and Evans producing. It was planned that Towne was going to direct and Evans was to play the second Jake; as it turned out, neither did, and Nicholson directed it in 1990, with Harvey Keitel as the other Jake, a crooked real estate dealer. This time the script's convoluted, labyrinthine nature ensures the plot is impenetrable and it is a less-than-complimentary epilogue to the original film.

In retrospect, the *Chicago Sun-Times* said *Chinatown* 'was seen as neo-*noir* when it was released. Now years have passed and film history blurs a little, and it seems to settle easily beside the original *noirs*. That is a compliment.' *Empire* magazine called it 'the best private eye movie ever made...a timeless classic'. *Chinatown* is one of the most elegantly costumed, styled and photographed films ever made. It is also a melancholy work of art and a cinematic enigma.

16

'Keep your friends close, but your enemies closer'

— *The Godfather Part II* (1974)

Credits:

DIRECTOR AND PRODUCER – Francis Ford Coppola
CO-PRODUCERS – Gray Frederickson and Fred Roos
ASSOCIATE PRODUCER – Mona Skeger
STORY – Mario Puzo
SCREENPLAY – Mario Puzo and Francis Ford Coppola
DIRECTOR OF PHOTOGRAPHY – Gordon Willis
EDITORS – Peter Zinner, Barry Malkin and Richard Marks
PRODUCTION DESIGNER – Dean Tavoularis
ART DIRECTOR – Angelo Graham
SET DECORATOR – George R. Nelson
COSTUMES – Theodora Van Runkle
MUSIC COMPOSER – Nino Rota
MUSIC CONDUCTOR – Carmine Coppola
Technicolor
Interiors filmed at American Zoetrope
A Paramount/Coppola Company Production
Released by Paramount Pictures
200 minutes

Cast:

Al Pacino (Michael Corleone)/Robert Duvall (Tom Hagan)/
Diane Keaton (Kay Adams)/Robert De Niro (Vito Corleone)/
Talia Shire (Constanzia 'Connie' Rizzi)/John Cazale (Frederico
'Fredo' Corleone)/Lee Strasberg (Hyman Roth)/Michale V. Gazzo
(Frankie Pentangeli, alias 'Frankie Five-Angels')/G.D. Spradlin
(Senator Pat Geary)/Gaston Moschin (Don Fanucci)/Tom
Rosqui (Rocco Lampone)/B. Kirby Jnr (Young Clemenza)/John
Aprea (Young Tessio)/Frank Sivero (Genco)/Mariana Hill
(Deanna Corleone)/Dominic Chianese (Johnny Ola)/Amerigo

Tot (Michael's bodyguard)/Richard Bright (Al Neri)/Troy Donahue (Merle Johnson, Connie's boyfriend)/William Bowers (Senate Inquiry chairman)/Roger Corman, Richard Matheson and Phil Feldman (Senators at Inquiry)/Peter Donat (Senate lawyer Questadt)/Gianni Russo (Carlo Rizzi)/Morgana King (Carmella 'Mama' Corleone)/Tere Livrano (Theresa Hagan)/ Angelo Infanti (Fabrizio)/Joe Spinall (Willi Cicci, Pentangeli henchman)/Abe Vegoda (Sal Tessio)/Maria Carta (Vito's mother)/ Oreste Baldini (Vito as a boy)/Giuseppe Sillato (Don Francesco)/ Fay Spain (Marcia Roth)/David Baker and Harry Dean Stanton (Pentangeli's FBI guards)/Carmine Caridi and Danny Aiello (the Rosato Brothers)/Peter LaCorte (Abbandando, the grocer)/ Leopoldo Trieste (Signor Roberto, the landlord)/Mario Cotone (Don Tommasino)/Tito Alba (Cuban president)/Salvatore Po (Vincenzo Pentangeli)/Andea Maugen (Strollo)/Ignazio Pappalardo (Mosca)/Roman Coppola (Sonny as a boy)/James Caan (Santino 'Sonny' Corleone)

*   *   *

Two years after the release of *The Godfather*, Francis Ford Coppola unleashed a sequel. Following the original's success, he was initially reluctant to revisit 'the family', but was persuaded when the producers made him an offer he couldn't refuse: $1 million plus a percentage of the takings, the highest fee for a director up to then.

Again co-written by Coppola and Mario Puzo, *The Godfather Part II* tells the story of young Vito Corleone fleeing Sicily in 1901 following the murder of his father, mother and brother, and arriving as an immigrant on Ellis Island. Vito grows up in Little Italy, a district in New York, and is married in 1914. In 1917, he shoots Don Fanucci, the local overlord of the 'Black Hand Society', and usurps his protection rackets, becoming a don himself, in league with two allies: Peter Clemenza and Sal Tessio. In 1927, Vito avenges his family when he returns to Sicily and kills their murderer, landowner Don Ciccio.

This story deftly interweaves with updates on Michael's story, between 1958 and 1959. At the end of *The Godfather*, it's 1955 and the Corleone estate is about to relocate from Long Island (a sign on the front wall reads 'Future Commercial Development, Genco Land Co. 56 Acres – Sold' and John J. Bartek removals are loading a van with the family's belongings). At the beginning of *Part II*, it's 1958 and the family are living on Lake Tahoe, with their business interests now in gambling and casinos in Reno and Las Vegas. Michael later branches out into Havana, with Hyman Roth, a rival gangster. Roth claims to be grooming Michael to take over his empire: in fact Roth plans to assassinate him, but Michael remembers his father's advice: 'He taught me "Keep your friends close, but your enemies closer".' Fidel Castro overthrows the Batista regime and puts an end to Michael's Cuban adventure. Fredo betrays Michael, who is almost killed in an ambush at his Tahoe estate; later it transpires that Fredo is in league with Roth. The Corleones are investigated by a senate hearing, but the star witness, Frankie Pentangeli (also called 'Frankie Five-Angels'), pulls out at the last moment – it is a question of Sicilian honour. When his brother Vincenzo from Palermo appears in the courtroom, Frankie refuses to testify. The climax of the story sees a series of deaths, all caused by Michael: Roth is assassinated at an airport, Pentangeli commits suicide in a bath and Fredo is shot during a fishing trip on Tahoe. The Godfather sits alone in the grounds of his estate and reflects on the past: he has lost his brothers, his friends and his wife, but he still has his 'family'.

The parts of the film set in Sicily and New York, between 1901 and 1927, were present in Puzo's original book, as 'Book III' of the novel's nine sections. Puzo was also responsible for this early part of the script. The fifties section was largely the creation of Coppola, though Puzo collaborated on that too. It contained elements of real history, though names have been altered. When, for example, Coppola created the character of informant Frankie Pentangeli, he was partly thinking of Joseph Valachi, who famously turned informant on the Mafia, in exchange for immunity from mob reprisals. The Senate hearings depicted in the film investigating

Young Vito Corleone (Robert De Niro), on the rise in *The Godfather Part II* (1974).

mob corruption were actually headed by Democrat Estes Kefauver in the early fifties. Called 'The Senate Special Committee to Investigate Crime in Interstate Commerce', they were televised and became massive ratings winners. Mobsters who couldn't testify because of bogus illnesses had their mystery ailments dubbed 'Kefauveritis'. The Cuban scenes of the film are also historically accurate, with Michael finding himself caught up in the New Year's Eve coup d'état, when President Fulgencio Batista's regime was overthrown by Fidel Castro's rebels in 1959. The American nationals flee to the docks and the airport, or try to find sanctuary in the US Embassy.

Coppola was pleased that most of the original cast members agreed to reprise their roles in the sequel. Al Pacino, Diane Keaton, Robert Duvall, John Cazale and Talia Shire all returned for *Part II*. Pacino was still a hot property, following his performance as dishevelled cop *Serpico* (1973), for which he earned another Oscar nomination as Best Actor. Richard Castellano refused to reappear as Clemenza unless he could write his own dialogue, so Coppola wrote an explanatory line informing us of Clemenza's recent death. A new character, Frankie Pentangeli, played by Michael Gazzo, replaced him. Many of the supporting players also came back, including Richard Bright as Michael's hitman, Neri, and Morgana King as Mama Corleone. Italian actor Gaston Moschin (the murder victim in *The Conformist* – 1970) appeared as white-suited Don Fanucci. Mariana Hill was cast as Fredo's drunken wife, Deanna; Hyman Roth's wife Marcia was played by fifties starlet Fay Spain. Coppola's mentor Roger Corman had a cameo role on the senatorial hearing panel, as did novelist Richard Matheson, the screenwriter of many of Corman's Poe adaptations.

For the role of young Vito Corleone, Coppola needed the Brando of his generation, Robert De Niro. De Niro had played in cheap gangster movies such as *Bloody Mama* (1970) and *The Gang That Couldn't Shoot Straight* (1971), portrayed a dying baseball player in *Bang the Drum Slowly* (1973) and made a dynamic appearance as manic Johnny Boy in *Mean Streets* (1973). Lee Strasberg, the famous acting teacher and artistic director of the Actors Studio in New York, played Jewish gangster Hyman Roth; Coppola also considered director Elia Kazan for the role. As well as his sister Talia Shire, Coppola again cast family members: Mama Corleone's corpse was played by the director's mother, while curly-haired young Sonny is Roman Coppola, the director's son.

In the penultimate scene of *The Godfather Part II* Coppola wanted to reunite the original's cast in the Corleone's dining room. The scene depicts Carlo Rizzi's introduction to Connie by Sonny, while Tessio, Michael, Fredo and Tom Hagan are all present. It takes place in 1941 (Pearl Harbor has just been bombed) and Michael informs his family he has enlisted. Of the original actors, only Brando refused to take part; he reputedly wanted $500,000 plus 10 per cent of the gross for his cameo. In the finished version, the family has planned a surprise birthday party for the Don; 'Brando's' arrival in an adjacent room is thus unseen.

No expense was spared for *The Godfather Part II*'s settings; according to Coppola, the budget was $11 million. The shooting schedule was 104 days: from October 1973 to June 1974. In New York, production designer Dean Tavoularis and his team spent six months converting Sixth Street, on the Lower East Side of Manhattan, into Little Italy's 'Hell's Kitchen' in 1912. Even the lamp-posts were replaced with their old-fashioned shepherd's crook equivalents. The same street was re-dressed, festooned with arches of light bulbs and bunting, for the sumptuous Festa di San Genarro ('Feast of San Genarro'), with its cash-covered Madonna procession. The authentic period costumes were designed by Theodora Van Runkle, who had also worked on *Bonnie and Clyde*, *The Thomas Crown Affair* (1968) and *Bullit* (1968). The Sixth Street setting is seen to best effect when Vito emerges from the Abbandando Grosseria carrying a grocery basket on his shoulders, and weaves his way down the street, through market stalls and crawling traffic.

The Corleone's Nevada estate was filmed in the Henry Kaiser Estate, on the banks of Lake Tahoe, in Nevada. Coppola reported that finding such an ideal location was one of the several happy accidents that occurred throughout the film's making. The Ellis Island immigration depot was a fish market in Trieste; the courtroom scenes were staged in Los Angeles. The Dominican Republic subbed for Cuba; a 1958 New Year's Eve party was staged in the Embajador Hotel, in Santo Domingo.

The warmth of the family scenes, in particular the opening wedding scene, in the first *Godfather* film and the book is replaced in *Part II* by Michael's cold calculating nature, where his own family become secondary to his business interests. In the way most directors cross-cut between two different scenes, to increase tension, or speed the narrative, Coppola's dual story threads deliver two epic tales in just such a manner. *Part II* shows both the Corleone family's creation and, at the hands of Michael, its destruction.

The most effective scenes in the film are of De Niro, as younger Vito, establishing himself in New York. The period settings and costumes are sumptuous and the burnished photography, again by Gordon Willis, evokes sepia prints of the period. The opening scenes are set in Sicily, the largest island in the Mediterranean: the football kicked by the boot of Italy. The young boy, on the run from local tyrant Don Ciccio, is called Vito Andolini – he changes his name to Corleone when he arrives in New York, to reinforce his ties to the Sicilian village where he was born. Corleone, with the Sicilian coastal town of Castellammare del Golfo, is the best known and most prolific place of origin for Mafiosi. In New York, young Vito works for a grocer and gets married, and his upward rise through society is driven by the care of, and passion for, his family. Their tiny tenement room is hardly big enough for them, but as their family starts to grow, with the birth of Santino and Frederico, so does Vito's immersion in crime. In a key moment, having just murdered Fanucci, Vito sits on the steps outside his tenement with his wife and children. Holding his youngest son in his arms, Vito says, 'Michael, your father loves you very much,' underlining the importance of family to Vito over all else.

Vito's life of crime, like the rise and fall of cinema hoods of yesteryear, begins innocuously enough, when he is conned by Clemenza into inadvertently stealing a rug. When he loses his job at the grocers, because Don Fanucci wants his nephew to work there, Vito takes it personally. He later kills Fanucci when the Don demands protection money from Vito, Clemenza and Tessio's rising hoodlums; 'Just enough to wet my beak,' says Fanucci. Vito stalks the white-suited Don, who mingles with revellers at the Festa di San Genarro. Vito shadows him along the rooftops and shoots Fanucci at the door of his apartment, having silenced the pistol by wrapping a blanket around it. De Niro is totally convincing in the role. In the early scenes, he exhibits grace and poise, a nobility inherent in Vito's poor peasant stock; when he becomes the first Don Corleone, De Niro's mannerisms incorporate Brando's speech patterns and gestures, as Vito gains control of the neighbourhood: now landlords and shopkeepers fear him. Later Vito's violent temperament is established; he returns to Sicily to take revenge on the man who killed his family in typically ferocious Cosa Nostra style: while helpless, elderly Don Ciccio sits in an easy chair on his patio, Vito guts him like a fish.

The visual beauty of the early New York scenes somewhat overshadows those of the fifties section, which has the better story. If the later section has a fault, it is that Robert Duvall is underused, with Tom Hagan pushed into the background for much of the drama. The fifties segment details Michael Corleone's moral collapse, as he follows in his father's murderous footsteps. At the beginning of the film, during a celebration of his son Anthony's first communion, we are reintroduced to Michael; the Sierra Boys' Choir sing 'Mr Wonderful', as Michael hands over a cheque to Anthony's university. But in contrast to the homely, touching family scenes of the Vito sections of the film, the icy world of Michael Corleone is a brutal, callous place. On his return from Cuba, Michael is told by Kay that she has miscarried; later she reveals she had an abortion, which ends their relationship. She couldn't face bringing any more monstrous Corleones into the world – 'I didn't want your son ... I had it killed because this must all end.' According to Coppola, the abortion was Talia Shire's suggestion, so he included it in the script; originally Kay was only to have miscarried. After their separation, a door closes on Kay, like it had in *The Godfather* – this time more permanently.

Michael even orders the killing of his own brother. Fredo has always been something of an unknown quantity; a weakling, naive and easily influenced. Michael realises that Fredo is in league with Roth when Fredo lets slip that he has met Roth's henchman Johnny Ola before; as they embrace to celebrate New Year, Michael tells Fredo the betrayer: 'I know it was you Fredo. You broke my heart.' Later Michael cuts him out of the family altogether: 'You're nothing to me now ... you're not a brother, you're not a friend,' which destroys Fredo. With their mother's death, a reconciliation seems imminent, but when Michael reintegrates Fredo into the Lake Tahoe community, he's simply living by his father's credo: 'Keep your friends close, but your enemies closer.'

Hyman Roth was reputedly inspired by Meyer Lansky. Born in 1902, Lansky was a Polish Jew from Grodno, who originally worked with Bugsy Siegel, until Lansky and Lucky Luciano ordered his death in 1947, for skimming gambling money. Luciano also killed off 'Joe the Boss' Masseria and Salvatore Maranzano, making himself and Lansky the most powerful men in gangsterdom. With Luciano as the boss, they founded the National Crime Syndicate, the 'Unione Siciliano', though it was more commonly called the Outfit and the Combination. Expanding their interests, Lansky gave Batista $3 million, plus 50 per cent of the profits, to control gambling in Havana.

In the early seventies, Lansky fled to Israel and claimed citizenship under the Jewish Law of Return, but he was forced to leave in 1972. Although the US government made several attempts to prosecute Lansky, he never went to prison and died peacefully in 1983; in *Bugsy* (1991), Ben Kingsley played Lansky.

Hyman Roth was to have appeared briefly in the early De Niro section of *Part II*, but his scene was cut. Vito is introduced by Clemenza to a young man named Hyman Zuchawski, whom Clemenza is about to nickname 'Johnny Lips'. Vito christens him Hyman Rothstein, after Arnold Rothstein, the famous gambler, hood and mathematical genius. By the fifties, Roth is an elderly, Svengali figure who

'Keep your friends close, but your enemies closer': the new Godfather, Michael (Al Pacino) in *The Godfather Part II* (1974).

plans to kill Michael on his way home from the New Year's Eve party in Cuba, even when Roth is professing friendship and a business partnership. Roth was the childhood friend of Moe Green, the casino owner killed by the Corleones in *The Godfather* (Green loosely resembles real-life Lansky associate Gus Greenbaum, who ran the Flamingo for Lansky in Las Vegas). Roth laughs that his American criminal fraternity is 'bigger than US steel', with Michael's slice of the cake, the gambling operations, representing 'leisure and tourism'; the 'US steel' quip was made by Meyer Lansky.

Even after the Cuban setback, the Corleone dynasty continues to roll on. Kay reminds Michael that he promised her '"In five years the Corleone family will be completely legitimate"... that was seven years ago'. But Michael will not be manipulated like a puppet by anyone, not least Roth. As in *The Godfather*, Coppola's *Part II* depicts a series of murders at the climax, and Roth is the latest in a long line of the Don's victims. At the end of the film, Michael sits alone among the rustling autumn leaves and contemplates his sins, while Coppola movingly intercuts Vito as a young man, holding baby Michael, waving from a Sicilian train carriage. Michael has travelled a long way since then and it has been a violent journey. This is the only moment in the film where De Niro and Pacino briefly share the screen together, though a unique photograph taken by Steve Schapiro exists of Pacino (in character as Michael), standing behind De Niro (in his Don Vito persona), on-set in New York.

Coppola insisted the film be called *The Godfather Part II*, though footage taken on-set during filming in New York features sign boards with the working title, *The Second Godfather*. It was the first time a film sequel had a numerical designation, commonplace today. Usually sequels, even those featuring the same central characters, had different titles to the originals, or were called *Return* or *Revenge of...* When the 200-minute epic was released, the full title was *Mario Puzo's The Godfather Part II*. It was put on general release in the US in December 1974. The *New Yorker* declared, 'This is a bicentennial picture that doesn't insult the intelligence. It's an epic vision of the corruption of America...about midway I began to feel that the film was expanding in my head like a soft bullet.' The *Hollywood Reporter* said the film was 'less emotionally disturbing than its predecessor', which studied 'the nature of power in the United States' heritage'. *Women's Wear Daily* described the two films together as 'the equivalent of those great, panoramic 19th Century novels that relate the progress of a family and a society'. But it was much less successful than *The Godfather*, taking $57 million.

At the 1974 Oscars, Coppola pulled off the astonishing feat of winning the Best Film category again, the only time a film and its sequel have won this award. Coppola also won Best Director and he and Puzo won Best Adapted Screenplay. The film's other awards include Best Score and Best Art Direction-Set Decoration. Robert De Niro won Best Supporting Actor, for his role as young Vito. This was another first – an Oscar won for the same role, played by different actors. *The*

Godfather Part II gained nominations for Best Supporting Actor (Michael V. Gazzo and Lee Strasberg), Best Supporting Actress (Talia Shire), Best Costumes (Theodora Van Runkle) and Al Pacino for Best Actor.

When the original *Godfather* was shown on US Network TV in 1974, with an introduction by Coppola (then editing *The Godfather Part II*), the director explained that he had personally assembled the abridged version to be screened, toning down the violence. The 1977–78 season on US TV saw a new innovation: the movie miniseries. *The Godfather: The Complete Epic* was *Parts I* and *II* edited chronologically. It was shown by NBC as a four-part series in November 1977, augmented with material that was filmed but never used in cinema release versions of the two films. It was shown in the UK on BBC2 in the eighties as *The Godfather Saga*, with extra nudity and violence.

In these extended TV versions, additional scenes from the original *Godfather* include more footage of Connie and Carlo's wedding, a scene with Woltz giving a young starlet a pony on her birthday and Michael and Kay in bed in New York. More scenes set in Sicily were added, including a Communist parade and Michael, Fabrizio and Calo relaxing under a tree. There was more footage of Michael talking to Don Vito in the garden and a scene with Kay lighting a candle for Michael in the family church, having been lied to over the death of Carlo Rizzi. Other scenes were never reinstated, including a brief scene following the death of Apollonia, with shocked Michael calling for vengeance on Fabrizio.

Extra footage that was shot but not used in the cinema release version of *The Godfather Part II* included the first meeting between Tessio and Vito, prior to a visit to a gunsmith. Another scene depicts the attempted murder by three thugs of white-clad Fanucci; he has his throat slit, but not deep enough to kill him, and runs away, screaming and holding his hat under his chin to catch the blood. There is a further scene where Signor Roberto refers to 'Don Vito Corleone' for the first time. Two important Sicilian connection scenes were also missing from *Part II*. In 1927, before Vito gains revenge on Don Ciccio, he kills two Ciccio hoods. One has his throat slit under his mosquito net. The other, named Strollo, is battered to death with an oar in a quiet bay, lit by a beautiful Sicilian sunrise. In the fifties sequences, the murder of Apollonia has a postscript. Michael receives information that Fabrizio, the car bomber, is in the US. Now a restaurateur, Fabrizio is fittingly blown up in a booby-trapped car. Some of these missing scenes were reinstated in the TV *Godfather Saga*; others have since been made available as individual scene extras on DVD.

Following the success of the two *Godfather* films, there were many inferior derivatives, which attempted to cash in on the vogue for Mafia movies, with much of the violence but little of the familial drama and human emotion. The most high-profile was Dino De Laurentiis's production of *The Valachi Papers* (1972 – also released as *Cosa Nostra*), based on the book by Peter Maas. It was a superior, although blood-drenched, decade-spanning gangster saga, with Charles Bronson as Mafia informer Joseph Valachi, who betrayed his boss, Don Vito Genovese. On hearing that Valachi has turned informer, Genovese puts a $100,000 bounty on his head. Jill Ireland, Bronson's wife, played Valachi's on-screen wife Maria, Lino Ventura was Mafioso Genovese, while Lucky Luciano was played by Angelo Infanti, Fabrizio in *The Godfather*. In contrast to Coppola's faultless *mise-en-scène*, *Valachi* for example features thirties period cars driving down seventies streets, evidently lined with modern cars.

The Valachi Papers was partly filmed on location in New York and much was made in the publicity of the discovery that the real Mafia was keeping an eye on proceedings. It was a box-office smash, even though Paramount, the film's original distributors, wouldn't release it in direct competition with the original *Godfather* films. Columbia released it in the US instead. Perhaps this wrangle was the reason for Bronson's comments regarding *The Godfather* – he thought that Brando gave 'a fantastic interpretation', but it was 'the shittiest movie I've ever seen in my entire life'. Ironic then that Bronson's Italian-made *Violent City* (1970) cashed in on the *Godfather* films, when it was retitled *The Family* on its US release.

Further *Godfather* derivatives include the blaxpoitation *The Godfather of Harlem* (1973), *The Big Family* (1973), *The Don is Dead* (1973), *Il Consigliori* (1973), *L'Emigrante* (1973), *Honour Thy Father* (1975), *Corleone* (1977 – also called *Father of the Godfathers*), *From Corleone to Brooklyn* (1979) and the action-packed Alain Delon revenge vehicle *Big Guns* (1973 – also called *Tony Arzenta*), with Delon's Tony seeking vengeance on the four bosses responsible for his wife's death.

In 1990, Coppola himself made the final chapter of Michael Corleone's story, entitled *The Godfather Part III* – Coppola's original title was the cheerful *The Death of Michael Corleone*. The action takes place in 1979 New York, with diversions to Rome and Sicily. Michael attempts to 'go legit' with his business interests, becoming involved with the Vatican (to 'purify their money'), but eventually realises he'll always be a gangster, unlike Anthony, his son, who makes his opera singing debut. 'I don't hate you,' Kay tells Michael at one point, 'I dread you.' In the finale, Don Corleone dies alone, sitting in a chair in his garden in Sicily, not the violent death of so many of his enemies, but quietly and with dignity.

It was always going to be problematic for Coppola to make a third *Godfather* film to equal its predecessors' pedigree. Despite some good performances, by Pacino, Diane Keaton, Talia Shire and Coppola's beautiful daughter Sophia (as Michael's daughter Mary), this is a mess and adds nothing to the first two films. The narrative drags, the settings are forgettable and the film is a disappointment considering it was again co-written by Coppola and Puzo. Coppola reckoned that it was released six months before it was finished. *Part III*'s best moments refer back to *Parts I* and *II*, especially a scene where Michael listens to a Sicilian song and emotionally recalls his wedding dance, all those years ago, with Apollonia. But such reminiscences are an unfortunate reminder of the past glories, which the filmmakers failed to repeat.

Released at Christmas 1990, *Part III* took $66 million in the US; not much for a film budgeted at $54 million. The *New Yorker* opined: 'The picture isn't just unpolished and weakly scored; it lacks coherence. *Godfather III* looks like a *Godfather* movie, but it's not about revenge, and it's not about passion and power and survival. It's about a battered movie-maker's king-size depression.' Following *Part III*'s release, a further television presentation was assembled, *The Godfather Trilogy*, a mostly chronological re-edit of all three films.

   The Godfather Part II features a collection of fine performances, including De Niro and Pacino, both giving career-topping portrayals, in a uniformly outstanding cast. Not only does *Part II* neatly round off the story of Michael's Godfather career, it also tells us where he came from. It is that rarest of films: a sequel that is better than the original movie. Sometimes it is best to keep it in the family.

17

'Fat Moe's bone-yard boys'

— Once Upon a Time in America (1984)

Credits:

DIRECTOR – Sergio Leone

EXECUTIVE PRODUCER – Claudio Mancini

PRODUCER – Arnon Milchan

STORY – Harry Grey

SCREENPLAY – Leonardo Benvenuti, Piero De Bernardi, Enrico Medioli, Franco Arcalli, Franco Ferrini and Sergio Leone

ADDITIONAL DIALOGUE – Stuart Kaminsky

DIRECTOR OF PHOTOGRAPHY – Tonino Delli Colli

EDITOR – Nino Baragli

ART DIRECTOR – Carlo Simi

COSTUMES – Gabriella Pescucci

MUSIC COMPOSER AND CONDUCTOR – Ennio Morricone

Technicolor

Interiors filmed at Cinecitta Studios, Rome

A Ladd Company production

Released by Warner Bros

229 minutes (English-language director's cut)

Cast:

Robert De Niro (David 'Noodles' Aaronson, alias 'Robert Williams')/James Woods (Maximilian 'Max' Bercovicz, alias 'Secretary Christopher Bailey')/Elizabeth McGovern (Deborah Gelly)/Joe Pesci (Frankie Menaldi)/Burt Young (Joe)/Tuesday Weld (Carol)/Treat Williams (Jimmy Conway O'Donnell)/Danny Aiello (Police Chief Aiello)/Richard Bright (Chicken Joe)/James Hayden (Patrick 'Patsy' Goldberg)/William Forsythe (Philip 'Cockeye' Stein)/Darlanne Fleugel (Eve McClain)/Larry Rapp (Fat Moe Gelly)/Richard Foronji ('Fart-face', the policeman)/Robert Harper (Sharkey)/Dutch Miller (Van Linden, the diamond

merchant)/Gerard Murphy (Crowning)/Amy Ryder (Peggy)/
Karen Sallo (Mrs Aiello)/Scott Tyler (young Noodles)/Rusty
Jacobs (young Max and David Bailey)/Jennifer Connelly (young
Deborah)/Brian Bloom (young Patsy)/Adrian Curran (young
Cockeye)/Mike Monetti (young Fat Moe)/Noah Moazezi
(Dominic)/James Russo (Bugsy)/Julia Cohen (young Peggy)/
Arnon Milchan (Limo chauffeur)/Ray Dittrich (Trigger), Frank
Gio (Beefy) and Mario Brega (Mandy)

*   *   *

Italian director Sergio Leone had a special cinematic relationship with America,
taking their most sacred genres and turning them inside out. His career took off in
the mid-sixties with a series of ironic, iconic westerns filmed in Italy and Spain.
Dubbed the 'Dollars' trilogy, they starred Clint Eastwood as the gunfighter, 'the
Man With No Name', in *A Fistful of Dollars* (1964), *For a Few Dollars More* (1965)
and *The Good, the Bad and the Ugly* (1966).

Leone then began work on what would become a second trilogy about America.
During the making of his third western, he had read Harry Grey's gangster novel
'The Hoods' (as 'Mano Armata'). But with the massive success of his westerns,
producers weren't interested in 'the hood, the bad and the ugly'. So Leone made
the epic *Once Upon a Time in the West* (1968), which saw the railroads rolling
towards the Pacific and the businessman replacing the gunman. He followed this
with *Duck You Sucker* (1971), detailing a mechanised revolution in Mexico. But these
were less commercially successful than the 'Dollars' trilogy and it was another 11
years before Leone directed another film. In the intervening years, he made TV
adverts for ice cream and Renault cars, and ruminated on his cherished adaptation
of 'The Hoods'. By 1976 his regular musical collaborator Ennio Morricone had
even written a score – all that was needed now was a film to accompany it.

Once Upon a Time in America follows a gang of Jewish street kids, from childhood to adulthood, in a similar manner to biographical crime movies such as *Angels
with Dirty Faces*. Grey's book was written in Sing Sing prison and is loosely
autobiographical. It was first published in the US in 1953, and in 1965 in the UK
and Europe. The cover blurb boasted: 'The inside story of New York gangster life,
by one of the few men left alive to tell it'. Between 1967 and 1977, all Leone had
was a title and an opening scene; no script. When he began to work on it in earnest,
the adaptation was written by several contributors – Leonardo Benvenuti, Piero De
Bernardi, Enrico Medioli, Franco Arcalli, Franco Ferrini and Leone himself – with
English-language dialogue written by Stuart Kaminsky, a journalist and novelist.

Its screenplay told the story of five childhood friends, 'Noodles' Aaronson,
'Max' Bercovicz, 'Patsy' Goldberg, 'Cockeye' Stein and Dominic, the youngest. As
kids in 1922 Prohibition New York, they dabble in petty street crime, working

protection rackets and rolling drunks. Noodles is enamoured of Deborah, the ballerina sister of their friend Fat Moe. But the gang's rivalry with Bugsy, another street thug, leads to Dominic being shot and Noodles going to prison for nine years for knifing Bugsy. In 1932, Noodles is released from prison and joins his three friends, who have continued in the crime business, making the most out of Prohibition as members of the Combination, organised gangsters on the take. They agree to rob a jewellers in Detroit, for Frankie Menaldi, a hood, and his sidekick Joe. During the heist Noodles rapes Carol, a secretary, and then the gang double-cross Joe. They become involved with the unions and side with the strikers, led by Jimmy Conway. But with the end of Prohibition in 1933, the mobsters find them-selves high and dry, having amassed $1 million, which is placed in a locker in Grand Central station. For one final job, Max plans for them to rob the Federal Reserve Bank. First they carry out one more bootleg whiskey run in Westchester. Noodles doesn't take part and tips off the police; a gun battle ensues and the other three are killed. Noodles checks the locker – the suitcase full of money has gone, so he goes on the run, hiding out in a Chinese opium den; his girl Eve is killed by the Combination.

Noodles takes a train to Buffalo on the Canadian border and hides out there for 35 years, returning to a changed New York in 1968, having received a mysterious letter regarding the relocation of his three friends' graves. He visits the tombs in a mausoleum and finds the key to a locker in which is a suitcase full of money and a letter: 'Advance payment for your next job'. He accepts an invitation to attend a party at the Long Island mansion of Secretary of Commerce Christopher Bailey, but it becomes apparent that Bailey is Max, who had faked his own death. About to be investigated for misuse of the Transport Union pension fund, Max has contracted Noodles to shoot him, but Noodles refuses to acknowledge that Bailey is Max, and leaves. Outside the mansion's gates, Noodles watches as Bailey commits suicide by throwing himself into the grinder of a garbage truck.

Many changes were made to Grey's story, which takes place between 1912 and the early thirties. Max is 'Big Maxie' in the book, Cockeye's surname is Hymie (not Stein), Deborah is Dolores, and Carol was originally named Betty. Combination boss Frank Costello became Frankie Menaldi, who refers to the gang as the 'Four Horsemen of the Apocalypse'. Of the many narrative changes, Dominic was shot by the police in the book, not a rival gang, and the locker containing the cash-laden case was originally four separate safes.

Moreover, the book has a linear narrative, but the film does not. Leone's story traverses three separate time periods: the twenties, the thirties and the late sixties. It commences in 1933, with the murder of Eve (while Noodles hides out in 'Joey the Chinaman's' opium den), then winds back to the night of the gang's betrayal, then forward to 1968 and Noodles's return to the city, then back to 1922 to their adolescence, and so forth. This non-linear strategy is employed throughout the film, until finally all the story fragments fall into place. At the climax of *America*, we meet 'Secretary Bailey' and see his demise, then return to 1933. Noodles arrives at the opium den, inhales on a pipe as he reclines on a bed and smiles with satisfaction, as though he has solved the mystery, even though it isn't actually resolved for another 35 years. It is an audacious and complex narrative structure, which challenges the audience to puzzle through the story, linking pieces of information back and forth through tiny clues and teasers. This complicated structure was introduced into the script by Franco Arcalli, a renowned editor, who had forged complex narratives to many Italian films, notably *Django Kill* (1967), *The Conformist* (1970) and *The Passenger* (1975). A more rigid format for the story would have been date captions, but instead Leone carefully used bridging inserts between the time periods, with musical and visual clues to the eras evoked.

Leone spent a long time casting the film. Early choices were Gerard Depardieu for Max and Jean Gabin as older Max; then it was Depardieu as Noodles, Richard Dreyfuss as Max and even James Cagney as the older Noodles. Dustin Hoffman and Harvey Keitel were also mentioned, while Claudia Cardinale wanted the role of Carol. Leone finally settled on Robert De Niro as Noodles, who would age within the role. The 1922 Noodles would be played by youngster Scott Tyler; the 1932- and 1968-era Noodles by De Niro, who actually grew up in 'Little Italy' on the East Side of New York. His background had been useful in his breakthrough film, *Mean Streets* (1973), to Martin Scorsese, for whom De Niro became an alter ego. De Niro had

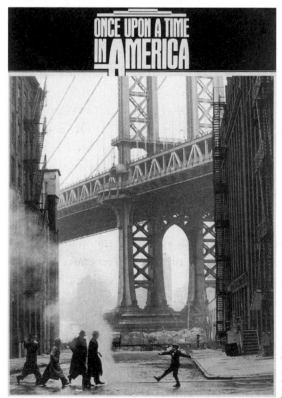

Sergio Leone's dead-end kids under the Williamsburg Bridge, on New York's Lower East Side, in *Once Upon a Time in America* (1984).

since appeared as young Vito Corleone in Coppola's *The Godfather Part II* and again for Scorsese in *Taxi Driver* (1976) and *Raging Bull* (1980 – as boxer Jake LaMotta). He also turned in a fine performance in Michael Cimino's *The Deer Hunter* (1978).

After 200 auditions, James Woods was eventually cast as Max; he had previously acted in *The Way We Were* (1973), *Night Moves* (1975) and David Cronenberg's controversial *Videodrome* (1983). Elizabeth McGovern, as Deborah, had appeared in Robert Redford's *Ordinary People* (1980). Tuesday Weld had debuted in Hitchcock's *The Wrong Man* (1956) and was a veteran of such classics as *Sex Kittens go to College* (1960) and *The Cincinnati Kid* (1965). Burly New Yorker Burt Young, cast as Joe, had appeared in *Chinatown* and the 'Rocky' boxing series. Joe Pesci had already shared the screen with De Niro in *Raging Bull*, as Jake LaMotta's brother and manager Joey. Of Italian-American descent, Pesci was ideal as boss hood Frankie Menaldi. Scott Tyler was well cast as young Noodles, while to add depth to the mystery, Rusty Jacobs played both the young Max and Secretary Bailey's teenage son, David. Producer Arnon Milchan had a cameo as a limo chauffeur.

Originally *Once upon a Time in America* was to have been filmed in 20 weeks, for $18 million, with $3 million going to De Niro. Shooting began on 14 June 1982 and finished over ten months later, on 22 April 1983. Leone lensed the film on a variety of locations in four countries: Italy, France, Canada and the US. Several sets were built at Cinecitta Studios in Rome, including the opium den, the jeweller's interior, the speakeasy, the brothel and the hospital. There were also painstakingly reproduced New York street locations in Pietralata at De Paolis Studios. The puppet theatre was Teatro la Cometa; Bailey's Long Island house was near Lake Como. The garbage truck scene was shot at Pratica Di Mare. Misty New York Bay was actually Porto Marghera, Venice; the grand Art Deco hotel for Noodles and Deborah's meal was the Excelsior, also in Venice.

In Paris, Gare Du Nord stood in for Grand Central Station; Hoboken Station housed the left luggage lockers, while the Brasserie Julien on Rue St Denis was the station's buffet area. Montreal locations include the news-stand arson, the prison exterior, an ambush on Crowning's henchmen and the Federal Reserve Bank. The rendezvous betrayal of Joe by the gang and Noodles driving into the bay were shot on the St Lawrence River, at the boatyard at Troise Rivieres, Quebec. In New York, Leone turned back the clock and dressed 8th Street on the Lower East Side in the architectural equivalent of period costume. In the background, the Williamsburg Bridge features prominently. Other scenes were shot on Bedford Avenue. The pub interior, where the boys decide which drunkard to roll, was McSorley's Alehouse. Another scene was shot in Chambers Paper Fibres, on Plymouth Street. The beach sequence was filmed in St Petersburg, Florida, at a hotel on Gulf Boulevard. Considering the broad range of locations and the long shooting schedule, the result is seamless, but at a price; the eventual budget rocketed to $30 million.

The sets are by Carlo Simi, who designed all Leone's films after *A Fistful of Dollars*, with the exception of *Duck You Sucker*. In Grand Central Station, 1933, a wall is adorned with a 'Visit Coney Island' mural advertising a circus sideshow, with such attractions as 'The Pip & Flip Twins' from Peru, 'Major Mite', the smallest entertainer on earth, 'Smoko the human volcano' and a seer, 'Fatalist Supreme'. This is replaced in the next scene by a giant Big Apple mural and 'LOVE' slogan, signifying the time shift to 1968, with an echo of the Beatles' 'Yesterday' on the soundtrack. The interiors are also painstakingly designed, from the quaint Chinese theatre, with its stalls and lanterns, to the opulent speakeasies, brothels and hotel interiors. The costumes were designed by Gabriella Pescucci, with a strong eye for detail; the assistant costume designer was Leone's eldest daughter Raffaella. The time periods are also differentiated by Tonino Delli Colli's cinematography (the twenties photography resembles a sepia effect, the sixties section is less stylised). This was Leone's first film not in the widescreen 'scope format – even his *The Colossus of Rhodes* had been in 'Supertotalscope', as befits its epic title.

Once Upon a Time in America sounds and looks great, but there are times when the narrative plods and the direction is unnecessarily self-indulgent. When young Cockeye sits down on a staircase and takes about five minutes to eat a charlotte Russe cream cake, you know you're in for the long haul. A similar scene occurs when Max has bought a throne and the tension mounts as Noodles sits in his office, slovenly scraping the bottom of a coffee cup with his spoon. The scraping is inexorable and is presumably to demonstrate that although Noodles is now rich, he still has no class. Elsewhere, Leone's pacing is exactly right, as in the opening scene, when Eve enters her darkened apartment. She finds the outline of a corpse traced in bullet holes on the bed and three threatening gunman soon make their presence known. But as scriptwriter Sergio Donati, who had worked on the 'Dollars' films, noted of Leone's style in *America*: 'Gangsters can't move like [gunslingers]; they can't take a quarter of an hour to get out of a car'.

Noodles's opium reverie combined with the ringing telephone at the beginning of the film is one example of Leone's approach to his westerns transposed to a modern setting. A telephone rings, loudly, 22 times, while a montage depicts the whiskey ambush in the rain and a celebration of the end of the liquor ban, with a cake-topped coffin inscribed in icing 'Prohibition' and four mocking champagne altar candles. After 20 rings, a hand picks up the receiver, but the phone keeps jangling, until finally it is answered by Sergeant P. Halloran. This ringing telephone is equivalent to the gunslingers waiting for the train in *Once Upon a Time in the West*, with Leone playing with the time frame and stretching Noodles's guilty flashback.

Leone looks at another American genre through European eyes. He makes use of cliché characters from American crime movies: the gang of street kids who become rich gangsters, corrupt cops, drunken molls, double-crossing, fast-talking conmen, duplicitous politicians, noble trade unionists, lumbering syndicate hitmen and perpetually smiling barmen. There is also a hint of De Niro's fast-talking 'wiseguy' persona from Scorsese's gangster films. In one exchange about the untrustworthiness of their job, Noodles tells Max, 'Today they ask us to get rid of

Joe, tomorrow they ask me to get rid of you. Is that OK with you, because it's not OK with me?'

Leone also stages archetypal elements of the America crime movie, including Tommy-gun massacres, jewellery hold-ups and Prohibition speakeasies. Max's front for the liquor trafficking is even an undertaking business (advertised with the slogan 'Why go on living when we can bury you for $49.50'). But if Leone occasionally slips into clichéd genre territory, other scenes are more original in their depiction of gangsterdom. For example, the visually arresting scene when the five boys walk from the station locker, having stashed their earnings. Dominic skips and dances ahead of the group, as they cross 8th Street South, below the imposing Williamsburg Bridge. Rounding the corner, rival Bugsy approaches, and the gang flees. Leone switches to slow motion, accentuating the chase, but also distending the moment when Dominic is struck with Bugsy's bullet and sprawls across the road.

The teenage gang scenes are reminiscent of Leone's own childhood on the streets of post-war Rome and also of the cinematic fantasies of Federico Fellini, in particular *Amarcord* (1974), Fellini's reminiscences of his growing up in Rimini, with many sexual references and adolescent fumblings. In Leone's film, a policeman is photographed having intercourse with a minor and is then blackmailed, while the boys buy sexual favours for cream cakes. Their sexual immaturity as boys is replaced by sexual sadism as men. Many of the most violent moments in the film unpleasantly mix brutality and sexual deviance, especially in Noodles's two rape scenes: of secretary Carol during the jewel robbery and Deborah in the back of a limousine. Such sexual violence immediately drew condemnation from critics and audiences alike.

Once Upon a Time in America has some powerful moments. Noodles looking at the riddled corpses of his best friends in Westchester is one of the best scenes in the film, with open umbrellas, pouring rain, shattered bottles of booze, cops in their drenched greatcoats and the cadavers laid out in a row for the photographer. The scene is lit by car headlights and a precariously angled shepherd's crook lamppost the whiskey wagon has collided with. In the crowd, Noodles, with rain dripping off his hat brim, looks guiltily at the bodies, not seeing the charred, bullet-riddled corpses they are, but the people they once were – dead through his betrayal. The impact of this scene is probably the only one that benefits in the re-edited US print of the film. This version moves the Westchester massacre towards the film's finale, where it is used as a fitting climax to the 1933 section of the story. We have met Max, Cockeye and Patsy, and their deaths in the ambush are much more effective than in Leone's original version.

The effortless way the story sweeps through time is revealed on multiple viewings to be outstanding, but on an initial viewing is virtually incomprehensible. Throughout *America*, memory and past events entwine with the present. Leone has characters passing through doorways that seem like portals to another era. At the end of the film, in 1968, Bailey apparently commits suicide by throwing himself into the back of Mr Geary's garbage truck. But there is a doubt in Noodles's mind as to his identity: James Woods's stand-in actually played the scene. Elderly Noodles watches the truck depart and its lights are replaced by three vintage cars carrying 1933 revellers, celebrating the end of Prohibition. It is the only moment in the film where the eras butt into one another.

Often these time shifts are facilitated with clever musical bridges from composer Ennio Morricone. Morricone had worked with Leone on all his westerns, rising to fame with him. Recorded in Forum Studio, Rome, this score is one of his most popular and enduring. In some instances he uses themes from the periods depicted: Irving Berlin's 'God Bless America' (sung by Kate Smith); George Gershwin's 'Summertime' (from *Porgy and Bess*) and Cole Porter's 'Night and Day'. The most famous of these was 'Amapola', written by Joseph M. La Calle and Albert Gamse, and arranged for the film by Morricone. This was used in a clarinet version for Deborah's rehearsal (spied on by Noodles) and the orchestra performs it in the restaurant for the couple to dance to as adults. In a scene where the gang pose as doctors and swap the tags on new-born babies in a maternity ward, to blackmail Police Chief Aiello, Morricone uses *La Gazza Ladra* (*The Thieving Magpie*) by Rossini.

Morricone evokes the Prohibition era with the knockabout ragtime of 'Childhood Memories' (which uses the gang's whistled theme tune as its root) and the funereal

Champagne Charlies: Fat Moe's bone-yard boys celebrate the end of Prohibition; left to right: Cockeye (William Forsythe), Patsy (James Hayden), Max (James Woods) and Noodles (Robert De Niro) in *Once Upon a Time in America* (1984).

'Prohibition Dirge', which leaps to life with a dynamic drum roll and chaotic wind work. Elsewhere, there are the eerie piano and ebbing violins of 'Poverty' and the happy-go-lucky 'Speakeasy'. 'Deborah's Theme' is a richly orchestrated piece reminiscent of 'Jill's Theme' from *Once Upon a Time in the West*, again highlighting the towering, bittersweet soprano of Edda Dell'Orso (this was an unused commission for a Franco Zeffirelli film). It also inspired Shane MacGowan, when he wrote the intro to the Pogues' Christmas hit 'Fairy Tale of New York'. The ghostly, menacing pan flute of 'Cockeye's Song' is used at its best as accompaniment to Dominic's murder. The pan flute was played by Gheorghe Zamfir, who had featured in the distinctive soundtrack to *Picnic at Hanging Rock* (1975).

On its release in the US in 1984, *Once Upon a Time in America*'s two major flaws, its length and its sexual politics, ensured its doom. Leone had already discussed the length of the film to be released with the Ladd Company and had even tried to release it in two parts. He chopped the film down from ten hours' worth of footage, to six hours, to finally 229 minutes. Scenes that didn't make it into this final version include a conversation between Noodles and the cemetery owner, Deborah's stage performance as Cleopatra, a further conversation between Carol and Noodles in 1968 at the 'Bailey Foundation' and the original opening scene in the Chinese theatre. It was rated R after two minutes' worth of violence and sexual content were excised from the US preview in February 1984, but the producers decided to cut the film further to improve the pace. Unfortunately, the two rape scenes make the film very difficult to praise and are the worst example of misogyny in Leone's films, an aspect of his work that escalated alarmingly with *Duck You Sucker* and destroys *Once Upon a Time in America*, making Noodles an alienating, unsympathetic protagonist.

UK and US posters announced that the film was 'The Epic and Powerful Story of an Unforgettable Era', with iconic images of De Niro's face and the gang members' bodies lying in the rain. Advertising copy said, 'As boys they said they would die for each other. As men, they did'. The trailer was edited to resemble an action-packed gangster film, invoking hits like *Borsalino* and *The Valachi Papers*. 'They forged an empire built on greed, violence and betrayal,' said the voiceover. 'It ended on a mystery that refused to die.' *America* played at the Cannes Film Festival in May 1984 to a 15-minute standing ovation, even though De Niro was harangued by a spectator who said, 'As a woman, I feel deeply embarrassed to have witnessed it'. Critics raved about this 'uncut' 229-minute version. But in the US, the film was re-edited and redubbed against Leone's wishes and cut down to 139 minutes. Its narrative was shuffled into chronological order, beginning with the childhood scenes in 1922, progressing to the 1933 and 1968 sequences, and ending with Bailey shooting himself. The missing half-hour was mostly explanatory dialogue, but predictably the violence remained. It was eventually released stateside in June 1984. Vincent Canby in the *New York Times* called it 'a lazily hallucinatory epic' that had been 'edited on a roulette wheel'; Ian Christie's *New York Times* review began, 'From bad to worse with the Kosher Nostra'.

It bombed in the US and was re-released in October 1984 in the 229-minute version. It grossed a measly $5.3 million in the US, $2.5million from the awful initial version. In the UK it was cut by 16 seconds for violence by the British censors and rated a certificate 18, the replacement for the old X certificate (abolished in 1982). A video release in 1986 removed a further ten seconds. *America* was a disaster and is Leone's least profitable film. For the US network TV showing there was a 192-minute version prepared; English-language DVD versions run at 222 minutes. In fact, the slated, chronologically edited print was the first version of the film I saw, in Liverpool in December 1989. It was far better than I was expecting from reviews, then raving about the 227-minute version. Even though some of the continuity is somewhat jumpy, it is still an absorbing, visually beautiful film. In Italy *C'era una Volta in America* was first screened in the Barberini cinema in Rome. It was distributed in Italy by Titanus and while not in the same financial league as the 'Dollars' films and *Once Upon a Time in the West*, it was still hugely successful and admired in Italy and throughout Europe.

The film even won a few awards: Morricone deservedly earned a BAFTA in 1985 for Best Score; Leone and Delli Colli missed out in their respective categories. Leone and Morricone were also nominated for Golden Globes and the Italian Film Journalists Syndicate awarded Silver Ribbons to Leone, Delli Colli, Simi and Morricone, as best in their fields for the year. Unbelievably, the US promoters forgot to register Morricone's score for an Oscar; it would certainly have won an award.

The critical reappraisal *America* has received and its availability on video and DVD led to Grey's 'The Hoods' being republished in the nineties as 'Once Upon a Time in America'. Leone had spent nearly twenty years thinking about, planning and shooting *America* and the later problems in releasing the film took a terrible toll on his health; he never directed a film again and died of a heart complaint in December 1989. When asked what is his greatest artistic achievement, James Woods answers, 'It was working with Sergio Leone...it was the Everest of my life'. Many of the cast feel the same way, but *America* is a strange film. At some moments it is a great film, the production design and costumes are exquisite, and De Niro and Woods deliver the best performances in a remarkable cast. But there is also an ingredient in his westerns that is missing here, leaving a hollowness. For example, rather than adding to and creating atmosphere, the long Leone silences do actually slow the film down. Elizabeth McGovern reckons that the most successful aspects of the film are those dealing with the gang's childhood. Perhaps Leone was more at home in this juvenile territory, a more straightforward world, with its children's bravado more in keeping with his simple western heroes, than the modern 'real world': a dream of America, rather than the harsh reality. After all, 'once upon a time' is how fairy tales begin.

18

'There's no more heroes left in the world'

— *Lethal Weapon* (1987)

Credits:
DIRECTOR – Richard Donner
PRODUCERS – Richard Donner and Joel Silver
ASSOCIATE PRODUCER – Jennie Lew
STORY AND SCREENPLAY – Shane Black
DIRECTOR OF PHOTOGRAPHY – Stephen Goldblatt
EDITOR – Stuart Baird
PRODUCTION DESIGNER – J. Michael Riva
COSTUME DESIGNER – Mary Malin
MUSIC COMPOSERS – Michael Kamen and Eric Clapton
Technicolor
Interiors filmed at Warner Bros Studios
A Warner Bros–Silver Pictures production
Released by Warner Bros
110 minutes
Cast:
Mel Gibson (Martin Riggs)/Danny Glover (Roger Murtaugh)/
Gary Busey (Mr Joshua, the albino)/Mitchell Ryan (General Peter
McAllister)/Tom Akins (Michael Hunsaker)/Darlene Love (Trish
Murtaugh)/Traci Wolfe (Rhianne Murtaugh)/Jackie Swanson
(Amanda Hunsaker)/Damon Hines (Nick Murtaugh)/Ebonie
Smith (Carrie Murtaugh)/Lycia Naff (Dixie)/Mary Ellen Trainor
(Dr Stephanie Woods, police psychiatrist)/Steve Kahan (Captain
Ed Murphy)/Ed O'Ross (Mendez)/Gustav Vintas (Gustaf)/Al
Loeng (Endo, the torturer)/Michael Shaner (McCleary, suicidal
jumper)/Donald Gooden (Alfred)/Jimmie F. Skaggs, Jason Ronard
and Blackie Dammett (Busted drug dealers)/Cheryl Baker, Terri
Lynn Doss and Sharon K. Brecke (Girls in shower video)/Paul
Tuerpe, Chade Hayes, Chris D. Jardins, Sven Thorsen, Peter

DuPont, Gilles Kohler, Cedric Adams and James Poslof (Shadow
Company mercenaries)/Burbank the Cat (himself)/Sam the Dog
(himself)

*   *   *

Lethal Weapon is the ultimate eighties action crime movie – an adult blend of laughs,
thrills and ultraviolence. It established actors Mel Gibson and Danny Glover as one
of the box-office partnerships of the decade. But *Lethal Weapon* is more than simply
a buddy movie with a million-dollar firework display. It has disparate influences,
including Vietnam veteran movies, *Dirty Harry* cop thrillers, *Death Wish* vigilantism, *Cosby Show* sitcom domesticity, *The Three Stooges* and *Lassie*.

Written by Shane Black and set over Christmas, *Lethal Weapon* is the story of two
sergeants in the LAPD who are partnered on a case. Since the death of his wife of
11 years in a car accident, ex-Special Forces expert marksman Martin Riggs is a
suicidal loner with a complete lack of self-preservation, who lives alone with his dog.
Roger Murtaugh is his polar opposite, just turned 50 and a settled family man who
keeps himself out of trouble. Amanda Hunsaker, the daughter of Michael Hunsaker
(one of Murtaugh's old Vietnam buddies), throws herself off the balcony of a high-
rise apartment, apparently under narcotic influence. Soon afterwards, the only
witness, Dixie, a prostitute, is killed in an explosion at her bungalow and it appears
Amanda was involved in pornography. Riggs and Murtaugh find out that Amanda's
death is a warning to her father, a drug smuggler – her cocaine had been spiked with
drain cleaner by Dixie. Eventually the two cops discover they are now the targets of
the traffickers: Shadow Company, ex-Special Forces mercenaries, led by General
McAllister and albino Mister Joshua. To curtail investigations they threaten
Murtaugh and his family and kidnap his daughter Rhianne. At a desert rendezvous,
they also capture Riggs and Murtaugh and torture them, before the heroes break
loose and exact their revenge on the gang, wiping them out in the process.

Lethal Weapon's director Richard Donner worked extensively in television and
moved into cinema with *X-16* (1961) and *Salt and Pepper* (1968), a Bond parody set
in 'Swinging London' with Sammy Davis Jnr as Charles Salt and Peter Lawford as
Christopher Pepper. In the seventies Donner directed *Kojak* on TV and then
became massively successful with *The Omen* (1976) and *Superman, the Movie* (1978).
The central protagonists of these two mega-hits anticipate Riggs in *Lethal Weapon*
– part Superman, part Antichrist.

Actor Mel Gibson was born in New York, but his family emigrated to Australia
in 1968. He made his film debut aged 21 in *Summer City* (1977) and was cast as *Mad
Max* (1979), a futuristic cop, whose wife is killed by bikers. The latter was released
in the US with redubbed American voices and wasn't a success. Gibson hit the
jackpot with *Mad Max 2* (1981); here a spent and desperate Max roams the desert's
post-nuclear wasteland, populated with biker punks, drag-buggy crazies, assorted
lunatics and boomerang-throwing children. Directed, like *Mad Max*, by George

Miller and also starring Bruce Spence (as an equally mad gyro pilot), the film was a huge success in the US (as *The Road Warrior*). Gibson struggled to find a character as widely popular as Max, until he was offered the part of Martin Riggs. Gibson hadn't made a film for a year and in the 'Making of' documentary *Pure Lethal* recounts that he was very nervous the night before shooting began.

Danny Glover, formerly of the Black Actors Workshop of the American Conservatory Theatre, was cast as Murtaugh. Glover made his film debut in *Escape from Alcatraz* (1979) and went on to appear in *Places in the Heart* (1984) and *Witness* (1985), before receiving critical acclaim for his role as Albert in *The Color Purple* (1985). *Lethal Weapon*'s malevolent villains were played by a pair of well-respected actors. Tall Kentucky-born Mitchell Ryan had appeared in *High Plains Drifter* (1972), *Magnum Force* (1973) and with great success as stetsoned Detective Harve Poole, who pint-sized motorcycle cop John Wintergreen (Robert Blake) literally looks up to, in *Electra Glide in Blue* (1973). Texan Gary Busey was the former drummer in the Rubber Band and later backed Kris Kristofferson and Willie Nelson. He appeared in the mud-and-rags western *Dirty Little Billy* (1972) and John Milius's cult surf epic *Big Wednesday* (1978), but is best remembered for another kind of buddy movie – his portrayal of the Crickets-fronting singer in *The Buddy Holly Story* (1978).

Lethal Weapon's budget was $15 million and despite its Christmas setting was filmed from August to November 1986 in and around Los Angeles and Long Beach, and at Warners' Burbank studio. The desert rendezvous was filmed in El Mirage dry lake, California. The suicide jumper is about to launch himself off Emser International Oriental Rugs & Ceramic Tiles on the corner of Santa Monica Boulevard and Orlando. The chase and shootout finale was filmed on Hollywood Boulevard, Los Angeles. The effective score was performed by Michael Kamen, Eric Clapton and David Sanborn, incorporating suspenseful Mantovani-esque strings, the distinctive picked tremolo of Clapton's blues guitar and an omnipresent sax solo that sounds like Gerry Rafferty's eighties hit 'Baker Street', perhaps, considering the detective work, via 221B.

Lethal Weapon's two central characters couldn't be more different. Murtaugh has a home life in suburbia, with a typical family, a boat in the drive and a cat called Burbank. In his introductory scene, Murtaugh is surprised in the bath by his family bearing his 50th birthday cake. His daughter tells him that his beard is going grey, so he shaves it off, and his catchphrase throughout the hectic investigation is 'I'm getting too old for this shit'. By contrast, Riggs lives on Long Beach in a trailer with his collie, Sam. The only thing that keeps him from committing suicide is his love of his job. In his introductory scene, Riggs wakes up with a cigarette dangling from his mouth. His Beretta sticks out from under his pillow, his first drink of the day is a Coors, and he lives on fast food and sandwiches. He served as an assassin on the Phoenix Project in 'Nam and is also schooled in the martial arts. As Murtaugh comments: 'I suppose we have to register you as a lethal weapon.' Riggs says that at 19 he 'did a guy in Laos from 1,000 yards out, rifle shot in high wind…it's the only thing I was ever good at.'

Their contrasts are reflected in everything from their dress sense to their weaponry. Murtaugh's a shirt-and-tie man, Riggs wears denims, cowboy boots, baseball cap and sticks his pistol in his waistband; when they first meet, Murtaugh wrestles him to the floor, mistaking him for a criminal, loose in police headquarters. Riggs carries a 16-shot 9mm Beretta automatic, Murtaugh a 4-inch Smith & Wesson revolver; 'A lot of old timers carry those,' notes Riggs. They approach their assignments in their own distinctive ways, with Murtaugh the, often ignored, voice of reason. But they bond and Murtaugh invites his new partner over to his house for a family dinner.

A police psychiatrist is trying to heave Riggs off the force, citing his suicidal tendencies, and Donner has him appropriately watching a Bugs Bunny *Loony Tunes* cartoon on TV. Murtaugh is aghast that he's been partnered with someone who has a death wish, asking, 'You ever met anybody you didn't kill?' Murtaugh moans that God must hate him; 'Hate him back,' advises Riggs, 'it works for me.' Riggs's rage rises uncontrollably and leaves him a shuddering, bulging-eyed wreck. In a scene originally cut from the film, Riggs empties an entire clip into a sniper, which is reminiscent of *Dirty Harry*. A detective comments, 'You're one psycho son of a bitch, but you're good'. Riggs later tackles an attempted suicide by handcuffing himself to the jumper and throwing them both off the roof – into an inflatable landing pad that the jumper didn't know was there – while Murtaugh has a nervous breakdown on the sidewalk.

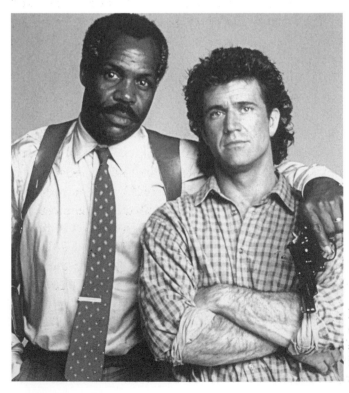

Danny Glover and Mel Gibson as Sergeants Murtaugh and Riggs, in a publicity still for Richard Donner's hit *Lethal Weapon* series.

Lethal Weapon's style is unmistakably of its time and this aspect of the film hasn't worn well. Amanda Hunsaker's suicide, which opens the film, is a good example. The bobbing optic-fibre lamp, her airy perm, white satin lingerie and coke chopped up on the glass table of her luxury apartment look like a scene from an eighties soft-rock video, until she jumps off the balcony and crumples on the roof of a car hundreds of feet below. Other dated touches include Murtaugh's mobile phone (with a hefty battery connected), the fridge sticker in the Murtaughs' kitchen ('Free South Africa – End Apartheid') and the hairstyles, particularly Gibson's lion king mullet; a credit in the titles even reads 'Mel Gibson's Hairstyle created by Ramsey'.

A vital ingredient of the buddy movie format was humour and there is plenty in Black's script. The drugs bust scene early in the film establishes this. A trio of pushers discuss business with their potential customer, Riggs. He asks how much for the whole consignment and is told 'a hundred'. Riggs begins to count out $100, but the pushers, amazed, clarify that they mean $100,000. He produces his LAPD badge; they don't believe him. Riggs does a quick Three Stooges routine on them, complete with slaps and pokes in the eye, then draws his gun: 'It's a real badge, I'm a real cop and this is a real fucking gun.' Gibson and Glover work very well together. After Dixie's house has been blown up, Murtaugh enlists the help of a little kid to do a sketch of a suspect and Riggs is convinced they are going to 'Put out an APB on Big Bird'. But from the humorous first half, *Lethal Weapon* becomes much darker when Murtaugh's daughter is kidnapped.

Their opponents are trained, ruthless professionals. The General is cold and detached, but his henchmen Mr Joshua, the albino psychopath, and Endo, the Chinese water torturer, have something of the ghoul about them (in this kind of eighties crime-movie drugs gang, an albino is almost obligatory). Mendez, a heroin dealer, asks if the General found his crew in 'Psychos are us' and the General demonstrates Mr Joshua's resilience by holding a cigarette lighter to his arm. During the investigation, Riggs and Murtaugh begin to fear the worst. The bomb that blows up their only witness is detonated with a mercury switch and a kid at the crime scene says the bomber had a tattoo identical to Riggs's – a snake coiled around a bayonet, with the motto 'NEVER QUIT' – which is peculiar to the Special Forces. The cops later learn the story of Air America in Vietnam, a CIA-fronted operation running the war from Laos. Hunsaker was involved with Shadow Company, who have re-formed under the General, and smuggle two huge shipments of heroin into the US a year. Hunsaker was about to go to the police, but they killed his daughter to stop him, and later, when Hunsaker informs Murtaugh of this, the albino assassinates him from a helicopter flying over Hunsaker's cliffside pad. Interestingly, Gibson later made *Air America* (1990), an action comedy, set in the Laos theatre of operations.

Donner handles the complicated action scenes well, as one would expect from the director of *Superman*. In a disastrous desert hostage exchange, Murtaugh stands alone as the convoy of mercenaries emerges from the heat haze; it makes a striking sight – a limousine, 4×4 and helicopter in convoy, speeding across the plain and leaving an immense dust trail. There are numerous kinetic car stunts, chases and explosions, expertly enacted by the huge stunt crew. In fact the film is dedicated to ace stuntman Dar Robinson, who worked on the film, but was killed in a freak accident shortly afterwards. Only in the final action scene, a punch-up between Riggs and the albino, does the film lose coherence, as Riggs asks his enemy: 'D'you like a shot at the title?' and their confrontation becomes a WBC bout, complete with flashing lights and pounding music. Elsewhere, there's a shootout in a warehouse-disco and a running battle on Hollywood Boulevard ending with the General's car being hit by a bus, flipped onto its roof and catching fire, before grenades in the back ignite and end the General's reign. In the most brutal scene in the film, Riggs is suspended under a showerhead, while torturer Endo pokes him with a sponge attached to a set of jump leads and a car battery. This shocking scene was edited for TV showings in the UK. Later, to escape his predicament, and by way of revenge, Riggs strangles Endo with his bare feet.

During the editing, two important changes were made. Riggs's opening scene (a Jack Daniels drinking session and punch-up in a bar) was cut out and the ending of the film was altered: in the initial cut, the two men part company, with Murtaugh saying he's going to quit the force.

Lethal Weapon opened in the US in March 1987, rated R. The poster taglines ran 'Two Cops…Glover carries a Weapon…Gibson is one. He's the only LA cop registered as a LETHAL WEAPON', with close-ups of Gibson and Glover, and their guns. Reviews were positive. *Variety* conceded it is 'one part "Rambo Comes Home" and one part *48 Hrs*. It's a film teetering on the brink of absurdity…but thanks to its unrelenting energy and insistent drive, it never quite falls.' It made $65 million in the US; it opened in the UK on August Bank Holiday weekend 1987 and grossed £2.5 million. The *Monthly Film Bulletin* reckoned it 'adroitly blends a whole range of current genres'. It was successful worldwide. In Spain it was *Arma Letal*, in Italy *Arma Latale*, in Germany 'Gibson und Glover' were *Zwei Stahlharte Profis* – 'Two Steel-hard Professionals'.

Lethal Weapon also enjoyed great success on home video and TV. The film was rated 18 at the cinema and UK TV showings usually edit the violence, nudity and expletives. US versions are uncut, except for the scene where Murtaugh and his daughter Rhianne discuss the merits of legalising marijuana – 'Beer is legal…grass ain't.' The original release version of the film was 110 minutes. A restored 'Director's Cut' is seven minutes longer, with five new scenes: in his trailer home, Riggs smashes his TV screen with a bottle of Coors; later he arrives back at his home with a brand new TV; Murtaugh goes to the firing range on his birthday, scoring five shots to the target's head; and after the family meal at the Murtaugh's, Riggs picks up a prostitute on his way home (he pays her $100 to watch *The Three Stooges* with him). The longest and most important addition is our first view of Riggs in action, when he is called to a sniper taking pot-shots at children in a playground. His wild disregard for his own safety, his marksmanship and his instability come over loud and clear, and the scene offers interesting comparisons with the subsequent Christmas tree drugs bust, though both scenes introduce Riggs's unconventional modus operandi. These additions slow down the introduction to the film, however; the pair are partnered on the case more quickly in the original version.

The film's popularity led to a trio of lethal sequels, all directed by Donner, which lent the series a consistency and development often absent from bandwagon-jumping follow-ups. Regular cast members were the Murtaugh family members: mum Trish (played by Darlene Love), daughters Rhianne and Carrie (Traci Wolfe and Ebonie Smith) and son Nick (Damon Hines). Other constants were Steve Kahan as Captain Murphy and Mary Ellen Trainor as Dr Stephanie Woods, the psychiatrist who is trying to get Riggs committed. Fans of Sam the dog and Burbank the cat should note they don't appear in episodes 3 and 4.

With an original story written by Shane Black, and with Kamen and Clapton again responsible for the score, *Lethal Weapon 2* (1989) was the now familiar mix of sax and violence. Riggs and Murtaugh are posted to guard helium-voiced key witness Leo Getz (Joe Pesci), who has embezzled half a billion dollars in mob drugs money. They get mixed up with a gang of South African smugglers claiming diplomatic immunity, led by Arjen Rudd (Joss Ackland) and Pieter Vorstedt (Derrick O'Connor), who Riggs discovers was responsible for running his wife's car off the road. The film benefits from big-budget set design, particularly in the South Africans' hillside hideaway, a state-of-the-art ellipse, and a dockside shootout aboard the money-strewn smuggling freighter *Alba Varden*.

In this sequel, there is less mullet and more action comedy, contrasted with sketches of Murtaugh family life. There's even some love interest for loner Riggs, in the villain's South African secretary Rika van den Haas, played by Patsy Kensit, though Julie Adams, billed as 'South African Dialect Coach', seems to have been unsuccessful. The sequel's action sequences are even more pyrotechnic – a car is driven from a suspended container into a harbour, there's a daring city centre helicopter rescue, a booby-trapped toilet seat and death by nail gun and poolside springboard. In an exciting car chase, one hood is impaled on a surfboard through his windscreen, and the villains must have cursed the genius who built their hideout on stilts; Riggs pulls the legs from under the building with his 4×4. Advertised as 'The Magic is Back', *Lethal Weapon 2* grossed $147 million at the US box office. As for its predecessor a 'Director's Cut' exists, with five minutes of extra footage. *Lethal Weapon 2* set the seal on the formula: this is genre filmmaking at its most exhilarating, with Gibson and Glover on top form. As wild-eyed Riggs says of their partnership: 'We're back, we're bad … you're black, I'm mad!'

Although Gibson wanted Riggs to die as a result of his wounds at the end of *Lethal Weapon 2*, another sequel followed in 1992. Advertised with the slogan 'The Magic is Back Again!' *Lethal Weapon 3* saw the series deteriorating, with Pesci returning as Leo Getz (now a realty agent, who is trying to sell Murtaugh's house) in what is one of the most irritating cameos ever to sully celluloid. Murtaugh is only eight days from retirement and Riggs seems determined to make his last week at work hell. Initially demoted to uniform cops on the beat, Riggs tells one dazed criminal, 'You have the right to remain unconscious.' Reinstated, the duo investigate a gang of gun traffickers who are stealing confiscated guns and ammunition from police depots. They suspect that it is an inside job and discover the chief culprit is Jack Travis (an evil turn by Stuart Wilson), ex-cop and front of the bogus Mesa Verde Construction company (Travis buries his enemies in the foundations). Having cracked the case in explosive fashion, Murtaugh decides not to retire, but to stay on the force with his partner.

Kicking off with a Bond-esque title sequence and bookended by two songs (Sting's 'It's Probably Me' and the Elton John/Eric Clapton duet 'Runaway Train'), *Lethal Weapon 3* has its moments, but too often settles for the easy option of laughs. A well-played subplot sees Murtaugh's son mixed up with local gangstas and shows Murtaugh's remorse when he kills a kid from his neighbourhood. 'Find the men who put the gun in my son's hand,' the dead teenager's father tells him. Riggs has his poignant moments too, telling his partner that when he retires, 'You're retiring us!' Riggs is also linked romantically with Lorna Cole (Rene Russo), a tough, karate-kicking internal affairs sergeant. In *Lethal Weapon 3*'s idea of a romantic interlude, Riggs and Cole compare bullet wound scars, but as expected the action scenes are most memorable. Riggs stifles a hostage situation, only to discover that it's a film set, with Rhianne Murtaugh making her acting debut in an action thriller, while in the finale, Riggs drives a truck trailing burning diesel and loaded with ammo at the bad guys. Takings were slightly down in the US, but the film still grossed almost $145 million. Gibson is dynamic and at last offers a reason why he's always running after cars: he's trying to quit smoking and has become addicted to dog biscuits.

Lethal Weapon 3 was generally regarded as the weakest of the series, until the arrival of *Lethal Weapon 4* in 1998. The UK press loved this fourth instalment regardless: 'This year's best action film,' noted the *News of the World*; 'The funniest and best of the series,' said the *Express*. Instead of the central buddy format, there was a whole gallery of characters, and some new ones, which detract from Gibson and Glover's chemistry. As well as the return of Pesci and Russo, toothy comedian Chris Rock appeared as Detective Lee Butters and martial artist Jet Li was cast as the leader of a gang of Snakehead Triads, the Chinese Mafia. Lorna Cole is expecting Riggs's child, while Murtaugh is about to become a grandfather. The loose plot sees Riggs and Murtaugh investigating the Triads, who are sneaking immigrants into the country and forcing them to work as slave labour in the gang's counterfeiting operation.

The action scenes are impressive, but the dialogue stinks and the comedy, finally, is forced, with Pesci and Rock the chief culprits. Riggs concedes that he too is 'getting too old for this shit' and the police force can't get insurance because of Riggs and Murtaugh's past exploits. In the opening scene, set in downtown Los Angeles, the duo take on a lunatic, who is heavily armoured and wielding a flame-thrower. Riggs convinces Murtaugh to strip down to his shorts and flap his arms like a bird, to distract the maniac, while Riggs gets a clean shot at his gas tank. Murtaugh has to put up with constant ribbing from his colleagues thereafter, with a newspaper headline reading 'Bird Man Fowls Human Torch'. The film was heavily cut before release (mainly for violence); audience reaction was positive and *Lethal Weapon 4* grossed $130 million in the US. But eventually the schmaltz is overwhelming and Pesci's final straight-faced graveside monologue about Froggy, his only true childhood friend, who he flattened under the back wheel of his bike, has to be seen to be believed.

Golan and Globus's *Number One with a Bullet* (1987) was probably the closest derivative in style to the original *Lethal Weapon*, with Robert Caradine and Billy Dee Williams pitted against drugs gangs. Many other films yoked together frictional cop duos to action-comedy effect: for example *Running Scared* (1986 – with Billy Crystal and Gregory Hines), *Tango & Cash* (1989 – starring Sylvester Stallone and Kurt Russell), *Red Heat* (1988 – with Arnold Schwarzenegger and James Belushi) and *Bad Boys* (1995 – Martin Lawrence and Will Smith). One of the more imaginative pairings was *Renegades* (1989), with Kiefer Sutherland's detective teaming up with Lou Diamond Phillips's Native American Lakota Sioux.

Such distinctive, stylised films were very easy to parody – especially Riggs's twitchy, live-wire mannerisms and way of negotiating any given action situation with his gun held out at arm's length, Special Forces-style. *National Lampoon's Loaded Weapon 1* (1993) targeted such action movies, with Emilio Estevez and Samuel L. Jackson as mismatched cops Jack Colt and Wes Luger, with Tim Curry and the ever-reliable William Shatner as the villains. Following an explosixe machine-gun shootout at 'Halim's Mini-Mart' during a bungled robbery, Colt aims his auto-matic pistol at a felon and hisses, 'I know what you're thinking, punk ... did he fire 173 times, or 174?' Other comedies saw humour in a cop–dog buddy partnership, as epitomised by *Turner & Hooch* (1989) – with Tom Hanks protecting a star murder witness, here a St Bernard dog.

Another interesting film in relation to the 'Lethal Weapon' series is *Deadly Force*, a very tough eighties exploitation B-movie, with cult actor Wings Hauser as Stoney Cooper, an ex-LAPD cop on a vendetta following the death of his friend's daughter. 'You don't call him in ... you turn him loose,' said the *Dirty Harry*-inspired trailer. In one scene Cooper faces a lunatic bomber, who yells, 'This is real dynamite,' and unhinged Cooper shouts, 'This is a real gun!' Even Hauser's mullet and manner seem reminiscent of Gibson's loose cannon Riggs. Most amazing is the fact that *Deadly Force* came out in 1983 – a full four years before Donner's film – and is a good example of B-movie crime films infusing the mainstream. But *Lethal Weapon* remains the best example of the genre, a highly successful, high–octane template that remains a formula today.

19

'I always wanted to be a gangster'

— *GoodFellas* (1990)

Credits:
DIRECTOR – Martin Scorsese
PRODUCER – Irwin Winkler
STORY – Nicholas Pileggi
SCREENPLAY – Nicholas Pileggi and Martin Scorsese
DIRECTOR OF PHOTOGRAPHY – Michael Ballhaus, ASC
EDITOR – Thelma Schoonmaker, ACE
ART DIRECTOR – Maher Ahmed
COSTUMES – Susan O'Donnell and Thomas Lee Keller
Technicolor
An Irwin Winkler production
Released by Warner Bros
148 minutes
Cast:

Robert De Niro (James 'Jimmy the Gent' Conway)/Ray Liotta (Henry Hill)/Joe Pesci (Tommy DeVito)/Lorraine Bracco (Karen Hill)/Paul Sorvino (Paul 'Paulie' Cicero)/Frank Silvero (Frankie Carbone)/Tony Darrow (Sonny Bunz)/Mike Starr (Frenchy)/Frank Vincent (Billy Batts)/Chuck Low (Morris 'Morrie' Kessler)/Frank DiLeo (Tuddy Cicero)/Gina Mastrogiacomo (Janice Rossi)/Catherine Scorsese (Tommy's mother)/Charles Scorsese (Vinnie)/Christopher Serrone (Young Henry Hill)/Henny Youngman (himself)/Debi Mazor (Sandy)/Jerry Vale (himself)/Michael Imperioli (Spider)/Robbie Vinton (Bobby Vinton)/Samuel L. Jackson (Parnell Steven 'Stacks' Edwards)/Anthony Powers (Jimmy Two Times)/John Williams (Johnny Roastbeef)/Frank Pelligrino (Johnny Dio)/John Manca (Nickey Eyes)/Margo Winkler (Belle Kessler)/Welker White (Lois Byrd)/Julie Garfield (Mickey Conway)/Elaine Kagan (Henry's mother)/

Beau Starr (Henry's father)/Kevin Corrigan (Michael Hill, Henry's brother)

*　　*　　*

In a career defined by urban dramas set in New York, *GoodFellas* is one of director Martin Scorsese's most successful and popular films. He takes the Warner Bros plots of the thirties, specifically *The Public Enemy*, and shows the rise and fall of Irishman Henry Hill through the ranks of the Italian mob in Queens, New York. It is the most hard-hitting of the 'rags to riches' biographical dramas, as Henry's free-fall descent is cataclysmic. *GoodFellas* depicts a grim underworld; a world in which tempers are so short that one wrong word can ensure you soon find yourself dumped in a wood with your brains blown out. They may be goodfellas, but they're bad men.

GoodFellas is based on the book 'Wiseguy' by Nicolas Pileggi. Pileggi was a writer and editor specialising in crime on the *New York Magazine*. *GoodFellas* tells the true story of Henry Hill, who grew up in East New York, Brooklyn. The action begins in 1955, when he starts working for a Sicilian family of 'wiseguy' gangsters, the Ciceros. There he meets Jimmy Conway, a racketeer, and Tommy DeVito, an up-and-coming hood. Paulie, the Cicero's headman, likes Henry and helps him out in any way he can. The Ciceros are 'a police department for wiseguys'. By the early sixties the gang are stealing everything they can from freighters landing at Idlewild Airport. Their centre of operations is the Bamboo Lounge, where they plan and pull off a $420,000 robbery of American cash, which has been exchanged for francs, from Air France. Henry marries Jewish girl Karen, who adapts to and adores Henry's life of crime. In 1970, following an argument in a Queens Boulevard bar, Tommy kills Billy Batts, a so-called 'made' man, an untouchable in the crime world. With Henry and Jimmy, he buries Batts in a wood.

Jimmy and Henry are sentenced to ten years in Lewisburg Federal Prison, for beating up a bookie in Tampa; Henry's out in four. Henry is warned by Paulie not to get involved in the drugs trade, but he ignores Paulie, setting up a trafficking business with Tommy and Jimmy, now also released . In 1978, Jimmy assembles a gang to pull off a heist at the airport, now renamed JFK, stealing $6 million in cash from the Lufthansa Cargo Terminal. But one of the gang, truck driver 'Stacks' Edwards, slips up and the cops find the robbers' lorry, which could lead them to Stacks. Playing safe, Jimmy and Tommy cover their tracks and kill everyone involved; later Tommy is told that he is going to be 'made', a great honour, to join the inner circle of gangsters, but in revenge for killing Batts, he's murdered. By the eighties, Henry is up to his neck in drugs and a paranoid addict himself. He is busted by the Narcs; betrayed, Paulie turns his back on Henry for ever. Henry and Karen decide to enter the Federal Witness Protection Program; he testifies against his former associates, putting Jimmy, Paulie Cicero and the gang away for a very long time.

Director Martin Scorsese read 'Wiseguy' while making *The Color of Money* (1986). He was keen to make a film of Pileggi's book, but Irving Winkler already owned the rights. Winkler had produced Scorsese's *New York New York* and *Raging Bull*, so they agreed on another collaboration. 'Wiseguy' was used as the working title for the project, but was eventually changed, to avoid confusion with Brian De Palma's misfire gangster comedy *Wise Guys* (1986), with Danny DeVito and Joe Piscopo. Pileggi wrote the *GoodFellas* screenplay in collaboration with Scorsese; it went through 12 drafts. The real Henry Hill received $480,000 two weeks before filming began in 1989, for the rights to his life story.

For the film version, Scorsese changed several names: Tommy DeVito is actually Tommy 'Two Gun Tommy' DeSimone, Paulie Cicero is Paulie Vario Snr, the head of the crew, and Jimmy Conway is cigarette racketeer Jimmy 'the Gent' Burke. Burke's daughter wanted money for the rights to use her father's name, so they changed it. Henry Hill's testimony against his former colleagues is part of the KENRAC trial (Kennedy Airport Racketeering trial). At the end of Scorsese's scenario, we discover that 'Paul Cicero'/Vario died in 1988 in Fort Worth Federal Prison, aged 73. 'Jimmy Conway,' we are informed, 'is currently serving a 20-years-to-life sentence in New York State prison... he will not be eligible for parole until 2004'; Burke never made parole – he died in prison in April 1996.

In the seventies, Martin Scorsese, along with George Lucas, Steven Spielberg and Francis Ford Coppola, was a member of the 'movie brat' movement of young, up-and-coming filmmakers. After a series of short films, Scorsese's directorial debut

The *GoodFellas* about to whack Billy Batts in a Queens' bar room; left to right: Henry (Ray Liotta), Jimmy (Robert De Niro) and Tommy (Joe Pesci).

was the Roger Corman-produced Depression-era train robbers drama *Boxcar Bertha* (1972). The most striking of his early films is *Mean Streets* (1973), a *tour-de-force* which established Scorsese's style. Made for $500,000 and originally called *Season of the Witch*, *Mean Streets* told the story of four friends, small-timers Charlie, Johnny Boy, Tony and Michael, in Little Italy, New York (although much of the action was shot in Los Angeles). Charlie, a good Catholic boy, is a debt collector for his Uncle Giovanni and is dating Johnny Boy's sister, Teresa. Johnny Boy owes everyone money, including Michael, who decides to collect, but Johnny Boy pulls a pistol on him. Later, as Charlie, Teresa and Johnny are driving out of town, Michael and his hoods pull up in a car and open fire, hitting Johnny in the neck and badly wounding Teresa and Charlie.

Mean Streets certainly wasn't a tale of crime aristocracy, of cons and dons, but rather the Dead End Kids grown up. Most memorable is Scorsese's casual attitude to violence (in particular a vicious poolroom bust-up, which explodes from nowhere) and his use of music. A stripper performs to 'Tell Her' by the Rolling Stones while Charlie looks on; later Johnny Boy swaggers into the bar with two pick-ups to the same band's 'Jumpin' Jack Flash'. Johnny does a goofy dance to 'Mickey's Monkey' by the Miracles; the poolroom fight is accompanied by 'Please Mr Postman' by the Marvelettes. The effect is electrifying, as is Robert De Niro's performance as Johnny Boy; Harvey Keitel is equally notable as Charlie. De Niro's first appearance in the film is memorable, as he mischievously blows up a street corner mailbox. Emphasising Charlie's Catholic guilt, *Mean Streets*' tagline was 'You don't make up for your sins in church. You do it on the streets'. *Mean Streets* was one of Henry Hill's favourite films; he even took Paulie to see it. Paulie usually only liked westerns, but he loved *Mean Streets*. Who knows how much these wiseguys were influenced in real life by *Mean Streets*? Then years later Scorsese went on to make another crime film about these very same gangsters.

Scorsese again cast De Niro in *GoodFellas*, as Jimmy Conway. De Niro was a regular collaborator with Scorsese. He was the lead in Scorsese's *Taxi Driver* (1976), *New York New York* (1977), the acclaimed boxing biography *Raging Bull* (1980) and *The King of Comedy* (1983). As Jimmy Conway he delivers one of his best gangster performances, a mature version of mad-ass Johnny Boy. Brooklyn-born Lorraine Bracco was a former model. She was married to Harvey Keitel from 1982–93; Karen Hill remains her best role to date. Handsome Ray Liotta, a dead ringer for Jeffrey Hunter, was cast as her husband Henry. Liotta had appeared in the short-lived TV series *Casablanca* (1983), and as Shoeless Joe Jackson in *Field of Dreams* (1989). He had turned down the role of the Joker (finally played by Jack Nicholson) in *Batman* (1989) to accept the role of Henry Hill. Both Liotta and Joe Pesci were born in Newark, New Jersey. Pesci had caught Scorsese's eye in *The Death Collector* (1976 – also called *Family Enforcer*), a very low-budget Mafia flick, which also starred Frank Vincent. Both Pesci and Vincent were cast in *Raging Bull*, with the latter playing Salvy Batts; in *GoodFellas* he played Billy Batts, while Pesci played Tommy DeVito.

Scorsese also cast his own family members in *GoodFellas*: his mother Catherine Scorsese played Tommy's mum, while his father Charles played elderly gangster Vinnie, who oversees Tommy's murder. Comedian Henny Youngman appeared as himself, as did singer Jerry Vale (singing 'Pretend You Don't See Her'); Robbie Vinton played his own father Bobby, miming in a Copacabana scene to Bobby's 'Roses are Red'. Real US attorney Edward McDonald played himself; it is he who persuaded Henry that the Witness Protection Program was Henry's only option to prevent him and Karen going to prison.

GoodFellas was filmed, like *Once Upon a Time in America* and *The Godfather* films, in the screen ratio of 1.85:1 (width to height – a ratio more often seen in TV movies), rather than the CinemaScope/Techniscope/Panavision letterbox ratio of 2.35:1. *GoodFellas* was photographed on location in Queens, New York and in New Jersey, during the spring and summer of 1989 for a budget of $25 million. JFK Airport, where the gang carry out the Lufthansa heist, doubled as Idlewild Airport; the airport's cargo buildings were used for the Air France hold-up and the Lufthansa job. The airport diner is Jackson Hole Diner, with its distinctive 'Airline' plane sign above the entrance. Henry's neighbourhood was filmed around Astoria in Queens, the railway bridge was the Long Island Railroad trestle in Queens. The Copacabana Club actually exists, and was filmed, on Fifth Avenue in Manhattan, while the 'Bamboo Lounge' was the Hawaii Kai restaurant. During the making of the film, the real Hill received ten phone calls a day from Scorsese and De Niro, although Liotta didn't really get to know Hill until after the film's release; he didn't want the real Henry to alter his take on the character during filming.

As with *Mean Streets*, Scorsese's soundtrack is littered with classics. Scorsese evokes the different decades through period music. Tony Bennett aptly croons 'From Rags to Riches' over the title sequence. Italian Mina sings the beautiful 'This World We Love In', in the scene where we are introduced to Paulie's crew in the sixties. Other classics include 'Then He Kissed Me' by the Crystals, 'Leader of the Pack' by the Shangri-Las and 'Frosty the Snowman' by the Ronettes, while Dean Martin sings the appropriate 'Ain't that a Kick in the Head'. The Rolling Stones provide 'Gimme Shelter', 'Monkey Man' and 'Memo from Turner' (from *Performance*). Cream's 'Sunshine of your Love', Donovan's 'Atlantis', George Harrison's 'What is Life' and the Who's 'The Magic Bus' all make an appearance. 'Mannish Boy', the blues song by Muddy Waters, was also performed by Waters in Scorsese's concert film *The Last Waltz* (1976). The end titles, following the shot of Henry in his new anonymous suburban identity, play out with Sid Vicious's version of 'My Way' from *The Great Rock and Roll Swindle* (1980).

The mob depicted in *GoodFellas* is the archetypal one big happy Italian family. The film is steeped in the Italian immigrant tradition of Scorsese's own childhood, growing up in the 'Little Italy' district. Their heritage is particularly noticeable through the Italian emphasis on the preparation and consumption of rich food. As Henry Hill himself noted, 'In 1957 grade-A imported prosciutto was all the evidence the government needed to prove there was a Mafia in the US'. Eating and wiseguys go together: you make better decisions on a full stomach; years later, Hill co-wrote 'The Wiseguy Cookbook'. There is also a lot of background dialogue based on language from the 'old country' – Sicilian slang from the older wiseguys (which is explained with footnotes in the published continuity script).

The gangsters' world is especially dangerous; there is an edge to some of the Bamboo Lounge scenes, for instance, where the threat of violence is omnipresent. The hoods, like Johnny Boy in *Mean Streets*, are constantly joking around; this ribbing, riling, violent horseplay is referred to in wiseguys' slang as 'busting' or 'breaking their balls'. In the film's most famous scene, Tommy tells a funny anecdote in his inimitable way and then flies off the handle when Henry says, laughing, that Tommy is 'really funny'. 'What do you mean I'm funny?' snaps Tommy, his rant escalating in venom: 'I mean, funny like a clown? I amuse you? I make you laugh. I'm here to fucking amuse you. What do you mean funny? Funny, how? How am I funny? What the fuck is so funny about me?' before revealing that he's just joking around. This scene was written and then improvised by Pesci himself.

Familial and gang loyalty is paramount in Scorsese's films and in this respect, *GoodFellas* is the middle film of his 'New York Gangs' trilogy: bracketed by *Mean Streets* (1973) and *Gangs of New York* (2002). When Henry is convinced he is about to become the target of his own kind, he recalls: 'They never tell you that they're going to kill you … so your murderers come with smiles. They come as friends, the people who have cared for you all your life, and they always seem to come at a time when you're at your weakest and most in need of their help.'

Henry's voiceover lends immediacy to his story and is highly effective; more so than the 'March of Time' framework that performed this function in the old Warners movies. 'As far back as I can remember, I've always wanted to be a gangster,' says Henry, as we see three hoods murdering a helpless elderly victim in the trunk of a car. 'To me, being a gangster was better than being President of the United States. You were treated like a film star.' Later, when Henry first meets Karen, her voiceover tells the story from her perspective. Everywhere the gangsters go, the red carpet is rolled out – the best seats, free drinks, kickbacks. In a memorable scene, Henry impresses Karen on a date by jumping the Copacabana Club queue, taking her down through the kitchens and whisking her to a table right beside the cabaret (this scene is impressively lensed in one long take by Scorsese).

An opening 'flash-forward' to 1970 depicts the killing of 'made' man Billy Batts and introduces us to Henry, Jimmy and Tommy in violent fashion; later the story is contextualised. In a bar, Batts riles Tommy. After hours, Tommy returns and with help from Jimmy and Henry he viciously beats up Batts. Hill notes that in reality Tommy pistol-whipped 'made' man 'Billy Bates' until the weapon fell apart. With Batts unconscious in the trunk of their car, the trio visit Tommy's mother in the middle of the night to pick up a shovel. The black comedy of these scenes is well played by the actors and Catherine Scorsese. Although they're in a rush, she insists they join her in the kitchen for pasta. Tommy says they've hit a deer and wants to borrow a butcher's knife; he explains she's seen him so little because 'I've been working nights'. Later the trio drive into woodland and hear banging in the trunk – they open it and Tommy stabs Batts, who is beginning to recover, with his mother's knife, and Jimmy shoots him. In Hill's actual recollections, they finished Batts off by clobbering him with a shovel and a tyre iron, then they buried him, covering him with lime. The coda to the story is also true: six months later they discover that the land is to be developed and they have to go back and disinter the body. As they dig, Jimmy and Tommy joke around: 'Here's an arm.' 'Here's a leg, here's a wing…' hey what do you like? A leg or a wing?'

The most memorable character in the film is Tommy DeVito. Pesci was well cast as the killer, a hood of whom it was said that he would shoot you 'just because he felt like trying out a new gun'. Pesci's machine-gun delivery, profuse swearing and violence put him in a different league to his co-actors: a Cagney for the nineties. Interestingly, the only scenes where Tommy doesn't swear are the ones with his mother. He is respectful, like mother's boy Cody Jarrett in *White Heat*, whom Tommy resembles in terms of his furiously volatile temper. Tommy is 'crazy… a cowboy'; the last image of the film is Tommy firing a pistol at the camera, echoing a scene in the silent western *The Great Train Robbery* (1903). As revenge for killing 'made' man Billy Batts without permission from his bosses, Tommy is 'whacked'

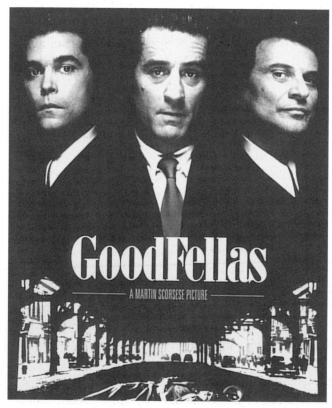

'I always wanted to be a gangster': promotional artwork for Martin Scorsese's *GoodFellas* (1990), starring Ray Liotta, Robert De Niro and Joe Pesci.

('whacking' or 'breaking an egg' was a mob euphemism for murder). On his happiest day, in his best suit, with his friends and mother proud of him, Tommy is blasted straight through the head; his assassins even shoot him in the face, 'so his mother couldn't give him an open coffin at the funeral'. Amazingly, Hill noted that Pesci's Tommy was a 'toned-down' version of the real one.

As Henry's voiceover informs us: 'Murder was the only way that everybody stayed in line…you got out of line, you got whacked.' In the most brutal passage of the film, Jimmy decides that he must cut all links between himself and the Lufthansa heist. Not following genre convention, we never see the actual heist and barely witness its planning – and this was at the time the biggest heist in the US. In an infamous sequence, blabbermouth accomplice Morrie Kessler is killed, with an ice pick in his neck, and then bodies start to turn up all over town. Stacks Edwards is riddled by Tommy in his apartment; Johnny Roastbeef and his wife are found shot in their pink Cadillac; behind the Airport Diner, Joe Buddha's and Frenchy's corpses roll out of a garbage truck; in Hunts Point Market parking lot, Frankie Carbone is found hanging in a refrigerated meat truck. 'Months after the robbery,' Henry intones, 'they were finding bodies all over. When they found Carbone…he was frozen so stiff it took them two days to thaw him out for the autopsy.' These gruesome discoveries are juxtaposed with the beautiful piano bridge from 'Layla' by Derek and the Dominos.

But Henry's life eventually disintegrates and is an archetypal 'dark side of the American dream' morality tale – from peeping out of the window as a child, watching the rich wiseguys at the cabstand across the street, to drug addiction, paranoia and betrayal. As the drugs take hold, he and Karen are reduced to freaked-out, drug-addled wrecks. Henry becomes convinced the police have tapped his phone and put a helicopter on his trail, following him around town, but everyone thinks he's paranoid. Later he discovers his suspicion is well founded: he's busted by Narcotics agents, his phone has been tapped and a helicopter has been following him around town. Finding out that Henry's involved in drugs, Paulie turns his back on Henry and pays him off: 'Thirty-two hundred bucks for a lifetime,' muses Henry. 'It wasn't even enough to pay for the coffin.' When Jimmy tries to send Henry to carry out a hit in Florida, Henry realises his number is up and 'I would never have come back from Florida alive'. So it seems he has only one course of action: to enter the Witness Protection Program, even if this contravenes both the pieces of advice Jimmy gave young Henry on his release from prison all those years ago: 'Never rat on your friends…and always keep your mouth shut.' He agrees to enter the Federal Witness Protection Program, with Karen and their two children, Greg and Gina, even though Karen will never be able to see her parents again. Perhaps this dénouement explains why non-Italians like Irish Henry can never become 'made' men – there is always potential for betrayal.

In some advertising material the film's title appears as *GoodFellas*, in others as *Goodfellas*. The poster depicted a portrait of Jimmy, flanked by Henry and Tommy, in smart-cut suits; below them was a railway trestle, with a body sprawled under it. The tagline read: 'Murderers come with smiles. Shooting people was "No Big Deal". We were…Goodfellas.' The cinema trailer was a potted biography of Henry, with the glamorous side emphasised, backed by Tony Bennett's 'Rags to Riches'. 'In a world that's powered by violence,' warned the solemn voiceover, 'on the streets where the violent have power…a new generation carries out an old tradition.' The *Washington Post* said there was 'a gutsy passion there, as well as a horrifying, unblinking view of humanity. Artistically at least, Scorsese has managed to make crime pay.' *New York* called it 'the greatest film ever made about the sensual and monetary lure of crime'; *Time* equated watching the film with a trip to the Bronx Zoo: 'You walk away tantalised by a view into the darkest part of yourself, glad that that part is still behind bars'.

GoodFellas was shown at the Venice Film Festival in September 1990, where Scorsese won the Silver Lion for best director; the film premiered in the US the same month. Rated R, it grossed $6.3 million in its opening weekend in the US and almost $47 million in total. It took almost £2 million in the UK and 3 billion lire in Italy, where it was released as *Quei Bravi Ragazzi*: literally 'Those Good Boys'. In Germany it was *Goodfellas: Drei Jahrzehnte in der Mafia* ('Three Decades in the Mafia'). In Spain it was *Un de los Nuestros* ('One of Ours' or 'One of Our Own'). The best foreign title was given to it by Argentina, where it was known by the literal but lively *Buenos Muchachos*.

On its 2004 special edition DVD release, a 'making of' documentary was assembled, entitled *Getting Made*. For TV showings, Scorsese himself prepared a sanitised version, no mean feat, considering the film contains 246 'fucks', a record it wrestled from Al Pacino's *Scarface*. In the UK it was passed uncut, but certified 18. Most of the expletives are uttered by Pesci, a one-man swear box, who won the 1991 Best Supporting Actor Oscar for his performance. There were also Oscar nominations for Bracco, editor Thelma Schoonmaker, and Pileggi and Scorsese's screenplay. *GoodFellas* won BAFTAs for Scorsese's direction and Best Film.

When Henry Hill saw *GoodFellas* in 1990, he said: 'That's really the way it was… it's all true.' In 2004 Hill published a book called 'Gangsters and Goodfellas: Wiseguys…and Life on the Run', which brought his story up to date and is essential reading for anyone interested in New York gangsterism. Hill also co-wrote 'A Goodfella's Guide to New York' and during the making of *GoodFellas* he also collaborated on a film treatment called 'Getting Gotti', about real-life mobster John Gotti, known as 'the Teflon Don' – so called because the police could never make charges stick.

The comedy *My Blue Heaven* (1990) was a variation on the Henry Hill story, with Steve Martin as an Italian New York hood entering into the FBI's Witness Protection Program, watched over by agent Rick Moranis. It was written by Nora Ephron, Nicholas Pileggi's wife. Other New York-set gangster stories have included the parodic *The Gang That Couldn't Shoot Straight* (1971), based on Jimmy Breslin's bestseller. Breslin was a crime columnist on *Daily News* who used to write about real wiseguys and the book is reputedly a parody of the goodfellas gangs. The film's cast includes Jerry Orbach, Lionel Stander, Jo Van Fleet, a young Robert De Niro and Herve Villechaize (Nick Nack in *The Man with the Golden Gun*).

GoodFellas is the only film mentioned in this book that has a pizza firm named after it. 'Goodfellas' pizzas, whose logo states 'We're New York Italian', litter their adverts with 'Bada-bings', capitalising on the link between the twin Italian cultural clichés of the Mafia and rich food. *The Sopranos*, an HBO TV series, has deployed the *GoodFellas* formula, populating its New Jersey setting with characters having the look and manner of Scorsese's protagonists. This highly popular mix of violent mayhem, comedy and drama follows the exploits of the Soprano Mafia family, headed by Tony Soprano, successfully played by James Gandolfini.

In 1995, Scorsese released *Casino*, depicting the Mafia's involvement in the Las Vegas gambling industry at the Tangiers casino, again co-written with Nicholas Pileggi. De Niro and Pesci both reappeared (as casino boss Ace Rothstein and hardman Nicky Santoro), with Sharon Stone as Ginger McKenna, Ace's wife. Singer Jerry Vale has a cameo as himself, while the strong cast includes James Woods, Don Rickles and L.Q. Jones. Ace Rothstein is based on real-life casino manager Frank 'Lefty' Rosenthal, while Scorsese beats his own 'fuck' record with *Casino*, with the expletive uttered 362 times.

Scorsese's latest addition to his New York gangster saga is *Gangs of New York* (2002), which depicted an earlier age of violence on New York's streets, from 1846 to 1862, between gangs with names like the Dead Rabbits and the Federation of American Natives. *Variety* first announced *Gangs of New York* as a Scorsese film in 1977, but it was finally made 25 years later. With Daniel Day-Lewis as gang leader Bill 'the Butcher' Cutting and Leonardo DiCaprio as his adversary, Amsterdam Vallon, it is Scorsese's biggest commercial success, taking $190 million worldwide.

But *GoodFellas* is the ultimate New York gangster movie, eclipsing even *Once Upon a Time in America* and the *Godfather* films. In 2005, *Total Film* magazine had *GoodFellas* topping its '100 greatest movies list' as 'the finest film ever made'; *The Godfather Part II* was fifth, *Chinatown* was twelfth and *The Godfather* was twenty-third. *GoodFellas*' massive popularity and clearly etched characters have ingrained themselves in the cinema-going public's consciousness. By the end of *GoodFellas*, the parallels between gangsterism and fame are even more pronounced. The last voiceover, as Henry picks up his morning newspaper in suburbia, bemoans his loss of privilege and the eminence that went with crime: 'There's no action. I have to wait around like everyone else. Can't even get decent food. I'm an average nobody. I get to live the rest of my life like a schnook.' As Hill notes at the beginning of 'Gangsters and Goodfellas': 'I became Joe Schmoe'. Schmoe or schnook, Henry Hill's story is incredible. Unlike so many people in his narrative, and thanks to the Witness Protection Program, he lived to tell his tale of life as a goodfella.

20

'Mon amour . . . l'aventure commence'

— *Pulp Fiction* (1994)

Credits:

DIRECTOR – Quentin Tarantino

PRODUCER – Lawrence Bender

ORIGINAL STORIES – Quentin Tarantino and Roger Avery

SCREENPLAY – Quentin Tarantino

DIRECTOR OF PHOTOGRAPHY – Andrzej Sekula

EDITOR – Sally Menke

PRODUCTION DESIGNER – David Wasco

COSTUMES – Betsy Heimann

MUSIC SUPERVISOR – Karyn Rachtman

Deluxe Color/Panavision

A Miramax presentation

A Band Apart/Jersey Films production

Released by Buena Vista International

154 minutes

Cast:

John Travolta (Vincent Vega)/Samuel L. Jackson (Jules Winnfield)/
Uma Thurman (Mia Wallace)/Harvey Keitel (Winston Wolf)/
Tim Roth (Ringo, alias 'Pumpkin')/Amanda Plummer (Yolanda,
alias 'Honey Bunny')/Maria de Medeiros (Fabienne, Butch's
wife)/Ving Rhames (Marsellus Wallace)/Eric Stolz (Lance, the
drug dealer)/Rosanna Arquette (Jody, Lance's wife)/Christopher
Walken (Captain Koons)/Bruce Willis (Butch Coolidge)/Laura
Lovelace (Hawthorne Grill waitress)/Phil Lamarr (Marvin)/
Frank Whaley (Brett)/Burr Steers (Roger 'Flock of Seagulls')/
Paul Calderon (Paul, alias 'English Dave')/Bronagh Gallagher
(Trudi)/Jerome Patrick Hoban (Ed Sullivan)/Michael Gilden
(Phillip Morris bellhop)/Gary Shorelle (Ricky Nelson)/Susan
Griffiths (Marilyn Monroe)/Eric Clark (James Dean)/Josef Pilato

(Dean Martin)/Brad Parker (Jerry Lewis)/Lorelei Leslie (Mamie Van Doren)/Emil Sitka ('Hold Hands, You Lovebirds' on TV)/Brenda Hillhouse (Butch's mother)/Chandler Lindauer (Young Butch)/Angela Jones (Esmarelda Villalobos, taxi driver)/Carl Allen (Dead Floyd Wilson)/Linda Kaye (Shot lady)/Duane Whitaker (Maynard, pawnshop owner)/Peter Greene (Zed, the cop)/Stephen Hibbert (The Gimp)/Alexis Arquette (Hidden fourth man)/Quentin Tarantino (Jimmie)/Vanessa Valentino (Bonnie)/Robert Ruth (Hawthorne owner)/Lawrence Bender (Long Haired Yuppie-Scum and 'Zorro')

*   *   *

In the late eighties, crime movies were stuck in a rut. In general, special-effects spectaculars, with brawn but no brain, were popular at the box office. It seemed that the task of crime films was to struggle straight to video, with imitation cop formula movies aping *Lethal Weapon*. Otherwise crime was the domain of Hong Kong action movies, featuring a new breed of kinetic, black-suited action hero. In the US, only Martin Scorsese stood out, with his idiosyncratic characters and sparkling dialogue, epitomised by *GoodFellas*, his anti-*Godfather* movie. Then in the early nineties, a filmmaker came along who changed the map and completely altered the way US crime films were made.

Quentin Tarantino was born in 1963 in Knoxville, Tennessee. He was named after 'Quint' Asper, the half-breed blacksmith played by Burt Reynolds in the TV series *Gunsmoke*. His family moved to Los Angeles and, before becoming a film director in 1992, he spent five years working in an LA video rental shop called 'Video Archives'. He wrote several stories and managed to sell a script called *True Romance*, which was later turned into a film by Tony Scott. In tandem with producer Lawrence Bender, Tarantino set to work on his directorial debut, *Reservoir Dogs*.

Made for $1.2 million, *Reservoir Dogs* tells the story of a six-man gang robbing a jewellery store of Israeli polished diamonds, in transit to Vermont. To maintain anonymity, the lowlifes are given by their employers, Joe Cabot and his spoilt son 'Nice Guy Eddie', colour-coded aliases: White, Orange, Blonde, Pink, Blue and Brown. But even though they steal the rocks, the gang have been set up ('We got a rat in the house') and the cops have laid an ambush. Blue and Brown are killed and Orange is badly wounded, as their escape turns into 'a fucking bullet festival'. Back at their warehouse rendezvous, White, Blonde and Pink argue over what went wrong, while Orange bleeds all over the floor. Eventually, Blonde is killed by Orange (actually an undercover cop) and 'Nice Guy' and his dad show up and try to retrieve the diamonds. In a three-way simultaneous 'Mexican stand-off', White shoots Dad, Dad shoots Orange, Nice Guy shoots White, and Pink waits for the smoke to clear before making off with the diamonds.

Reservoir Dogs was an assured debut. The story is told with snatches flashing back to the robbery, intercut with the gang licking their wounds in the vacant, echoing warehouse. Tarantino's snappy, harsh and very strong language is a significant aspect of his style. During high-tension, high-volume discussions, there is a profusion of gesticulating and grandstanding, often filmed in medium shot, giving the film a stagy, hysterical quality, like a lunatic theatre workshop. The gang bicker constantly about everything, from whether to execute a captive cop to who is going to have which colour as their 'cool-sounding name' (everyone wanted to be 'Mr Black'). But this verbal violence is often offset with humour: 'I bet you're a big Lee Marvin fan, aren't you?' asks Blonde of White, following a blazing row in which they've almost shot each other.

Two scenes in particular demonstrate Tarantino's visual and aural style. In the title sequence, the gang, dressed like mourners, in iconic black suits, ties and shades, stride down the street in slow motion to the George Baker Selection belting out 'Little Green Bag'. Incidentally, this scene is only preceded by the oft-quoted line 'Let's go to work' in the theatrical trailer, not in the actual film. In another pivotal scene, the gang have captured a cop. Mr Blonde, left alone with the officer, determines to torture him to death: 'All you can do is pray for a quick death… which you ain't gonna get.' Blonde begins the ordeal by severing the cop's ear with a razor, while performing a shuffling dance to Stealer's Wheel's rendition of 'Stuck in the Middle with You', before dousing him with gasoline. The music is linked throughout the film by a fictional radio show 'K–Billy's Super Sounds of the Seventies', introduced by a monotonous DJ played by deadpan comedian Steven Wright.

Reservoir Dogs's vivid colour scheme is red, white and black. By the end there is blood everywhere, with the murdered, mono-eared cop slumped in the chair and life seeping out of Orange, down a loading ramp and pooling on the floor. The actors' performances are very good, in particular the central quartet of Steve Buscemi, as motormouth Mr Pink, Tim Roth as undercover cop Freddy (Mr Orange), Harvey Keitel (as too-trusting Mr White) and most significantly Michael Madsen, infusing a little of maniacally grinning Jack Palance into fanatical Mr Blonde.

In interviews, Tarantino cites directors Howard Hawks, Sam Fuller, Brian De Palma, Martin Scorsese, Sergio Leone, Jean-Luc Godard and Jean-Pierre Melville as influences. Joseph H. Lewis's *The Big Combo* (1955) inspired the scene where a cop is tortured in a chair, while Tarantino's plot was suggested by an earlier B-movie, *Kansas City Confidential* (1952); here a crook recruits three no-goods (Neville Brand, Lee Van Cleef and Jack Elam), to rob an armoured car. There is complete anonymity within the gang, as they all wear masks throughout. Later they reassemble at the Borados resort in Mexico to split the loot with their boss, who turns out to be an ex-cop.

Reservoir Dogs was one hell of a surprise for the Sundance Independent Film Festival and was particularly popular in the UK and France, where its funeral suits, cowboy boots and big guns struck a chord; it took £6 million in the UK. It was less popular in the US, earning only $3 million, possibly because it was an independent feature and lacked the backing of a major studio to promote and distribute it.

For his next film, *Pulp Fiction*, Tarantino originally envisaged three separate stories, filmed by three directors, like an old-fashioned portmanteau film, but the stories ended up overlapping into one continuous, albeit non-chronological, narrative. The film begins in the Hawthorne Grill coffee shop, where Ringo and Yolanda prepare to relieve the patrons of their wallets. The first story, 'Vincent Vega and Marsellus Wallace's Wife', sees two hitmen, Jules and Vincent, arrive at an apartment to retrieve a valuable briefcase for crime boss Marsellus Wallace from a gang of college boys. They kill two of the kids and take the case. Vincent has to take Marsellus's wife Mia out for the evening while his boss is away; they go to Jack Rabbit Slim's retro theme bar and win a twisting contest. Back at home, Mia overdoses on heroin and Vincent saves her life by taking her to his dealer's house and giving her an adrenaline shot. In the second story, 'The Gold Watch', boxer Butch Coolidge has been told by Marsellus to take a dive in a fight, but instead he wins and goes on the run with his French girlfriend, Fabienne. When Butch goes back to retrieve his father's gold watch from his apartment, he kills Vincent, who has been sent by Marsellus to kill him. Butch runs into Marsellus, but they are both captured by Maynard, a deranged pawnshop owner, and his mates, Zed and the Gimp, who proceed to sodomise Marsellus. Butch escapes and saves Marsellus, squaring things between them; Butch leaves town with Fabienne, on Zed's chopper bike. In the third story, 'The Bonnie Situation' occurs when Vincent accidentally shoots Marvin, their contact in the college gang, on the back seat of Jules's Chevy Nova. They hide out at Jimmie's, but his wife Bonnie is due home at any moment. Marsellus sends over Mr Wolf ('I solve problems'). Wolf barks instructions to ensure the clean-up runs smoothly; 'A please would be nice,' says Vincent. Wolf points out that he's doing them a favour: 'So pretty please, with sugar on top...clean the fucking car.' They clean up the mess and dispose of the corpse before Bonnie arrives. In the end, back at the Hawthorne Grill during the robbery, we discover that Vincent and Jules are having breakfast in there, shortly after leaving Jimmie's. Jules convinces Ringo not to steal the briefcase and the thieves leave, before Jules and Vincent stroll out of the diner with the case.

Following the success of *Reservoir Dogs*, appearing in a Tarantino movie was very cool, so the director had an extraordinary cast for his next film, headed by John Travolta. A worldwide superstar at 24 as a result of the TV series *Welcome Back, Kotter*, the disco movie *Saturday Night Fever* (1977) and the screen adaptation of musical *Grease* (1978), Travolta's star had descended somewhat by 1993. He received only $100,000 from Tarantino, but the director's instinct was well founded and Travolta is terrific as Vincent Vega, the brother of Vic Vega (Michael Madsen) in *Reservoir Dogs* (also considered for Vincent Vega were Daniel Day-Lewis and Bruce Willis).

Prospective Mias were Joan Cusack, Meg Ryan, Michelle Pfeiffer and Daryl Hannah, but the role of the mobster's moll went to Uma Thurman. Born in 1970 in Boston, Thurman had appeared in *Dangerous Liaisons* (1988), the ill-fated *The Adventures of Baron Munchausen* (1989), the controversial *Henry & June* (1990) and the slated *Even Cowgirls Get the Blues* (1994). In *Pulp Fiction* she was Mia to a T, with her chic outfits and jet black fringed, bobbed hairstyle, influenced equally by fifties bondage pin-up Betty Page and Jean-Luc Godard's muse, Anna Karina. Harvey Keitel and Tim Roth both returned from *Reservoir Dogs*; Keitel played black-suited fix-it, Mr Wolf, who looks like a pencil-moustached relative of Mr White, while Roth was cast with Amanda Plummer as the thieves exploring the possibilities of robbing restaurants: Ringo and Yolanda. Rosanna Arquette, her face here riddled with piercings, looked very different from her eighties heyday in such movies as *Desperately Seeking Susan* (1985); in *Pulp Fiction* she portrayed Jody, the wife of grungy drug dealer Lance (Eric Stolz). Christopher Walken, who'd appeared in *The Deer Hunter* (1978), *Heaven's Gate* (1980) and the Tarantino-scripted *True Romance* (1993), had a cameo as Vietnam vet Captain Koons, who spent the last two years of the war in a prison camp with a valuable wristwatch concealed in his rectum.

Matt Dillon and Sylvester Stallone (cinema's 'Rocky') were both mentioned for boxer Butch, but Tarantino eventually made the right choice with Bruce Willis. Hugely popular, Willis had received $15 million for his 'Die Hard' action movies, but worked for $1,400 – minimum wage – just to secure a part in the film. New Yorker Ving (full name Irving) Rhames had debuted in the Vietnam movie *Casualties of War* (1989); in *Pulp Fiction* he was suitably monstrous as club owner and mobster Marsellus Wallace. Paul Calderon almost played Jules, but ended up in a supporting role as English Dave. Samuel L. Jackson, eventually cast as hitman Jules, had a small role in *GoodFellas* and had appeared in Spike Lee's *Jungle Fever* (1991). As the hitman, Jackson wears a Jheri curl wig and a Ron O'Neal moustache (he compares himself at one point to *Superfly TNT*). He had already auditioned for *Reservoir Dogs*.

Hitmen Jules and Vincent en route to a contract; Samuel L. Jackson and John Travolta in Quentin Tarantino's *Pulp Fiction* (1994).

Pulp Fiction was budgeted at $8 million, with $5 million going to the actors. It was filmed between September and November 1993. Halfway through filming cinematographer Andrzej Sekula (who'd also shot *Reservoir Dogs*) smashed his leg in a car accident and completed filming in a wheelchair. The biggest set was the Jack Rabbit Slim's fifties theme restaurant interior, including a Scalextrix track, replica cars converted into dining tables and a tachometer-shaped stage; the exterior was a disused bowling alley. Many of the interiors were built in two warehouses – which also contained the film's production office – including the hotel room set, Mia's monitor room and the basement of the pawnshop. The boxing arena for the 'Battle of the Titans' was the Olympic Arena, also used in *Rocky*. Monster Joe's Truck & Tow yard is in Pacoima; the Hawthorne Grill is on Hawthorne Boulevard. For Vincent's car to crash into Lance's house, a fake extension was attached to a real bungalow. Marsellus's house was an actual house in the Hollywood Hills; the pawnshop exterior was in the San Fernando Valley.

Tarantino's choice of soundtrack is influenced by Scorsese's use of songs and music. *Pulp Fiction* opens with Dick Dale and His Del-Tones' pounding surf-stomp 'Misirlou', with stuttering guitars and soaring Mariachi trumpet. Halfway through the titles the music tunes out, like a radio dial, and 'Misirlou' is replaced with the funky brass 'get-down' of 'Jungle Boogie' by Kool and the Gang. Dusty Springfield's sultry 'Son of a Preacherman' accompanies Vincent's arrival at Mia's. The cool bass, tremolo chords and sax of 'Bullwinkle Part II' by the Centurions play as Vincent injects heroin and feels the hit on the way to Mia's. Mia and Vincent twist to Chuck Berry's 'You Never Can Tell'. Urge Overkill's 'Morricone-meets-Jan and Dean' rendition of Neil Diamond's 'Girl, You'll be a Woman Soon' accompanies Mia dancing in her lounge, while Vincent and Jules coolly walk out of the coffee shop at the film's close to the shimmering 'Surf Rider' by the Lively Ones. The soundtrack was one of the top sellers of 1994.

Despite the absorption of a myriad of generic film styles, Tarantino's movies are unmistakably his, through a variety of narrative, aural and stylistic flourishes and in-jokes. For instance, there is always a point-of-view shot from inside the boot of a car, the so-called 'Tarantino trunk shot'. Both hitmen wear the black suit 'uniform' of *Reservoir Dogs*, a style borrowed from John Woo Hong Kong movies. There are also several in-jokes from the director. For instance, at the 'Battle of the Titans', the supporting bill is 'Vossler versus Martinez', two of Tarantino's old video-store mates.

There is also a strange morality to Tarantino's films. Here Jules, despite his profanity, is a moral person, quoting Ezekiel 25:17 with hellfire-sermon-style venom, before plugging his victims. Tarantino rewrote the Bible extract for his script to better suit his purpose: 'And I will strike down thee with great vengeance and furious anger, those who attempt to poison and destroy my brothers.' The moment when the hitmen witness a miracle (a gunman ambushes them, but misses at point-blank range) affects Jules: 'I felt the touch of God...God got involved.' It changes the way he feels about his vocation and later Jules retires, to 'walk the earth', as he puts it: 'Like Kane in *Kung Fu*, walk from place to place, meet people, get into adventures.' Vincent ignores the 'sign from God' and dies.

Pulp Fiction is jammed with knowing pop references. Vincent and Jules drive classy cars: Vincent a red Chevrolet Malibu and Jules a 1974 green Chevy Nova. Everyone uses Zippos, the coolest of lighters, and smokes 'Red Apples' cigarettes, a Tarantino-concocted brand that also appears in his other scripts. Vincent reads 'Modesty Blaise' on the toilet. A dealer peddles Bava heroin (a reference to Italian director Mario Bava, who made the three-part film *Black Sabbath*); college kids enjoy Big Kahuna Burgers (Kahoona and Moondoggie are the surfers in the Sandra Dee comedy *Gidget* – 1959) and one of the college boys shot by the hitmen has a floppy fringe and is referred to by Jules as 'Flock of Seagulls', after the eighties UK band, who had a hit with 'I Ran So Far Away'.

Undoubtedly the most referential section of the film is Vincent and Mia's date in Jack Rabbit Slim's, peopled by lookalike icons of the fifties and sixties. Marilyn Monroe, Mamie Van Doren, James Dean and Zorro wait tables; Martin and Lewis crack jokes at the bar, Ricky Nelson strums on stage, emceed by Ed Sullivan and the Phillip Morris tobacco company midget bellhop. Actor Steve Buscemi takes orders as Buddy Holly and producer Lawrence Bender is dressed as Zorro. Tarantino claimed in interviews that the twisting competition was already in the script before Travolta was cast, but a note in the published screenplays states that the scene was 'added during filming' (the energetic Japanese trailer for the film has Mia and Vincent dancing to Urge Overkill instead of Chuck Berry). Vincent orders a Douglas Sirk steak (named after the director of Hollywood melodramas like *Written on the Wind*) and is offered the serving options: 'Burnt to a crisp or bloody as hell'; Mia orders a Durwood Kirby burger (named after the host of *Candid Camera* in the sixties). Tarantino peppers the film with such references and the effect is a little like David Bowie watching several TV sets simultaneously in *The Man Who Fell to Earth* (1976). Jack Rabbit Slim's is a collision of images and the most visually impressive scene in the film; inevitably, like all retro-obsessed places, it looks fantastic, but as Vincent observes, it's 'a wax museum with a pulse'.

Pulp Fiction's briefcase, which links the stories together, is what Hitchcock called a McGuffin, a meaningless element in the film that advances the plot without ever being explained. What is in the case? When opened it emits a golden glow and, in the coffee shop, Ringo is transfixed, asking Jules, 'Is that what I think it is? It's beautiful.' Various different theories were advanced in the TV special *Hollywood's Best Kept Secrets*, the most imaginative of which was the diamond haul from *Reservoir Dogs*. The most ridiculous was Marsellus's soul, which has been removed through the back of his neck – hence the sticking plaster on Marsellus's neck and the 666 case combination. Most convincing was actor Jackson's explanation to a magazine: 'A twelve-volt battery and a light bulb'.

Pulp Fiction won the Palme D'Or at the Cannes Film Festival in May 1994, as the year's best film – it was presented by Kathleen Turner and announced by Clint

Eastwood, the chairman of the jury. The edge was taken off the moment by a woman in the audience shouting 'Fascist!' during Tarantino's speech; afterwards Bruce Willis threw a dinner to celebrate the win.

Pulp Fiction was released on 23 September 1994 in the US, rated R (for violence and drug use); it grossed $9.3 million in its opening weekend and almost $108 million in all. It grossed £10 million in the UK when it came out on 21 October, rated 18. *Pulp Fiction*'s poster was a ten-cents schlock-novel pastiche, depicting Thurman stretched out alluringly on a quilt, elbow propped on a cushion, coolly smoking a cigarette. Littered before her are classic pulp ephemera: an automatic pistol, a packet of Red Apple cigarettes and a lurid paperback, entitled 'Pulp Fiction'. The taglines included 'Girls like me don't make invitations like this to just anyone'. The satirical trailer began as a highbrow, arthouse parody, complete with piano accompaniment, praising the film's success at Cannes, before being shot full of bullet holes, as 'Misirlou' bursts onto the soundtrack – 'You won't know the facts until you see the fiction'. The UK trailer also included the caption 'From the creator of *Reservoir Dogs*'. It took $212 million worldwide – a massive profit on the $8 million 'art movie' investment – and was the hippest must-see of the year.

Roger Ebert recalled that Tarantino had been hailed as 'the first director who's a rock and roll star', while *Variety* called *Pulp Fiction* a 'startling, massive success' and 'the *American Graffiti* of crime pictures'. *Entertainment Weekly* saw it as 'a Martin Scorsese film written by Preston Sturges'. The *New York Times* voted it 'The best movie of the year – tremendous fun', while the *Washington Post* compared Travolta and Jackson to 'modern-day Beckett characters'. In the UK, the *Financial Times* hated it, while *The Sunday Times* compared Tarantino's approach to a 'cinematic Heimlich Manoeuvre'. It was nominated for six Golden Globes (winning Best Screenplay for Tarantino) and seven Academy Awards (it won for Tarantino and Avery – Best Story written for the screen). Best Picture went to *Forrest Gump*. At the MTV awards *Pulp Fiction* won Best Movie and Best Dance Sequence. In the UK, Jackson won a Best Supporting Actor BAFTA, while the soundtrack won a BRIT music award. *Pulp Fiction* also topped many end-of-year 'best of' lists on both sides of the Atlantic.

According to some sources, *Pulp Fiction* was re-edited into a linear narrative for the United Arab Emirates and other Middle Eastern countries. This version begins with Jules and Vincent's hit and the 'Bonnie Situation', continues with Vincent and Mia's night out and ends with 'The Gold Watch'. Chronologically, the last line is Bruce Willis saying 'Zed's dead baby, Zed's dead' as he and Fabienne ride off on the chopper. In the original release version, Travolta's 'hero' dies two-thirds of the way through the film, only to be 'resurrected' by Tarantino's narrative structure, to walk out of the coffee shop with Jules in the finale.

In some UK and US video and TV releases, the film's running time was uncut, but it was reframed and the image zoomed, in a variation of TV's pan-and-scan, to censor violence and drug abuse: for the cinema version, three seconds of the needle going into Travolta's arm was reframed so that the entry was out of shot. The profanity and abuse were considerably redubbed for Network TV showings, while the violence and drug abuse were excised where possible. This truncated version is quite different to the cinema release, missing some important scenes and inserting dialogue footage from scenes never incorporated into final versions of the film. There are also several key filmed scenes, which feature in the published screenplay, and have been included as extras on DVD special editions. These include Mia interviewing Vincent with a video camera (where she expounds her theory that you either like Elvis or the Beatles; you can't like them both equally), a longer taxi ride scene with Butch and an extended Jack Rabbit Slim's sequence, with more information about Mia's *Fox Force Five* pilot; the varying length of Mia's cigarette is an indicator of the cuts herein.

More significantly, because of Tarantino's highly quotable dialogue, the screen-play, published in tandem with the film, sold very well, as the *Reservoir Dogs* screenplay had. *Pulp Fiction*'s screenplay was billed as 'Three Stories…About One Story'. There are quite a few minor dialogue changes between the scripted version and optimum-length prints of the finished film.

Pulp Fiction quickly found its own place in pop culture. For example: the Hawthorne Grill robbery dialogue sampled at the beginning of 'Scooby Snacks' by Fun Lovin' Criminals. The Black Eyed Peas' 2005 hit 'Pump It' uses 'Misirlou' as a backing track, for the Peas to shout over. In 1995, there was also a craze for Uma Thurman's 'Chanel Rouge Noir' nail varnish. The conversations between the hitmen were also influential and easily parodied. Films infused with the hip dialogue include *Destiny Turns on the Radio* (1995), while the unrelenting pop culture barrage mixed with extreme violence is best seen in the Tarantino-scripted *From Dusk till Dawn* (1994), a trashy vampire road movie, and the sexy spoof *Bikini Bandits* (2001), who take out their aggression on the hated consumerism of G-Mart. Tarantino's narrative

Pulp Fiction (1994): Mia and Vincent arrive at Jack Rabbit Slim's; Uma Thurman and John Travolta in retro heaven.

tongue-twisters were adopted by the labyrinthine *The Usual Suspects* (1995). But now Tarantino's influence is everywhere in cinema, as the 'Indie' fringe has infiltrated the mainstream so comprehensively.

Tarantino's next directorial effort was *Jackie Brown*, an adaptation of Elmore Leonard's 1992 'Rum Punch'. He cast Pam Grier as smuggler Jackie Brown – named Jackie Burke in the book, but renamed Brown in honour of Grier's blaxploitation classic *Foxy Brown*. Grier was originally up for the role of Jody in *Pulp Fiction*. Tarantino also cast Robert De Niro, Robert Forster and Bridget Fonda, and reused Jackson, but the film was subtler than his previous work and didn't meet with the same success as *Pulp Fiction*, grossing $39 million in the US. Travolta meanwhile starred in another Leonard adaptation, the hitman comedy *Get Shorty* (1995). Tarantino scripted *Natural Born Killers* (1994), the ultraviolent 'Bonnie and Clyde' for the MTV generation, and went on to direct *Kill Bill*, *Volumes One* and *Two* (2003–4). Here his love of spaghetti westerns and kung fu movies came to the fore, with some pyrotechnic action scenes; *Volume One* outshines *Volume Two*, but *Two* has the better soundtrack. Tarantino isn't just a director, he's a film historian, social commentator and pop culture-vulture, with a vast knowledge of cinema, which infuses his films with inimitable atmosphere and élan.

21

'Off the record, on the QT and very hush-hush'

— *L.A. Confidential* (1997)

Credits:

DIRECTOR – Curtis Hanson

PRODUCERS – Curtis Hanson, Arnon Milchan and Michael Nathanson

STORY – James Ellroy

SCREENPLAY – Brian Helgeland and Curtis Hanson

DIRECTOR OF PHOTOGRAPHY – Dante Spinotti

EDITOR – Peter Honess

ART DIRECTOR – Bill Arnold

COSTUMES – Ruth Myers

MUSIC – Jerry Goldsmith

Panavision/Technicolor

Interiors filmed at Lacy Street Production Centre

A Regency Enterprises/Arnon Milchan/David L. Wolper
    production

Released by Warner Bros

137 minutes

Cast:

Kevin Spacey (Sergeant Jack Vincennes)/Russell Crowe (Officer
Wendell 'Bud' White)/Guy Pearce (Detective Lieutenant
Edmund Exley)/James Cromwell (Captain Dudley Smith)/Kim
Basinger (Lynn Bracken)/Danny DeVito (Sid Hudgens, editor of
Hush-Hush)/David Strathairn (Pierce Morehouse Patchett)/Ron
Rifkin (District Attorney Ellis Loew)/Matt McCoy (Brett Chase,
star of 'Badge of Honor')/Paul Guilfoyle (Mickey Cohen)/Paolo
Seganti (Johnny Stompanato, Cohen's henchman)/Graham
Beckel (Sergeant Dick Stensland)/Alan Graf (Wife beater)/
Precious Chong (Wife)/Will Zahrn ('Nick's Liquor' owner)/
Amber Smith (Susan Lefferts)/Darrell Sandeen (Leland 'Buzz'
Meeks, the ex-cop)/Tomas Arana (Detective Michael Breuning)/

Michael McCleery (Detective William Carlisle)/Gere Wolande
(Forensic chief)/Brenda Bakke (Lana Turner)/Nectar Rose
(Marilyn Monroe)

*   *   *

The novel 'L.A. Confidential' was written by James Ellroy between 1988 and 1989, and was published in 1990. It was originally an 809-page manuscript, which he edited, chopping the sentences down to their bare minimum – some of the chapters are only one page long. Ellroy said of the book, even in its edited form, 'It was big, it was epic, it was huge' and described it as suitable for 'the whole family' if the name of your family was 'Manson'.

Ellroy was born in 1948 and his mother was murdered when he was a child; the case is still unsolved and he wrote a book about it in 1996, called 'My Dark Places'. His novel 'The Black Dahlia' (1987) also looks at an unsolved real-life murder mystery from the forties, of an actress who was cut in half. Ellroy grew up a petty thief and his first book was the semi-autobiographical 'Brown's Requiem', published in 1981. 'The Black Dahlia', written in 1987, was the first book of his LA Quartet. It was followed by 'The Big Nowhere' (1988), 'L.A. Confidential' (1990) and 'White Jazz' (1992). His other books include 'Blood on the Moon' (1988), 'American Tabloid' (1995), 'Crime Wave' (1999) and 'Destination: Morgue' (2004), some of which have been adapted for the screen.

Director Curtis Hanson loved Ellroy's book. Hanson brought in Brian Helgeland to write the screenplay and he expertly telescoped Ellroy's extraordinary style. Their screen adaptation of 'L.A. Confidential' follows three very different cops of the Los Angeles Police Department (LAPD) in the early fifties. Sergeant Ed Exley is the bright son of legendary cop Preston Exley, now deceased. Exley wants to become a detective on Homicide and plays it strictly by the book. Officer Bud White is the antithesis of Exley, a tough nut who does what he has to do to uphold the law, administering his own brand of rough justice with his partner Dick Stensland. Sergeant Jack Vincennes is a showbiz narcotics cop, who loves the celebrity kudos his stint as 'technical adviser' on the hit TV show *Badge of Honor* brings him. Vincennes also works in cahoots with Sid Hudgens, the editor of *Hush-Hush* magazine, a seedy tabloid exposé of life in the dark corners of Hollywood; Vincennes is often the arresting officer in Hudgens's scams to humiliate various Hollywood stars and minor contract players.

The scenario opens with mobster Mickey Cohen beginning his ten-year incarceration on McNeil Island for tax evasion. On Christmas Eve 1951, during a drunken party at LAPD headquarters, a group of Mexican prisoners are beaten up by the cops. The story makes the papers, dubbed 'Bloody Christmas', and several officers are disciplined for their involvement. Vincennes is demoted to Vice, ringleader Stensland is made a scapegoat and is fired a year before his pension, while

White is pushed to the Homicide department. As a reward from his superiors for testifying against his colleagues over the 'Bloody Christmas' scandal, squeaky-clean Exley is promoted to detective lieutenant. His first call-out is to the Nite Owl coffee shop at 2 a.m. He discovers there has been a shotgun massacre; the proprietor is dead behind the counter and the gent's toilet is full of corpses – one of them is Stensland. Captain Smith, the head of Homicide, is in charge of the case. They arrest and interrogate three black youths who have a maroon Mercury coupé matching one at the scene; later two detectives discover shotguns that match those used in the massacre at the youths' house. But something doesn't quite add up and Vincennes, White and Exley all pursue their own leads and begin to unravel the case.

Vincennes investigates a vice racket called 'Fleur de Lis', involving prostitutes made up to look like famous film stars, and White becomes involved with one of them, Lynn Bracken, who resembles pin-up Veronica Lake. Eventually, all roads lead to Pierce Patchett, a rich LA resident with his fingers in several pies, including the planned Santa Monica Freeway, heroin smuggling, vice and the 'Fleur de Lis' racket. Eventually it becomes obvious that the black youths have been set up. The real culprit behind the Nite Owl slayings was Captain Smith. Smith and his accomplices are trying to capitalise on Mickey Cohen going to jail by taking over his rackets. Smith kills Vincennes, Patchett (in a faked suicide) and Sid Hudgens, who knows too much. In a trap, White and Exley are ambushed by Smith and his men at the Victory Motel, but the duo prevail and kill Smith. Exley is awarded a medal for valour, White leaves town with his lover Bracken and Smith is afforded a hero's death, to cover up the LAPD's incompetence.

In interviews, the scriptwriters of *L.A. Confidential* said they wanted to keep Ellroy's main characters and set pieces – including 'Bloody Christmas', the Night Owl massacre, the interrogation of the three black suspects and Bud's relationship with Lynn. But they also had to remove or alter many details. The book covers a much longer timescale: the events in the prologue take place in 1950, the Nite Owl massacre in 1953 and the dénouement in 1958. The most significant differences between the novel and the film are that Exley's father is alive at the beginning of the book (he commits suicide later on), and it is Ed's brother who was killed in the line of duty on the force. Ex-cop and heroin dealer Buzz Meeks dies in the prologue and Dudley Smith survives the book to fight another day. Only in the book does Exley send Stensland to the gas chamber, Vincennes get married and Mickey Cohen feature more prominently; in the book he is released from prison in 1957.

David L. Wolper had already bought the rights to 'L.A. Confidential' and had tried unsuccessfully to turn it into a miniseries for Network TV. To finance his film adaptation, Hanson went to producer Arnon Milchan. Milchan, himself a passionate movie fan, liked Hanson's enthusiasm (he had previously bankrolled Sergio Leone's *Once Upon a Time in America* and Michael Mann's *Heat*). Eventually the film got off the ground, with Hanson signed to write and direct it at Warner Bros, with Wolper and Milchan producing.

Hanson deployed some well-chosen actors to flesh out Ellroy's already established characters. Kevin Spacey, cast as showbiz cop Jack Vincennes, had made his breakthrough as Verbal Kint, who was the key to the riddle in *The Usual Suspects* (1995). He was also the monstrous serial killer John Doe in *Se7en* (1995 – though he appears unbilled) and is an accomplished theatre actor. For the two main protagonists, casting director Mali Finn chose two antipodean actors from very different film backgrounds. Born in New Zealand, Russell Crowe had moved to Australia and made a splash as a neo-nazi in the controversial *Romper Stomper* (1992), concerning racially motivated gang violence. *L.A. Confidential* was his third film in the US (following *The Quick and the Dead* and *Virtuosity*, both 1995). A tough guy on- and off-screen, he jumped to superstar status with his appearance as Maximus in *Gladiator* (2000) and later won a Best Actor Oscar for *A Beautiful Mind* (2001).

Guy Pearce was born in Ely, England in 1967 and emigrated with his family to Australia in 1970. Pearce rose to fame as heart-throb Mike Young, opposite Jason and Kylie, in *Neighbours* from 1986 to 1989 and also appeared in its competitor, *Home and Away*, as David Croft (from 1991 to 1992). His breakout role was as Felicity Jollygoodfellow in the cult movie *The Adventures of Priscilla, Queen of the Desert* (1994), opposite Terence Stamp and Hugo Weaving. For *L.A. Confidential*, both Pearce and Crowe had long hair and were unshaven in their respective screen-test try-outs for the cop roles; by the time filming began, both were clean-shaven, and Crowe had a crew cut, while Pearce's cropped hair was neatly slicked back.

James Cromwell, cast as nefarious Captain Smith, had previously played the farmer in the hit children's comedy *Babe* (1995), following the adventures of a talking pig. Former Bond girl Izabella Scorupco (from *GoldenEye*) was first offered the part of Lynne Bracken; former Bond girl Kim Basinger (from *Never Say Never Again*) accepted the part. Basinger, born in Athens, Georgia, was a model who had posed for *Playboy* and appeared in the 1979 TV miniseries *From Here to Eternity*. Her stardom in the eighties was consolidated by roles opposite Mickey Rourke in the sexy *Nine½ Weeks* (1986) and as photojournalist Vicky Vale in *Batman* (1989), with Michael Keaton as the caped crusader. Hanson wanted Basinger for the role; the actress agreed and thought the script was wonderful. The part of weasely Sid Hudgens, who also narrates the film off-screen, went to Danny DeVito, who played comedy roles in *Romancing the Stone* (1984), *The Jewel of the Nile* (1985) and *Twins* (1988). He has also become an accomplished director, with the successful *The War of the Roses* (1989).

With a budget of $35 million, 45 different locations and almost 80 speaking parts, *L.A. Confidential* was a mammoth production. It was shot on location around Los Angeles, in a startling early fifties *mise-en-scène*. Hanson played the songs he'd already chosen for the soundtrack on set, to establish mood. Many real LA places appear in the movie. The Frolic Rooms (on Hollywood Boulevard, next to Pantages Theatre) and the famous Hollywood hangout the Formosa café (on Santa Monica

Boulevard, opposite Warner Brothers Studios) can both be seen. The distinctive rocket tower of the 'Crossroads of the World' shopping centre on Sunset Boulevard (with its 'When Worlds Collide' logo) and the Church of the Blessed Sacrament (next to the shopping centre) are easy to spot. Pierce Patchett's beautiful white luxury abode was the Lovell Health House. Boardner's of Hollywood, the cocktail bar with distinctive arches, and the steps of Los Angeles City Hall were also used. Studio facilities at Lacy Street Production Center provided interior and exterior sets. The Victory Motel, a set, was largely destroyed during the final shootout.

The obvious model for *Hush-Hush* magazine was the gossipy *Confidential* exposé, published in New York. It appeared countrywide in 1952; like *Hush-Hush*, it had a motto: 'Tells the Facts and Names the Names'. In *L.A. Confidential*, editor Sid Hudgens (Danny DeVito) signs off each issue with 'You heard it here first… off the Record, on the QT and very Hush-Hush' ('on the QT' is an abbreviation of 'on the quiet'). *Confidential* became famous for blowing the lid on the movie stars. Its publisher, Robert Harrison, employed call girls with tape recorders hidden in their handbags, to bait unsuspecting stars. *Confidential* printed such headlines as 'Errol Flynn and his two-way mirrors' and 'The Best Pumper in Hollywood? M-M-M Marilyn M-M-Monroe!' Its other victims included Jayne Mansfield, Lana Turner, Ava Gardner and Frank Sinatra. In *L.A. Confidential*, *Hush-Hush* magazine promises 'exposés and exclusives': 'In the joint with Mickey Cohen – Bribes, Babes and Booty!'; on the QT: 'Ingenue Dikes in Hollywood' and 'Exclusive: The Women of Howard Hughes!' Unscrupulously Hudgens peeps through windows or jumps out from behind bushes to surprise his victims, with his camera snapping away. Director

'Hush-Hush': showbiz cop Jack Vincennes (Kevin Spacey) in Curtis Hanson's *L.A. Confidential* (1997).

Hanson described Hudgens as 'the Christopher Columbus of tabloid journalism'. Hudgens tells Vincennes, his partner in grime, that he is proud of his 36,000-issue circulation and adds: 'Once you whet the public's appetite for the truth, the sky's the limit'.

Hanson wanted to make a film 'in Los Angeles, the city of manufactured illusion', and *L.A. Confidential* is one of the best depictions of the 'Dream Factory' and its skewed way of life. At a morgue identification following the Nite Owl killings, a mother doesn't recognise her starlet daughter's profile because she's had a nose job to look like Rita Hayworth (her bandaged nose is a visual reference to *Chinatown*). *L.A. Confidential* also shares a retro chic style with *Pulp Fiction* (1994): its Jack Rabbit Slim's sequence, with movie lookalikes, is mirrored in the Formosa café, with its Marilyn and Lana Turner imitators. Hudgens describes Patchett's 'Fleur de Lis' (whose motto is 'Whatever you desire') as 'primo tail, fixed up to look like movie stars'. The bar and its clientele reputedly had some basis in reality, a place where clients could go to meet and sleep with facsimiles of their idols.

This theme extends to Lynn and her convincing Veronica Lake impersonation. Lynn even screens Lake movies for her clients to complete their experience of sleeping with a star. Veronica Lake was at her best opposite Alan Ladd, in films such as *This Gun for Hire* (1942), Dashiell Hammett's *The Glass Key* (1942) and *The Blue Dahlia* (1946). She was launched in 1939 with the name 'Constance Keane' and then again, successfully, in 1941 as 'Veronica Lake' (her real name was Constance Ockelman). Her distinctive 'S'-curl hairstyle across one eye earned her the name 'the girl with the peek-a-boo bang'. In *L.A. Confidential*, Lynn notes that White is the first man she's ever met who hasn't told her within a minute that she looks like Lake; 'You look better than Veronica Lake,' says White, who dissolves her Hollywood façade. He sees it as just another retro illusion in the factory of dreams.

Lynn is a small-town girl from Bisbee, Arizona, who plans to quit prostitution and return there to open a glamorous clothes shop; that's her only motivation for working for Patchett. At the end of the film, as White and Lynn leave together, Lynn tells Exley, in a direct quote from the last page of Ellroy's book, 'Some men get the world', as rising star Exley has done, 'Others get ex-hookers and a trip to Arizona'. In the last scene she appears as herself, with a shorter hairstyle, regular clothes and shades. Her transformation back to Lynn Bracken is complete, in preparation for her new life with Bud White.

L.A. Confidential has a historical backdrop. Gangster Mickey Cohen and his sidekick Johnny Stompanato were real people; in *Bugsy* (1991), Harvey Keitel appeared as Cohen. In *L.A. Confidential*, Cohen is incarcerated for tax evasion, like Al Capone. At the Formosa café, Exley tries to question Stompanato and tells the gangster's platinum date, 'A hooker cut to look like Lana Turner is still a hooker... she just looks like Lana Turner'; 'She is Lana Turner,' points out Vincennes, as Turner throws a drink at the impudent cop. Stompanato (also called 'Johnny Valentine') did date Lana Turner. Turner's daughter stabbed Stompanato to death in self-defence on Good Friday 1958. This was one of the biggest scandals of the day, with *Confidential* subsequently publishing many of Stompanato and Turner's love letters.

L.A. Confidential's style closely resembles *Chinatown*. Basinger's costumes evoke the grand Hollywood style of the thirties and forties; most memorable were her green satin dresses and a black velvet hooded cape with cream lining. Fifties details include Pantages Theatre screening *The Bad and the Beautiful* (1952), and White takes Lynn to see Audrey Hepburn in *Roman Holiday* (1953). The TV show *Badge of Honor* was inspired by early fifties US TV cop shows, in particular *Dragnet*, following the adventures of Sergeant Joe Friday (Jack Webb) and Officer Frank Smith (Ben Alexander). There are even references to this show's catchphrase, with characters jokingly quoting 'Just the facts' to technical adviser Vincennes.

Hanson uses period songs, often to ironic effect. Over the titles, we hear 'Ac-Cent-Tchu-Ate the Positive', written by Johnny Mercer and Harold Arlen, sung by Mercer. Accompanying a 'Greetings from Los Angeles' postcard and numerous newsreel clips of fifties American suburban life and film stars, Sid Hudgens tells us how great LA is: 'Life is good…it's Paradise on earth. That is what they tell you anyway…but there's trouble in paradise.' The town is riddled with drugs, racket-eering and prostitution. 'Ac-Cent-Tchu-Ate the Positive' also appeared prominently in the Veronica Lake film *The Blue Dahlia*; the partygoers are singing it as Alan Ladd returns home from the war to find his soon-to-be-dead wife has been unfaithful and his son has been killed in a drunken car smash. Other songs used in *L.A. Confidential* include 'Hit the Road to Dreamland', 'Wheel of Fortune' and George Gershwin's 'But Not for Me'. In a bar room, a radio emits Dean Martin's 'Powder Your Face with Sunshine (Smile! Smile! Smile!)', his first hit for Capitol in 1949. 'The future's brighter,' sings Dino, 'when hearts are lighter', as Vincennes wrestles with a moral dilemma. Martin's 'The Christmas Blues' accompanies a drugs bust. The film's incidental music is by Jerry Goldsmith; he uses a jazz trumpet in the lead, referencing the era, just as he had in *Chinatown* (1974).

Hush-Hush magazine sarcastically asks in the film's preamble: 'How can organised crime exist in the city with the best police force in the world?' The police force in *L.A. Confidential* is riddled with corruption and vice, although there are a few good men. The three cop protagonists couldn't be more different and epitomise the varying facets of the force – a force, by its own admission, in transition, as the departmental superiors try to root out the police's corrupt elements.

Spacey was told by Hanson to play Vincennes in the manner of Dean Martin, enjoying the showbiz limelight. In the film Vincennes is referred to as 'Hollywood Jack' and 'The Big V', living the life but 'on a night train to the big adios'. Vincennes tells *Badge of Honor* star Brett Chase how to act like a cop and tells his female fans he was the arresting officer on the Robert Mitchum marijuana case. Spacey's deliberate pronunciation – as in the scene when he asks Exley, 'Why do you want to go digging any deeper into the Nite Owl killings, Loo-ten-ant?' – has the effect of making Vincennes almost identical to the TV cop character he inspired. Initially, Vincennes is happy to cream money from Sid Hudgens and be present at his stage-managed pot busts of MGM contract players. 'Celebrity crime stopper Jack Vincennes,' laughs Hudgens, 'the scourge of grasshoppers and dope fiends everywhere.' Later, as he investigates 'Fleur de Lis', Vincennes's enthusiasm for the high life sours, especially following the throat-slitting of a young actor sent to seduce the DA, during yet another celebrity sting.

Bud White is a tough guy and a moral protector of women, almost to the point of obsession. This is because White saw his father beat his mother. Lynn asks if White saved his mother; 'Not for long,' replies White flatly. He also has a terrific temper, tending to act first and think later – for example, he's involved in the 'Bloody Christmas' fracas, he dangles the DA out of his high-rise office window and in his opening scene he intervenes in a domestic argument by hauling the illuminated Santa Claus, reindeer and sleigh down off the roof. Exley calls him 'a mindless thug'.

Bespectacled Edmund Exley is something of a contradiction. He appears to be straight as an arrow and a good politician within the force, but he also snitches on his comrades' behaviour in order to get ahead in the bureau. Exley is extremely vain. In a running gag, he has been told to stop wearing his glasses (it's bad for a detective's image), and Exley keeps showing up at crime scenes and action spots without them; he also removes them for publicity photos. As the son of star cop Preston Exley he has a hard act to follow, though he has joined the force reacting to his father's random murder. Preston was killed off-duty by a purse-snatcher. The culprit was never caught, but Exley has given him a name, 'Rollo Tomassi', just to provide himself with someone tangible to hate.

When faced with Dudley Smith's deception and given the chance to kill him before the police arrive (just as White had executed a suspect earlier at a crime scene), Exley shows that he is learning. He shoots his captain in the back. It is one of the most satisfying bullets-in-the-back in crime movies. 'Maybe Dudley Smith died a hero?' Exley's superiors observe; Exley answers, 'In this situation, you'll need more than one,' ensuring he receives a medal for valour. Simultaneously a headline praises Smith: 'Hero's Death for famed police captain'.

The film's intertwined mysteries are well handled by Hanson. The chief culprits turn out to be heroin smuggler Meeks – who first appeared in Ellroy's 'The Big Nowhere' in 1988 – and Smith, who was introduced in Ellroy's 'Clandestine' (1982). White instinctively knows 'There's something wrong with the Nite Owl', but doesn't think he's 'smart enough' to prove it, yet it is he who figures out that the rotten body of Buzz Meeks is under old Mrs Leffert's house. The clues soon pile up, and so do the bodies. There is blood on the wall of the Nite Owl, indicating that cop Stensland was killed in the café and then dragged to the toilet. The rendezvous was a drug deal that went wrong – Meeks had heroin for sale, Stensland was seeing Susan Lefferts, who was being transformed by Patchett into 'Rita Hayworth' for 'my little studio'. They are all interlinked and Smith has received a tip-off. The shotgun massacre was carried out by Smith and his two crooked cohorts, detectives Breuning and Carlisle, who later plant the shotguns at the black suspects' house. Patchett is involved with B-movies, heroin and call girls. Hudgens is also in league with Smith and Patchett, until Smith quietly smothers him, murmuring 'Hush, hush'. Earlier, having mortally wounded Vincennes, Smith asks him, 'Have you a valediction, boyo?' 'Rollo Tomassi,' replies Vincennes, with his last breath. Later, Smith informs Exley they are going to try and find 'Rollo Tomassi', an associate of 'crooked cop' Vincennes. This reveals to Exley that Smith is the real culprit.

At the film's first screening the producers loved it. *L.A. Confidential* was released in the US in September 1997, rated R. Basinger's 'peek-a-boo' Veronica Lake impersonation featured prominently in the film's ad work. Posters led with the tagline 'Everything is Suspect…Everyone is For Sale…And Nothing is What it Seems'. Spacey, Crowe, Pearce and the 'Hollywood' sign were also highly visible in the publicity. Warners prepared a trailer, introducing the three cops 'with nothing in common': one wanted to get ahead, one dispensed his own brand of justice and one loved the spotlight. Now they're all investigating one crime: 'They thought they had it all figured out…'

L.A. Confidential took $5 million in its opening weekend and $64 million in all in the US. In the UK the film gained an 18 certificate; it was released uncut in October 1997 and grossed almost £7 million. The *Mail on Sunday* raved: 'Movie

Blonde Ambition: Kim Basinger as Lynn Bracken as Veronica Lake, the girl with the peek-a-boo bang, in *L.A. Confidential* (1997).

of the year, thriller of the decade'. Critic Barry Norman, on BBC TV's *Film 98*, named it 'The best film of last year'. *Cahier du Cinéma* noted, 'It's striking to see how the elegance and lightness of touch in the atmosphere of *L.A. Confidential* seem both to derive from and influence the actors'. At the 1998 Oscar ceremony, *L.A. Confidential* was nominated for Best Picture, Director, Cinematography, Editing, Art Direction, Set Decoration and Sound, but won Oscars for Basinger, as Best Supporting Actress, and Best Screenplay Adaptation, for Helgeland and Hanson. A 'making of' documentary appeared in 1998 called *Off the Record*, while a TV pilot also called *L.A. Confidential* was made in the US in 2003, but the series never got off the ground. Kiefer Sutherland played Jack Vincennes, with David Conrad as Ed Exley and Melissa George as Lynn Bracken.

Ellroy said that his book 'L.A. Confidential' was 'unconstrainable, uncontainable and unadaptable'. When he saw the finished movie, he changed his mind: 'Here was a compatible vision, unique on its own terms, of a book that I wrote, characters and a milieu that I created, that assumed a brilliant alternative life and I was flabbergasted and startled by the experience'. Hanson now refers to the film as a 'labour of love' and it remains a unique achievement in modern cinema – a commercial art film, intelligently handled and beautifully made, with assiduous attention to detail on a grand scale. It's a complete one-off – but that's strictly off the record, on the QT and very hush-hush.

22

'You're either in or you're out'

— *Ocean's Eleven* (2001)

Credits:
DIRECTOR – Steven Soderbergh
PRODUCER – Jerry Weintraub
EXECUTIVE PRODUCERS – John Hardy, Susan Elkins and Bruce Berman
CO-PRODUCER – R.J. Louis
ORIGINAL STORY – George Clayton Johnson and Jack Golden Russell
ORIGINAL 1960 SCREENPLAY – Harry Brown and Charles Lederer
SCREENPLAY – Ted Griffin
DIRECTOR OF PHOTOGRAPHY – Peter Andrews
EDITOR – Stephen Mirrione
PRODUCTION DESIGNER – Philip Messina
ART DIRECTOR – Keith P. Cunningham
COSTUME DESIGNER – Jeffrey Kurland
MUSIC – David Holmes
Technicolor/Panavision
Interiors filmed at Infinite Horizon Studios and Universal Studios
A Jerry Weintraub/Section Eight Production
Released by Warner Bros Pictures in association with Village
    Roadshow Pictures and NVP Entertainment
Cast:
George Clooney (Daniel Ocean)/Matt Damon (Linus, alias
'Sheldon Willis')/Andy Garcia (Terry Benedict)/Brad Pitt
(Robert Charles 'Rusty' Ryan)/Julia Roberts (Tess Ocean)/
Casey Affleck (Virgil Malloy)/Scott Caan (Turk Malloy)/
Elliott Gould (Rueben Tishkoff)/Eddie Jemison (Livingstone
Dell, alias 'Radio Shack')/Bernie Mac (Frank Catton, alias
'Ramon Escalante')/Shaobo Qin (Yen, the acrobat)/Carl Reiner
(Saul Bloom, alias 'Lyman Zerga')/Don Cheadle (Basher
Tarr)/Lennox Lewis (himself)/Wladimir Klitschko (himself)/

Jerry Weintraub (High roller)/Henry Silva and Angie Dickinson (Guests at ringside).

*   *   *

In January 1960, at the very start of the Swinging Sixties, the Rat Pack called a 'summit' at the Sands Casino, Las Vegas. It starred the boozed-up, rowdy, sharp-suited 'pack', a nightclub act evolving into a continuous party and for some a lounge lizard lifestyle. The gang were the 'chairman of the board', Frank Sinatra, Italian crooner Dean 'Dino' Martin, song and dance man Sammy Davis Jnr, English faux-toff Peter Lawford and stand-up comic Joey Bishop. During their Sands nightclub act, Martin was usually announced on stage as 'Direct from the bar'. They drank, they smoked, they told irreverent jokes. The singers rarely finished their songs; 'You want to hear the whole song…buy the record,' laughed Dino, the joker in the pack. And while they were there, Sinatra, in questionable taste considering his carefully cultivated, mob-influenced tough-guy image, produced a heist film for his own Dorchester Productions, called *Ocean's Eleven*.

The film is the prototype for the comedy crime caper sub-genre. It details an elaborate simultaneous New Year's Eve heist on five Las Vegas casinos: the Flamingo, the Desert Inn, the Riviera, the Sahara and the Sands. Danny Ocean (Sinatra) assembles a group of his ex-comrades-in-arms – paratrooper buddies from the 82nd Airborne Division – 'to liberate millions of dollars', apparently out of boredom. 'In any other town they'd be the bad guys,' claimed the posters. The group includes Lawford, Martin, Bishop and Davis Jnr (effectively playing themselves) and financier Spyros (Akim Tamiroff). At midnight they blow up an electricity pylon, plunging the city into darkness. When the auxiliary circuit switches on, the gang have hot-wired the system to open the vaults. With some help from a tin of luminous paint (so they can follow their footprints in the darkness), the job passes without incident, until one of their number has a heart attack on the street outside. The money bags are deposited in dustbins and are collected by a bin wagon driven by Davis Jnr, with the mob and the police close behind. The gang plan to ship the money back to San Franciso in their dead comrade's coffin. But his wife decides to inter him in Las Vegas and the service is a cremation.

Ocean's Eleven hasn't worn well and is now best viewed as a snapshot of those swinging days and nights in the Nevada desert. Dino gets the opportunity to burst into song on a couple of occasions; he says at one point: 'I used to be Ricky Nelson… I'm Perry Como now.' Only the final shot of the gang, dressed for the funeral, walking away from the chapel in world-weary resignation, has passed into cinema heist-ory as an iconic moment. As the camera pans up, the Sands' billboard announces the Rat Pack's five stars. But the film had huge box-office appeal and several cameo appearances, including thirties gangster star George Raft as Jack Strager, a casino owner, and Shirley MacLaine as a drunken reveller. *Ocean's Eleven* made a fortune for all concerned and was the first in a group of films made by the Rat Pack with numerical titles: *Sergeants 3* (1962), *Four for Texas* (1963) and *Robin and the Seven Hoods* (1964). But the pack became more complacent, pampered and self-indulgent as the series progressed – on *Four for Texas*, Sinatra had a 'hairpiece handler'.

Immensely influential, *Ocean's Eleven* spawned dozens of cinematic imitators, knocking off banks, museums, trains, art galleries and private collections. But in 2001, shooting began on a remake of the grandfather of them all, on a suitably grand scale. The director was Steven Soderbergh, who made his directorial debut with the critically acclaimed *sex, lies and videotape* (1989). Soderbergh went on to commercial success with *Erin Brockovich* (2000) and *Traffic* (2000). Based on the original 1960 story and script, the new version of *Ocean's Eleven* was written by Ted Griffin, who changed all the character's names, except for Ocean. Griffin had previously written the screenplay for *Ravenous* (1999), a cannibal western starring Guy Pearce and Robert Carlyle, and *Best Laid Plans* (1999). For *Ocean's Eleven* Griffin recalled his favourite ensemble movies of the sixties, *The Magnificent Seven*, *The Great Escape* and *The Professionals*, and tried to evoke their macho camaraderie in his scenario.

In Griffin's *Ocean's Eleven* the gang prepare to rob the marginally more realistic three casinos and one vault. Daniel Ocean is released after four years in North Jersey State Prison and sets about embarking on an ambitious $150 million heist. He visits Atlantic City, then Hollywood, and picks up his old cohort, a cardsharp named Rusty Ryan. His plan is to rob the Bellagio, the Mirage and the MGM Grand, all casinos owned by Terry Benedict, during a world heavyweight boxing match staged at the MGM arena. Benedict is formidable opposition, but isn't well liked, and there's no shortage of conmen willing to join in Ocean's scheme. He gains finance from Reuben Tishkoff, who lost his casino to Benedict. He also recruits Basher Tarr, an explosives expert, the Utah Malloy brothers, Virgil and Turk, Los Angeles electronics expert Livingstone Dell, card dealer Frank Catton, pickpocket Linus, acrobatic 'grease man' Yen and ulcer-ridden retired thief Saul Bloom. They will pull off a whole series of 'cons' that will fleece the casinos of a fortune. Planning is further complicated when the gang discover that Ocean's ex-wife, Tess, is now partnered with Benedict, making the score personal. Some of the gang infiltrate the casino, Yen the acrobat accesses the vault hidden in a cash trolley and breaks out from within. Eventually the money is literally walked out through the front door by a SWAT team (the gang in disguise), called to the premises by Benedict to defuse a bomb that the robbers claim is about to detonate the safe. Unlike the sixties original, the gang are successful. The police are unable to link Ocean to the heist and, following a short sentence for breaching his parole, he is reunited with his wife – though Benedict's thugs are already on his trail.

Ocean is played by George Clooney, the nephew of singer Rosemary Clooney. Born in Kentucky, Clooney was Dr Ross in TV's *ER*, then made the difficult transition to the big screen, in films ranging from the romantic *One Fine Day*

(1996) to the vampire road movie *From Dusk Till Dawn* (1996) and the Coen brothers' comedy *O Brother Where Art Thou?* (2000). He'd even turned caped crusader in *Batman and Robin* (1997) and appeared in the *Kelly's Heroes*-influenced heist *Three Kings* (1999).

For the rest of the cast, Soderbergh assembled a veritable all-star who's who. Brad Pitt was better known for his pretty-boy looks than his acting ability, as epitomised by his breakthrough role as drifter JD in *Thelma and Louise* (1991). He had refuted this, however, with his convincing transformation into the wild-eyed pikey Mickey O'Neil, the boxer in *Snatch* (2000). His role as cardsharp Rusty Ryan called for the most laid-back playing of his career. Julia Roberts had made a splash in the successful *Pretty Woman* (1990) and had consolidated her fame with a selection of massive hits: *My Best Friend's Wedding* (1997), *Notting Hill* (1999), *Runaway Bride* (1999) and *Erin Brockovich* (2000), the last for Soderbergh. In *Ocean's Eleven*, she was billed as 'Introducing Julia Roberts as Tess' – Roberts was probably the biggest female star in Hollywood at the time and also the highest paid.

Matt Damon (as pickpocket Linus) had appeared in *Good Will Hunting* (1997) and *Saving Private Ryan* (1998); Cuban-born Andy Garcia, as ruthless Benedict, had appeared as Don Vincent Mancini-Corleone in *The Godfather Part III*. Don Cheadle, unbilled in all prints of the film, had appeared in Soderbergh's *Traffic* (2000). As Basher Tarr, Cheadle adopts the most unconvincing cockney accent since Dick Van Dyke swept a chim-er-nee. Seventies icon Elliott Gould starred as the outrageously dressed hippy casino owner, Rueben. One of the outstanding performers was legendary New York comedian Carl Reiner as Saul Bloom, a retired con artist out for one last job, though Reiner was a late choice for the role. He was Sid Caesar's feedman in *Your Show of Shows* in the early fifties and appeared in the classic '200-year-old man' sketch with Mel Brooks. He also featured in the crazy treasure hunt movie, *It's a Mad Mad Mad Mad World* (1963). He directed the cult film *Where's Poppa?* (1970) and three Steve Martin movies: *The Jerk* (1979), *Dead Men Don't Wear Plaid* (1982) and *The Man with Two Brains* (1983). Producer Jerry Weintraub, whose connections facilitated filming in the actual Bellagio, has a cameo as a high-rolling gambler. Holly Marie Combs (from TV's *Charmed*) and Topher Grace (*Traffic*) are two of the Hollywood actors learning to play cards with Rusty Ryan. Original 1960s cast members Angie Dickinson (who played Beatrice, Ocean's estranged wife) and Henry Silva (as gang member Roger Corneal) appeared ringside at the boxing match.

Ocean's Eleven was budgeted at $85 million. It was filmed from February to June 2001, with much of the footage filmed on location. The Bellagio casino, whose setting was based on an Italian lakeside village, was used for interior and exterior filming; the beautiful Fountains of Bellagio can be seen in the finale (accompanied by the Philadelphia Orchestra's moving rendition of Debussy's 'Claire de Lune'), while Tess and Ocean dine in the Picasso restaurant. Other scenes were filmed on the Las Vegas Strip, outside a prison in New Jersey, on the streets of Los Angeles, at McCarran airport and in Atlantic City, notably Trump Plaza. The boxing match was filmed in the arena at the MGM Grand, with 2000 extras deployed. Reuben's luxury house was filmed in Palm Springs, Florida. Interiors were lensed at Infinite Horizon Studios, Florida, where the casino vault was constructed, and Universal Studios, for the casino floor and various offices, corridors and rooms. Reuben's recollection of the attempted casino robbery in the eighties was filmed at the entrance to Caesar's Palace; the scene is accompanied by 'Take My Breath Away' by rock band Berlin, as the hapless robber shuffles out of the foyer clutching wads of bank notes, only to be shot by security.

Exquisite Panavision cinematography by Peter Andrews captures these well-chosen locations and the constant sunshine, almost placing the movie as *film soleil*, the sun-drenched nineties movement initiated by *Wild at Heart* (1990). Andrews's photography of structures, particularly the exterior of the Bellagio, recalls Philip Lathrop's work on *Point Blank*. The sharp suits and glittering locales could have reduced the good-looking protagonists to catalogue models. But Griffin's script ensures that each character has a defined personality – some achievement, considering the large ensemble cast and the frenetic pace, though this is helped somewhat by the fact that the gang members are played by already familiar famous faces. Editor Stephen Mirrione used several visual tricks to sustain the film's

A Pair of Aces: master thieves Danny Ocean and Rusty Ryan recruit nine more accomplices; George Clooney and Brad Pitt in Steven Soderbergh's *Ocean's Eleven* (2001).

velocity, including jump cuts, a skip frame technique and speeded-up footage. There is also a voiceover, like heist movies such as *The Killing* (1956), keeping the audience informed of the rapid on-screen developments.

In the 1960 original, the eleven aren't really a group of individual 'specialists' as dictated by heist movie conventions, simply a bunch of army buddies, though Sammy Davis Jnr does play a singing, dancing binman, which is quite specialised. Similarly, in the original the gadgetry used is decidedly low-rent; the gang manage to clean out five casinos by inducing a power cut and deploying some glow-in-the-dark paint. In the post-*Matrix*, CGI-era remake, this just wasn't good enough: hi-tech gadgetry and hardware were bound to feature heavily.

In the new version, Daniel Ocean is a convicted conman and fraudster, who is released from prison at the beginning of the film. He blames his wife leaving him on his 'self-destructive pattern' and assures the parole panel that he won't re-offend. He's released from jail in his tuxedo and bow tie – exactly the same outfit he wears at the end of the movie, when he is yet again released from jail (implying that he was initially inside for attempting a similar heist). As agreed, he rings up his parole officer in Atlanta and assures him that he hasn't been getting into trouble or drinking, adding, 'No sir, I wouldn't even think about leaving the state,' before heading for California. There, he hooks up with Rusty Ryan (a cardsharp wasting his time teaching Hollywood brats how to gamble), who suggests that for such a heist to succeed, they need a group of crooks pulling a combination of cons. They are financed by Rueben, an ex-casino-owner; Benedict 'torpedoed' his Xanadu casino and is about to demolish it. He tells them: 'You gotta be nuts...and you're gonna need a crew as nuts as you.' The specialists they enlist are hand-picked for their expertise and work seamlessly as a team. The gang's professionalism and focus is epitomised by a brief scene featuring Basher. He's working on a method of disabling the Las Vegas power supply, while watching the demolition of the Xanadu on TV; just over his shoulder, out of the window, the real Xanadu collapses into rubble.

The romantic subplot sees crook Ocean trying to woo back his wife Tess from Benedict; this was perhaps suggested by Hitchcock's *To Catch a Thief* (1955). When Ocean and Tess are first reunited following his spell in prison, she calls him a thief and a liar; 'I only lied about being a thief'. The tension between Benedict and Ocean is intensified by their rivalry for Tess, but Benedict is not a man to mess with. As Rueben says: 'He'll kill you and then go to work on you. He'll destroy not only your life, but your family's and everyone else you know.' With the robbery in full flow and with Tess beginning to have second thoughts about her relationship with Benedict, Ocean slips a cellphone into Tess's pocket. As the gang cleans out the vault, the phone rings and Ryan asks to speak to Benedict. 'Who the hell is this?' asks Benedict. 'The man who's robbing you.' 'Congratulations,' hisses Benedict, when he realises what is happening. 'You're a dead man.'

Ryan calls the Bellagio vault 'the least accessible vault ever designed'. It's protected by the very latest in security measures, from fingerprint security encoded technology to trusty standbys, like armed guards. The robbery takes place during a world heavyweight boxing match between Lennox Lewis and Wladimir Klitschko (Lewis's opponent was originally to have been Mike Tyson). This time, the power cut is induced by a 'pinch', a device that knocks out the whole of Las Vegas with a power surge. The pinch does exist, though it is much larger and doesn't look like the bright green, glowing, state-of-the-art fish tank deployed here.

The gang makes a replica of the vault and film part of the robbery beforehand. Yen, the Chinese acrobat, is hidden inside a cash box on a trolley and deposited into the vault, while Linus (posing as a Nevada Gaming Commission official) and Ocean gain access to the vault through the ducting. They are suspended over the lift shaft leading to the vault, which is criss-crossed with laser beams, exactly like the vault in the caper movie *Grand Slam* (1967). When the pinch whirrs into action, the lasers are disabled and the pair are able to abseil down the shaft and break into the vault. As part of the plan, Saul (posing as high roller Lyman Zerga) fakes a heart attack, Ryan poses as a doctor and Livingstone Dell hacks into the Bellagio's closed-circuit TV system and runs a recording of events that never happened inside the Bellagio vault (the giveaway is that the word 'Bellagio' is missing from the floor of the fake footage). The gang then threaten to blow up all the money if they're not allowed to leave with half of it and the sequence goes into overdrive for the ingenious *coup de grâce*. It's a very clever heist scene, packed with twists and suspense – one of the best movie robberies of all time.

These images are accompanied by an apt score. Not simply a cut-and-paste montage of classic tracks, the non-original cues deployed here complement the film well. 'Cha Cha Cha' by Jimmy Luxury and the Tommy Rome Orchestra, 'Papa Loves Mambo' by Perry Como and Quincy Jones's take on 'Blues in the Night' evoke the Rat Pack original, without calling upon its members for background assistance. David Holmes, who oversaw the score and composed the incidental music, also uses a souped-up remix of Elvis Presley's 'A Little Less Conversation', which continues:

> A little more action please. All this aggravation ain't satisfactioning me.
> A little more bite, a little less bark. A little less fight, a little more spark
> Don't procrastinate, don't articulate … Girl it's getting late

This song accompanies helicopter shots of the neon-lit gambling Mecca ('America's Playground') and recalls Elvis's own trip to the Strip, *Viva Las Vegas* (1964).

As the plan crystallises, the music cranks up the tension, but also adds a sensation of effortlessness. When the SWAT team whisk the money away from under Benedict's nose, Holmes's '$160 Million Chinese Man' (an instrumental, brass-led 'A Little Less Conversation' remix) is used as accompaniment. Tess's theme is an expansive looped chill-out, as Julia Roberts makes her entrance, descending the sweeping Bellagio staircase. The bouncy, big-beat 'Gritty Shaker' and classic lounge shuffle 'Rodney Yates' are both taken from Holmes's 1999 album 'Let's Get Killed'. For the soundtrack, released on Warner Sunset, some of the tracks are abridged, with snatches of dialogue inserted between cues and even overdubbed throughout them. In addition, there is the odd omission of the 'Rodney Yates' track, which has become synonymous with the film. Holmes's other standout track, '69 Police', plays over the end titles, as Ocean, Ryan and Tess drive away from prison, where Ocean has just served a pitifully short sentence for breach of parole. The sugar rush of '69 Police', with its sixties Hammond organ groove and punchy drumming, produces the most satisfying coda in caper cinema.

Harry Potter and the Sorcerer's Stone and *Ocean's Eleven* were the big Christmas 2001 hits in the US. *Ocean's Eleven* was premiered on 5 December 2001, with a general release two days later. Energetic trailers (touting 'The Con of the Century') prepared audiences for hip, slick entertainment. The modish poster advertising depicted several black-suited individuals, photographed from the neck down (very reminiscent of the *Reservoir Dogs* poster), with a large red '11' in the foreground. The taglines asked 'Are you In or Out?'; other slogans included 'Place Your Bets' and 'Three Casinos, 11 guys, 150 million bucks...Ready to Win Big?' It did win big at the box office. Rated PG-13, the opening US weekend's takings was $38 million; it ended up taking $183 million domestically. A novelisation by Dewey Gram was published in 2002 to tie-in with the film and a 'making of' documentary (*The Look of the Con*) captured the hectic shooting conditions. In the UK *Ocean's Eleven* was granted a certificate 12 and released in February 2002, taking £24 million. In Italy it was *Ocean's 11: Fate il Vostro Gioco*, in France *Ocean's 11: Faites vos Jeux*, which translates as 'Make your Play'. It made $450 million worldwide and is the highest-grossing caper film to date.

In 2004, Soderbergh reunited the team for *Ocean's Twelve*. Clooney, Pitt et al. returned, as did Roberts, Garcia, composer Holmes, cinematographer Andrews and many of the main crew. How, then, did it all go so wrong – not in terms of the heist, which is as successful as the first film, but in terms of the drop in quality? A clue could be the absence of the talented Griffin, whose dialogue was pitch-perfect in *Ocean's Eleven*. In the sequel, Benedict catches up with Tess and informs her that he wants his $160 million back, with interest, even though he has been reimbursed by the insurance company. Ocean has 14 days to come up with the money. Regrouped, the gang embark on a crime spree, jetting off to Amsterdam and Rome in an effort to steal enough to pay off what is owed. Following one of the most needlessly confusing and incoherently convoluted plots in modern cinema, during which they jack up a house and replace a Fabergé egg with a hologram, they eventually hand over a cheque for £198,427,084.32 to Benedict, paying the debt in full.

'They're All Back...Yes, All Of Them,' said posters, disbelievingly, though most of them aren't on screen for long. *Ocean's Twelve* is much more like its sixties counterparts than *Ocean's Eleven*, with a flabby, nonsensical plot line and an in-joke star cameo by Bruce Willis (as himself). The twelfth member of the gang is Ryan's girlfriend, a 'Europol' detective, played by Catherine Zeta Jones. Moreover, in a highly improbable plot twist, Tess (as played by Julia Roberts) impersonates film star Julia Roberts, to gain access to a museum for a photo opportunity – Tess even calls Julia up on the phone. The best gag in the film comes in the end titles, where a caption reads 'And Introducing Tess as Julia Roberts'. David Holmes's score, so effective in the first film, sounds like outtakes from *Starsky and Hutch*, while the action doesn't gel in the effortless way its predecessor's had. Actually, *Twelve*'s trailer is much more entertaining than the finished movie, conning the audience into believing it is going to be quite coherent. With the taglines 'It's Payback Time!' and 'Twelve is the New Eleven', it made a fortune: $125 million in the US alone.

Heist and caper stories have proved to be consistently popular at the box office. Examples include *Entrapment* (1999), with insurance investigator Catherine Zeta Jones the baited trap to catch art thief Sean Connery, and *The Thomas Crown Affair* (1999), a remake of the 1968 Steve McQueen–Faye Dunaway movie. Here master thief Crown (Pierce Brosnan) appears to be a rich businessman and consequently above the law. He is investigated by insurance agent Rene Russo, whose company won't pay out until they are satisfied a recovery of the artwork is out of the question.

The caper sub-genre's enduring appeal is easy to fathom, with its mixture of derring-do, romance, ingenuity, gadgets and thrills. Audiences love roguish criminal heroes who come out on top. To paraphrase Dean Martin, whose appearance in the original caper movie inspired many imitators: everybody loves to see somebody getting away with something, sometime.

Danny Ocean outlines his hi-tech plan to rob the MGM Grand, the Bellagio and the Mirage in *Ocean's Eleven* (2001).

CRIMOGRAPHY: THE CRIME WAVE FILMOGRAPHY

This is a chronological filmography of 130 international crime films referenced in the text, with brief credits: title, original year of release, directed by (d) and starring (s). For non-English-language releases, the original language title is in parenthesis. AKA = also known as.

Little Caesar (1930)
d: Mervyn LeRoy
s: Edward G. Robinson, Douglas Fairbanks Jnr

M (1931 – *M: Moerder Unter Uns*)
d: Fritz Lang
s: Peter Lorre, Ellen Widmann

Scarface, Shame of a Nation (1932)
d: Howard Hawks
s: Paul Muni, Ann Dvorak, Boris Karloff, George Raft

The Thin Man (1934)
d: W.S. Van Dyke
s: William Powell, Myrna Loy

G-Men (1935)
d: William Keighly
s: James Cagney, Robert Armstrong, Ann Dvorak

The Petrified Forest (1936)
d: Archie Mayo
s: Leslie Howard, Bette Davis, Humphrey Bogart

Angels With Dirty Faces (1938)
d: Michael Curtiz
s: James Cagney, Pat O'Brien, Humphrey Bogart, the Dead End Kids

The Roaring Twenties (1939)
d: Raoul Walsh
s: James Cagney, Humphrey Bogart, Pricilla Lane

They Drive by Night (1940)
d: Raoul Walsh
s: George Raft, Ida Lupino, Humphrey Bogart

Out of the Fog (1941)
d: Anatole Litvak
s: Ida Lupino, John Garfield

The Glass Key (1942)
d: Stuart Heisler
s: Brian Donlevy, Veronica Lake, Alan Ladd

This Gun for Hire (1942)
d: Frank Tuttle
s: Alan Ladd, Veronica Lake

Double Indemnity (1944)
d: Billy Wilder
s: Barbara Stanwyck, Fred MacMurray, Edward G. Robinson

Farewell My Lovely (1944 – AKA:
Murder, My Sweet)
d: Edward Dmytryk
s: Dick Powell, Claire Trevor, Anne
Shirley

The Mask of Dimitrios (1944)
d: Jean Negulesco
s: Peter Lorre, Sidney Greenstreet

The Big Sleep (1946)
d: Howard Hawks
s: Humphrey Bogart, Lauren Bacall

The Blue Dahlia (1946)
d: George Marshall
s: Alan Ladd, Veronica Lake

The Killers (1946)
d: Robert Siodmak
s: Burt Lancaster, Ava Gardner,
Edmond O'Brien, Charles McGraw,
Albert Decker

The Spiral Staircase (1946)
d: Robert Siodmak
s: Dorothy McGuire, George Brent

The Verdict (1946)
d: Don Siegel
s: Peter Lorre, Sydney Greenstreet

Kiss of Death (1947)
d: Henry Hathaway
s: Victor Mature, Coleen Gray, Richard
Widmark, Brian Donlevy

Out of the Past (1947 – AKA: *Build My
Gallows High*)
d: Jacques Tourneur
s: Robert Mitchum, Jane Greer, Kirk
Douglas

Key Largo (1948)
d: John Huston
s: Humphrey Bogart, Edward G.
Robinson, Lauren Bacall, Claire Trevor

T-Men (1948)
d: Anthony Mann
Dennis O'Keefe, Alfred Ryder, Charles
McGraw

The Treasure of the Sierra Madre (1948)
d: John Huston
s: Humphrey Bogart, Walter Huston,
Tim Holt

Border Incident (1949)
d: Anthony Mann
s: George Murphy, Ricardo Montalban

Force of Evil (1949)
d: Abraham Polonsky
s: John Garfield, Thomas Gomez,
Marie Windsor

Gun Crazy (1949)
d: Joseph H. Lewis
s: John Dall, Peggy Cummins

Panic in the Streets (1949)
d: Elia Kazan
s: Richard Widmark, Barbara Belle
Geddes, Jack Palance

Armoured Car Robbery (1950)
d: Richard Fleischer
s: William Talman, Charles McGraw

Roadblock (1951)
d: Harold Daniels
s: Charles McGraw, Joan Dixon

Kansas City Confidential (1952 – AKA: *The Secret Four*)
d: Phil Karlson
s: John Payne, Jack Elam, Neville Brand, Lee Van Cleef

Narrow Margin (1952)
d: Richard Fleischer
s: Charles McGraw, Marie Windsor

Beat the Devil (1953)
d: John Huston
s: Humphrey Bogart, Jennifer Jones, Robert Morley, Peter Lorre

The Big Heat (1953)
d: Fritz Lang
s: Glenn Ford, Gloria Graham, Lee Marvin

The Ladykillers (1955)
d: Alexander Macendrick
s: Alec Guinness, Herbert Lom, Peter Sellers, Katie Johnson

Rififi (1955 – *Du Rififi chez les Hommes*)
d: Jules Dassin
s: Jean Servais, Carl Mohner, Robert Manwell, 'Perlo Vita' (Jules Dassin)

The Harder They Fall (1956)
d: Mark Robson
s: Humphrey Bogart, Rod Steiger

The Killing (1956)
d: Stanley Kubrick
s: Sterling Hayden, Coleen Gray, Marie Windsor, Elisha Cook Jnr, Vince Edwards

The Bonnie Parker Story (1958)
d: William Witney
s: Dorothy Provine, Jack Hogan

Machine-Gun Kelly (1958)
d: Roger Corman
s: Charles Bronson, Susan Cabot, Jack Lambert

Touch of Evil (1958)
d: Orson Welles
s: Charlton Heston, Janet Leigh, Orson Welles, Marlene Dietrich

Breathless (1959 – *À Bout de Souffle*)
d: Jean-Luc Godard
s: Jean-Paul Belmondo, Jean Seberg, Roger Hanin

Ocean's Eleven (1960)
d: Lewis Milestone
s: Frank Sinatra, Dean Martin, Sammy Davis Jnr, Peter Lawford, Angie Dickinson

Salvatore Giuliano (1962)
d: Francesco Rosi
s: Frank Wolff, Salvo Randone, Federico Zardi

The Killers (1964)
d: Don Siegel
s: Lee Marvin, Angie Dickinson, John Cassavetes, Ronald Reagan

Topkapi (1964)
d: Jules Dassin
s: Melina Mercouri, Maximillian Schell, Peter Ustinov

Second Breath (1966 – *Le Deuxième Souffle*)
d: Jean-Pierre Melville
s: Lino Ventura, Christine Fabrega, Michel Constantin

Tokyo Drifter (1966 – *Tokyo Nagaremono*)
d: Seijun Suzuki
s: Tetsuya Watari, Chieko Matsubara, Tsuyoshi

Branded to Kill (1967 – *Koroshi no Rakuin*)
d: Seijun Suzuki
s: Jo Shishido, Mariko Ogawa, Koji Nambara

Grand Slam (1967 – *Ad Ogni Costo*)
d: Giuliano Montaldo
s: Edward G. Robinson, Janet Leigh, Robert Hoffman, Adolfo Celli, Klaus Kinski

Le Samouraï (1967 – AKA: *The Godson*)
d: Jean-Pierre Melville
s: Alain Delon, Nathalie Delon, François Périer, Cathy Rosier

The St Valentine's Day Massacre (1967)
d: Roger Corman
s: Jason Robards, George Segal, Ralph Meeker

Targets (1967)
d: Peter Bogdanovich
s: Boris Karloff, Tim O'Kelly

Bullit (1968)
d: Peter Yates
s: Steve McQueen, Robert Vaughn, Jacqueline Bisset, Robert Duvall

Coogan's Bluff (1968)
d: Don Siegel
s: Clint Eastwood, Lee J. Cobb, Don Stroud, Susan Clark

The Detective (1968)
d: Gordon Douglas
s: Frank Sinatra, Jacqueline Bisset, Lee Remick, Ralph Meeker

Madigan (1968)
d: Don Siegel
s: Richard Widmark, Henry Fonda, Inger Stevens, Harry Guardino

The Split (1968)
d: Gordon Flemyng
s: Jim Brown, Diahann Carroll, Ernest Borgnine, Gene Hackman, Warren Oates

The Thomas Crown Affair (1968)
d: Norman Jewison
s: Steve McQueen, Faye Dunaway

The Italian Job (1969)
d: Peter Collinson
s: Michael Caine, Noël Coward, Benny Hill

Marlowe (1969)
d: Paul Bogart
s: James Garner, Carroll O'Connor, Rita Moreno

The Sicilian Clan (1969 – *Les Clans des Siciliens*)
d: Henri Verneuil
s: Lino Ventura, Alain Delon, Jean Gabin

Borsalino (1970)
d: Jacques Deray
s: Alain Delon, Jean Paul Belmondo

The French Connection (1971)
d: William Friedkin
s: Gene Hackman, Fernando Rey, Roy Scheider

Cool Breeze (1972)
d: Barry Pollack
s: Thalmus Rasulala, Judy Pace, Jim Watkins

The Getaway (1972)
d: Sam Peckinpah
s: Steve McQueen, Ali MacGraw, Ben Johnson, Al Lettieri

Hit Man (1972)
d: George Armitage
s: Bernie Casey, Pamela Grier, Roger E. Mosley

Shaft's Big Score (1972)
d: Gordon Parks
s: Richard Roundtree, Moses Gunn

Superfly (1972)
d: Gordon Parks Jnr
s: Ron O'Neal, Carl Lee

The Valachi Papers (1972 – *Joe Valachi: I Segreti di Cosa Nostra*)
d: Terence Young
s: Charles Bronson, Lino Ventura, Jill Ireland, Joseph Wiseman

Coffy (1973)
d: Jack Hill
s: Pam Grier, Booker Bradshaw, Robert DoQui

The Long Goodbye (1973)
d: Robert Altman
s: Elliott Gould, Sterling Hayden, Henry Gibson, Nina Van Pallandt

The Mack (1973)
d: Michael Campus
s: Max Julien, Dan Gordon, Richard Pryor

Magnum Force (1973)
d: Ted Post
s: Clint Eastwood, Hal Holbrook, David Soul

Mean Streets (1973)
d: Martin Scorsese
s: Robert De Niro, Harvey Keitel, David Proval

Serpico (1973)
d: Sydney Lumet
s: Al Pacino, John Randolph, Jack Kehoe

Shaft in Africa (1973)
d: John Guillermin
s: Richard Roundtree, Frank Finlay, Vonetta McGee

The Sting (1973)
d: George Roy Hill
s: Paul Newman, Robert Redford, Robert Shaw

White Lightning (1973)
d: Joseph Sargent
s: Burt Reynolds, Ned Beatty, Matt Clark

Death Wish (1974)
d: Michael Winner
s: Charles Bronson, Hope Lange,
Vincent Gardenia

Thieves Like Us (1974)
d: Robert Altman
s: Keith Carradine, Shelley Duvall

Bugsy Malone (1976)
d: Alan Parker
s: Scott Baio, Jodie Foster

The Enforcer (1976)
d: James Fargo
s: Clint Eastwood, Harry Guardino,
Tyne Daly

Illustrious Corpses (1976 – *Cadaveri
Eccellenti*)
d: Francesco Rosi
s: Lino Ventura, Alain Cuny, Max Von
Sydow, Fernando Rey

The Big Sleep (1978)
d: Michael Winner
s: Robert Mitchum, Sarah Miles,
Oliver Reed, James Stewart, Joan
Collins, John Mills

The Driver (1978)
d: Walter Hill
s: Ryan O'Neal, Bruce Dern, Isabelle
Adjani

The Long Good Friday (1980)
d: John Mackenzie
s: Bob Hoskins, Helen Mirren, Dave
King

Sharky's Machine (1981)
d: Burt Reynolds
s: Burt Reynolds, Vittorio Gassman,
Rachel Ward

48 Hrs (1982)
d: Walter Hill
s: Eddie Murphy, Nick Nolte

La Balance (1982)
d: Bob Swaim
s: Nathalie Baye, Philippe Léotard

Deadly Force (1983)
d: Paul Aron
s: Wings Hauser, Joyce Ingalls

Scarface (1983)
d: Brian De Palma
s: Al Pacino, Steven Bauer, Michelle
Pfeiffer

Sudden Impact (1983)
d: Clint Eastwood
s: Clint Eastwood, Sondra Locke

Beverley Hills Cop (1984)
d: Martin Brest
s: Eddie Murphy, Judge Reinhold

City of Fire (1987)
d: Ringo Lam
s: Chow Yun Fat, Danny Lee

Number One with a Bullet (1987)
d: Jack Smight
s: Robert Carradine, Billy Dee
Williams

The Untouchables (1987)
d: Brian De Palma
s: Kevin Costner, Sean Connery, Robert
De Niro, Martin Smith, Andy Garcia

The Dead Pool (1988)
d: Buddy Van Horn
s: Clint Eastwood, Liam Neeson

The Killer (1989)
d: John Woo
s: Chow Yun Fat, Danny Lee

Lethal Weapon 2 (1989)
d: Richard Donner
s: Mel Gibson, Danny Glover, Joe
Pesci, Patsy Kensit

Dick Tracy (1990)
d: Warren Beatty
s: Warren Beatty, Al Pacino, Dustin
Hoffman, Madonna

The Godfather Part III (1990)
d: Francis Ford Coppola
s: Al Pacino, Diane Keaton, Talia Shire,
Andy Garcia, Eli Wallach, Sofia
Coppola

The Krays (1990)
d: Peter Medak
s: Gary and Martin Kemp, Billie
Whitelaw

The Two Jakes (1990)
d: Jack Nicholson
s: Jack Nicholson, Harvey Keitel, Meg
Tilly, Eli Wallach

The Silence of the Lambs (1991)
d: Jonathan Demme
s: Jodie Foster, Anthony Hopkins

Lethal Weapon 3 (1992)
d: Richard Donner
s: Mel Gibson, Danny Glover, Joe
Pesci, Rene Russo

Reservoir Dogs (1992)
d: Quentin Tarantino
s: Harvey Keitel, Tim Roth, Steve
Buscemi, Michael Madsen

Carlito's Way (1993)
d: Brian De Palma
s: Al Pacino, Sean Penn, Penelope Ann
Miller

Natural Born Killers (1994)
d: Oliver Stone
s: Woody Harrelson, Juliette Lewis

Casino (1995)
d: Martin Scorsese
s: Robert De Niro, Joe Pesci, Sharon
Stone, James Woods

Get Shorty (1995)
d: Barry Sonnenfeld
s: John Travolta, Gene Hackman, Rene
Russo, Danny DeVito

Heat (1995)
d: Michael Mann
s: Al Pacino, Robert De Niro, Val
Kilmer, Jon Voight

The Usual Suspects (1995)
d: Bryan Singer
s: Stephen Baldwin, Benicio Del Toro,
Gabriel Byrne, Kevin Spacey, Kevin
Pollak

Face/Off (1997)
d: John Woo
s: John Travolta, Nicholas Cage

Lethal Weapon 4 (1998)
d: Richard Donner
s: Mel Gibson, Danny Glover, Rene
Russo, Joe Pesci

Lock, Stock and Two Smoking Barrels
(1998)
d: Guy Richie
s: Jason Flemyng, Dexter Fletcher,
Nick Moran, Vinnie Jones, Sting

Payback (1998)
d: Brian Helgeland
s: Mel Gibson, Gregg Henry, Kris
Kristofferson, James Coburn

The Thomas Crown Affair (1999)
d: John McTiernan
s: Pierce Brosnan, Rene Russo, Denis
Leary

Get Carter (2000)
d: Stephen Kay
s: Sylvester Stallone, Michael Caine,
Miranda Richardson, Mickey Rourke

Shaft (2000)
d: John Singleton
s: Samuel L. Jackson, Vanessa
Williams, Richard Roundtree, Jeffrey
Wright

Snatch (2000)
d: Guy Richie
s: Jason Statham, Alan Ford, Brad Pitt,
Vinnie Jones, Benicio Del Toro

Traffic (2000)
d: Stephen Soderbergh
s: Michael Douglas, Benicio Del Toro,
Catherine Zeta Jones, Don Cheadle

Gangs of New York (2002)
d: Martin Scorsese
s: Daniel Day-Lewis, Leonardo
DiCaprio, Cameron Diaz, Liam
Neeson

City of God (2003 – *Cidade De Deus*)
d: Fernando Meirelles
s: Alexandre Rodrigues, Leandro
Firmino da Hora

The Italian Job (2003)
d: F. Gary Gray
s: Mark Wahlberg, Charlize Theron,
Jason Statham

Maria Full of Grace (2004)
d: Joshua Marston
s: Catalina Sandino Moreno

Ocean's Twelve (2004)
d: Stephen Soderbergh
s: George Clooney, Brad Pitt, Julia
Roberts, Andy Garcia, Matt Damon

Kiss Kiss Bang Bang (2005)
d: Shane Black
s: Robert Downey Jnr, Val Kilmer

Sin City (2005)
d: Robert Rodriguez, Frank Miller and
Quentin Tarantino (uncredited)
s: Bruce Willis, Mickey Rourke, Elijah
Wood, Clive Owen, Benicio Del Toro

BIBLIOGRAPHY AND SOURCES

Adams, Mark, *Mike Hodges* (Pocket Essentials, 2001)

Andrews, Emma, *Heroes of the Movies: Michael Caine* (LSP Books, 1982)

Anger, Kenneth, *Hollywood Babylon* (Arrow, 1986)

Beacher, Milton Daniel, *Alcatraz Island: Memoirs of a Rock Doc* (Zymurgy Publishing, 2003)

Bergen, Ronald, *The United Artists Story* (Octopus, 1986)

Bishop, David, *Starring Michael Caine* (Reynolds & Hearn, 2003)

Biskind, Peter, *Down and Dirty Pictures: Miramax, Sundance, and the Rise of Independent Film* (Bloomsbury, 2004)

— *Easy Riders, Raging Bulls: How the Sex-Drugs-And-Rock 'n' Roll Generation Saved Hollywood* (Simon & Schuster, 1998)

— *Gods and Monsters: Thirty Years of Writing on Film and Culture* (Bloomsbury, 2005)

Brode, Douglas, *Money, Women, and Guns: Crime Movies from Bonnie and Clyde to the Present* (Citadel, 1995)

Buford, Kate, *Burt Lancaster: An American Life* (Aurum, 2001)

Burrough, Bryan, *Public Enemies: Bonnie and Clyde, Machine Gun Kelly, Baby Face Nelson, Ma Barker's Gang and America's Greatest Crime Wave* (Penguin, 2004)

Burt, Robert, *Rockerama: 25 Years of Teen Screen Idols* (Blandford, 1983)

Cameron, Ian, *The Movie Book of Film Noir* (Studio Vista, 1994)

Chapman, James, *Saints and Avengers: British Adventure Series of the 1960s* (I.B.Tauris, 2002)

Chibnall, Steve, *Brighton Rock* (I.B.Tauris, 2005)

Cole, Gerald and Peter Williams, *Clint Eastwood* (W.H. Allen, 1983)

Cork, John and Bruce Scivally, *James Bond: The Legacy* (Boxtree, 2002)

Cox, Alex and Nick Jones, *Moviedrome – The Guide* (Broadcasting Support Services, 1990)

Crane, Douglas and Harold Myers, *Hollywood–London Film Parade* (Marks & Spencer, 1949)

Crawley, Tony, *Bébé – The Films of Brigitte Bardot* (BCA, 1979)

Crowe, Cameron, *Conversations with Wilder* (Faber and Faber, 1999)

Cumbow, Robert C., *Once Upon a Time: The Films of Sergio Leone* (Scarecrow Press, 1987)

De Agostini, *The Clint Eastwood Collection, Volume 1: Dirty Harry* (De Agostini, 2004)

De Fornari, Oreste, *Sergio Leone: The Great Italian Dream of Legendary America* (Gremese, 1997)

Donnelley, Paul, *Marilyn Monroe* (Pocket Essentials, 2000)

Duncan, Paul, *Film Noir: Films of Trust and Betrayal* (Pocket Essentials, 2000)

— *Martin Scorsese* (Pocket Essentials, 2004)

— *Noir Fiction: Dark Highways* (Pocket Essentials, 2000)

Eames, John Douglas, *The MGM Story: The Complete History of over Fifty Roaring Years* (Octopus, 1977)

— *The Paramount Story* (Octopus, 1985)

Ellroy, James, *L.A. Confidential* (Arrow, 1994)

Falk, Quentin, *Cinema's Strangest Moments* (Robson Books, 2003)

Fiegel, Eddi, *John Barry: A Sixties Theme – from James Bond to Midnight Cowboy* (Boxtree, 1998)

Fitzgerald, Martin, *Orson Welles* (Pocket Essentials, 2000)

Fleming, Ian, *On Her Majesty's Secret Service* (Jonathan Cape, 1963)

Fox, Keith and Maitland McDonagh (eds), *The Tenth Virgin Film Guide* (Virgin, 2001)

Franchi, Rudy and Barbara, *Miller's Movie Collectibles* (Octopus, 2002)

Frank, Alan, *Frank's 500: The Thriller Film Guide* (Batsford, 1997)

— *The Films of Roger Corman: 'Shooting My Way out of Trouble'* (Batsford, 1998)

Frayling, Christopher, *Clint Eastwood* (Virgin, 1992)

— *Sergio Leone: Something to Do With Death* (Faber & Faber, 2000)

Freer, Ian (ed.), *Bond – the Legend: 1962–2002* (Empire, 2002)

Friedman, Lester D., *Bonnie and Clyde: BFI Classics* (BFI, 2000)

Graysmith, Robert, *Zodiac* (St Martin's Press, 1992)

Grey, Harry, *Once Upon a Time in America* (Bloomsbury, 1997; first published as *The Hoods*, 1965)

Guérif, François, *Clint Eastwood: From Rawhide to Pale Rider* (Roger Houghton, 1986)

Hall, Angus (ed.), *Illustrated Library of Crime and Detection* (No. 1, Phoebus Publishing, 1974)

Hammett, Dashiell, *The Big Knockover and Other Stories* (Penguin, 1969)

— *The Four Great Novels* (*The Dain Curse*, *The Glass Key*, *The Maltese Falcon*, *Red Harvest*) (Picador, 1982)

Hardy, Phil (ed.), *The Aurum Encyclopedia of Science Fiction Movies* (Aurum, 1984)

— *The Aurum Film Encyclopedia: The Western* (Aurum, 1983)

— *The BFI Companion to Crime* (Cassell/BFI, 1997)

— *The BFI Companion to the Western* (André Deutsch, 1996)

— *The Aurum Film Encyclopedia: Gangsters* (Aurum Press, 1998)

Hasted, Nick, 'Repo Man' (*Uncut Magazine*, July 2005)

Hill, Henry with Gus Russo, *Gangsters and Goodfellas: Wiseguys … and Life on the Run* (Mainstream Publishing, 2004)

Hirschfeld, Burt, *Bonnie and Clyde* (Hodder and Stoughton, 1967)

Hirschhorn, Clive, *The Warner Bros. Story* (Octopus, 1983)

Hughes, Howard, *Once Upon a Time in the Italian West: The Filmgoers' Guide to Spaghetti Westerns* (I.B. Tauris, 2004)

Jewell, Richard B. and Vernon Harbin, *The RKO Story* (Octopus, 1982)

Johnstone, Iain, *The Man With No Name* (Plexus, 1981)

Kaminsky, Stuart M., *Don Siegel: Director* (Curtis, 1974)

Katz, Ephraim, *The Macmillan International Film Encyclopedia* (HarperCollins, 1998)

Koven, Mikel J., *Blaxpoitation Films* (Pocket Essentials, 2001)

Lane, Brian and Wilfred Gregg, *The Encyclopedia of Serial Killers* (Headline Publishing, 1992)

Lane, John, *The Themes of 007: James Bond's Greatest Hits* (Columbia Pictures Publications, 1985, sheet music of John Barry's scores)

Leonard, Elmore, *Rum Punch* (Penguin, 1992)

Levy, Sean, *Rat Pack Confidential* (Fourth Estate, 1998)

Lewis, Roger, *The Life and Death of Peter Sellers* (Arrow, 2004)

Lloyd, Ann (ed,), *Good Guys & Bad Guys* (Orbis, 1982)

— *Movies of the Sixties* (Orbis, 1983)

— *Movies of the Fifties* (Orbis, 1982)

Lloyd, Ann and Graham Fuller, *The Illustrated Who's Who of the Cinema* (Orbis, 1983)

Love, Damien, 'Way of the Gun: The Making of Dirty Harry' (*Uncut Magazine*, Take 53, October 2001)

— 'Blown Away: The Making of The Getaway' (*Uncut DVD*, Issue 1, November–December 2005)

Luck, Steve (ed.), *Philip's Compact Encyclopedia* (Chancellor Press, 1999)

Luck, Richard, *Sam Peckinpah* (Pocket Essentials, 2000)

Macnab, Geoffrey, *Key Moments in Cinema* (Hamlyn, 2001)

Madsen, Axel, *John Huston: A Biography* (Robson Books, 1979)

Maltin, Leonard, *2001 Movie and Video Guide* (Penguin, 2001)

Malyszko, William, *The Godfather, the Ultimate Film Guide* (York Press, 2001)

Masheter, Philip, 'This Never Happened To the Other Feller: The Making of On Her Majesty's Secret Service' (*Movie Collector Magazine*, Volume 2, Issue 2, 14 March 1995)

Mathews, Tom Dewe, *Censored: The Story of Film Censorship in Britain* (Chatto and Windus, 1994)

Matthews, Roger, *Armed Robbery* (William Publishing, 2002)

McCabe, Bob, *Clint Eastwood: 'Quote Unquote'* (Parragon, 1996)

McGilligan, Patrick, *Clint: The Life and Legend* (HarperCollins, 1999)

Medved, Harry and Michael, *Son of Golden Turkey Awards: The Best of the Worst from Hollywood* (Angus & Robertson, 1986)

— *The Fifty Worst Films of All Time (And how They got that Way)* (Angus & Robertson, 1978)

Muller, Eddie, *Dark City: The Lost World of Film Noir* (Titan Books, 1998)

Müller, Jürgen (ed.), *Best Movies of the 90s* (Taschen, 2005)

— *Movies of the 70s* (Taschen, 2003)

— *Movies of the 60s* (Taschen, 2004)

Naughton, John, *Movies* (Simon & Schuster, 1998)

Nourmand, Tony and Graham Marsh (eds), *Film Posters of the 60s: The Essential Movies of the Decade* (Aurum, 1997)

O'Brien, Daniel, *Clint Eastwood – Film-Maker* (Batsford, 1996)

Pfeiffer, Lee and Dave Worrall, *The Essential Bond: The Authorised Guide to the World of 007* (Boxtree, 1998)

Puzo, Mario, *The Godfather* (William Heinemann, 1969)

Reeves, Tony, *The Worldwide Guide to Movie Locations* (Titan Books, 2001)

Reynolds, Burt, *My Life* (Hodder & Stoughton, 1995)

Rock, Phillip, *Dirty Harry* (Star, 1977)

Rogers, Dave, *The Prisoner & Danger Man* (Boxtree, 1989)

Rose, Simon, *Classic Films* (Harper Collins, 1999)

Rye, Graham (ed.), *007 Magazine: On Her Majesty's Secret Service 25th Anniversary Special* (1995)

Scheuer, Steven H. (ed.), *Movies on TV* (Bantam Books, 1977)

Sciascia, Leonardo, *The Day of the Owl / Equal Danger* (Paladin, 1987)

Scorsese, Martin and Nicholas Pileggi, *GoodFellas* (Faber & Faber, 2000)

Shipman, David, *The Movie Makers: Brando* (Macmillan, 1974)

Sifakis, Carl, *The Mafia Encyclopedia: Second Edition* (Checkmark Books, 1999)

Silver, Alain and James Ursini, *Whatever Happened to Robert Aldrich? His Life & His Films* (Limelight, 1995)

Slide, Anthony (ed.), *De Toth on De Toth – Putting the Drama in Front of the Camera* (Faber and Faber, 1996)

Sperber, A.M. and Eric Lax, *Bogart* (Weidenfeld & Nicholson, 1997)

Spillane, Mickey, *I, the Jury* (Arthur Barker, 1952)

Stacey, Jan and Ryder Syvertsen, *The Great Book of Movie Villains: A Guide to the Screen's Meanies, Tough Guys, and Bullies* (Contemporary Books, 1984)

Stewart, John, *Italian Film: A Who's Who* (McFarland, 1994)

Tarantino, Quentin, *Pulp Fiction: Original Script* (Faber and Faber, 1994)

Tchernia, Pierre, *80 Grands Succès du Cinéma Policier Français* (Casterman, 1989)

Thomson, Douglas, *Clint Eastwood, Sexual Cowboy* (Warner Books, 1993)

Tonks, Paul, *Film Music* (Pocket Essentials, 2003)

Tosches, Nick, *Dino: Living High in the Dirty Business of Dreams* (Secker & Warburg, 1992)

Weddle, David, *Sam Peckinpah: 'If They Move…Kill 'Em'* (Faber & Faber, 1996)

Weldon, Michael J., *The Psychotronic Video Guide* (St Martin's Griffin, 1996)

Whitehead, Mark, *Roger Corman* (Pocket Essentials, 2003)

Whitney, Steven, *Charles Bronson, Superstar* (Dell, 1975)

Wiegand, Chris, *French New Wave* (Pocket Essentials, 2001)

Wilkinson, Frederick, *Handguns: A Collector's Guide to Pistols and Revolvers from 1950 to the Present* (Apple, 1993)

Witcombe, Rick Trader, *Savage Cinema* (Lorrimer, 1975)

Zmijewsky, Boris and Lee Pfeiffer, *The Films of Clint Eastwood* (Citadel Press, 1993)

FURTHER SOURCES

Soundtrack recordings:
> *Ocean's Eleven* (David Holmes and various artists), *Once Upon a Time in America* (Ennio Morricone), *Themeology: The Best of John Barry* (liner notes by Jonathan Ross), *Dirty Harry* (Lalo Schifrin), *On Her Majesty's Secret Service* (John Barry; liner notes by Jeff Bond), *Get Carter* (Roy Budd – liner notes by Mike Hodges, Paul Fishman and Charlie Galloway) and *Pulp Fiction* (various artists).

Documentaries, audio commentaries and booklets from DVDs:
> *On Her Majesty's Secret Service*, *Get Carter*, *Shaft*, *Dirty Harry*, *The Godfather*, *Once Upon a Time in America*, *Lethal Weapon*, *GoodFellas*, *Pulp Fiction*, *Ocean's Eleven*, plus the documentaries: *James Cagney: A Hard Act to Follow*, *Clint Eastwood: the Man from Malpaso*, *Easy Riders, Raging Bulls* and *Lee Marvin: A Personal Portrait*.

Also, travel guides and maps of the United States and the United Kingdom. The following websites proved useful:
> The Internet Movie Database (www.imdb.com), the official British Board of Film Classification site (www.bbfc.co.uk), the Motion Picture Association of America (www.mpaa.org) and Turner Classic Movies: in the US www.turnerclassicmovies.com and the UK www.tcmonline.co.uk.

INDEX

Film titles in bold type denote a chapter devoted to the film; page numbers in bold denote an illustration.

TV = TV series

doc. = documentary